Army Life

The Civil War in the West

Series Editors: T. Michael Parrish
and Daniel E. Sutherland

Army Life.

From a Soldier's Journal.

By Albert O. Marshall

INCIDENTS, SKETCHES AND RECORD OF A UNION SOLDIER'S ARMY LIFE, IN CAMP AND FIELD.

1861–64

Edited and Annotated by Robert G. Schultz

The University of Arkansas Press
Fayetteville • 2009

Manufactured in the United States of America

ISBN-10: 1-55728-917-4
ISBN-13: 978-1-55728-917-9

13 12 11 10 09 5 4 3 2 1

Text design by Ellen Beeler

♾ The paper used in this publication meets the minimum requirements of the American National Standard for Permanence of Paper for Printed Library Materials Z39.48-1984.

Library of Congress Cataloging-in-Publication Data
Marshall, Albert O., 1840–1914.
Army life : from a soldier's journal : incidents, sketches, and record of a Union soldier's army life, in camp and field, 1861–1864 / by Albert O Marshall ; edited and annotated by Robert G. Schultz.
p. cm. — (The Civil War in the West)
Originally published: Joliet, Ill. : Printed for the author, 1883.
Includes bibliographical references and index.
ISBN-13: 978-1-55278-917-9 (pbk. : alk. paper)
ISBN-10: 1-55728-917-4 (pbk. : alk. paper)
1. Marshall, Albert O., 1840–1914. 2. United States—History—Civil War, 1861–1865—Personal narratives. 3. United States. Army. Illinois Infantry Regiment, 33rd (1861–1865) 4. United States—History—Civil War, 1861–1865—Regimental histories. I. Schultz, Robert G. II. Title.
E505.533rd .M37 2009
973.7'81—dc22

2009020256

Contents

Series Editors' Preface

The Civil War in the West has a single goal: to promote historical writing about the war in the western states and territories. It focuses most particularly on the Trans-Mississippi theater, which consisted of Missouri, Arkansas, Texas, most of Louisiana (west of the Mississippi River), Indian Territory (modern-day Oklahoma), and Arizona Territory (two-fifths of modern-day Arizona and New Mexico), but encompasses adjacent states, such as Kansas, Tennessee, and Mississippi, that directly influenced the trans-Mississippi war. It is a wide swath, to be sure, but one too often ignored by historians and, consequently, too little understood and appreciated.

Topically, the series embraces all aspects of the wartime story. Military history in its many guises, from the strategies of generals to the daily lives of common soldiers, forms an important part of that story, but so, too, do the numerous and complex political, economic, social, and diplomatic dimensions of the war. The series also provides a variety of perspectives on these topics. Most importantly, it offers the best in modern scholarship, with thoughtful, challenging monographs. Secondly, it presents new editions of important books that have gone out of print. And thirdly, it premieres expertly edited correspondence, diaries, reminiscences, and other writings by participants in the war.

It is a formidable challenge, but by focusing on some of the least familiar dimensions of the conflict, The Civil War in the West significantly broadens our understanding of the nation's most pivotal and dramatic story.

Even among Civil War historians, Albert O. Marshall's *Army Life* is an extremely rare and little-known work, which makes Arkansas's annotated edition all the more welcome in the literature. *Army Life* is a richly detailed and lively memoir by a Union soldier who served from 1861 through 1864 throughout the Mississippi Valley, southern Louisiana, and along the lower Texas coast. Marshall describes his service in the Thirty-third Illinois Infantry, illuminating that unit's crucial contributions to important campaigns in Missouri and Arkansas, the siege of Vicksburg, the invasion of the Teche country in Louisiana, and subsequent attempts to invade Texas at Brownsville and Matagorda Bay.

Marshall includes a wide range of interesting comments and candid evaluations of soldier life. He criticizes his commanding officers, evaluates Yankee strategy and politics, and describes several interesting encounters with Confederate civilians of various classes and conditions. He also delineates quite candidly the invading Union army's destruction of property and seizure of cotton, and he gives vivid pen pictures of the dangerous and difficult plight of runaway slaves who flocked by the thousands to the safety of Union lines. Marshall also makes it clear that the great majority of Union soldiers viewed emancipation primarily as a military policy meant to win a war to save and restore the Union and to ensure that slaveholders would no longer control the national government.

Based substantially upon information gleaned from original diaries and letters written during the war, Marshall's *Army Life* provides an extremely valuable primary account by an intelligent and insightful Civil War soldier. Robert G. Schultz, the volume editor, has done a commendable job of introducing and editing the text and of adding a variety of maps, portraits, and other illustrative material that enriches the memoir. As such, it is an excellent addition to the Civil War in the West series.

T. Michael Parrish
Daniel E. Sutherland
Series Editors

Editor's Introduction

In 1884, Albert O. Marshall published his memoirs of service, entitled *Army Life.* This memoir is a rarity in what it is not. It is not a complete story of the Thirty-third Illinois Regiment. It is not a complete roster of regiment members, nor a list of killed and wounded. It is not written from an officer's point of view. It is the story of the experiences of a twenty-year-old (in 1861), written from a private soldier's point of view. He describes the battles he fought, but also the games he played. He comments on his friends and fellow soldiers and also gives his opinion of his officers.

Marshall does all this with a skill in writing that belies his youth—but also allows his youth to shine through. This is not a stuffy tome, but rather an easy to read, enjoyable volume that covers a military experience in mainly the Trans-Mississippi Theater. Marshall describes actions of the Thirty-third Illinois in Missouri and Arkansas, at Vicksburg, and then in Louisiana and on the Texas Gulf Coast.[1]

Albert O. Marshall was born in 1840 on a farm near New Lenox, Will County, Illinois. He was educated in the local school and at age nineteen entered Lombard University in Galesburg, Illinois. War intervened and in 1861 he enlisted in Company A of the Thirty-third Volunteer Infantry Regiment, the Normal Regiment, made up mainly of students and teachers. (Upon his enlistment, Marshall declared himself a "farmer.") Marshall was one of seven children (five boys and two girls). His father went to California with gold fever in 1849 and died in 1850 while returning home.

Marshall was discharged in October 1864. After the war he attended what is now the School of Law of Northwestern University, graduating in 1866. He began a successful law practice in Joliet, Illinois. He was elected to a four-year term in the Illinois State Senate in 1874. From 1894 to 1902 he was elected

Albert O. Marshall. From Elliott and Way, History of the Thirty Third Regiment Illinois Veteran Volunteer Infantry in the Civil War.

judge of the county court, and in 1905 he was elected circuit court judge. He also served on the Joliet school board and on the township high school board. Marshall died October 20, 1914, and is buried in the Marshall Cemetery in New Lenox Township.[2]

In this edition, Marshall's original work has been left untouched with the exception of a few spelling corrections. In the original there was only one drawing. Illustrations and maps have been added. These are from *The Official Atlas of the Civil War,* contemporary *Harper's* and *Leslie's* weekly newspapers, the later *Harper's* and *Leslie's* Civil War histories (that reproduce items from the original 1861–1865 weekly issues), or the *Battles and Leaders of the Civil War* volumes.[3] Footnotes were added to explain and identify places and people mentioned in the text.

The Trans-Mississippi Theater, where the Thirty-third spent most of its time, has been under-reported in Civil War literature. When "war in the west" is mentioned, it turns out that this means west of the Appalachian Mountains. In order to better understand Marshall's narrative, it is necessary to give background on the war west of the Mississippi. One fact, often unknown, is that Missouri had the third largest number of battles and skirmishes of all the states in the Civil War (after Virginia and Tennessee).

BACKGROUND OF EVENTS LEADING UP TO MARSHALL'S NARRATIVE.

In August 1861, the official formation of the Thirty-third Illinois began in Bloomington. Companies began forming and drilling. These companies were periodically forwarded to Camp Butler near Springfield, and the Thirty-third was officially established on August 30. Drilling continued until September 19, when the regiment left Camp Butler for duty in Missouri.

In the ten months prior to the Thirty-third's establishment, much had occurred in the United States: Lincoln's election and inauguration, secession of the southern states, the fall of Fort Sumter, and the first battle of Bull Run. And over this same time in the Middle West, other events, also driven by Lincoln's election and the secession, had occurred. The loyalty of the southern part of Illinois ("Little Egypt") was questioned because of the many residents there with southern roots.

But the main concern of many Illinoisans was Missouri. Missouri was a slave state and just west across the Mississippi River from most of Illinois. But Missouri was also a state divided. Most of the original settlers of Missouri had come from southern states (Kentucky, Tennessee, Virginia, and North Carolina), and the original commerce extended southward by steamboats on the Mississippi River. However, with time, the nature of the state in both population and commerce changed. The original southern population had often settled along the Missouri and Mississippi Rivers. Cotton was not a practical crop in Missouri, but tobacco and hemp were popular crops requiring slave labor.

As Missouri grew, farming spread into the northern counties away from the rivers and many new settlers came from northern states (Illinois, Indiana, Ohio, New York, and the New England area). Another factor came into play at the same time, immigration. Gottfried Duden's book caused a great increase in German immigration to Missouri.[4] Some counties, particularly Gasconade, Franklin, Warren, St. Charles, and St. Louis, received great numbers of immigrants. The immigration increased with the failed revolutions of 1848. These changes altered the complexion of the state of Missouri.

St. Louis became a major urban center with a population of 160,773 in 1860.[5] Manufacturing also grew in St. Louis to supplement its commercial operations. The city's population was listed as well over 50 percent "foreign born," mostly German and Irish.[6] In addition, the city was shifting its ties from the South to the Northeast. One of the influencing factors was the arrival of railroads on the east side of the Mississippi River. Railroads were also built westward from St. Louis: south to the iron mines at Pilot Knob and Ironton; southwest to Rolla; west to Jefferson City and beyond; and northwest through St. Charles to connect with the Hannibal and St. Joseph railroad at Moberly. Financing for these railroads and other manufacturing ventures came mainly from the Northeast. (There were no bridges over either the Mississippi or Missouri Rivers until well into the 1870s. Railroad car ferries were used.)

Many of the German immigrants who arrived in the 1850s were fleeing the failed revolutions of the 1840s in the various German states. They, as well as many of the earlier German immigrants, were at first attracted to the Democratic Party, rather than the Whigs (which was dying out) or the nativist American Party (the "Know Nothings"). However, as the Democratic Party increasingly drifted to a southern orientation, many Germans shifted allegiance to the new Republican Party.

Slavery, while well established in Missouri, did not have as much economic importance as in the other slave states bordering the Mississippi River. While the other slave states ranged from 24.2 percent slave (Kentucky) to 55.2 percent slave (Mississippi), slaves in Missouri represented only 9.7 percent of the population.[7]

In 1860, Missouri, as well as the rest of the nation, was facing a crisis. The Democratic Party split in two and ran two candidates. A new party, the Constitutional Union Party, was formed, and the Republican Party ran a presidential candidate for the second time.[8] A similar situation obtained in Missouri. Elections for governor and the state legislature were held in August, and four sets of candidates under the national banners were competing. The winner, Claiborne Fox Jackson, ran as a northern (Douglas) Democrat, but many saw him as really a southern Democrat. The results in Missouri for governor in August and for U.S. president in November were similar (see table).[9] In both these elections, Missourians voted for middle-of-the-road, moderate candidates.

Governor, August 1860	No. of votes	% of vote	Party	No. of votes	% of vote	President, November 1860
Claiborne Fox Jackson	74,446	46.9	Northern Democrat	58,801	35.5	Stephen A. Douglas
Hancock Jackson	11,415	7.2	Southern Democrat	31,317	18.9	John C. Breckenridge
Sample Orr	66,583	42.0	Constitutional Union	58,372	35.3	John Bell
James Gardenhire	6,135	3.9	Republican	17,328	10.3	Abraham Lincoln

With Lincoln's election and the beginning of southern state secession, the question arose, "Where does Missouri stand?" Newly elected Governor Claiborne Fox Jackson, in his inaugural speech on January 4, 1861, stated, "Missouri must stand by her sister slave-holding states."[10] The new lieutenant governor, Thomas C. Reynolds, went even further in support of secession. Jackson requested that the legislature call for a state constitutional convention to determine Missouri's relationship to the Federal Union.[11] Jackson fully expected that secessionist candidates would be elected and vote for secession. He had good reason to expect such a result. Districts had not been re-apportioned and the Republican stronghold of St. Louis was seriously underrepresented. The makeup of the state legislature also led Jackson to this belief. The state election of August 1860 produced a majority of Democrats (including senators not up for election, see table).[12] Many of the Douglas Democrats were Claiborne Jackson followers, and Jackson was sure they would vote for secession.

	House of Representatives	Senate	Total
Douglas Democrats	37 (28.0%)	9 (27.3%)	46 (27.9%)
Constitutional Unionists	36 (27.3%)	8 (24.2%)	44 (26.6%)
Breckenridge Democrats	47 (35.6%)	15 (45.5%)	62 (37.6%)
Republicans	12 (9.1%)	1 (3.0%)	13 (7.9%)
Total	132	33	165

The state legislature voted for a constitutional convention, but those elected to the convention were not whom Jackson expected. Most were either staunch Unionists or conditional Unionists. Few outright secessionists were elected. Most of the delegates were "solid, substantial and conservative businessmen."[13] Sterling Price, a former governor and conditional Unionist, was elected president of the convention. The convention met February 28 to March 22, 1861, and resolved "that at present there is no adequate cause to impel Missouri to dissolve her connection."[14]

Jackson was greatly disappointed and continued his less overt efforts to force Missouri's secession. The prize in this contest, besides secession, was the St. Louis Arsenal on the south side of the city. It was the main depository for all the army units serving in the West. It supposedly contained sixty thousand stands of arms, numerous cannon, cannon and musket shot, and powder.[15] Southern states had emptied Federal arsenals. (For example, Louisiana troops had taken over the lightly defended arsenal at Baton Rouge.)

Governor Jackson began working on strengthening and arming the state militia. But he was not alone in planning for troops. Frank Blair and his friends began considering how to form and arm a pro-Union force. Many Germans enlisted and formed units led by German officers. Many of these Germans, both officers and men, had military experience in the failed revolutions in Europe.[16]

Then, the U.S. Army transferred an army company from Ft. Leavenworth to St. Louis to increase security in the city. It was led by Captain Nathaniel Lyon, a career office and ardent abolitionist.[17] Blair and Lyon became fast friends, united in the Union cause and in the defense of the arsenal.

After Fort Sumter fell, Abraham Lincoln called for troops from the states to suppress the rebellion.[18] Missouri's quota was 3,123 officers and men. Governor Jackson's response was direct and negative:

> Hon. Simon Cameron, Secretary of War:
>
> Sir: Your dispatch of the 15th instant, making a call on Missouri for four regiments of men for immediate service has been received. These can be, I apprehend, no doubt but the men are intended to form a part of the President's army to make war upon the people of the seceded States.
>
> Your requisition, in my judgment, is illegal, unconstitutional, and revolutionary in its object, inhuman and diabolical, and cannot be complied with. Not one man will the State of Missouri furnish to carry on any such unholy crusade.
>
> C. F. Jackson, Governor of Missouri.[19]

On April 20, the small Federal arsenal in the western Missouri town of Liberty was ransacked by secessionists.[20] Over the months of February through April 1861 in St. Louis, arsenal defenses were strengthened and permission was obtained from Washington to arm and enlist ten thousand men into Union service. Frank Blair and Nathaniel Lyon were only too happy to provide these men. They were not sent East, but rather kept in St. Louis for defense of the city. In addition, thousands of stands of arms were requisitioned by Governor Yates of Illinois and transferred without notice to Illinois and safety.[21]

Fear grew about the safety of the St. Louis Arsenal. On April 22, Governor Jackson called for a special session of the legislature, to begin on May 2, to "perfect the organization of the militia and provide for the defense of the state."[22] He also called for the state militia to meet in each of the militia districts for "Camps of Instruction."[23] Normally, these camps were light-hearted affairs with the men drilling and target shooting, drinking, playing cards, visiting, and enjoying the attention of young ladies visiting the camp.

This year, all of these factors were present, but things were also different. Brigadier General Daniel M. Frost, commanding the Ninth District, established his camp in Lindell's Grove on the western edge of the city and named it "Camp Jackson in honor of Governor Jackson."[24] Blair and Lyon viewed this encampment with suspicion since Frost and many others, but not all, in the camp were avowed secessionists. On May 10, Lyon called up his volunteers, surrounded the camp, and forced its surrender without a fight. However, on the march to return to the arsenal with the prisoners, the watching crowd grew unruly. Stones were thrown, and shots fired. Lyon's poorly trained volunteers responded, and before the troops could be brought under control, twenty-eight civilians lay dead in the streets of St. Louis.[25]

An attack against the arsenal had been prevented, but at what cost? First, it was improbable at this late date that an attack would have even been attempted, much less have been successful. Second, if an attack had been ordered by Frost, it is probable a significant number of the militia would have refused the order. And finally, and most importantly, the Camp Jackson "affair" drove a significant number of conditional Unionists into the secession camp. The most prominent of these was Sterling Price, who, after Camp Jackson, accepted the appointment as major general, commanding the Missouri State Guard.

Uriel Wright, the preeminent criminal lawyer in St. Louis and unconditional Unionist, stated, "If Unionism meant such atrocious deeds as had been that day witnessed, he was no longer a Union man."[26] Since most of the Union troops were German, secessionists began to compare themselves with the minutemen of 1775 and the Germans with the Hessian mercenaries of the Revolutionary War. Secessionists took to calling the Union soldiers the "Dutch" or, more often, the "damned Dutch."

On June 11 a conference was held at the Planter's Hotel in St. Louis. On one side were Governor Jackson, Major General Price, and Thomas Snead (aide de camp). On the other side were Nathaniel Lyon, no longer captain, U.S. Army, but brigadier general of volunteers; Frank Blair; and Horace A. Conant, aide de camp to Lyon. After six hours of fruitless negotiations, the conference broke up. Jackson and Price returned to Jefferson City and ordered the railroad bridges to be burned to delay pursuit. The next day Jackson issued a proclamation calling for fifty thousand men to repel the invasion.[27]

Jackson, Lieutenant Governor Reynolds, the secretary of state, and some members of the legislature fled Jefferson City, first westward to Boonville, then further southwest. General Lyon put his troops on steamboats and on June 15 occupied the capital city.[28] Leaving a detachment under Colonel Henry Boernstein to occupy the city, Lyon continued westward and met and routed the Missouri State Guard under Colonel John Sappington Marmaduke at Boonville.[29] (Price was further west seeking recruits.)

After Boonville, Missouri was on a total war footing. Jackson and Price with state guard troops, many unarmed, began moving to the southwestern part of the state, hoping to link up with Arkansas forces. Colonel Franz Sigel[30] and a small force attempted to interpose themselves across the state guard's path but were pushed aside at the battle of Carthage, July 3, 1861.[31] Lyon moved his forces southwest and occupied Springfield. There, he united with Sigel's troops. Price succeeded in merging with the Arkansas forces under General Ben McCulloch.[32] After some disagreement on tactics, they moved upon Springfield. Lyon was badly outnumbered but decided on a surprise attack on the Confederate camp at Wilson's Creek. While the attack was indeed a surprise, it was also a failure. There were heavy casualties on both sides, averaging 23 percent killed, wounded, and missing, considerably higher than the casualties sustained at First Bull Run (10 percent). Among the casualties was Nathaniel Lyon, the first general killed in the Civil War.[33]

Politically, things also changed in Missouri. The constitutional convention was recalled into session, meeting July 22–31, 1861. The convention declared the office of president vacant, replacing Sterling Price with Robert Wilson. It also declared all the state offices vacant: governor, lieutenant governor, and secretary of state. In addition, it declared the entire general assembly vacant and decided that it (the convention) should name provisional state officers.[34] Hamilton R. Gamble was named provisional governor.[35]

The Federal government was also active in Missouri affairs. The Western Department was created with St. Louis as headquarters city. General John C. Fremont was named as department commander and took command July 25, 1861.[36] Fremont stirred considerable controversy. He was criticized for not reinforcing Lyon at Springfield. He rented a mansion in St. Louis (from his wife's aunt) at a rate of six thousand dollars annually for residence and headquarters. He was quite inaccessible and maintained a fancy bodyguard led by Colonel Charles Zagonyi. Resentment against Fremont and his inaction grew and he even succeeded in alienating Frank Blair and his supporters.[37]

The situation in Missouri was thought to be deteriorating. Confederate forces held much of western Missouri or at least prevented Union control there. Guerrilla bands were active north of the Missouri River and attacked railroads. A Confederate army was also said to be massing in southeast Missouri. This then was the situation in Missouri when the Thirty-third Illinois received its marching orders.

After getting their training and arms, they took part in the battle of Fredericktown and did guard duty until the spring of 1862. The Thirty-third then began a foray into Arkansas under General Frederick Steele and united with General Samuel R. Curtis, who had moved eastward to Batesville after defeating Earl Van Dorn at Pea Ridge. The initial aim was to occupy Little Rock. However, there was considerable flooding between Batesville and Little Rock, making the route impassable. Rebel action took its toll on Curtis's supply lines from Rolla and Pilot Knob. Foraging expeditions were attacked. Then General Henry Wager Halleck recalled part of Curtis's army to take part in the advance on Corinth after Shiloh. Curtis decided to try for naval resupply up the White River. After this failed, the army marched to Clarendon and then Helena, Arkansas, on the Mississippi River. Along the way, the Thirty-third fought an engagement at Cache River.

From Helena, the Thirty-third returned north by steamboat and train to

Pilot Knob. They spent the next months keeping order in southeastern and southern central Missouri, chasing guerrillas and escorting supply trains to out posts like West Plains, Missouri. Spring 1863 saw the Thirty-third and other units sent to support Ulysses S. Grant's attack on Vicksburg, and the Thirty-third was in the midst of the battles. After victory at Vicksburg, the Thirty-third, unlike many other units that went east, went south to New Orleans.

New Orleans was chosen for the Thirty-third and several other units to suppress Confederate action in south Louisiana. They were under the overall command of General Nathaniel Banks. One of the major thrusts in planning the suppression of the Confederacy was to gain control of Texas and stop the importation of arms and exportation of cotton that was occurring along the Rio Grande River. Several routes were proposed to strike into Texas. The Red River from the Mississippi River to Shreveport was suggested but rejected. A foray up the Teche River (or Bayou) was attempted using the railroad that extended from Algiers to Brashear City. The Thirty-third and other units moved out, skirmished, and advanced as far as Vermilionville (now Lafayette, Louisiana). But then the Union forces were withdrawn and plans changed. An assault on Sabine Pass in East Texas was decisively routed in September 1863.

Banks then decided to attack at the source of the import-export problems, Brownsville on the Rio Grande River. The Thirty-third and other units took transports from New Orleans, and some landed near the mouth of the river and occupied Brownsville, meeting little opposition. The Thirty-third was ordered further north and landed on Mustang Island and then crossed to Matagorda Island. At the north end of the island the Union captured Fort Esperanza and then occupied the important port town of Indianola. Indianola had become a major port on the Texas Gulf Coast and an important jumping-off point to the interior. However, by the spring of 1864 it was decided to abandon this area but continue to occupy the Brownsville area.

Additional comments on the broader military situation will also be added as footnotes to the appropriate chapters in Marshall's text. Marshall's comments concern mainly the small, everyday events of "army life," but when he comments on larger events, his comments are remarkably close to the events reported in other official sources.

Army Life.

From a Soldier's Journal.

BY

ALBERT O. MARSHALL

INCIDENTS, SKETCHES AND RECORD OF A UNION SOLDIER'S ARMY LIFE, IN CAMP AND FIELD.

1861–64

SECOND EDITION

PRINTED FOR THE AUTHOR

JOLIET, ILL.
1884

Stereotyped, Printed and Bound
By the
Chicago Legal News Company

CONTENTS

PREFACE

Books are merely word pictures. The true artist makes the scene upon the canvas appear life-like and actual.

It has been truly said, that if the biography of any man, however humble his station, were written so truthful and complete as to display his whole inner and outer life, from the cradle to the grave, it would be immortal. To write such a biography is impossible. The writer, like the painter, only produces a likeness; neither creates the real.

Many histories of the late war have been written, a perusal of which calls to mind my own soldier life; and in reading of the brave deeds of many officers, as recorded, the thought has often occurred to me that the simple story of the private soldier's actual army life would not be devoid of interest.

Turning occasionally to my army journal, after these many years, the sketches written from time to time by the light of the evening camp fires, appear to me, deeply interesting. They may, perhaps, be entertaining to others.

The preservation of the little memorandum books in which my army journal was written is almost miraculous. The knapsack in which they were carried, was often left behind on some forced march, or just before a battle. Other knapsacks were lost. But through all the varied changes, dangers and vicissitudes of three years of a soldier's life at the front, on the march, in bivouac and battle, this knapsack was never so mislaid or lost as not to bring along its little army journal. These memoranda are simply jottings, made rather as a pastime than with any thought of future use, or of their being of sufficient value to send home for safe keeping; an army blanket was then more highly prized and carefully guarded; yet with all the neglect and hazard attending its journey, this journal always returned and was at the muster out, or these pages could not have been presented.

No published histories nor public records have been consulted in compiling this volume. It contains only such matters as were, at the time, deemed of sufficient interest to be noted in my army journal.

In reviewing this army journal, I discover that many things written at the age of twenty appear crude and incomplete, twenty years thereafter. At this time I have sometimes felt inclined to erase the words of youthful enthusiasm, wild extravagance, or, perhaps, boyish foolishness, found therein. Such correction would, however, leave the picture less vivid, distinct and real. Hence, with but little change, or even verbal alterations, and omitting only such peculiar personal matters as no one need ask nor expect to see, these pages are presented as they were written twenty years ago.

When it is remembered that a majority of the private soldiers were, at enlistment, between the ages of sixteen and twenty-three, it will be realized that a true picture of their soldier life must, of necessity, portray a youthful and immature one.

If my comrades of the great Union army, when reading these reminiscences are carried back, in memory, to the old camp fires and army scenes—if their friends in reading the story can, in imagination see what the soldiers endured and what they accomplished, my object is attained. I have made no attempt to write a war, nor even a regimental history; but this little book is submitted for simply what it claims to be—A PICTURE OF A PRIVATE SOLDIER'S ARMY LIFE.

A. O. M.

Joliet, Ill., 1883.

Army Life.

From a Soldier's Journal.

CHAPTER I.

LEAVING HOME.

The eleventh day of September, during the eventful year of 1861, found me riding at railroad speed down the Chicago and Alton road, on my way from my Will County home to Camp Butler[1] at Springfield, Illinois, where I was to join the army, shoulder a musket, and go forth to the bloody fields of battle to fight for the grand cause of Country and Liberty.

I will not attempt to portray the varied emotions I felt upon this, to me, long to be remembered day. Such emotions as any young man must feel when leaving the dearest of home associations, the kindest of friendly relations, the most cherished and valued school privileges; leaving all of these for the first time, and that, too, not as fond anticipation had often promised, to mingle in the common contests of active life, but for the uncertain, desperate battle field, by and by to return, perhaps—perhaps not. Attempting to throw the veil of forgetfulness over these memories I will let this journal recount other thoughts and scenes.

The day was bright and beautiful; one of the fairest of early Autumn. The journey passed swiftly and pleasantly.

FIRST IMPRESSION OF THE THIRTY-THIRD.

I had decided to join the Thirty-third Illinois (Normal) Regiment. At Bloomington two intelligent and accomplished ladies joined the passengers for Springfield. I was much pleased to learn that they were acquainted with the Normal Regiment, to which, in fact, they were on the way to make a visit. One was the wife of Colonel Hovey of the Thirty-third and the other a sister of a young man, lately from the Normal school, and now orderly sergeant of the company I intended to join. With one exception they were the first members of the Normal Regiment—which they were in spirit and interest, if not in fact—I had ever met.

If the regiment sustains even a small part of the good impression created in its favor by this first meeting with any of its members, it will prove to be one of the best regiments that Illinois or any State can send to the field.

We arrived at Springfield at sundown. Jumping into a carriage I was soon in Camp Butler and the camp of the Thirty-third shown to me. I then found Company A and was furnished with soldier quarters for the night.

FIRST NIGHT IN CAMP—YOUNG SOLDIERS ON GUARD.

I lay down with the soldiers, but sleep was out of the question. Of all the strange and queer racket and sound ever heard, none could exceed the unearthly clamor made by a large number of young volunteers during the first few nights they are in camp. One soldier near my tent kept up a continual yell, of, as I thought, "corporal-of-the-guard-want-something-to-eat." This early evidence of starvation in camp raised rather dubious suggestions when I thought of our future prospects. As he continued to yell louder and louder, instead of ceasing, at last I became vexed, as I supposed he was only yelling for fun, and was about ready to go out and try the virtue of throwing a brick at his head, merely as a gentle hint for him to cease such unreasonable midnight howling, when one of the boys in our tent, Charley Huston, *an old soldier*—he had been in the army three full weeks—informed me that the soldier was on guard and was only trying to utter the simple call of "corporal of the guard No. 17," which meant that he wanted such officer to come to his post for some reason or other. Thus, it appeared that the soldier was only doing his duty and not merely yelling nonsense as I had supposed. How he had been able to give such a plain call the sound I first heard I am unable to understand.

Although the commotion appeared to subside a little as night advanced, yet it seemed to be only so that it could become more dismal and hideous. Thus the night's confusion continued with all the wild and weird variations possible until the early *reveille* of the next morning called up those thousands of enthusiastic young soldiers, who soon transformed the hideous, fantastic scene of a dark, foggy night camp, into a grand and bewildering sea of life, action and labor. Thus passed my first night in camp.

THE NORMAL REGIMENT.

The original idea of having the Normal Regiment contain only young men of literary aspirations and habits, had not been insisted upon as strictly as at first had been intended. And yet, the regiment contained many who had left schools and colleges to join the army; may who well deserved the name of "Student soldiers of Illinois." Taken altogether, the regiment appears to well deserve the honor of carrying through the war the name, Normal Regiment, and being thus identified with that favorite school of the Prairie State, the Normal University.[2]

My first acquaintances were among Company A. Of course, I was more interested in them than in others, as they were to be my immediate associates and comrades for the next three years. Among them were quite a number of students from the Normal University—and a noble class of young men they were—some from other colleges, others were school teachers, and quite a large number had come from the best class of farmer boys, who were, many of them equal, if not superior, in intelligence and all soldierly qualities to their college comrades.

Many good people would regret to see so many bright and promising young men rushing to meet the deadly exposure of camp life and the battle field. It is indeed, a sad, a terrible thought. Still if it proves to be the will of Heaven that they should fall, why should friends at home mourn? If they were to live for ages, when could they again have an opportunity to give their lives to support and uphold a nobler, a better cause. In these trying days how often has the thought been repeated in thousands of earnest hearts: If I have not my loved country to live in, I have nothing to live for. If this is to be its end, let it also be mine. Such a cause thus supported, thus maintained, must be right and in the end must surely win.

SWORN IN.

I was sworn into the service on the fourteenth day of September. Only four others were sworn in at the same time. The medical examination was skipped in my case. The doctor simply bowed to me pleasantly and said: "I guess you will make a good soldier." The company had been mustered and fully organized before I joined it. All the officers had been elected, commissioned and appointed, and every thing was in working order.

I was somewhat amused to see the reluctance with which our officers, at my direction, inserted the word "farmer" instead of "student" in the column of the muster-rolls headed "occupation." They were anxious to have all who had left universities to join the army entered on the rolls as "students." But being a farmer boy I preferred to enlist as one.[3]

MY FIRST SABBATH IN CAMP.

Sunday, the fifteenth, was my first Sabbath in camp. There was not any religious services in our regiment, so I sought relief from the long, dull hours by visiting, reading and writing letters home. As if to remind us of the holiness of the day, which seemed to have been almost forgotten, one of our regiment was called from among us to meet his Maker. This was the second death in the regiment.[4]

A FULL DRESSED SOLDIER.

On Monday I drew my uniform and soon was in full soldier trim. Got a very good, well fitting suit of clothes. Felt quite solder-like. From what prouder position could a young man of this noble country desire to commence active life than that of a free American soldier? And should he die in this cause, every good Christian will admit that he ought to go right straight to Heaven.

MARCHING ORDERS—HURRAH!

On Tuesday, September seventeenth, in answer to the sudden call, "Fall in," our company was immediately assembled together. We were then informed that we were likely to soon move to the front, and ordered to be ready to march at an hour's notice. "Hurrah! Hurrah, boys!! Hurrah!!!" What a yell rang and echoed and re-echoed through the camp and woods, until the staunch old oaks themselves seemed to have caught the inspiration and vibrated with the wild enthusiasm. The boys threw their hats high in the air, ran, jumped, tumbled, hallooed and yelled until they were hoarse and exhausted. In fact, I never saw boys or men so wild, so enthusiastic, so delighted as those of the Thirty-third were when the order came for them to leave Camp Butler and start for the seat of war. All the afternoon every thing and every one was in the greatest commotion. The strange excitement and enthusiasm continued at the highest pitch. And such excitement, such enthusiasm! It seemed in fact as though each and every one was a powerful electric battery charged to the full and overflowing with the electricity, created by the wild enthusiasm of that hour. It appeared as though they thought that the greatest events of a thousand eventful years had been combined and condensed into one brief moment of time, and the victory of them all given to the boys of the Thirty-third in those brief commands: "To the front," "Prepare for active service."

LEARNING TO USE THE KNAPSACK, ETC.

Our knapsacks, haversacks and canteens were issued to us at once. Many funny scenes occurred as the young soldier boys were trying to understand the new, and to them, curious soldier trappings. Each commenced trying to solve the unknown mystery at once. Most of the soldiers could, at first sight, understand the use for which the different articles were designed, but the more awkward ones made some laughable blunders. The canteens being simply a round tin water flask with flat sides and a strap attached to carry it by, so plainly showed for what it was intended that all could understand its use at once, except a few of those odd fellows who never understand anything, and who were laughed at for the way in which they explained their supposed powder horns. This was the only mistake made with the canteens, unless the enthusiastic endorsement of one soldier could be called a mistake, who, when he received his canteen, earnestly embraced it and spontaneously exclaimed, "What a neat and convenient thing to carry a drop of whisky in to have in case of accident."

The knapsacks with their different parts, pockets, and straps, puzzled them more. The haversacks being simply a canvas bag with a strap attached long enough to go over the shoulders, were so plain and simple that they could, as they erroneously supposed, understand its use at once. By the time a single blanket was crowded into it, the haversack, never intended for such a purpose, was full and running over, and the perplexed and bewildered soldier would look with blank astonishment and comical dismay at the large pile of necessary blankets and clothing for which he had no room. By this time the more dexterous ones had solved the mystery of their knapsacks and with them fully packed were trying them in position on their backs. Upon looking at the more ingenious ones, the unhappy and confused soldiers began to see where they were wrong, and soon understood that the haversacks they had been trying to use as a bag for their blankets and clothing was only designed for a dinner bag. With the help of their more efficient comrades the awkward soldiers learned how to pack their knapsacks. In this way even the dullest volunteer was set right as to the different and proper uses of the knapsack, haversack and canteen, and we were soon pronounced to be all in marching order.

GOING—BUT WHERE TO? STRIKING TENTS.

Although we have received orders to be ready to march at an hour's notice, we do not know when we will start nor whither we are to go. Some try to guess, but it is no use. Already every place from Washington to Texas has been mentioned. The only thing we seem to be certain about is that we are going somewhere.

The next day we completed our arrangements for leaving Camp Butler. Many of the soldiers had clothing, books, etc., which they could not take with them. Such things were disposed of in different ways; some were given or thrown away; some, Yankee like, traded off; and others sent to friends at home. Every thing being ready we impatiently waited for marching orders.

At five o'clock in the afternoon the welcome, anxiously-waited-for order came: "Strike tents." No sooner said than done. Even now the laugh went round at the expense of two or three wildly enthusiastic, awkward ones who, this being the first time they had heard this command, had taken the order exactly as given and with the nearest clubs at hand were hastening to vigorously perform their share of "striking tents." Our zealous friends soon learned that to "strike tents" did not mean, like "whipping carpets," to vigorously pound them with a stick, but to take them down. A thousand willing hands seized the tents, took them down, rolled them up and loaded them on the wagons and we were ready to start.

It was now generally understood that we had been ordered to Washington. We marched out to our last parade at Camp Butler. Colonel Hovey[5] was absent from camp. He was in the city of Springfield arranging for our departure. Major Roe on horseback was in command of the regiment. He made a few happy remarks which were enthusiastically cheered by the command. We marched from the camp to the public road, and supposed that we were now fairly on the way; but just as we were starting for the railroad depot we were ordered to stop a few minutes. The few minutes ran into hours. It turned out that we had to stay waiting on the roadside all night expecting every moment to start forward. Waiting for what?

Waiting, as we afterward learned, for Uncle Sam to make up his mind where he wished to send us. Colonel Hovey and our other officers, so it was

Charles E. Hovey. Courtesy of the Illinois State University Archives.

Edward R. Roe. From Elliott and Way, History of the Thirty-Third Regiment Illinois Veteran Volunteer Infantry in the Civil War.

understood, were anxious to cast their fortunes and the future of the regiment with the Western army and not with that of the East. Finally the order for us to go to Washington, in response to much telegraphing, was countermanded and we were sent to Missouri.[6]

FIRST MARCH.

After lying upon the roadside all night we got up at an early hour and returned to our old camp, where we took an early breakfast and then marched to Jimtown,[7] the nearest railroad station.

Our first march, although a short one, only two and a half miles, was to us a hard one. Lying as we did by the roadside all night, expecting every moment to be called into line to go to the supposed waiting railroad train, with little chance to sleep or keep warm during all the long hours of a chilly September night, did not have a tendency to put us in an extra good marching trim. Besides this, we were all heavily overloaded. Each was carrying about as heavy a load as he could lift. And then our knapsacks, the awkward things, would not set right; or rather perhaps we did not know how to make them do so; something was wrong. Going in this condition, by the time our little march was ended, many of the young and unseasoned soldiers were completely exhausted. This, it must be confessed, was rather a poor beginning for soldiers who had such high expectations of the great wonders they were to accomplish when opportunity offered.

JIMTOWN.

We took the cars at Jimtown; such at least was given as the name of the place where we took the cars when leaving Camp Butler. The city—if it is ever to be one—at the time we were there consisted, according to my recollection, of quite a number of substantial, erect and well preserved white oak stumps, one corn crib and a small house upon the side of one of the hills.

ON THE ROAD FROM SPRINGFIELD TO ST. LOUIS.

The train was waiting for us. Embarking took but a short time. The sight of the snorting railroad engine waiting to start us on our journey to some more war-like lands, seems to bring back the enthusiasm of the previous day. Every one was revived as if by magic and at once forgot the weariness caused by our first march. All were soon on the cars, the tents and everything loaded, all ready, and away we went.

We had a very pleasant ride over the grand prairies of Illinois, down to Alton and thence along the river to St. Louis. The sympathy and earnest good will extended to us by the noble-hearted, loyal and true people of Illinois, whose free and happy homes we were so rapidly passing, was unbounded. At every city, village and farm house the citizens and inmates, man, woman and children, all would come out to cheer us on our way and bid us an earnest, heartfelt "God bless you." From Springfield to St. Louis our route was lined with flying flags and waving handkerchiefs. It seemed as though all the people were our own, well known neighbors and friends.

The neatest, best part, was to see the pretty girls, the blooming maidens, the farmer's daughters as they came tripping across the fields to wish us—many of us hoped that it might not prove to be the last—timid yet earnest "good-by." Perhaps there is more truth than would at first appear in the spontaneous words of one soldier, who could not help exclaiming: "If every man in the United States was a farmer's daughter, there would not be any rebels for us to fight." Most certain it is that, if all hearts were as loyal and true as those that beat within the breasts of the kind and noble daughters of our Illinois farmers, there would not be any bloody, treason-stained hands in the land.

At Alton we stopped a short time. This delay gave the soldiers an opportunity to buy a fresh supply of fruit, cakes, pies, etc. It was strongly suspected that a few had something stronger than "cold coffee" in their canteens, which they insisted was what they had purchased. A peculiar kind of cold coffee no doubt. One which, the colder it was, the hotter it became. Its use was not general. One intoxicated man was all I saw in our entire regiment. (This was, please remember, before we had learned to be old soldiers. At that time it was thought to be very wrong for a soldier to get drunk.)

When we first arrived at Alton we expected to take a steamboat and sail down the river to St. Louis. As the boat which was to take us would not be ready to start for several hours, it having part of a cargo to unload, it was decided that we should continue by rail. This was quite a disappointment to the soldiers, especially those, of whom there were many, who had never had a steamboat ride. We were soon under way again and arrived at Illinoistown[8] on the Mississippi River, opposite St. Louis at night. As it was now too late to cross over the river, we took up quarters in the railroad station houses, where we passed the night quite comfortably.

The next morning we went aboard the steamboat Louisiana and crossed over to St. Louis. This little trip somewhat reconciled the boys to the loss of yesterday's anticipated ride. Although it was a short one, not quite two miles in length, still it will bear the name of a steamboat ride, and by many of us will long be remembered, not only as our first steamboat ride, but also as the first time we were ever upon the waters of the grand old Mississippi River.

FROM ST. LOUIS TO PILOT KNOB.

We stopped in St. Louis only long enough to unload from the steamboat and re-load on the railroad cars. As our freight consisted only of camp equipage and a small supply of rations, the work of transferring was soon done and we were ready to start forward. The sharp railroad whistles sounded, Colonel Hovey acting as railroad conductor for our train, cried, "All aboard," and we were on our way for Pilot Knob.

Through that part of Missouri which we passed the people seemed to be loyal at heart and cheered us with nearly the same hearty enthusiasm as that which greeted us in Illinois. If we had not known the fact, we would not, from what we saw, have believed that we were traveling in a slave State.

CHAPTER II.

AT PILOT KNOB.

It was late at night when we arrived at Pilot Knob, too late to pitch tents, so we spread them on the ground for a bed and slept upon them with nothing over us except the starry sky during our first night in Missouri. "Pitch tents," does not, like "pitching quoits," mean to throw them as far as you can but, to erect them. In the army the order is, "pitch tents," when they are to be put up, and "strike tents" when they are to be taken down.

We found the Seventh Nebraska, the Twenty-first Illinois Infantry and part of the Seventh Indiana Cavalry at Pilot Knob.[1] They talked mysteriously of unknown bands of rebels being in force at various surrounding points and in threatening proximity. They appeared anxious upon one point at least, that it should be understood that they were doing very important duty in a military point of view.

To judge by the talk of volunteers who have for the first time found themselves within fifty miles of an armed enemy, one would think that all the great issues of the entire war depended upon their valor. Of course we soon learned to do our part in this line. But a few weeks had passed before every circle in camp was nightly enlivened by the recital of the important and eventful exploits that some of our young heroes had performed. Every scouting expedition of even two miles distance multiplied the numbers of wondrous deeds accomplished. He was a poor soldier, indeed, who could not at least add his one little story to the countless number nightly recounted. It was estimated by the more prudent and wise ones, that our regiment had, to say the least, already done enough to make its name historic.

The Twenty-first Illinois put on airs because their first colonel, an officer by the name of Grant, was acting as a brigadier-general and in command of a small force at Cairo.[2]

ON PILOT KNOB.

We arrived at Pilot Knob at a late hour on Friday, September twentieth. As we were not to move on Saturday, the noted mountain of iron, Pilot Knob, from which the village received its name, claimed our first attention. Every one was anxious to climb over its iron sides and surmount its highest point. Permission was granted and we started forward in high glee. In a short time that gigantic mountain of iron was a grand sight to behold. It was completely covered with curious and impetuous soldiers. Upon every point and crag they could be seen, clambering, laughing and racing until they swarmed upon the topmost peaks. As they gathered at the top they could be seen swinging their hats high in the air as they gave cheer after cheer for the Union, for the flag and for the country we all love so well, until the stern old iron mountain seemed itself to reply with redoubled echoes. To see these earnest young men thus faithfully remembering their country and their country's flag in the midst of the enjoyment caused by their first visit to a place they had so often read about in their schoolboy days, was enough to warm the coldest heart to the highest enthusiasm.

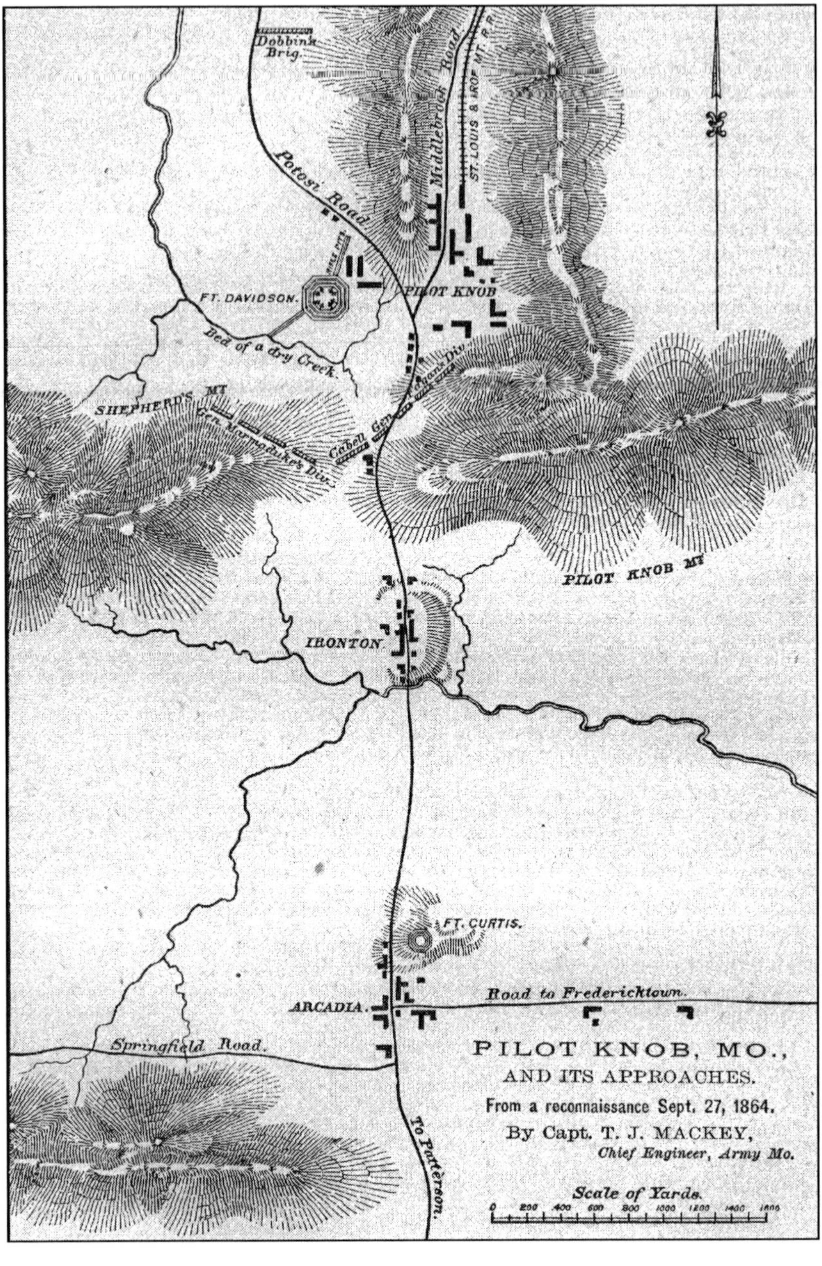

Pilot Knob map. This map was drawn by a Confederate officer in 1864 during Price's expedition. For purposes of this chapter, Fort Davidson had not yet been built and Fort Curtis was called Fort Hovey, but the general appearance of the area is correct. From *War of the Rebellion: Official Records.*

Pilot Knob in 1861. Note train in far background. Fort Davidson at Pilot Knob was built later. This view is from near the base of Shepherd Mountain. From Guernsey and Alden, *Harper's Pictorial History of the Civil War.*

OUR GUNS.

The time granted for us to visit the mountain expired, and we returned to our camp at the village. Upon arriving there we were called into line and marched to the quartermaster's quarters and he issued our guns to us. Colonel Hovey had procured them at the arsenal in St. Louis when we came through. There was no time to issue them to us then, so they were brought down on the cars in the same trains with us in the boxes as received. It seems strange soldiering this. A lot of green country boys, undrilled, undisciplined and without a single weapon in their hands, with no training as to how to use them if they had, going as it were into the very face of an armed enemy in such a destitute and helpless condition. Thus it was our war commenced.

The guns we drew were muskets of a European make, said to be some of those purchased for our Government by General Fremont.[3] The boys were very much disappointed. They had expected to get some of the best rifles in use. They had enlisted with the understanding that this regiment was to be armed with the Enfield rifles, or better, if better were to be had. It was to be the crack regiment of the State, you know. Every regiment organized was formed upon the idea that *it* was without fail to be number one, the especial favorite and pride of the Union army.

Expecting to get the best rifles and then to get a musket—and such a musket! Phew! A musket that needed the services of a skillful engineer to run it successfully. To load one of them: commence by taking a cartridge out of the cartridge-box, tear off the end of it and pour the powder down in the gun, then place the ball in after the powder; now go for the long iron ramrod, which must be pulled out of its pocket, inserted in the mouth of the gun, and with it drive the ball down upon the powder; then take out the ramrod and return it to its own pocket. At this stage of the proceeding, with a decent gun, a percussion cap would be taken from its box, the hammer of the gun raised, and the cap placed upon the gun tube, but these guns do not go off with a simple little percussion cap such as we are acquainted with. No, indeed. First, the hammer must be raised and then a little trap door must be opened, then a funny little primer about two thirds of an inch in length with a pretty little wire string attached, must be taken from its box and inserted "just so" in a cunning little pocket, and then the amusing little trap door must be carefully closed down over it, and thus go through all of this elaborate ceremony before the gun can be loaded. These guns must be intended for soldiers who go out and fire one shot and then return leisurely to camp and go back the next day to fire the second volley. But they are so cunning. Yes, just as cunning as a little red wagon and probably about as dangerous. They are a smooth bore gun and the charge contains one ball and three buck shot. They are good for nothing except at short range, and even at that but little better than a common shot gun and much more complicated and unhandy. In every respect except for use as a club, where their weight would be available, a double barreled shot gun would be far more desirable. These guns were a poor apology for those the members of our regiment had expected; the promised rifles with which they could pick off a rebel with perfect ease at a distance of nine hundred yards.

AN ACCIDENT.

This morning, Saturday, a serious accident occurred in the Seventh Nebraska.[4] A lieutenant was carelessly handling his revolver when it went off and wounded two men, one quite badly through the leg and the other mortally. The latter died during the day and was buried this evening. Such carelessness as this ought to be severely punished.

CAMP HOVEY.

Our chaplain not having arrived, our first Sabbath in Missouri was passed without any religious services being held in our regiment.

On Monday we moved and established a permanent camp. Our new camp lay between Ironton and Arcadia, two little villages near Pilot Knob. It was named Camp Hovey. It was upon dry ground, shaded with some fine old oaks, and upon the whole a very pleasant place. Just beyond our camp was a commanding hill upon which the trees were being cut preparatory to building a fort. The boys went to work earnestly, and soon had made a fine army camp.

It would surprise any one not acquainted with the inexhaustible resources and utility of Yankee ingenuity, to see how soon apparently useless pieces of board and planks and even the broken remains of deserted secesh buildings were transformed into articles of convenience and utility. Tent floors, bunks, tables, writing desks, seats, etc. were made with surprising rapidity and skill. Three hours after our tents were pitched our camp presented the appearance and contained all of the conveniences of an old and well arranged camp. The easy-going people of Missouri were surprised and astonished. "Why," they exclaimed, "if these men stay here six months they could build a big city." They had never before seen men work in earnest.

GOOD WATER.

One of the best things of this country is the quality and abundance of good water. Flowing springs pour forth their streams of cool and clear water from every mountain side. The springs are unnumbered and their supply of good water is inexhaustible. Good water is necessary to preserve the health of an army. The bad water of Camp Butler no doubt did much to impair the health of the soldiers camped there. Unhealthy water frequently destroys more soldiers than the enemy's bullets. A commander who would allow his soldiers to use bad water when good can be had without fighting too hard, ought to be drummed out of the service.

A SUICIDE.

Shortly after we were established in our new quarters at Camp Hovey, fourteen men came from Illinois and joined our company. Some of them were new members who had lately enlisted, and others those who could not come with us when we left Camp Butler. They brought us the sad news that Henry Johnson, a fine, intelligent young man who had been left in the hospital at Camp Butler, had committed suicide by drowning himself in the small lake at that place.[5] This sad information seemed too incredible for belief. I saw and had a talk with him just before we came away and he appeared to be in good spirits. He said that he was gaining nicely and would be with us in a few days. When I expressed my regret that he could not go with us he replied in a happy, lively manner and laughingly anticipated the pleasant time he would have going down to Missouri in a nice comfortable passenger coach, while we would have to go in crowded freight cars. In these rushing times passenger cars for the transportation of soldiers had to be extemporized out of freight cars. Some new, discouraging memories and thoughts must have occurred to the young soldier after we came away or he would never have sacrificed his life so vainly. With a big war on hand and his command going to the front, it would seem that a soldier would know that he could have lots of good chances of being killed and to die in an honorable and useful way, and that he need not commit suicide. Young Johnson left a short note bidding his friends good-bye and telling them that he was "going to the happy land above." Poor boy! Let us pity although we may not understand him.

BUILDING A FORT.

The early building of a fort upon the hill near our camp was deemed a pressing and important matter. The work was placed in charge of Colonel Hovey, who took hold of it in earnest. He examined the plans and estimated the work to be done. He then appealed to the members of his regiment; mentioned the importance of the work, the desire and necessity that it should be done immediately; explained that it must be done either voluntarily or by regular detail. He would prefer to work with us as volunteers rather than otherwise; would the Thirty-third volunteer to do the work and have the honor of building the fort, instead of assisting others to build it as detailed soldiers? The boys of the regiment most willingly assented, and to work we went. Additional inducement was given by a promise of twenty-five cents per day in addition to our regular pay as soldiers. Those who worked as mechanics to have forty cents per day. All of us who could use an ax, saw or hammer, were put down on the list as mechanics. Eight hours to be credited a day's work. Every one more than that to be credited as double time. Thus twelve hours' work in one day would be credited as two days' work. We usually put in the full twelve hours. Thus many of us were earning eighty cents per day extra. Trustworthy sergeants were appointed to keep these *important time tables* with strict impartiality and military exactness. The boys jokingly called this promised extra pay "boat money," a name derived from the case of the always insolvent man who was continually bargaining for the purchase of a farm which he would pay for "when his boat came in." (Of course, nothing was ever paid upon these carefully kept accounts.)

The work was pushed forward with the utmost rapidity. Officers and men all worked together. In this work all rank is ignored. The best workmen were our recognized leaders. The timber in the woods near at hand was freely used. Large trees were cut and the logs hauled to the fort and placed in the walls.

By the time the week ended the walls of the fort were so well established and the work in such a state of progress, that the chaplain of our regiment who had now arrived, thought that the fort ought to have some sort of a dedication, so he obtained permission and held religious services in it on Sunday.

As seemed proper and appropriate the fort was named after the colonel of our regiment and called Fort Hovey.

COLONEL HOVEY AND THE WORKMAN.

One day while the work on the fort was being carried on with its accustomed vigor, Colonel Hovey, as was usual with him, was around among the boys to see how the work progressed, lending a helping hand now and then as he saw occasion. Among others, he came across a man who was working with considerable difficulty by reason of not having the proper tools to use. The man did not recognize the Colonel, who was dressed in a plain way, and looked, it must be confessed, more like a common soldier than like what we would expect to see in the person of the commander of the famous Normal Regiment. Colonel Hovey noticed this workman a moment and then asked: "Could you not do that work better if you had a good hand-saw to use?" "Why, yes," said the man; "I believe that I could. Say, old chap, won't you go over to the tool house and get one for me?" The Colonel trudged off to the tool house, nearly a quarter of a mile distant, and promptly returned with a hand saw. The workman praised him for his promptness and continued his work. The Colonel stood looking on and soon again suggested: "I should think that you could do that better if you had a good ax to use." "Yes, I never thought of that; won't you run over to the other side of the fort and see if you can find one for me?" Colonel Hovey went as before and soon returned with the desired tool. His apt suggestions and willingness had completely won the workingman's good will. "Well, old hoss," said he, in his warmest, friendliest manner, "you are a might handy chap, and if you will come around and see me this evening I will go with you to headquarters and have you assigned to help me as a carpenter, and you will then get better wages than you do now as a common laborer."

At this time, seeing that some of those who knew him were beginning to notice the interesting interview, Colonel Hovey passed to some other part of the work. The honest workman's astonishment, when informed who his "handy chap" actually was, can be well imagined.

SOLDIER DYEING.

One evening after our work for the day was done, our jovial little comrade, Elisha Burrows, was seen walking down toward the officers' quarters. His face, always the picture of mirth and fun, was now covered with sadness. He had just come from his tent. Corporal Lewis was one of his tent mates. Lewis, one of our best soldiers, was a general favorite, and especially so with Lieutenant Burnham, one of the warmest hearted and most sympathetic men in the army.

As Burrows came near Lieutenant Burnham, his face grew more sad and in mournful tones he asked: "Lieutenant, did you hear about Corporal Lewis?" In his quick, impulsive way, the Lieutenant answered: "No, what is the matter with him?" With a voice trembling with emotion Burrows slowly replied: "He is now in his tent dyeing." With tears of heartfelt sorrow and sympathy coursing down his cheeks, Burnham rushed to the soldier's tent, exclaiming: "Poor Lewis!" and found him—sitting before a glass dyeing his new-grown mustache.

OLD SECESH AND HIS PIG.

Although we were quite well supplied with provisions by the Government, some of the boys would persist in having a relish for the many little knickknacks which the farms and larders of Missouri furnished and not included in the army rations. No doubt they were in error in their belief, yet some of the boys were actually foolish enough to affirm, and the extreme ones even to go so far as to really believe, that fat chickens and plump pigs were good to eat even in the army. Whether or not any of them ever attempted actual proof is another question. As a general thing our soldiers were, in those early days of the war, very generous and exact in respecting the Union citizen's right of property, but woe to him who was known to be a secesh sympathizer. Although military rules and orders would not allow anything to be disturbed unless properly and formally confiscated, yet the soldiers' ingenuity enabled them in many ways to show their respect to rebel sympathizers.

One of the wealthiest men living in the vicinity of Arcadia was of this stripe. One day this rebel sympathizer when passing through the woods near camp saw one of his fattest shoats fall down not far from him, it having met with a severe accident in the shape of a ball from an unseen gun. The Missourians allow their hogs to run at large in the woods, and he was no doubt slipping slyly around to see that nothing happened to his pigs. There being no hunter in sight to claim the game, and being unable to find from what part of the thick brush the shot was fired, the owner picked up his pig, a good sized one, and started home.

He was soon met by a soldier without any gun. "Goodness," the soldier said, "are you foolish enough to tire yourself out carrying that fat pig home when all you have to do is to go to Colonel Hovey who will not only make the rascals who shot it carry it home and dress it nicely for you, but also punish them severely in the bargain?" "Yes," he replied, "but how will he know who shot the pig?" "Oh, that is easy enough. He keeps a list of all the boys out of camp. He can spot the lads for you." This plan tickled old secesh hugely. The idea that he could go to camp and then come back marching proudly at the head of the despised Yankee soldiers, who would have to do the drudgery of lugging the pig to his house and perform the dirty work of scraping and cleaning it, with him in command to see the work well and thoroughly done, and then to send them back to camp to remain with ball and chain in the guardhouse, while he, old importance himself, was at home eating his fresh meat, was too great a temptation for him to withstand. He quickly assented to the plan. The friendly soldier kindly helped him to place the pig in a nice shady place where it would safely remain until the owner's anticipated, victorious return. The old cove then went briskly into camp to find Colonel Hovey.

The sequel can be easily imagined when we add that the pig was soon transferred and keeping company with an unloaded gun, which the kind soldier had hid before volunteering his unselfish and valuable advice.

Suffice it to say that Colonel Hovey impatiently listened to the complaint, more than half intimated that he doubted its truth, and then sent some men to investigate.

When the owner got to the place and looked for the dead pig, to his great astonishment there was no pig there, and the officers returned and reported old secesh to Colonel Hovey as an old fraud.

That day at supper a fine piece of fresh pork steak was furnished the Colonel. As he finished it with much relish he said to his cook: "How did you get this, Sam?" "Selled eggs and byed it," said Sam. As it was not dignified for a great man like the commander of the Thirty-third to have an extended confab with his cook, the Colonel finished his supper in peace. But it is said he shortly afterward sent to the owner of the lost pig and bought two of his best—the value was not large—and forgot to ever send for one of them; in this way paying for the confiscated pig.

WARLIKE TIMES.

While the work on the fort was being pushed forward with the utmost rapidity, many other things claimed our attention.[6] We were in many ways made to appreciate the fact that armed forces of the enemy were within threatening distance of us. Countless wild and exaggerated rumors were circulated day and night. Among them were some stubborn facts.

A squad of men went to Arcadia and took two prisoners and 22,000 secesh gun-caps. The men protested that they were true Union men and that the rebel who was trying to take the ammunition through our lines to the enemy was another fellow who could not be found. They were given the benefit of the doubt and discharged and the gun-caps confiscated.

Two negroes were brought in by our picket guard. They claimed to have been connected with the rebel army as servants, from which they had escaped and come to the Union army. They were taken to headquarters and freely gave all the information of the enemy they could.

Three companies of our regiment, E, B, and K, were as soon as they had received their guns, after our arrival at Pilot Knob, sent back toward St. Louis to guard the railroad bridges. They were the first of our command to get into trouble. Quite a large force of the enemy had been hovering around us. Not being bold enough to attack the Union troops in the vicinity of Pilot Knob, they had passed up between us and the Mississippi River and then thrown a force around in our rear to destroy the bridges on the railroad and thus cut us off from communication with St. Louis.

They were too strong for the small force we had at those places and our soldiers were soon driven away and the bridges burned. Those of our troops nearest to us made their way back to Pilot Knob, those nearest to St. Louis fell back toward that city, and Captain Elliott and his company (E) were captured.[7]

Captain Lippincott had command of those that fell back to Pilot Knob. When he and the men of Company K came in and we were told of the fighting they had seen, we began to appreciate what it was to be in a warlike country. Captain Lippincott received much credit for the able manner in which he saved his little force from being captured by the large band of rebels by which they were surrounded.

Two men of Company C were outside our lines to hunt in the woods and were captured by some straggling band of the enemy.[8]

Our cavalry now began to get in their work in feeling out the enemy. They were sent out in every direction and met roving bands of rebels almost every day. These small forces when found were easily driven by our men. When the neighborhood of the main rebel army was reached, our cavalry would have to skip back. Our cavalry scouts soon learned so that they could tell as soon as they saw a rebel picket whether or not it was supported by a large force. If it was, the rebels would only fall back on their supporting guard and show fight. If it was only a part of a detached force they would go pell-mell over the hills and out of reach, and it would be as impossible to get a second sight of them as it would be to get a second shot at a flock of wild turkeys.

JUST BEFORE THE BATTLE.

It will be remembered that we did not get our guns until the twenty-second of September. The next day we moved and established a new camp, and then went to work building the fort. Soon threatening movements of the enemy near us admonished our officers that the new soldiers needed some training in the use of their guns. On the twenty-eighth we commenced drilling in the manual of arms. From this time, all of the leisure moments that could be taken from other duties were spent in drilling. With building forts, drilling and watching rebels, the last of September and the first of October, 1861, were very busy times with us.

Toward the last of October, all of our available force was called into line and we started out fully expecting to meet the enemy near at hand. After going a short distance a halt was called, and in a short time a march back to camp ordered. Two or three days afterward the same movements with the same expectations of a battle were repeated.

On the fifteenth of October it seemed that the so often expected engagement would certainly take place. News from our cavalry told us that they were being driven back toward camp. It was believed that the enemy were moving upon us with their entire force. At four o'clock we started out on the Fredericktown road to meet them. We did not expect to go more than one or at most two miles before being obliged to select a battle ground. Instead of this we went seven miles without seeing any rebels, but we met our returning cavalry. They had met some of Jeff Thompson's forces with whom they had quite a severe brush. Our men were repulsed but they succeeded in bringing off their wounded. From the cavalry it was learned that the enemy were in force at or near Fredericktown. We now halted and a council of war was held by our commanding officers. After a session of two or three hours it was decided that we should return to our quarters at Pilot Knob and Ironton and wait for future arrangements. So we turned and marched back again.

It was upon this march that Lieutenant Burnham who for a short time had command of our company gave the order which afforded considerable amusement and came near making him famous. While we were descending a steep hill, for some reason the front of the column stopped which made it necessary for us to halt. Burnham, like the rest of us, was new in military life, and in the confusion of the moment the proper command "Halt!" escaped his memory, and thus in its place in thundering tones upon the night air came the command: "Mark time!" The idea of stopping upon a sharp march to a supposed battle field, with the enemy perhaps within hearing distance, to go through the idle ceremony of "marking time," which is to take up one foot after the other in succession and replace it in the same place was so absurd that the entire company caught the spirit of the joke and obeyed the command. And there stood Company A, in battle array, upon a steep hill in sight of their comrades and the enemy near, vigorously "marking time" until one of his brother officers suggested the right word, when Burnham stopped the interesting ceremony by the command "Halt!"

Other troops had followed us to Pilot Knob so that we now had quite a respectable force at this point. Among the new arrivals was the Thirty-eighth Illinois, Colonel Carlin commanding.[9] By some means his commission had been issued so that it bore a prior date to the one held by Colonel Hovey, which made him the senior and commanding officer of the army at this point. This led to considerable unpleasant feeling, but nothing serious grew out of it. The Thirty-third having been organized so as to take the earliest number, it did not seem just right that it should be outranked by the Thirty-eighth. Our soldiers being volunteers took a deep interest in these matters. For a time excitement ran high. At one time Colonel Carlin for some trifling reason put Colonel Hovey under arrest. That is he went so far as to order Hovey to consider himself under arrest. This continued for a few days. The lively times the surrounding rebels were now giving us claimed our undivided attention, and other reasons served to smooth over the misunderstanding for the time being, but it can be safely said that Carlin and Hovey never became very loving to each other so long as they remained in the same command.

BATTLE OF FREDERICKTOWN.

It now became known that Jeff Thompson was fast concentrating an army of considerable force in the neighborhood of Fredericktown, and between us and the Mississippi River.[10] This large force of the enemy and its position made an attack upon us more than probable. It seemed certain. All military rules demanded. The bridges between us and St. Louis had been burned. The enemy had successfully thrown himself between us and the only Union troops within supporting distance. The situation of affairs demanded that General Thompson should attack us, and do it at once. We expected it. Orders were given for us to keep our guns loaded and ready for use. We "slept on arms" every night. We were frequently called out expecting an immediate battle.

At last, however, it became certain that Thompson would not attack us in the strong position we held. His movements were strange indeed. To occupy the position he did required great bravery, if not absolute recklessness. To remain where he was inactive was at once both dangerous and silly. He should have immediately come on and made an attack upon the forces at Pilot Knob before reinforcement could have reached them, or else have promptly retired to a safe position. His delay gave time for communication to be made with the

M. Jeff Thompson. From Johnson and Buel, *Battles and Leaders of the Civil War.*

Union forces upon the Mississippi river. A force large enough to compete with Thompson, under command of Colonel Plummer, had crossed the river from Illinois, and coming northwest from Cape Giardue [*sic*] were within easy striking distance of the rebels. Another force from Cairo had crossed to Bird's Point. It was easy to be seen that Thompson's entire force could easily be captured. The boys were now in high spirits. Soldiers in the ranks talk of and study military points almost as much as the officers in command. By going to the southeast from Pilot Knob and having the force from Bird's Point move to the northeast and then let the Union troops from Cape Giardue [*sic*] come up and strike him from the east, Jeff Thompson would not only have been defeated but would also have been cut off from all chance of escape.

Such was the condition of affairs when the force at Pilot Knob, with Colonel Carlin in command, started out to join in the attack upon the enemy under General Thompson, who had now concentrated his entire force at

Fredericktown. We were aware of the fact that the Union troops under Colonel Plummer were on the way and within striking distance of the rebel army.

On the twenty-first of October the troops came up and a sharp brisk battle was fought in which Thompson was quickly and severely defeated. Most of the fighting on the Union side was done by the soldiers under Colonel Plummer. As he outranked Colonel Carlin he was the ranking officer of the united command. Plummer's own soldiers did most of the fighting. Most of the Pilot Knob forces, however, participated in the battle; some of them in the thickest of it. Company A was on the skirmish line. The balance of the Thirty-third was held in reserve at first, but they were so anxious to go in that they were permitted to do so. The fight was, however, so soon over that they only came up in time to fire one volley at the retreating rebels. It was a short, sharp and decisive contest. As I was confined in the camp hospital at Ironton, during this time, with a severe attack of typhoid fever, I will not attempt to give incidents of the contest.

Instead of falling to the south of the enemy as they could easily and safely have done, the troops from Pilot Knob had kept to the north so as to form a junction with the troops under Colonel Plummer. This left an open road for Thompson to the south, and with his defeated army he retreated in hot haste toward the Arkansas state line. In war if you are sure to defeat the enemy, strike so as to cut off his retreat and make the victory complete.

Although the enemy's entire force was not captured as it ought to have been, still the battle of Fredericktown was in many respects a very important one. It gave us undisputed possession of all of Southeastern Missouri and was the first battle of the war that could be claimed as a decided Union victory.

The loss upon the Union side was small. That of the rebels comparatively large. It is claimed that our soldiers buried over 200 of the rebel dead, left by them upon the field. The enemy's severest loss was that of Colonel Lowe, who was second to General Thompson in command of the rebel forces. He was one of the most promising young officers in the rebel army. He was killed in the early part of the battle. His death had a very depressing effect upon the rebels of Southern Missouri and Northern Arkansas, where, before the war, he was well known as a brilliant, promising and popular young lawyer.

The beginning of the contest shows that Thompson attempted to lead the Union army into an ambush. When Colonel Plummer arrived at Fredericktown,

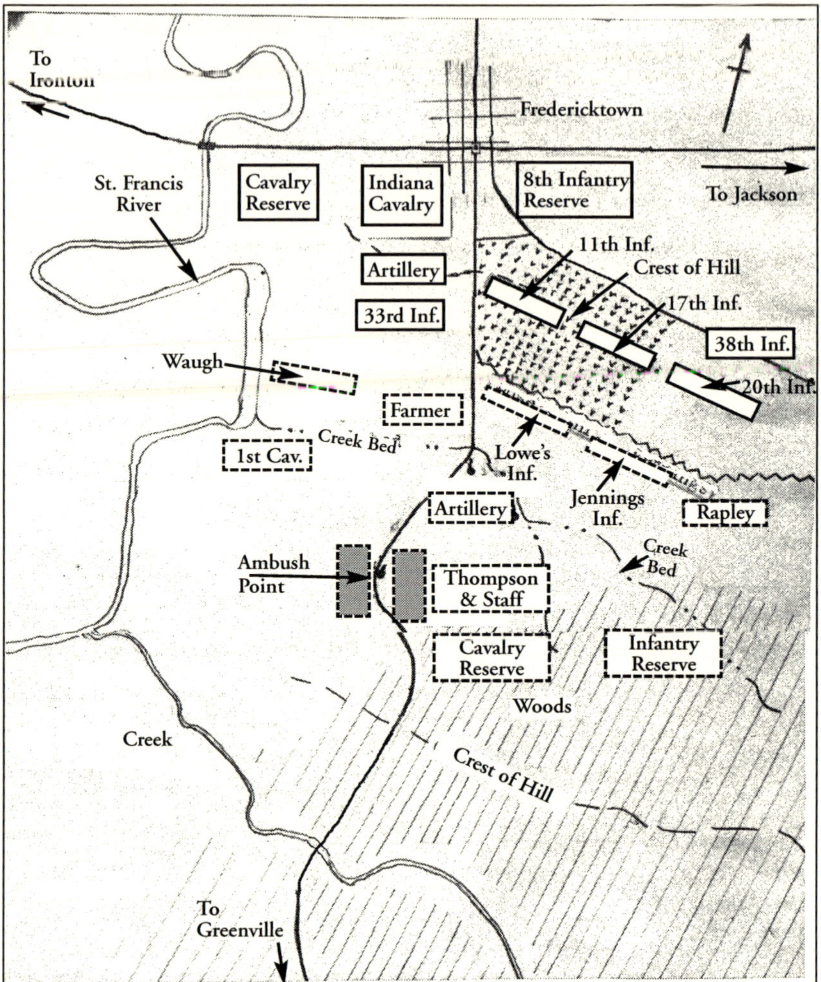

Battle of Fredericktown
Adaped from Westover

Battle of Fredericktown. From Westover, "The Civil War Experiences of General M. Jeff Thompson in 1861."

he found that Colonel Carlin had preceded him and been near the town since morning. It was believed by Carlin that the enemy had beat a hasty retreat. Colonel Plummer desired to advance and see what had become of the confederates. As arrangements were being made for this movement, Colonel Plummer directed Captain Stewart, the captain of an independent cavalry company, and A. J. Sanger, a solder of the Twentieth Illinois, to go forward and take observations.[11] The two rode forward and from the brow of a hill saw some smoke arising from the distant woods. Stewart used his field glass but could discover no evidences of a large force. They now passed on down the road, which was narrow and enclosed on both sides by a high old-fashioned rail fence. The high and thick weeds and grass growing along the fence were not easy to be seen through. As they passed down in this narrow road the Captain, in a clear, distinct voice, discussed the strength of the force in the woods beyond, giving it as his opinion that it was nothing more than a detached band of rebel scouts. Just at this moment Sanger's keen eyes peered through the fence and weeds, and there discovered the rebels in full army line lying still as mice upon the ground. At the same moment the thought flashed through his mind that the rebels had planned an ambush and were waiting for the Union troops to come in solid column down this road, when they would raise up and slaughter them. Rightly guessing that they were waiting for larger game and would not care to discover themselves by firing upon two men, Sanger assumed not to see them and coolly continued the talk with the Captain, in a tone easily heard by the rebels within a rod of them; agreeing that there were no rebels worth noticing near, and that our soldiers could come down without being disturbed. "Yes," said the Captain, "I guess that we will not see any more secesh in these parts." "That is so. Suppose we cross into that field, go up over that hill, and tell our boys to come on," suggested Sanger. "All right," was the reply. They had by this time passed quite a distance along by the heavy ranks of rebels lying upon the other side of the fence. They were near enough to almost have reached our scouts with their sabers and heard every word spoken. Sanger dismounted, let down the fence to the field opposite, let their horses through and slowly put the fence up again, all the time chatting about the situation as though there was not a rebel within a hundred miles of them. Re-mounting, both rode up the hill on a slow walk and as they passed over and out of sight of the rebels, Sanger for the first time spoke of what he had seen and asked the Captain if he saw the rebels by the fence. "No, did you see any?" The situation was explained in a few words, a brisk trot under cover of the hill was made back to the Union lines, Colonel Plummer informed of the situation and the rebels themselves were soon surprised by a sudden and destructive fire, which told them that their well laid plans to get the Union troops into a pocket and slaughter them had failed.

CHAPTER III.

IN WINTER QUARTERS.

After returning from Fredericktown our regiment remained in Camp Hovey until the middle of November and then took up winter quarters, in which we remained until the first day of March.

We took possession of the vacant houses in Arcadia, of which there were quite a number and they made us very good and pleasant quarters.

Three companies, A, C and D, went into the seminary building. Schoolhouses, colleges, churches and all kinds of public buildings are vacant and unused in this part of the country during these war times. The seminary was a large and roomy frame building.[1]

Our company had a number of small rooms. When we were divided into squads, there were from eight to twelve men in a room, according to its size.

In each room there was either a stove or a fireplace. The one I was in had a good large fire place. These old-fashioned fire-places, relics of the past in more civilized lands, are yet in quite general use in Missouri. These are, as all pioneer people will well remember, simply an open fire-place at the end of the room, built of brick or stone and connected with a chimney running to the top of the house for the smoke to escape. Filled with large pieces of wood and a rousing fire well under way, there is a degree of sociability in the glowing coals and the sparkling fire of these old-fashioned open fire-places that the modern invention of iron stoves can not approximate. During a long winter evening a bright sparkling fire in an old-fashioned, open fire-place would be far more pleasant company than a smoking stove and a scolding wife. One can sit before such a fire and easily imagine that it talks.

We built bunks three tiers high in one end of the room to sleep on. This left us considerable room for other purposes. Seats, writing desks, etc., we made to suit our taste and convenience. That is, my comrades did this. Having myself just left the camp hospital and the typhoid fever, both of which I was right glad to get away from, I was not in a condition to take much part in heavy work. When fairly settled we had as good winter quarters as soldiers could wish for, the best in the army.

Our conveniences and means for entertainment and amusement were varied and simple. Here we remained having jolly, good times until the first of March. In fact the only thing we had to grumble about was the easy, inactive times we were having, and to envy those who were suffering untold hardships elsewhere. Many were fearful that the rebels would all be whipped and the war ended by others, while we remained here and simply performed garrison duty. It seems to be a natural desire to be at the work to be done. Even the well-fed, thoroughbred race horse will jump and pull and bruise himself in his frantic attempts to escape from the well supplied stall, where he could eat and sleep and take his comfort, to join his mates when he sees them hard at work in a contested race. And so with soldiers enlisted for the war, they are never contented except when trying to accomplish something.

RELIGION IN THE ARMY.

During the first part of our soldier life a steady, deep and increasing religious interest was maintained. Each new camp we established usually made it necessary to form new squads. At Camp Butler, Camp Hovey, and at this place, I was connected with three different squads in all of which it was customary each evening before retiring for the night to observe some short religious exercise such as reading a chapter in the Bible and acknowledging our accountability to our Maker. In the seminary our squad continued this during the winter. All were nominally Christians, although not all professors of religion. All creeds were ignored. Even church members rarely if ever knew to what church or denomination others belonged. Each one of our members would in turn lead in these evening services by reading his own selection from Scripture and end with a short prayer. Whenever this duty fell to one of us common sinners who was not a member of any church, he would do the reading and then turn to some one of our professed Christians with the request: "Brother ——— will please lead us in prayer."

It may be added that with a few noble exceptions but little assistance was derived from the army chaplains in maintaining this or any other religious interest in the army. The fault was probably more in the want of adaptation to the work before them than in the lack of inclination to perform it.

The field was a large one. A deep religious feeling prevailed. It could not have been otherwise. The religious sentiment of a country will, during a war, always be strongly represented by its soldiers. A great war never was, and never will be, fought by those who do not believe in anything. Those who do not believe in a future existence can not believe any reward sufficient for the loss of this life. Unbelief doth make cowards of all. He that hath no hope in his soul hath no bravery in his heart.

SETTLING REBEL CLAIMS.

During the winter some of the disloyal owners came to claim rent for the buildings occupied by the Union soldiers. Colonel Carlin, who had joined the army as a strong Democrat in politics, had at this time much faith in the effect of kind and liberal treatment to the erring Southern brothers, and freely listened to them upon all occasions. (He became radical enough before the war ended.) Thinking that it was right to pay rent, he directed Captain George R. Dyer, the post quartermaster, to investigate and make out proper vouchers. Captain Dyer looked the buildings over and made out vouchers for such rent as they would have commanded before the war. At this time there was no demand for them at any price. Colonel Carlin approved the vouchers and sent them forward. Soon the owners of the buildings learned the amount and loudly insisted that it should be increased. They wanted to rob the Government. Captain Dyer would not change the figures, having already allowed liberally for the use of buildings which would have been vacant if we had not occupied them. To Carlin the owners went, talked sweet to him, and soon got him to order Captain Dyer to make out new vouchers for an increased amount.

Remembering that he was post quarter-master and not fully accountable to Colonel Carlin, he at once wrote a statement of the case to General Allen, then department commander. Promptly the answer came back ordering Captain Dyer not to make any vouchers for an increase of rent but to allow the owners to apply to the department at Washington if they felt aggrieved. Soon in came the secesh owners. "We want our new vouchers," they demanded. "We have concluded not to make any," said the Captain. In hot haste they went to Colonel Carlin and reported that his orders had not been obeyed. Threatening to place the quartermaster under arrest he sent for him. He came. "Do you intend to obey my orders?" he fiercely demanded. "All proper orders," meekly answered the Captain. "Sir, I want you to understand that as commander of this post I am the judge of what are proper orders. Have you made the vouchers I ordered for these men?" "I have received other directions upon that matter," said the quartermaster, handing the Colonel the order from General Allen. Colonel Carlin read the order and then simply said: "You may return to your quarters." He never referred to the matter again. The grasping owners did not dare to send their fraudulent claims to Washington, and thus a large sum was saved to the Government.

READING MATTER.

During the winter we spent in Arcadia Seminary we were well supplied with reading matter. A nice little library had been selected and sent to us by kind friends, mainly by the good people of Bloomington and Normal, Illinois. It contained good and interesting books which were well adapted to our use. In addition to the books of larger size a neat box came full of Harper's and other good and instructive magazines. The latter were sent to us by the fair inmates of the Rockford Female Seminary. Those good girls had thoughtfully re-covered the magazines with their own hands and expressly for the soldier boys. Such true, unassuming kindness as this, and from personal strangers, will always be remembered. The soldier's motto is, Hurrah for the flag—God bless the ladies! And it is hard to say to which the simple fellows can be the most faithful. A brave soldier will be a true lover. Added to the books and magazines we received the daily papers promptly each day.

LETTER WRITING.

The ever faithful source of improvement, pleasure and happiness, letter writing, filled an important place with us.[2] Our conveniences for writing were so good; the leisure time we had at hand; the anxiety to hear from absent friends and the desire to tell them of ourselves; the force of example and the inclination to do as we see others doing; all these things combined, served at one time to make letter writing almost a panic with us. If one could get a copy of all the letters written during this time he would have a voluminous if not interesting collection. It was no uncommon thing for some of the boys to write as many as from five to ten letters per day. Weekly correspondence home was changed to semi and tri-weekly, and often, especially if there was a girl in the case, to daily. Many new correspondences were commenced. Common kind of friends at home were no doubt annoyed with the ceaseless flow of letters. The amount of soft sentiment that was sent to the fair ones was truly amazing. Letters were written and sent upon the smallest pretext. No doubt many of Illinois' fair daughters were surprised to receive an unexpected letter from some soldier in Missouri. Those who had left a girl at home pushed their suit with all the ardor and impetuosity of a soldier lover. And then, in those cases where there was actually a confessed sweetheart—mercy save us! Turn the pages down; do not let even imagination attempt to uncover those sacred secrets. Let no ruthless hand ever dare to break the seal of a soldier's letter to his own true sweetheart.

AMUSEMENTS.

Our means for and sources of amusement were various and sufficient. We indulged in all of the different games of chess, checkers, backgammon, dominos and card playing. Cards as usual in the army being the most patronized; while chess with us, as elsewhere, was recognized as a game of art and skill, requiring thought and good judgment to play successfully.

Nothing in the nature of actual gambling was permitted in our company. In fact the vice of gambling was soon and effectually driven out of our army. No officer should ever allow gambling to gain a foothold in his command.

A little contest, "for the treats," was not considered actual gambling. One day the officers of our company concluded that the boys were entitled to a treat of a box of cigars. After the cigars were ordered, Lieutenant Norton, who was a very good player, proposed to Captain Potter who was not, that they should play checkers to decide who should pay for the cigars; the one first getting five games to win. The Captain assented and they commenced. After easily winning four games, seeing that he could decide the contest at his pleasure, Norton allowed Potter to take two games. In the next he played still more carelessly, so that Potter not only won but was also able to prevent Norton from making a king. The Captain now claimed that a "skunk" always counted as three games, which made him five, and the winner, and declared the contest ended. Norton paid for the cigars and tried to get satisfaction with another contest, but Potter insisted that his record as the champion checker player was established, and from that time ceased to indulge in the game.

In front of the seminary was a fine lawn upon which, in fine weather, we had rousing times playing ball and other athletic school-boy games.

Among other things we sent to St. Louis and procured a set of boxing gloves. They were well patronized by the company and gave the boys much amusement and healthy exercise in learning the manly (?) art of self-defense.

When we wanted a real huge time we tried the blanket game. This consisted of taking two large, strong blankets spread together to give them the needed strength, and surrounded by a lot of soldiers all taking hold of the sides and ends of the blankets, and then capture some victim, throw him into the center of the blanket and commence lively throwing him up into the open air, carefully catching him as he came down. The height to which a person can be thrown in this manner and safely caught as he comes down is truly surprising. We first commenced by taking the smaller men and throwing them up but a little distance. In time we freely threw them higher and became indifferent as to the size of the one thrown. Sergeant Ed Pike, one of the heaviest men in the company, and as big hearted as he is large, was often a leader in this game of throwing up the boys. One day as he had hold of the blanket, having just finished with one and waiting to toss up the next, before he knew what was coming, some others had come up behind him and Pike himself was tumbled into the center, two stout lads had taken hold of the blanket in his place, and to his great surprise he was immediately flying sky-wards. His look of dismay as he went into the air the first time was comical enough. He expected, of course that his heavy weight would, in the fall, carry him through the blanket as easy as though so much paper and that his neck was liable to be broken upon the hard ground below. He came out all right and after a few flights twenty feet or more high, began to like it and was willing to give the boys all the exercise they wanted in throwing him up. In fact this is the way it always worked. After being thrown up a few times they all seemed to enjoy it, so that when we wanted to send up some one who would look wild as he went into the air, we had to pick out a new chap, one who had never been sent up.

Another source of rare amusement was what we called "stag dances"—soldier filling the place of both ladies and gentlemen. The smaller, best looking lads taking the women's part of the dance. The part each assumed was designated by the gentlemen appearing on the floor bare-headed, while those who represented the ladies wore their caps with the front piece behind. At best the prettiest boy, in place of a girl, is a sorry partner for a dance. These dances were, of course, delightful—I never dance.

Sometimes, to change the programme, we would get some limber-toed negro to come in and dance a lively old-fashioned Southern break-down. If a colored man is strong in any part it is in his legs. Why in thunder they did not, long ago, all run away and save us from this fearful war upon the slavery questions, I cannot understand. At this time Company A gloried in the possession of two violins and half a dozen fiddlers, so that we could indulge in these dancing amusements whenever we chose.

Add to all of these the endless number of camp jokes and never-ending plans of play and fun that soldiers are always, day and night, inventing, and it will be readily conceded that we had no reason to complain for lack of amusements during the winter we spent in Arcadia.

OUR RATIONS—MISSOURI PIE—GOOD THINGS FROM HOME.

We had a convenient cook and dining room in which the rations for the whole company were prepared and served. The supply furnished by the Government was liberal and excellent, that is, for army rations.

We were supplied with good bread, a liberal quantity of beef, pork, beans, rice, coffee, tea and sugar, and occasionally with potatoes and other vegetables. The cooking was not the best in the world, but as good as could be expected by our soldier-boy cooks. Audible complaints about the cooking were not often made. The prompt and decisive answer to such complaints always was: "If you do not like this cooking come and do it yourself." Improperly cooked food is one of the greatest evils of a volunteer army. A lot of young boys who never had the least experience in cooking, are brought from their homes and given a supply of raw provisions to cook or eat raw as best they can. No doubt the fearful amount of sickness and loss of life by disease in the army during these early days could be justly traced to this cause. It became an oft-quoted maxim, that: more soldiers are killed by raw beans than by bullets.

If another war ever calls such a mass of the raw and inexperienced youth of our land into the soldiers' ranks, let it be seen to that competent cooks are at hand to give them assistance and instruction in the beginning of their army life. If nothing else can be done, let some of the mothers go to their first camp and show their boys how to cook. No officer should ever venture to lead a thousand young men from their homes to the army who is not alive to the importance of preventing improperly cooked food from killing more of his soldiers than do the enemy's bullets.

This part of Missouri is a good fruit country and the surrounding farms were well supplied with apples of an excellent quality. The farmers were right glad to trade fruit for our extra pork, coffee and sugar, so that we had good apples nearly all winter. The women folks wanted to trade for tea while their husbands were trading for pork and coffee, so they commenced making pies to sell us. They sent the pies into camp by their children. In a short time the little folks could every day be seen around camp with their basket of pies—and such pies—goodness save the mark! If the women of Missouri know how to cook, making pies certainly is not their strong point. It would be a tough man who could eat one of their pies and live. Well cooked leather would be a luxury in comparison. One day Captain Potter felt a hankering for something extra to eat. Seeing a boy with a basket of pies the Captain's mouth began to water for one. A pie was soon bought, a round one of common size, about a foot in diameter. When in his hands the Captain thought that the pie looked suspicious and he commenced to pull it. The tough, half cooked crust stretched like rubber. As his pie extended in his hands a cloud spread over his face. "What do you call this?" he asked the boy. "It's pie." "Who made it?" "Mother." Growing more fierce as his pie extended, which was not all of two feet in length, in fierce tones he exclaimed: "Does she want to kill our soldiers with such stuff as this?" The bare-headed boy's hair was by this time standing straight up, and as the last word was said he turned and scampered away as for dear life. The story he told his mother was no doubt a confused if not an exaggerated one. It at least was effective. In a short time it was reported among all the women folks around, that the Union officers believed that some of the Missouri women were trying to kill the Yankee soldiers with poisoned pies, and fearing that it might be true, not knowing what some of their extreme rebel sisters might attempt, and not wishing to be themselves under suspicion if it was so, they quit the business and the pie trade was ended.

Being in easy railroad communication by way of St. Louis with our Illinois homes, we were often remembered by something good to eat, cooked by our own kind of folks. The cakes, fruits, preserves and knickknacks of all kinds they sent us were delicious. Every few days a well filled box would come to some one of our boys. Each would of course share with his comrades. Thus we had good things nearly all the time. Every thing sent was excellent, but after all nothing else was quite as nice or tasted as good as those which came in a big box, crowded full, sent to me by my mother. No one else can cook quite as well as she. But this I found the same with all the boys. When a boy is away from home he can never find anything that is as nice as those his own mother used to make for him.

STANDING PICKET AND CATCHING APPLES.

In these days standing picket was considered a desirable and pleasant, instead of being a tiresome and unpleasant duty. Among the mountains that surrounded us it was found necessary to have picket guards posted only upon the few different roads that led out into the country. A picket guard is that which is sent to the farthest outpost to give the alarm in case of the approach of the enemy. The high mountains around us rendered all directions of approach, except the roads through the valleys, impracticable. The necessity for picket duty was limited. A guard was sent out upon each road to perform this duty, remaining out for a week at a time. The reason was discovered why the boys were partial to this kind of duty.

A Missourian was chided for charging such exorbitant prices for his produce. "Wall," said he, "'pears like you oughten to complain, seeing as we have to pay such big taxes." As all civil government was completely disorganized in this part of the country and no one in office or authority to collect taxes or do anything else, this reply was a surprise. "Taxes, what kind of taxes do you pay?" "Why, every time we come in we have to give your soldiers out on the road, part of our chickens, butter and apples for taxes." As he did not have any other taxes to pay, this burden, waiving the mode of its collection, was not a very heavy one.

One day a practical joke of this kind was carried almost beyond pardonable limits. A country-man from the backwoods was coming in with a wagon box full of apples. As he was ascending a steep hill near the picket guard, a mischievous trick was played upon him. The rear end-board of his wagon fell out, *accidentally, of course,* and the whole load of apples came pouring down to the foot of the hill. The man came back and commenced securing his load. At this moment one of the boys claimed his attention, and in an earnest, solemn manner took a piece of writing paper from his pocket and proceeded to read a supposed order, stating that all property of whatever kind falling from a wagon to the ground within the army lines should be forfeited to the Government. The man could not read a word and supposed that what he had heard was actually true. He then sorrowfully started homewards to muse by the way upon the beauty of a decisive Government and cogitate upon the profit of attempting to drive a load of loose apples up a steep hill with a loose end-board in his wagon box.

Before going he promised to return soon. The boys set to work and saved the apples. In a few days the same man, ignorant and good-natured, returned with another load of produce. After he had treated the boys to some of his new load of apples they produced and gave him a lot of coffee, sugar, etc., for which they had traded the apples he had lost on the former occasion. They had run a temporary store with his load of apples and had lots of fun. He was greatly surprised and went his way the happiest man in Missouri.

UNPOPULARITY OF THE NORMAL REGIMENT.

It must be confessed that the Normal Regiment did not at first have the best opinion of its comrades in other regiments, as to its soldierly qualities. Its fame as a school-boy organization had preceded it and created an unfavorable opinion. The heavy work done by the regiment in building Fort Hovey and its known anxiety to be in the fight at Fredericktown had in a measure dispelled this feeling, but our cosy [*sic*] winter quarters and jolly times in Arcadia revived it. During the winter, however, the prompt and willing way in which the Thirty-third boys performed their share of every duty that fell to the lot of our army, re-established on a firm basis the more favorable feeling. The men of the different regiments were also becoming personally acquainted with each other. Our boys made many warm personal friends in the other regiments. These things all helped to increase the growing good will in favor of the Thirty-third. Still many a little joke was cracked at the expense of the Normal Regiment. "Pretty school-boys," "nice ladies' men," "school-master's regiment," and like expressions were often used. Each good story told of us was taken good naturedly and often repeated by our own boys in a more graphic shape than when first invented.

DRESS PARADE AT CAMP HOVEY.

The story of our dress parade was one of these that did not lose anything in the telling. The foundation for it was small, at the same time I do not think that any military man having had experience with young volunteers would discredit it as improbable. I will give the story as our own boys learned to repeat it:

Soon after we had gone into Camp Hovey as we had drawn our guns, our ambitious adjutant, Crandall,[3] who was the only West Point officer our regiment could boast, and who was the general director and manager in all little military points, thought that we ought to have a dress parade. Of course we should. What could a regiment do without a dress parade?

He proceeded. First calling the officers together, Crandall instructed them in the part they and their men were to perform. The time appointed was four o'clock P. M., our regular supper hour. The time came and we formed upon the parade ground. As we went from our quarters we could see and smell our supper steaming hot and waiting.

Dress parade is not as elaborate an affair as a high-toned dress party. The companies simply form in line with their guns in hand and march to the parade ground where the entire regiment forms in line. The first part of the parade is performed by the entire regiment performing some simple movements, mainly going through the manual of arms.

The parade went on bravely, each part was properly performed, until the adjutant gave the command, "Parade dismissed," which means that the officers shall all leave the men standing in line and at rest while they march up in front of the center of the regiment and then forward to the commanding officer, who stands quite a distance in front, to receive from him such instructions as he has to give, or perhaps a "curtain" lecture if he has anything to scold about, after which the officers return each to his own company, which is then to be marched back to quarters. The men had not yet learned all of this and when the adjutant in his full, sounding voice said: "Parade dismissed," they took him at his word and promptly dismissed themselves and broke for quarters and supper like a lot of wild school-boys just let loose. The adjutant wisely concluded not to make matters worse by attempting to recall the fleeting soldiers; but at our next dress parade the men were informed that they were not to "break ranks" until such command was given, and that "Parade dismissed" did not mean the same as "school dismissed."

OUR DEAD COMRADES.

Many of our noblest boys sickened and died during our sojourn in Missouri. A quiet, pleasant, dry piece of ground was selected for our army burial place. Ere the winter had passed, the rows of little mounds of earth covering our dead increasing day by day, became long in length and many in number. Often we were called upon to make our sad march to the hallowed place to add to the number sleeping there; with guns reversed, keeping step to the sad dirge of the funeral march, we would slowly, sadly follow the remains of our dead comrade to his last resting place, stand with uncovered head as the body was lowered into its lonely grave, tenderly cover it with mother earth, listen to the last prayer for the departed one, fire a farewell shot over the grave, and then return to our quarters wondering whose turn would come next.

Of those who died, A. M. Brookfield was my most intimate friend. He was in the same squad and room with me. His death was almost as sudden to us as though he had fallen in battle. He had been quite sick but it was thought had fully recovered, and he had returned to quarters from the hospital rejoicing in being again at home, as it were, with us. He was taken with a relapse and died in a few short hours. It was a sad event to our little number, his roommates. Living he was loved by all who knew him, dying, mourned by them as a brother. He was buried on the twenty-second of December. On the twelfth of January his sad, gray-haired father came, and we, the special friends of his dead boy, went with him to perform the sad, pleasant duty of taking up the remains so that the sadly stricken father could remove them to his Illinois home. Although a sad duty, still it was one we were glad to do, so that the last sleep of our dead comrade could be at his own home and beneath the grass that will grow, and the flowers that will bloom over his grave in our own Prairie State.[4]

WAR RUMORS.

During the winter numerous reports came in of an advancing enemy. We became so familiar with such reports that but little attention was given to them, except the strife to see who could make the most exaggerated additions to them. One can imagine the terrific heights to which these reports would in this manner sometimes reach in passing through the army. The well-known fact that a large rebel force was wintering near the Arkansas state line immediately south of us, and occasionally made some demonstrations, was sufficient to cause us to keep well on guard, and was all ample foundation for all the war rumors that it was found necessary to invent and circulate. About the middle of January the rebels became more aggressive and began to push their scouts up toward our lines. Things began to look quite warlike. On the twenty-sixth affairs appeared so pressing that orders were issued for us to "sleep on arms" which means to sleep with our clothes on and a loaded gun by our side. We did so for three or four nights. The work of finishing Fort Hovey was also pushed forward, with renewed vigor. It would have taken a large force to have dislodged us from the strong and well fortified position we held. In a few days the threatenings of the enemy were over and we were not troubled with any more war alarms.

WINTER MARCH OF THE TWENTY-FIRST ILLINOIS.

On the twenty-ninth day of January, 1862, the Twenty-first Illinois Infantry[5] started south for Greenville. It was decidedly one of the worst times ever known for soldiers to march. It had been raining for nearly all of the preceding week filling the roads with mud and water. The weather now suddenly turned freezing cold and a heavy coat of snow was thrown upon the deep mixture of mud and water. This made the surface look, fair enough, like a body of innocent snow, but woe to the luckless one who trusted to appearances and risked himself upon the covered but not less dangerous swamp of slush. This was the condition of the roads when the Twenty-first started. As they went by our quarters a new and terrific snow storm had burst upon them. For two or three days in this freezing cold weather with a fierce storm pelting them they marched through the cold, soft, wet snow six inches deep beneath which lay the much worse mixture of almost unfathomable mud. Surely a worse time for marching was never known. Some of the men died in the attempt to go through, but the regiment reached its destination. It was a march almost unequalled in the hardships under which it was undertaken and one which well deserved the place it filled by being the subject of an historic picture of the war in one of the leading New York illustrated papers.

NEW GUNS AND A SHOOTING MATCH.

About the middle of February we exchanged our old muskets for good rifles. Our regiment got guns of three or four kinds, and part were supposed to be better than others. Our colonel decided to arm Companies A and K, the right and left flank of the regiment, with the best ones. Of the best there were two kinds. Hovey concluded to have a shooting match by A and K for first choice. The contest was arranged, twenty men of each company to participate. Two large, pine board targets were erected, one for each company. The boys went out and fired away, one after the other, until the entire twenty of both sides had shot. The result was then decided by taking the two targets and measuring from the center to the place where each ball hit. If twenty holes were not found the missing shot was measured to the outside of the target. Company K had one or two of this kind of shots and Company A three or four. After considerable time the referees had figured it up, and decided that Company K had won by about three inches in the aggregate distance of the shots from the center of the target. Thus a side with five plump center shots and one miss could be defeated by others who had not made a single center shot out of six; a manner of determining such contests that would not be countenanced by any well advised authority. The shots found upon the targets showed the best for Company A, but the larger number of outside shots made the case against them. Another blunder was discovered. As none of the bullet holes had been closed, it occurred to some that perhaps the missed shots might have sent a ball through a hole previously made. Upon looking at the target evidence of this was found. Had it been so counted the decision would have been for Company A. But as the referees had decided, and there not in reality being any first choice so far as the quality of the new guns was concerned, the targets were split up for kindling wood.

We got the Dresden rifles. They were a very good gun and the boys were much pleased with them. They were a great improvement upon the old worn-out lumber wagons in the shape of muskets we had been carrying for the preceding four months.

CHAPTER IV.

LEAVING ARCADIA SEMINARY—THE FAREWELL SPEECH.

On the twenty-seventh day of February we received marching orders. These orders were received with glad enthusiasm. It is not necessary to describe the wild scene. It was almost an exact repetition of the scene at Camp Butler on a like occasion. All were anxious—wildly so—to go forward. To attempt to interest and satisfy soldiers who enlist only for war, with dull, idle camp duties, while others are doing the real soldiering in the active field, is as useless as it would be to attempt to satisfy a hungry, *growing* boy with thin porridge while his brother upon the other side of the table is devouring ham and eggs. And it is well known that if there is anyone who does get hungry clear down to his boots it is a *growing* boy.

On the first day of March, 1862, the order to start was given. Our company with arms, knapsacks, etc., formed in front of the seminary building.

Among the cheers that we then gave, such cheers as only soldiers can give, none were given with a more hearty good will than the one proposed by Captain Potter: "Three cheers for the seminary and the good old times we have had here." We then formed with the regiment, Major Roe, strangely enough, as at the time when we started from Camp Butler on horseback, was again in command of the regiment. We of course expected the last and best speech from him. He had given us a rousing one upon the former occasion. He was at this time the recognized orator of the Normal Regiment. We were not disappointed. The speech he made upon this occasion was one of the shortest, best and most eloquent ever made. I will give it in full. In tones that rang down the entire line and up over the hills, as clear and sharp as the bright steel sword he waved in his hand, he made the farewell speech and gave the last command in Arcadia in these words: "Forward, *to Dixie,* march!" The speech itself consisted of only two words. The other two were a military command. How much these words suggested. They meant everything. The entire object of our existence as soldiers; the object and aim of the entire Union army was expressed in them. Forward to all of Dixie's land meant that the Union army was to successfully march from Northern borders to Southern gulf, from Western land to Eastern sea; that every force of armed rebellion was to be crushed; that our glorious Union was to be preserved unimpaired; that every star upon our banner waving above us was again to shine with its old-time luster and glory; that victory, complete victory was to be ours, and that we were to help win and share in it. The soldiers were satisfied, more than satisfied. The speech they had expected, and far better than they had hoped for, had been made. A multiplicity of words, the most eloquent words of mortal tongue at this time on this occasion, would have been tame in comparison. A few words fitly spoken will live a thousand years. Had the historian been there to have recorded the words they would long have lived; yea, have become immortal in the world's poetry, song and history. As it was, upon many a hard and tedious march, through many a cane-brake wild, across many a dark and dismal swamp, during many hungry and weary hours, through many long, sad days and upon many crimson and bitter battle fields, they were carried in soldier memory. With a rousing cheer oft repeated, as over the hills and through the valleys we went with the brightest hopes and lively step, we indorsed the words, and obeyed the command: "Forward, to Dixie, march."

Thus we left Arcadia Seminary.

FIRST MARCH TO DIXIE—OUR TENTS AND THE TRICKS THEY PLAYED US.

As already stated, we commenced our march southward on March first. We started with light hearts, banners flying, boys hurrahing and high hopes for the future. We had become so tired of the dull monotony and sameness of soldier life in winter quarters that almost any hardship elsewhere would be welcomed as a relief. Besides this the men of our command thought that we were hardly doing our duty by remaining inactive while our brothers in arms were doing all the fighting. It became a common expression and complaint "that the war will be over before we have a chance to see an armed rebel." Thus when marching orders finally came, they were gladly received and promptly obeyed by the soldiers of the Thirty-third. We willingly started out to participate in the most tedious duty of soldier life—foot marching.

We started at three o'clock P.M. and marched five miles the first day. At night we camped in the woods upon the banks of a small stream of clear water. As soon as we stop for the night lively work commences. Tents have to be unloaded from the wagons and pitched; fuel must be found, fires built and supper prepared and eaten. All the cooking we do while on a march is to make some coffee and fry some bacon.

The tents we brought with us were a new kind, known by the name of "Sibley tents". Their form is circular. A strong center pole standing in the middle of the tent supports its top. The bottom is stretched out in equal distance all around from the center, and fastened to the ground. Thus the tent when standing presented the appearance of a perfect cone. The bottom of the center pole is supported upon a set of iron legs which unites at the top and spreads apart at the bottom. This gave room in the center between the legs for a small sheet iron stove—also in the shape of a cone—which had been furnished us. A hole at the top of the tent permitted the smoke to escape.

To sleep we lay with our feet toward the middle of the tent and near the fire. This made a complete circle of soldiers with their feet all toward the center and heads toward the outside. We were very crowded. There were from eighteen to twenty men in each tent. In the morning the boys of one of the most crowded tents claimed that they had commenced sleeping all lying upon their right side closely packed together, and that during the night becoming tired and wishing to rest by changing to the left side, it was found necessary for the soldier nearest the door and go outside in order to give the others room to turn over.

Sibley tent. From Marcy, *The Prairie Traveler.*

This story was probably as nearly true as the other one afterward repeated in camp as having occurred upon this march, and which I will give here. It runs thus: One morning, as the Colonel was about to give the order, "Forward, march," he was chagrinned to see one tent belonging to his regiment still standing. Without ceremony he ordered it pulled down, which was promptly done, whereupon all were greatly surprised to see the whole squad of its occupants lying there upon their backs in a complete circle. Upon lying down each one had, unwittingly extended his arms under his comrades on each side making a complete network of the entire circle and they were so crowded that not one could move enough to break the chain holding them together. Comprehending the situation the Colonel directed his soldiers to surround the helpless squad and take each one by the shoulders and pull them outward, which of course enlarged the circle and released the unhappy members who formed it.

ON THE ROAD—REBEL CAVALRY—UNION MEN—BRAVE GIRLS.

Sunday, March second, we started at 8:30 A.M. and marched ten miles. The roads were very bad. The late heavy rains had rendered them almost impassible. The mud was fearful. Mud reigned supreme here. The little rivulets coursing down the hillsides were changed into mountain streams; while streams usually of moderate width were now raging, sweeping rivers. Crossing them was very difficult and sometimes dangerous. Through the valleys which we were obliged to follow, as the mountains are impassable, the number of swift and rapid streams seemed unlimited. At one time, after we had with much difficulty crossed five large streams in going four miles, our wonder was turned into vexation by learning that each was only a different crossing of the same stream. When we came to other like streams we attempted to evade some of the crossings by going around, but the rough hills and stubborn mountains made it impracticable. The only safe way in a mountainous country is to follow the road others have traveled, no matter how much it may, seemingly, take you out of the course you wish to go.

The next day we started at eight o'clock and made a good day's march. Profiting by our previous difficulties, men were sent in advance to fell trees across the streams. By means of these temporary foot bridges we had but little difficulty in crossing. Wet logs, however, do not make the safest kind of a foot bridge. Every now and then, as the soldiers were running over them, some luckless chap would lose his footing and go into the swiftly running water. All of these were fished out and placed upon dry land and no lives lost. A gun now and then and some other small property was all the tribute the raging streams succeeded in requiring our army to pay for the privilege of crossing over their mad waters. Only three days out and yet the boys begin to complain of short rations.

After we had started on Tuesday morning, we were surprised to learn that a force of one hundred and fifty rebel cavalry had been within sight of our camp fires during the night. They captured a lieutenant who was carrying dispatches to some of the Union troops. But, as luck would have it, they did not get the dispatches. He took the chance, the only one left, and slyly placed the papers in the hands of a citizen of Missouri standing near. It proved that he had trusted the right man. The citizen concealed the dispatches and gave them to Colonel Hovey the next morning as we came up. This proves that some true Union men live in this part of Missouri. He ought to be remembered. Am sorry that I did not learn his name.

Full and reliable information was given us of this rebel force. Most of it by two young ladies, whose home we passed. The rebels had made a lengthy halt at their home. This gave the girls an opportunity to become well posted as to the numbers and doings of the rebel troops. A few months previous to this time these two young ladies had become quite noted by making, raising and protecting a Union flag and that, too, in the midst of a large number of desperadoes who wished and threatened to tear it down. It was believed, probably was true, that the plucky Missouri girls would shoot the first one who touched their flag, and it was not disturbed. We made a halt of some length at their home, and as they were delighted to talk with the Union soldiers, most of us exchanged a few words with them. They were actual heroines in the eyes of our soldiers. Woman never received a more earnest and respectful ovation than our soldiers gave these two true, loyal girls.

Had they wished it every soldier in the command would have sworn to come back when the war was over to marry either of them. And they might do worse than to have kept such a pledge had it been made. Each will make some one a splendid wife. A woman who is loyal and true to the land of her birth will be faithful and loving to the husband of her heart. One who is willing to risk her life for the flag she reveres, will, if necessary, die for the husband she loves. None but brave soldiers are fit to wed such girls.

The bravery of these two young girls was wonderful. For two farmer's daughters, living in the mountain wilds of Missouri, with no one near to help them, to stand and protect the flag of our country and bid defiance to a large band of desperate rebels who swear they will tear it down, shows a degree of bravery that may well claim the admiration of all. It was an event rarely, if ever, equaled, and never excelled in the world's history. All honor to these brave daughters of Missouri.

AT GREENVILLE—A LIEUTENANT-COLONEL—A VOTE.

We reached Greenville at sundown Tuesday, March fourth, and camped there for five days. During the first day of our camp at Greenville we were reminded of an almost forgotten fact, namely: that we have had a lieutenant-colonel. In organizing our regiment the office of lieutenant-colonel was the one reserved to be filled by executive appointment. The other officers had been chosen by members of the regiment. Of course all commissioned officers had to be appointed by the Governor of the State, but the custom was to allow the members of volunteer regiments to designate their choice for officers, usually leaving one for the executive to fill by his own selection. In our case our good Governor made an unfortunate selection. After some delay in making the appointment, Lockwood[1] was sent to us as lieutenant-colonel. His brief stay with us was not the most pleasant. He did not have the facility to correctly learn military commands. When attempting to drill us he was sure to make some blunder, run one company into another, get one company started away from the rest and lose it, not knowing what command to give to get it back in place. Undoubtedly much of his perplexity arose from the propensity of the officers and men to increase instead of helping him out of his difficulties. One day he was in command at a dress parade. He had brought the command to "present arms." According to our tactics, when a battalion is at "present arms" the only command that can properly be given is to "carry arms." Lockwood gave the improper command, "Right shoulder, shift, arms!" Not a gun was moved. The entire command stood in line still presenting arms. With more care as to clear pronunciation he repeated the command. No one moved. Turning to the adjutant he said: "It don't fetch them yet, does it?" At another time, while we were at Arcadia, in attempting to drill the regiment he ran the command into a heavy rail fence. The boys were watching and as they struck it, all pushed together and the entire fence was thrown flat before them, much to his disgust. The only command he could think of was: "What in h—— did you go through that fence for?" He was said to be a man of ability. If so, the Normal Regiment gave him no chance to show it. He soon became disgusted. He asserted that: "Unless a command is spoken grammatically, punctuated correctly and each word emphasized properly, the Normal Regiment will not pay any attention to it, and as I did not come to the army to teach grammar or rhetoric, I do not want a d—— thing more to do with it." And he kept his word good by promptly resigning.

Having virtually crowded Lieutenant Colonel Lockwood out of the regiment, it was thought as a vote had never been taken for that office, that the men of the regiment had the right to take a vote for his successor and ignore all questions of regular promotion. A vote was taken on March fifth. The candidates voted for were: Major Roe, Captains Potter, Lippincott and Elliott, and Adjutant Crandall. To the surprise of all, especially the officers, Captain Elliott received a majority of the entire vote cast. Two or three causes helped to give Captain Elliott his unexpected large vote. Among them were his supposed military experience, he having had a fight with, been whipped and taken prisoner by Jeff Thompson and afterward been exchanged, his very pleasant and social way among the soldiers, he having in a short time formed the personal acquaintance of every member of the regiment, and last, but not least, his good looks, he being the handsomest officer in the Normal Regiment.

One of the strangest votes was that of Company A, which gave its own Captain, Potter, only six votes out of about seventy cast. And stranger still, the six votes were cast by the six men in the company the least friendly to him. The majority voted against him because they wanted him to remain in command of their own company.

Major Roe got a light vote because he was, you know, the orator of the regiment. The only proper office for a regimental orator to hold is that of major

Isaac H. Elliott. From Elliott and Way, *History of the Thirty-Third Regiment Illinois Veteran Volunteer Infantry in the Civil War.*

of the regiment or a second lieutenant of a company—those with the least duties attached.

Captain Lippincott could well claim to at least equal Captain Elliott in military experience, he had safely brought his men to camp when surrounded and threatened with capture by Jeff Thompson's troops, and had been at the battle of Fredericktown.

The result of the vote was sent off to the Governor of Illinois. It was of course of no binding force, but was supposed to be a recommendation that would be complied with.

A REBEL CAMP GROUND.

During the afternoon some of us visited Jeff Thompson's drill and camp ground. This is the place where his army went into camp after being driven from Fredericktown. Judging from the lines, or rather all absence of lines, the rebel troops did not take much pride in the order or regularity of their camp. After attempting to trace the lines our boys declared that it was impossible to find where more than two tents had stood in a line. The rule with the rebels seemed to have been for each to pitch his tent where he chose. The only interest connected with the ground was the uninteresting fact that it had been, for a time, a rebel camp ground.

At Greenville our company was divided into small messes, each mess to do its own cooking. Until this time the rations for the entire company had been cooked together.

ON THE ROAD.

Sunday, March ninth, we left Greenville to go further south. Found the roads much improved. Marched nine miles. The next day we started at eight o'clock and reached Black River by noon. It was quite a good sized stream. The water was high, caused by the late heavy rain-fall. We had to cross on a slow ferry boat and it took until a late hour for the regiment and its wagon train to pass over.

Tuesday we lay still. Wednesday we moved up the river and camped at Reaves Station. The Thirty-eighth Illinois and one company of artillery had preceded us.

This ended what might be called our first real march. It told a little upon some of the boys, but upon the whole was a very easy march. Our regiment came the entire way alone. Our wagons were always with us and we generally stopped at noon each day and made some warm coffee for dinner.

IN CAMP AT REAVES STATION.

Our camp at Black River was known as Reaves Station Camp.[2] Our regiment pitched their tents about half a mile from the river. Simple camp duties such as standing guard, drilling, etc., occupied our time.

F. M. Gasthman, of our company, died on March twenty-second. He was a talented, good hearted young man, one of the Normal University students. Even when it became certain that he must die and that, too, in this inhospitable land, his pleasant, buoyant spirits sustained him. One day he said: "It does seem rather hard to have to die so early and in this lonely land." Except this no word of regret ever passed his lips. He simply joins the many that have gone before. The entire regiment went to his funeral and followed him to his grave. It is very unusual for the entire regiment to follow a soldier to his burial; doing so showed the high esteem all had for our lamented young friend.

The Eleventh Wisconsin Infantry arrived on March twenty-seventh. It was to be in the same brigade with the Thirty-third. The entire command was to be put into more army shape. Brigades were to be formed and the division was to be commanded by a brigadier-general. His name was General Steele.[3]

Friday, March twenty-eighth, General Steele arrived. He was a fine-looking officer. He did not put on extra fine airs like some of our fancy generals. The soldiers seemed well pleased with their new commander. He had at least their good will to commence with.

The next day after the arrival of General Steele the assignment of troops to brigades was announced. This division under the command of General Steele was divided as follows: First Brigade, Twenty-first and Twenty-eighth Illinois, Colonel Carlin commanding; Second Brigade, Thirty-third Illinois and Eleventh Wisconsin, Colonel Hovey commanding; Third Brigade, Fifth and Eighth Indiana and First Indiana Cavalry, Colonel Baker commanding.

Our vote at Greenville was ignored and Captain Lippincott[4] appointed lieutenant colonel. With Colonel Hovey in command of the brigade, Lippincott will be in command of our regiment.

March thirty-first the First Brigade of this division started forward. The army telegraph was completed to this place. One of the first dispatches was: "Island No. 10 is ours."

Maj. Gen. Frederick Steele. Courtesy of the Library of Congress.

On April first, a drove of pack mules arrived from Pilot Knob. This was a new feature in the transportation of army supplies with us. The mules were wild and hard to manage. Three of them ran away and were lost, packs and all. Upon the whole the experiment was claimed to be a tolerable success.

On the third of April a company of our cavalry came in with some rebel prisoners. Our advance guard was attacked by a band of bushwhackers. None of our soldiers were hurt. Some of the enemy were killed and others taken prisoners and brought in.

Considerable excitement was created on the ninth of April by the drumming of a man out of camp because he was found to be guilty of stealing. He belonged to the cavalry that was acting as the General's body-guard. With one side of his head shaved clean with a sharp razor, his coat turned wrong side out, the word "thief" in large letters upon his back, with the guards close behind him, with the sharp points right close up to his rear, making him take quick steps or get pricked; with the drum and fife playing the rogue's march, he was marched all through camp amidst the hoots and jeers of the entire army, then out of camp to the top of a hill in sight, and then with a vigorous kick from the butt of a heavy gun in the hands of a stout soldier, he was sent over the hill and out of sight and never again seen by his army comrades.

While at Reaves Station Captain Potter appointed some non-commissioned officers. Our big, jolly sergeant, Ed Pike, was promoted to orderly sergeant in place of Baker, who had been discharged on account of failing health. Pike would get good rations for us if anyone could. Willis was appointed fifth sergeant, and Riggs and Harris corporals.

On the twenty-first we came near having a serious accident in our company. Whited was handling Riggs' revolver when it was accidentally discharged and hit Bovee. But as good fortune would have it, Bovee's substantial foot was in front of him, so that the ball struck the bottom of his solid army boot. The boot got well. No one else was hurt. Some more cavalry joined us at Reaves Station, so that we now have the most of four cavalry regiments with our division.

FORWARD AGAIN.

We started forward again on the twenty-second of April. Marched twelve miles and camped for the night upon the banks of the Little Black River.[5] We found a grist mill there which some of our men had taken possession of and were running. It is easy enough to find men in our army who can run a grist mill. The roads are very bad. The backwoodsman with his ox team, pressed in for the occasion, bringing our tents, was all night in getting through the deep mud, so we had to pass the night without any tents.

Our transportation being so much delayed by the condition of the almost impassable roads, we had to wait and only went six miles the second day.

On the third day we went through to Pitman's Ferry.[6] During the day I had charge of and ran an independent command. It was a unanimous command and was not troubled by any differences of opinion as to where the best walking was to be found—in truth there was no best, each side of the road was the worst—nor when a halt was to be made, nor how fast to push forward. All were agreed. The "command" consisted of myself only. Three different detachments of the army were upon the road but I made the march alone, selecting such paths through the woods as suited me best. I had delayed when the regiment advanced to give Seybold, one of our mess, his breakfast and rations for the day. He had been on the rear picket guard during the night, and according to the rule of this time, was to be part of the rear guard during our day's march.

After I rejoined the company at night, as the usual day's adventures, real and imaginary, were being recounted around our evening camp fires, my comrades insisted that, having been on a separate march, I ought to have some incident of the day to relate. After telling the many little incidents of the day, which were numerous for the reason that "the natives" took more liberty to stop my "command" with curious questions than they would a larger force, the boys insisted that it should end with a romance. The one given was in substance as follows: adding two short sentences to the beginning to make it readable should it ever be found alone. Perhaps it is true. As to that, no confession is required. Let the story be repeated as then told.

ROMANCE OF MISSOURI, IN THE BACKWOODS.

One day I stopped to give one of the boys of our mess his breakfast. He had been on rear picket the night before and consequently would be with the rear guard of the army that day. Our regiment having the advance, made an early start and I did not expect to rejoin it until a late hour at night. After finding our comrade and giving him his morning coffee, I pushed forward. In course of the day, wishing to rest a short time, I ventured to call at a dwelling by the roadside. The house was simply a log hut like all others in the backwoods of that part of Missouri. Entering I found it had but one room and that furnished in the plain, rough style common to such localities.

In one part of the room sat—what shall I call her? How shall I describe the charming creature who sat before me? A woman; an angel beautiful as day; fairer than the fairest; in age just passed beyond charming, sweet sixteen to lovely womanhood. No, I will not attempt to describe this most beautiful one. Let it suffice that my highest idea of angelic perfection was more than realized in the person of the lovely being before me. Being a young and enthusiastic volunteer, such a feast of beauty completely captivated me. Numerous remembrances of stories where I had read of princesses of beauty being found elsewhere by some singularly fortune-favored knight flashed through my brain. All my faith in love at first sight returned with redoubled force. Although enrapt I had not yet heard her speak; had not heard the enchanting tones of her sweet voice.

Her mother—could it be? Was it possible that this plain, coarse woman was the mother of one so divine? No! I would not believe it. I would believe that she was the child of love—a being of heavenly, not of earthly origin, and I almost trembled for fear she would suddenly vanish from my sight and soar to her far-off home above. Her mother went to the door and called: "William, come here; your sister wants to see you." Her brother would come, *she* would speak to him. Then, oh then! I should hear the delicious music from that sweet angel's tongue. The bare anticipation intoxicated me. What, then, would the sweet reality be? Would it then be possible for me to control myself? Could I then refrain from throwing myself at her feet and praying to be her slave forever. She rises to speak to her brother. Oh! Sweet anticipation! One moment now is an age of bliss. She opens her mouth. Oh sweet, charming, delight—what? The words she spoke were: "Bill, you little cuss, give me a chew of tobacco." Thrusting his dirty hand down into his greasy pocket he brought forth a filthy piece of the vile weed, and—words are worthless—the romance was bursted.

AT PITMAN'S FERRY.

On Friday, April twenty-fifth, we remained at Pitman's Ferry. On Saturday we crossed the river. General Steele and his staff came up during the day.

Captain Potter got "on his ear" because, as he thought, the boys did not obey his orders as fully as he thought they should and ordered a company roll-call every two hours. Not a very severe punishment.

The rebel General Hardee was in command of a force of rebels at this place for some time. Visited his drilling and camp ground. All that remains here now to mark the stay of the rebel army is their burying ground. Its size plainly shows that they, as well as we, suffer much by sickness and death in the army.

THE MAJOR AND CHAPLAIN HOLD MEETING.

On Sunday the regiment was ordered into line and marched out under military orders to a convenient place to attend religious services. When soldiers are lying quietly in camp a regiment never can be ordered into line, it matters little what the occasion may be, unless for a fight, but that there are sure to be some of the men who would prefer to do something else rather than to "fall in." As we were marching to the preaching ground one soldier was heard to impatiently say in a side remark that he "wished that the chaplain was in h——," or words to that effect. In some strange way the words happened to strike Major Roe's quick ear. As soon as we were assembled in preaching array the Major commenced the services by referring to the remark that had been made by the thoughtless soldier, refraining, however, from calling him by name. The Major regretted to hear such remarks, and reminded the soldiers that the Chaplain held a position above insult, given him by the Government; referred to the importance of religion to those who, like us, go forth every day with our lives in our hands, and after a proper amount of scolding with his pleasant voice and eloquent words, even talked himself into a happy frame of mind and finally ended with the suggestion that probably he had misunderstood the words used, and that the soldier meant "to wish the Chaplain in heaven instead of h——."

Dr. Eddy, our very able and conscientious chaplain, was evidently much affected by this unexpected circumstance. He was sorry to think that any member of the regiment held such feelings against him. I did not believe that any in reality did. Assured us "that he had none but the kindest feelings toward each and everyone of the Normal Regiment." Of course he did, we all knew that without his mentioning it. And finally the Doctor freely gave his permission for those who did not wish to hear him preach, to leave the meeting. Of course no one accepted the offer. The Chaplain, you see, had got the wrong idea. He did not well understand soldiers. Getting up out of his tent, where he was lying upon his back and reading some story and taking his ease in true soldier style, to fall into line and march out to the meeting place was what disgusted the most indolent soldier and not the Chaplain's preaching, for he was in fact one of the most pleasant clergymen to listen to. Now that they were sitting upon the green grass and ready, all, even the soldier who made the emphatic remark —if it actually was made—would rather stay and hear Dr. Eddy preach a good sermon, which he was sure to do, than get up and walk back to camp.

None wishing to leave, the Chaplain, as the Major had done, got into a happy frame of mind and gave us a splendid sermon.

In time our good Chaplain, no doubt, learned to better understand soldiers. They all respected him and his calling. Brave soldiers are naturally religious. Some religious belief is necessary to create good soldiers. Faith and hope always are a soldier's steadfast friends, while infidelity and ignorance are but sorry comrades in a battle. .

OUR MARCH RESUMED.

On the twenty-ninth of April we resumed our march, went fifteen miles and camped on Focia Creek,[7] Here we found Company C of our regiment. They had been sent in advance to fix up the roads.

The next morning we started at eight o'clock and marched five miles, to Pocahontas.

Received news of the capture of New Orleans. The soldiers gave three cheers for General Butler and three times three for the success of the Union cause.[8]

We laid over in Poca, as the people here call the place, one day.

On Friday, May second, marched down the river twelve miles and camped at the ferry. Found the first good ferry-boat we have yet met upon our travels and as for bridges, they are absolutely out of the question in this indolent, heathen country.

A CYPRESS SWAMP.

On Saturday we crossed the river and marched through a cypress swamp.

A cypress swamp is quite a curiosity. The cypress is, like the pine and cedar, an evergreen tree. They seem to thrive best in a swamp upon which the water stands most of the year. From the roots, "knees," grow up without number. The knees have a smooth, round top without any limbs or other projections. In fact they are like small stumps running up a foot or two out of the water, over the round top of which the smooth bark has grown, and are from a few inches to half a foot or more in diameter. They annoyed us fearfully. In taking our wagons through, the wheels would sink down in the soft mud and the cypress knees would catch the axletree and hold the wagon fast. We had to turn in and cut them off. As they had to be cut off from one to three feet under water it was a very difficult and unpleasant task. Fortunately we were well supplied with saws. Axes are no good to chop a log under three feet of water. By wading out into the water, often waist deep, and running the saws under water we were able to cut open the necessary passageway for our wagons. For a few men the undertaking would have been an hopeless task, but we had a thousand willing soldiers and the tedious and difficult work went on merrily.

On Sunday we marched twelve miles, part of the way through cypress swamps, but the bottom being formed of a firmer substance than the soft muck over which we passed the day before, it did not break through as much and we did not have to stop so often to cut roads for our wagons and artillery. It was during this Arkansas march that one of the Union officers decorated some of his soldiers. In riding up he suddenly came upon five or six of his men who in passing the garden of a rebel sympathizer had each pulled a handful of onions and turnips. With the tell-tale evidence in their hands there was no doubt of their having been trespassing, which was against orders. Feeling that he must punish them in some manner he at once ordered that a label with the word "onion" should be pinned to each cap. It was done. But the result was contrary to expectation. Instead of being a disgrace, the men of the regiment construed the labels to be a decoration of honor. The word was willfully misread and wherever the "onion" boys appeared, the men cheered and praised them as "Union" boys. This play upon the word took so well, and the boys of the army not believing that it was actually any great harm to pull an onion or two from a secesh garden, it was soon seen that the attempted punishment had miscarried, and a request was quietly sent asking the boys to remove their "onion" labels, This was done, but the badges were preserved as an interesting trophy of army life.

MISSOURI AND ARKANSAS LAND.

By marching fifteen miles, on the fifth of May, we reached Jefferson City, or Bird's Point,[9] as it is called. We have now entered upon lands which will, no doubt, some day prove to be rich farming lands. Having come on foot all the way has given us a good opportunity to see the country. From Pilot Knob down to Arkansas the country is very rough and broken, the high hills often running up into small mountains. Through this section the valleys generally have a deep, rich soil and appear to be specially adapted to the growth of all kinds of fruit and rich blue grass. A field of the latter left uncut will keep hardy stock in fair condition all winter without any other feed. Corn and other kinds of grain will, no doubt, also do well.

As we strike the lands of Northern Arkansas, it is not so broken nor to such an extent entirely worthless, but the soil is not as rich as the Missouri valleys. As we near Jefferson City it greatly improves. Here the land is nearly all fit for tilling and the soil very good. With an enterprising, willing-to-work class of people, like our Northern farmers, these rich valleys would soon be the paradise of the world. As it is, we find but little that is desirable except the land, timber, springs and water-courses, often with a fine water power, and these are so only when seen as nature left them, with none of the natives or their habitations in sight. The indolent, go-easy, do-nothing squatters who encumber much of this land would, if they were upon it, make the fairest, sunniest land in the world look dark and gloomy.

A UNION WOMAN.

Most of the people in this vicinity are bitter secessionists, but there are among them a few true Union folks. As we were coming into Jefferson City, we passed the humble home of an old couple, an old man and his wife who had remained true to the flag they had learned to love in the good old days of the past. She stood at her humble door as we marched by, with a glad welcome for us all, waving in her hand the cherished and loved Union flag she had herself made, in her long since passed girlhood days, and which she and her husband had brought with them when in early life they had come to this wild land to make themselves a home. During these many long years she had kept the little flag, but little larger than a stout man's broad hand, and then this fierce, dark storm of treason came on when this aged couple, as if putting their firstborn in his cold grave, had been obliged to hide away the little flag where it could not be found by their rebel neighbors, and thus it had remained during the days when fierce rebellion swept every thing before it. But now the Union troops have come, and the little flag can again in triumph wave. There she stood at her own door as the afternoon sun was going down, her white hair like a wreath of silver loosely floating in the wild wind and like a crown of glory, shining in the golden sun, while her aged hand proudly waved her own Union flag above her devoted head. By her side stood her husband, old and feeble, and yet his arm seemed to move with the strength and vim of youth as round and round he swings his hat to cheer on their way those who were bearing aloft the flag, he himself had once fought for and helped to maintain. As each regiment passed and as each large, beautiful and proud regimental flag was waved in salute to her and her little flag, tears of joy would start afresh and course down the old woman's cheeks. The two happiest people in the State on this day was this loyal old man and his Union loving wife. Many a rousing cheer was given to them by our soldier boys as they passed by.

RAISING A LIBERTY POLE—LOOKING FOR A REBEL FLAG.

We laid over at Jefferson City a few days. These delays became necessary to let our supplies be brought up. The roads are so bad that our wagon trains have hard work to get through.

The rebels had made arrangements to raise a grand liberty pole at this place. The pole, an elegant piece of timber, had been selected and dressed with much care, and was on the ground ready to be erected. But the approach of the

Union troops had alarmed the rebels so that they had skipped away, leaving their liberty pole lying like a stick of common timber on the ground. Finding it thus we concluded to proceed with the good work. Our soldiers promptly and merrily erected the flag-staff, and with a brass band playing a loyal national tune, dedicated the liberty pole for our secesh brethren by running to its top a good Union flag, where it waved for the balance of the day, high over their heads and in sight of all the people of the town.

The Johnny Rebs had not only run away, leaving their flag-staff in the dust, but had gone in such hot haste that the Confederate flag which was to wave upon it, a large one already made and at hand, had also been left behind. This fact soon became known to our soldiers. Now for the flag. There is nothing soldiers will attempt with a more lively zeal than to capture an enemy's flag. To tell them where one is to be found is like putting a zealous hunter upon a fresh deer track. The location of the flag was soon learned—too well learned. Its location made its capture impossible—that is, impossible to gallant soldiers like those of our army. The house containing the flag was soon known. As the search for it was being made, a little colored girl, a little pickaninny, so small that she ran around among the men without attracting any attention, and who probably thought that it would be huge fun to see the rebel flag captured, privately gave information where it was, by slyly lifting up the corner of the dress of a young lady of the house. It was at once seen that the young woman had extemporized the rebel flag into an undergarment and was wearing it as part of her underclothing. The location of the flag was soon whispered around and the soldiers promptly came away, leaving the flag in triumph to wave around the brave but disloyal maid.

Had the flag been guarded by a thousand armed men it would have been brought away. As it was, I do not believe there was one soldier in our army who desired to have it taken. If the young woman had known that the Yankee soldiers had discovered its hiding place, knowing as she did how anxious they were to capture a rebel flag, she would undoubtedly have fainted on the spot. As it was our soldiers came away so quietly that she flattered herself with the idea that the flag had been hidden so cunningly that it could not be found.

The nearest approach to a desire to have the flag captured after its location had been discovered, was the suggestion of one who had not been there: "She could have been requested to retire to a private room and disrobe." "Yes," was the fully indorsed answer, "but who in thunder would ever want to show a flag, which when captured, was only a piece of cloth in use as a woman's petticoat?"

When doing duty as part of a woman's under clothing, a rebel flag can remain undisturbed; but when waving as an emblem of rebellion it must come down.

AT JACKSONPORT—EXCITEMENT CAUSED BY A SLAVE-CATCHER IN CAMP.

At the hour of six o'clock in the morning on May tenth, we started forward again and marched to Jacksonport. This place is at the junction of Black and White Rivers. We remained in the place four days. The soldiers consider it the meanest secesh place we have yet found. And they have to guard the stores and property of the miserable rebels. They would much prefer to guard the disloyal owners as prisoners of war. But that we can not do because they never have courage enough to fight. Brave Southern Soldiers command our respect for their bravery, but these sneaking, cowardly, stay-at-home rebels are contemptible in every respect.

On Tuesday, the thirteenth, much excitement was created in camp by a rebel slave owner. Some of his slaves had attempted to run away. He found one within the lines and tied him to his wagon and led him away. This was bad enough and he ought, in all conscience, to have gone away in peace, but he was one of the domineering kind and could not go away without throwing back vile names at the soldiers, calling them "nigger dogs," and the like. The story passed swiftly through the entire command. Soon another active young negro told some of the soldiers that he belonged to the same owner. He was not sent away. His absence was soon discovered and in came the lordly slave owner. The army officers had felt the rising storm and wisely declined to attempt to find any soldiers who would go through camp to find the runaway. No matter who might have been detailed for this purpose no military commands would have been obeyed. The soldiers could have been placed under arrest; in such case the entire army would soon have been in disgrace, as all would have refused to act as sentries to such a guard-house. Not a step would have been taken for the slave owner who wished to use the soldiers as "dogs" to catch his slaves. As property in slaves was yet acknowledged, the army rules required it to be protected. This our officers could not well ignore. They could not kick the slave owner out of camp. Their only course was evasion. By some means knowing the feeling prevailing in the ranks, the officers to whom the slave owner applied informed him that they knew of no runaway slaves, that they would not look for them, and that if he had lost any he would have to hunt them up himself. Having two or three of his low, contemptible lackeys with him, some of those indigent "poor white trash" who never own so much as a dead chicken's feather, but who do all the fighting for their masters, the slave owners; this slave owner thought that a trip and search through the soldiers' quarters was just what he most desired. He started. By this time the soldiers became aware of his presence and its object. In a brief moment a fierce commotion was raging. The slave owner did not search a single tent; but was hooted and driven out of camp in hot haste. The last seen of him, with all of his boasted bravery oozing out at his finger ends, white as a sheet and trembling, like the coward that he was, he was running for dear life to escape the threatened hanging he so well deserved and feared he would get. Even after he was safely away from our lines, it is said that he was still so badly scared that he traded his high-toned coat and hat with a poorly dressed negro he met upon the road so as to be in disguise if by chance any union soldier should meet him. He never again returned to our camp.

This is the first real excitement or interest that has been awakened in our army on the slavery question; on all other occasions, when any slaves have strayed around camp the owners have come in a quiet, manly way, treated the soldiers respectfully, and generally by pleasant talk with the runaway himself, got him to go back without difficulty. One case happened in Missouri where an uncommonly intelligent slave had run away. His owner having found him, they sat down and talked the matter over together. The negro argued that Missouri would soon be a free State and said that he was afraid of being sold and sent South. The owner settled this by promising that the negro should not be taken out of the State. He was known to be a man who would keep his word, and the slave trusted him fully and went back and took charge of his master's stock and farm as before.

Considering the existing condition of affairs, this Jacksonport incident plainly shows what a fierce storm a very small thing can start. The right of an owner to take his slaves away was not questioned. It frequently occurred without attracting the least attention. Now a quick-tempered slave owner, in the heat of the moment, had termed the soldiers "nigger dogs." His words had been reported in camp. From this small matter such a fierce storm arose that an entire army of the most loyal and obedient soldiers the world ever produced would have refused to obey their own officers and incurred the severest penalty, rather than to allow that particular slave owner to talk one of his slaves out of the army lines. Men are strange beings. Things that move the feelings of men strike a deeper chord than those that only reach their reason. During the world's history, mere sentiment has led to more wars, than matters of substance.

CHAPTER V.

IN CAMP AT BATESVILLE.

During the afternoon of May fourteenth we crossed Black River.

General Curtis, who had come down from Southwestern Missouri, through Northwestern Arkansas is near us and we have crossed to the north side of Black River on the way to join him.

We made two easy marches and camped near Batesville on the evening of the sixteenth. Our division is now with and actually a part of General Curtis' army.[1]

Maj. Gen. Samuel R. Curtis. From Johnson and Buel, *Battles and Leaders of the Civil War.*

A curious incident happened on Sunday. By invitation, some of our soldiers met with and joined in a prayer meeting at the residence of a widow who lived near our camp. The widow, a very zealous, religious old lady was there and participated with the Union soldiers. In fact it was her prayer meeting. The soldiers were there by her invitation. At this very time, her own son was away from home and serving in the rebel army. This old lady's religion is so strong that she is much more anxious about the soldiers' souls than she is as to which side they fight upon. Probably she is right. All good people will, no doubt, agree with her. But, nevertheless, it appears to me that she is rather over-zealous. For a woman to entertain a number of Union soldiers as her invited guests, even though it be to a Sabbath evening prayer meeting, while her own son, with all his hopes for the future, is in the rebel army, and fighting for a cause she is in sympathy with, seems strange to me. I did not go to her prayer meeting.

On the twenty-first of May the members of our regiment voted upon the adoption of the proposed new Constitution for the State of Illinois. The vote of our regiment was nearly solid against it. There were only six votes for it in the entire regiment. This was undoubtedly the first vote many of our soldiers ever cast. A very large share of our number were not old enough to vote at the last election in 1860.

Our first camp at Batesville was upon very low and wet ground. By general consent it was called "Mud Camp." Owing to the uncertainty of our future movements we lay at Mud Camp nearly two weeks before looking for a better camp ground. As it began to appear that our stay was to be a protracted one, a high, dry piece of ground was selected for a new camp. The only desirable place we could find was in the woods thickly covered with hazel brush and small trees. We went to work and cleared it off and soon had a first-class camp ground.

A WIND CAVE AND THE AGUE.

A few miles from our camp there were some natural caves. Many of the boys being anxious to visit them, it was arranged that the soldiers should go in companies, so as to avoid all danger of being captured by roving bands of rebels, of which there were many in the surrounding country.

Companies A and B went together. Only those who wished to do so, made the march. The first cave we came to was a small one; the second a more interesting one, known as the "bone cave." The third and last one we visited was the somewhat celebrated "wind cave." It is so named from the fact that a strong wind is always blowing out of its mouth. We stopped at its mouth to rest and then explored it to our satisfaction. It proved to be much more interesting than we had anticipated.

(Even at this late day I am tempted to interpose a line to say confound that wind cave. It was there I got the ague. The exposure to the unhealthy swamps we had marched through had probably planted the seed, but this wind cave certainly sprouted it into action. When we reached the cave at the end of a warm march I thought it refreshing to sit in the cold, damp wind coming from its mouth. In a short time I commenced to realize that I was very chilly and began to feel some queer little fellows running over me sometimes they appeared like a drove of frisky mice playing a game of ball, then like lively crickets going with a hop, skip and jump; at times like a more active leap-frog going from knee to elbow, from head to foot with a single jump; and again sometimes, worse than all, like some vile viper slowly winding up and down my bones, the entire crowd of which I found to consist of only one—the ague. Soon such entries as this began to appear in my journal: "Sick with the ague this week." For a year and more thereafter I was a liberal patron of Uncle Sam's quinine box. .Although it was no doubt the swamps that laid the eggs, I always believed that this wind cave, with its unhealthy breath, was the old hen that hatched them into a full grown ague shake.)

HARD TIMES.

We now began to see hard times. The distance between us and Pilot Knob was so great that roving bands of rebels fell in our rear and effectually cut off all communications by that route. It would take a large force to guard a wagon train through. To attempt to capture these bands of the enemy was useless. At the approach of a large force they would scatter and disappear from sight and hide among the heavily timbered hills and mountains, and thus be ready to come out and again assemble to capture and burn any of our supply trains that might unhappily lie on the road. The still longer and more difficult route by which General Curtis had come, had long since, by the same causes, and by reason of its length, been rendered impracticable, and was totally abandoned. The fearful condition of the roads and the long distance to be traveled would well nigh have rendered it impossible to supply an army by over land even if the enemy had let our supply trains alone.

The supply trains that our army had brought from Pilot Knob, when we came, were virtually the last that came through. These supplies were quite large when we started, but our long march had seriously reduced them. General Curtis' army was nearly destitute when our division reached him. The surrounding country is poor and destitute. The most successful foraging expedition can barely find enough to last themselves back into camp. As for clothing, we had not drawn any to speak of since we left Pilot Knob, on March first. Thus we found ourselves in Batesville, ragged and hungry, with no supplies within reach to draw from.

All communications being cut off we know nothing of what is going on elsewhere. Conjecture is all that is left us. Has McClellan's grand army marched on to Richmond and even now virtually ended the rebellion, as was promised when last we heard from the East? Or has another Bull Run disaster overtaken our army and again placed Washington in danger, as the enemy were equally confident of doing? Between the two our hope is for fear that it may be worse, that both sides have remained facing each other and are still as when last we heard from them, standing like two bad boys with a good wide road between them, each vigorously telling the other that if he will "come over, I will knock your eyes out."

No letters from home can reach us. We have no tidings of our individual friends and relatives in other armies. How are they? How are our own folks at home? What do they think has become of us?

In the midst of all of this we while away many a tedious hour with some pleasant game, and at times I become almost gay over some jolly army jest. It was during these days that Company A's claim to superiority in one respect was acknowledged. In bringing in good, fat chickens, our march through Missouri and Arkansas had established the fact that Peverly, of Company A, and Hayes, of Company I, had no equals. These two surpassed everything and swept the board clean. Between them it was hard to decide. Either of them could start out after a hundred soldiers had returned, certain that there was not a chicken within twenty miles of camp, and in less than an hour return with a sack full. One day a plump but badly frightened chicken was seen running and flying through camp. Where it came from or to whom it belonged no one cared. The question was who would own the chicken by catching it. Twenty boys or more were after it. It was wild and active and led the boys a lively race. Peverly lay under his tent, the side of which was slightly raised, reading. He would not get up for one little chicken. As it was flying past he reached out one arm and took it in, without losing his place in the book he held in the other hand, and still continued to read. His mess had the chicken for dinner and the entire regiment conceded that Company A's man was entitled to the belt until Company I's man could publicly show that chickens would also voluntarily run to him to be killed.

LEAVING BATESVILLE.

All communication overland being cut off, and our provisions being about exhausted, it was fast becoming necessary for us to act and to act promptly. To return within reach of supplies by way of the Missouri railroads was out of the question. The railroad only came to Pilot Knob. We had nothing to live upon while making that long march, and the produce of the country would not avail toward feeding so large a force. A like want of supplies would prevent us from marching on to Little Rock and the Arkansas River valley country. The success of the Union forces in clearing the upper part of the Mississippi River of all formidable obstructions led us to hope that the Union boats would soon be able to reach the mouths of the White and Arkansas Rivers and come up them so that we could establish a base of supplies upon one or both of these streams. On the fourteenth of June we heard that Memphis had been captured, and soon thereafter that our gun-boats had cleared the way as far as the mouth of White River. This river is not, as we understand it, obstructed by any strong rebel works, and the water is high enough for boats of light draft to reach Jacksonport.[2]

At last it is decided that we must move. Marching orders are issued on June twenty-first. By night everything is ready. There was not much to do except to look up conveyances for our sick soldiers. This being done we went to sleep as usual. Less interest was felt in this preparation for a march than ever before. But for the anxiety felt to be once more where we could hear from home and friends and get some food to eat and clothes to wear, there was nothing in our expected march to excite attention. We simply expected that by easy marches we would go down the river and meet our boats at or a little below Jacksonport; get an abundance of supplies; receive letters and newspapers from home; go into camp, rest and recruit and then strike out and capture Little Rock and all of Arkansas. We felt sure that we would meet our boats. News that they were well up the river had been received. Such were the prospects with which we left Batesville.

FROM BATESVILLE TO JACKSONPORT.

Sunday morning, June twenty-second, the reveille beat at two o'clock. We got up. When the reveille drum beats, that means soldiers wake up. We had a lively time getting breakfast, packing knapsacks, filling canteens—our lean haversacks did not require much attention—and striking tents at this early morning hour. It is truly an interesting scene to see an army packing up and starting on a march at night.

At half-past three we started and marched until ten o'clock, and then camped for the day. The reason why we start and then stop so early is to avoid traveling in the heat of the day. This is the plan we will have to adopt if we do much marching during the summer in this Southern climate. To march in the hot summer dust at mid-day would be next to impossible.

The secesh, the lazy fellows, who never work and can hardly endure the hot summer weather of their own climate, have said and fully believe that the Northern soldiers could not live through the summer season in this hot and sultry climate. As for marching, it was the height of absurdity to think of such a thing. When this hot weather struck us at Batesville they believed that we were as effectually penned as though enclosed within impassable walls. That all they had to do now was to prevent supplies from reaching us and then all whom the heat did not kill would die of starvation. Thus they have been looking upon us as virtually prisoners of war and for this reason are making such desperate efforts to prevent us from getting any provisions. They will no doubt be much surprised to see how well we enjoy starting out at two or three o'clock for an early morning walk.

To make these early morning walks more pleasant we do not have to carry our knapsacks. Plenty room in the wagons now. All the supplies they have to carry is a few boxes of hard-tack. This is all the provisions we have left and not much of that. Hard-tack is the soldier name for army crackers. It is simply flour and water baked into hard crackers. So we use the provision wagons to carry our sick men and knapsacks and every thing except our guns and accoutrements, canteens and lean haversacks. We think it mighty lucky if we can find a hard-tack or two to put with our drinking water for one day's lunch. We put only a small load in each so as not to overload the wagons as the army mules are not in prime condition. We begin to look them over now and then as they are driven by to see what chance there is for mule steak for breakfast, but the prospect is not promising. Hide and bones are about all there is of the mules.

The hot weather has dried up the roads so that they are as dry and hard as a barn floor, and as long as the mules can walk six of them run a lightly loaded wagon without much effort.

Monday we started at four o'clock and marched eight miles to Black River near to Jacksonport. We then threw our pontoon bridge over the river and the next two days were spent in crossing over to Jacksonport. Our rations are hard-tack and water.

LIVELY TIMES.

Our division started forward on June twenty-sixth, and marched down the river and camped at a small stream called Village Creek.[3]

We are obliged to send out forage trains in every direction to gather up enough provender to keep our mules alive, and of course we take every thing we find for men to eat. We do not find much in this country for man or beast.[4]

On the twenty-seventh we sent out a forage train with a strong guard. It was attacked by a band of four hundred rebels. Our men stood their ground, whipped the rebels and brought their forage into camp. We lost four killed and thirty wounded. The rebels left eight of their dead upon the field. How many dead and wounded they took away is unknown. Our men returned to camp at night.

The next day General Benton[5] took the Thirty-third Illinois and Eighth Indiana, one battery and part of the Seventh Indiana cavalry, and went in pursuit of the rebels. We went over the battle ground of yesterday's fight, and after marching twelve miles found that the rebels had passed out of reach. As we returned to camp the night became fearfully dark and we had much difficulty in finding our way through the dark woods.

On Sunday our forage train, out in another direction, was attacked by a small band of rebels. The Eleventh Wisconsin went out to assist our men but found the train and guard coming in all right. A few shots had driven the enemy away. It is thought that some of them were hit. None of our men were hurt.

Monday, June thirtieth, Company A went out as guard to a forage train. We kept our eyes open for rebels but did not see any. Had good luck. We got some corn fodder, rye in the straw, etc., for the mules, and some bacon, molasses, lard and potatoes for the men. Our officers settled with the owners for every thing taken. It seems strange to pay for what we get first and then fight for it afterward. The rebel soldiers and rebel citizens seem to well understand each other—so well that there is not usually much danger until the owner has been settled with and passed out of sight—then look out. Every piece of woods is then liable to prove to be filled with a band of hiding rebels ready to fire upon us.

Having waited at Village Creek until all of General Curtis' army had crossed Black River, we started forward again on July first and marched twelve miles before noon, our advance driving the rebels before them. At four o'clock six companies of our regiment went ahead to reconnoiter. Two miles from camp we found that the rebels had blockaded the road by felling a large number or trees across it. We supposed that the rebels were in force upon the other side and crawled through the fallen timbers to see what they were about. We soon came to their picket guard which we drove in and then chased the rebels until dark but could not catch them. We then slowly picked our way through the dark woods back to camp. Rather risky business this. The enemy had force enough to have easily captured us. We did not fire through this blockade as they expected but were upon their side and right upon them when they first saw us. They probably thought that none but a very strong force would thus venture into their very teeth, and left the field, one in which they had a capital position for a good fight, without firing a gun. Where our six little companies would have been if they had turned upon us is hard to tell. Probably swept off at the first fire. How disgusted that rebel army would have been if they had learned that they had been driven from their chosen field by a little band of less than three hundred men. In war, as in love, audacity often wins, while superiority is asleep.

The next day our soldiers went to work and soon cut a road through the woods. The alarmed rebels did not return to annoy us. We made a new road and will leave the one the rebels have blockaded with so much trouble for them to repair when they get ready. With dry hard ground and no bridges to make, it was easy work to cut a new road through the woods, and it was soon done. The First Indiana cavalry went ahead and had a sharp brush with some of the enemy. None of our men were lost, but a number of the rebels were killed by our cannon.

We made an early start on the morning of the third of July and went through to Augusta. We expected a tilt with the rebels here as they had loudly threatened that we should not enter the town. Some heavily timbered hills that we had to pass through before reaching the city gave them the choice of many capital places for a battle. Our company was on the skirmish line and we made our rapid advance with much interest, but as we approached the nimble rebels skipped out so lively that we could not catch any of them. We got in at noon. Other troops continued to come in during all of the afternoon.

JULY FOURTH.

We celebrated the fourth of July in good style in Augusta. A salute was fired, speeches were made, and this place treated to the first good, honest fourth of July celebration it ever had. The Declaration of Independence is always indorsed with mental reservations by the people of the South. The declaration that "all men are created free and equal" never was popular with slaveholders. Why should it be?

During the day an advance guard was sent ahead and they had a sharp skirmish with the enemy. The rebels were severely punished with our "little bull-dogs" (steel guns) and it is reported that about sixty of them were killed.

As it was known that the enemy was gathering a large force in front of us, to block our advance, it was deemed prudent for the army to move in a more compact form, so we remained in Augusta on July fifth. This gave all of General Curtis' army time to come in or at least to reach within supporting distance of us.

Considerable interest was created by the arrival of the First Arkansas Regiment, one raised by General Curtis since he came to Batesville. It was the first time they had met our division.

July sixth we started at four o'clock and marched fifteen miles to Cache River. The advance came upon a force of the enemy who had commenced to blockade the road. If they expect to seriously annoy us, why do not the lazy fellows do their mischief before we get to them? After a short, sharp skirmish they skipped across the river. At night they commenced to annoy us by firing into our camp from their side of the river. Our artillery opened and soon cleared those woods and we slept in peace the rest of the night. Our army is supplied with much the best artillery, and whenever we can get two or three good batteries into play upon them the rebels always skip out of reach. Rebels do not like cannon balls.

CHAPTER VI.

BATTLE OF CACHE RIVER.

The early morn of a summer day, as the light began to break in the eastern sky on Monday morning, July 7, 1862, found us camped on the west side of Cache River.[1] Work was commenced at an early hour and our pontoon bridge was soon thrown over the river. The army immediately commenced crossing. Our guards had been thrown some little distance ahead, but we were not troubled by the enemy. Our effective artillery work of the previous night had taught them to keep at a safe distance.

At eleven o'clock four companies of the Thirty-third Illinois and four of the Eleventh Wisconsin, with one piece of light artillery, belonging to a cavalry regiment, all under command of Colonel Hovey, went forward to see what the enemy in front of us were doing.

With a skirmish line in advance, we went forward on a rapid walk. Nothing occurred until we had marched about seven miles. Here we came upon a rebel picket so suddenly that they were obliged to take to the woods, leaving their guns and other traps upon the ground. At the point where this picket guard had been posted another road crossed the one we were upon at right angles. This picket post was to our left as we advanced or upon the north side of our road. They disappeared in the woods in front of us, keeping to our left. Believing that they had gone to join the command to which they belonged, we were confident that the main force of the enemy was in the woods directly in our front.

Upon the south side of our road and just beyond the cross road was an old frame house. It was unplastered and the side boards were so loose and cracked that a person inside could easily look out upon the road in front. Some of our men made a hasty search of this house, but failed to find any rebels. It afterward proved that a rebel officer was at the time secreted in one of the rooms upstairs. He had been aided by the good, honest woman of the house who earnestly assured our men, "upon the word of a pious Christian woman," that there had not been any rebels at her house and none in sight. In reply to a question she asserted that the men who had run into the woods, as we came up, were only a small hunting party who had stopped by the road to make some coffee. While no reliance was placed upon her earnest statements it was not thought worth while to leave any guard to watch the house or her. As soon as our men withdrew, she of course promptly notified the rebel officer upstairs.

About three quarters of a mile in front of us were very heavy woods, thick with underbrush. We were sure the rebels were in these woods waiting for us. We would go and see them. Without a moment's delay we pushed forward, our entire force passing in front of the frame house. The rebel officer in one of the upper rooms, with the woman below acting as his sentinel, peeked through a convenient hole and saw and counted our entire force. We had by actual count three hundred and eighty-two men all told. It is understood that the observing rebel's report to his commanding officer was "not quite four hundred men." This shows that he was reasonably accurate.

Passing rapidly by the house and the partly cleared field we soon reached the heavy woods where we expected to find the rebels. We did not find them. We did, however, find two negroes who had been hiding in the thick brush. They were frightened almost to death. As soon as we came near enough so that they were sure we were Yankee soldiers, they ran toward us exclaiming: "Lord a-golly, massy! Big Lord bless you'uns! We's mighty glad to see you'uns! Don't shoot! Oh Lord a-massy; look out! I'se afeared of dem big guns. Don't, don't let 'em big mouths come dis way. Swallow up dis darkey sure." They were quieted with the assurance that they should not be harmed and their excited exclamations cut short with the questions: "Are there any rebel soldiers near here?" "Oh, Lord-a-mighty, bless you lots of 'em. Woods chuck full of 'em. More dan hundred thousand. Oh, d'ey eat you all up sure, sure as you live d'ey will, massy! All the woods full of 'em." "Are they in these woods?"—Jumping five feet high in terror at the bare thought.—"In dese woods! Lord a save you, no; dese darkies nebber hide in dese woods if de rebs be here—Dead darkey sure—Woods full of 'em, eat you'uns all up sure, sure as you live a minute, you'uns all dead men sure. Sure as you live you is! Dis darkey dead, too! Oh, golly save us; let dis darkey take to the woods! Dey be here mortal minute sure! Dis darkey must go!" Of course all this took place in much less time than it can be written. By a few questions we learned that the rebel force, whatever it was, was not far from us. By looking in the direction their hands most eloquently pointed, we could easily see the deep woods in which the rebels were undoubtedly covered. That these poor frightened negroes, who all their lives had been the slaves of their rebel masters, told us the truth, we did not for a moment doubt. We can always depend upon the colored folks to tell us the truth about the rebels.

It was now plain that if we wanted to find the enemy the place to go was to retrace our steps nearly a mile to the frame house we had passed, then take the cross road leading into the woods lying off to the south of the road by which we had come.

In the meantime the rebel officer secreted in the house when we passed it had not been idle. Having carefully noted our strength as we passed, he hastened to rejoin the rebels massed in heavy force in the woods near at hand. Here was a glorious opportunity—for them. A force of Union troops of less than four hundred men had gone past and left off to their right a rebel force of more than as many thousand nicely hid in the thick woods and not two miles distant from the road the Union troops had taken. No more of the Union army was within hearing distance. A cavalry guard could easily be thrown in that direction to give warning if danger arose. All they had to do was to come up rapidly, turn in our rear, and slaughter our little force. Of course they at once resolved to do it. A band of rebel cavalry was sent through the woods toward the road by which we had advanced to watch and give warning if reinforcements should be coming to us. Their main force was put in shape to march up and capture us.

By this time unknown to them, we were rapidly upon our way to meet them. The rebels had not calculated upon our finding some negroes in the woods, and thus becoming posted as to their position. They expected to give us a complete surprise by coming up in our rear. They calculated, and with good reason, that by coming up in our rear we would believe that it was some of our own troops and that they could fall upon and slaughter us with a single volley. We had been warned in time, but none too soon. With a rapid march we had hastened back to the road crossing. Here we left two companies of the Eleventh Wisconsin as a reserve guard. The rest of our little force started south to enter the woods where we knew the rebels were. The two other companies of the Wisconsin regiment were placed in front as skirmishers. The four little companies of the Thirty-third followed solid column. What an army column, hardly two hundred strong! With this force we went into the thick woods to meet an enemy of unknown strength. Of course it was not for a moment supposed that we would meet an enemy that would stand and make a stubborn contest. Our daily experience in the past had been that when found, the enemy would fire only one volley and then seek safety by rapid flight into the depths of the wild woods. Colonel Hovey, always ready and ever anxious for a fight, had so little hopes of any thing but a deserted rebel camp being found that he started leisurely to ride back toward the main army at Cache River to give the information that the road was open. Ere he had gone far his quick ear caught the first sound of clashing arms, and dashing the spurs into his steed with headlong speed he returned to his little command and joined in the wild conflict that was then raging, as we shall presently see.

Our rapid march had brought us back so that we turned toward them by the time the rebels had fairly started for us. Discovering our approach they quickly adopted another plan. Their strong advance in solid line of battle was hid by lying close upon the ground well covered by fallen logs and thick underbrush. In this way they expected to lie concealed until we were within reach when they would rise up and sweep us off at the first fire. Back of them, further out of sight, was a heavy body of mounted men who were to rush in at the proper time and complete the slaughter. That a slaughter was their design was plainly shown. Had they simply wished to capture us, able as they were to surround us with such an overwhelming force, they could, and by all rules of civilized war ought to at once have sent in a flag of truce, informed us of their large force, advised us of our real condition and demanded our immediate surrender. Their action showed that it was not a capture but a slaughter they desired. But their last well laid plan, like the first, was doomed to fail.

We advanced in column and without any line of battle, having in front only a line of skirmishers. Our keen-eyed skirmishers, many of whom had been successful hunters in the wild woods of Wisconsin, were too quick for the hiding rebels. Profiting by our repeated experience in the woods of Arkansas with the rebels who at first sight would shoot and run away, our established rule had become to fire at the enemy as soon as we got near enough. Some of our skirmishers soon saw the heads of the prostrated and hidden rebels and commenced firing at them. Now the wild music commenced. Seeing that they were discovered the entire rebel line rose up and fired a terrific volley at our skirmishers. The distance was so great that their poor guns did no serious damage, while the powerful rifles in the hands of our men told with deadly effect upon the enemy. But it was only our skirmish line of a few men engaged. They had no time to reload their guns and fire a second shot. Many of the rebels had double-barreled shotguns and thus each had a charge still in reserve. Their heavy support on horseback had started rapidly forward at the first shot. Now the entire rebel force, cavalry and infantry, came forward upon a fierce run. Wisconsin's little band of skirmishers had to skip back at a lively rate. They were now out of the fight. Our time had come. Company A was in the advance. The ground upon which we stood was some higher than that over which the rebels were advancing. Standing at the brow of the hill our one little steel gun had commenced a lively play upon the advancing rebels. As our skirmishers came back on the run we barely had time for part of the company to turn into line in support of the cannon and face the enemy when they were upon us. They came upon a fearful charge and with but little attention to military order. The heavy lines of the enemy's infantry breaking up to let through a more dense mass on horseback. In this way they were right upon us before they saw our line. Now a terrific clash of arms followed. Here we were but a few yards apart. Into the dense throng our trusty rifles were fired with fearful effect. They replied with a volley that made the timber roar and the ground tremble. Lead enough went screeching over our heads to have swept off an entire army. In front of our few guns, horses, horsemen and footmen were falling to the ground. In front of theirs our men stood unharmed. Hardly a man upon our side was hit by this first volley. We were standing waiting for them. They were surprised to meet us face to face when they supposed that our entire line was upon the run to the rear. In the thick woods numbers could not be accurately estimated, and our little line of skirmishers had given the advancing enemy such a warm reception that they believed our entire force was in the advance line and had been driven back, and the rebels rushed madly on, never dreaming of the stubborn resistance they were yet to meet. In surprised confusion they fired wildly. Standing as we did upon higher ground also helped to save us. In firing they aimed too high. A few feet above our heads the trees were almost swept clean by the leaden balls fired above us. Leaves and twigs and limbs severed from the trees by the leaden storm dropped upon us like hail. Had the rebel guns been aimed so as to have sent the bullets five or ten feet lower none of us would have been left alive to tell the tale of our defeat. Their lines wavered and trembled at the fearful punishment they received, but the force of the heavy mass coming so swiftly impelled them on, on into our very midst. Fortunately their guns, like ours, had been fired and were now unloaded. But close at hand fast rushing upon us, were still other heavy forces of the enemy with lead in their guns.

Let no one suppose that Company A, a mere handful of men, stood there in formal army line, with these hosts of fresh rebels coming up to shoot at us, while we went through all of the motions of reloading our empty guns. No, indeed! Plenty of good trees to get behind were too near at hand. But ere we fell back there was a little work to do. As soon as it became certain that we must fall back, the first thought was to save the little steel cannon. The driver swung his team into place, the gun was hooked on the caisson, the gunners scampered back under cover of the woods, and yet, oh, misery! there stood our little cannon. The soldier heart always bleeds to see a flag or a piece of artillery fall into the enemy's hands. At the first jump of the team, the quick start had thrown the cannon from its fastenings. The bold driver was wounded and could not at once bring his horses to a stand. In the midst of the fierce storm raging about us, Captain Potter coolly said: "Steady, boys; save the gun." Sergeant Ed Pike, of our company, ran up and grabbed hold of the cannon with one hand, his own rifle in the other, and with the strength of a giant and the assistance of one comrade ran the cannon down the road, hooked it on the caisson, and the team galloped to the rear and saved the gun. The rebels were all around. The nearest horseman was almost close enough to have struck Pike with his saber. The rebels were, however, completely dashed by the supreme audacity of the movement. Half a dozen of us, the tallest members of the company, and thus thrown near to Pike, our orderly sergeant, were all that were near enough to witness the strange scene. A strange scene, indeed! With one false step, or the loss of a single second of time, it would have been a tragedy. With our heavy guns in hand we were ready to aid our brave comrade, if we could, had the rebels raised their sabers to strike, but, it may be confessed, we had no desire to enter into a clubbing fight with unloaded guns unless compelled to do so. As soon as the cannon was hitched to the caisson and saved by the galloping team, we made lively time to join our comrades in finding good places and friendly trees behind which we could stop and reload our rifles. As I dodged under a limb it caught my cap and it fell to the ground behind me. Pike had saved a cannon. A pretty story it would be if I could not save a little army cap. Without scarcely any thought other than the appearance of coming out of the fight bare-headed I turned back for the cap. The faces of the rebels who had witnessed our audacious actions in taking the steel from their very teeth were covered with amazement. They looked as though they were in doubt whether we were really fighting or only engaged as two parties in some huge play. As I looked up with the recovered cap in hand, and the real situation began to appear to me, while overwhelmed with astonishment, I could not help returning the surprised smiles of the nearest rebels and then scampered back, right lively to find my tree. It was more thoughtlessness than any thing else that caused me to save my cap from such a place. As I was reloading behind a good, stout tree, and began to fully realize the situation, a thousand miserable army caps could have lain there at their leisure and I would have gone bareheaded twenty years before I would have run in to the teeth of that rebel host to get one of them.

All of this had hardly taken more than a second of time. Upon occasions like this, actions and events are swifter than passing time. The terrific rebel volley had answered our fire; almost at a single jump Pike had taken the gun to its place; and into the woods we went hardly a pace behind the rest of our company. At this point the woods were, fortunately, so thick with underbrush that two rods distance completely hid us from our foes.

And still on came the crowding mass of anxious rebels who had not yet fired a gun. We had not been a moment too soon. Company A had barely time to scamper into the thick woods to our left, when this seething, rushing horde of fresh rebels came up, passed the ground where we had stood, and fell upon the three other companies of the Thirty-third. Each had turned partly into line. There had been no time to change from column into line by battalion. The scene our company met a moment before was now re-enacted. Steadily, coolly and with deadly aim the large rifle balls were sent into the dense rebel ranks. The effect was too terrible. Flesh and blood could not stand it. Brave men though they were, the rebel lines wavered, halted and then rushed back in wild dismay.

By the time this desperate charge was over we had ceased to pay any great attention to mere company lines. Officers and men all fought together. About the only indication of rank was the fact that wherever our lines were the thickest an officer would generally be seen in the midst of them. Scattered through the deep woods, only watching that we kept in the general line of the Union soldiers, we sought such shelter as we could, and rapidly loaded our rifles and fired at the best mark we could see. Thus the rebels withdrew, suffering at every step until they were out of reach of our long range rifles.

Do not think that this retreat of the enemy was the end of the battle of Cache River. We thought so for a brief moment. Colonel Hovey, who had now reached the front, said to his orderly: "Report to camp that one officer and two men are severely wounded and that we want a surgeon immediately." He was standing near me when he said this and evidently had as little thought of a renewal of the attack as any of us. More from a soldierly spirit, than from any thought of necessity, our lines had been somewhat re-formed by the soldiers changing places and getting nearer to their own officers and company comrades. But a brief moment was, however, allowed for this. Before formal lines could be planned, much less made, we were clearly advised of our error in believing the battle ended. So soon that it seemed but an echo of the departing cry we had so lately and with so much satisfaction heard, the returning rebel yell, rapidly coming nearer and nearer, told us that all was not yet over. Their cavalry guard had informed the rebels that no reinforcements were yet at hand to rescue the little band of Union soldiers. For a large army, thousands in number, to be baffled by a few hundred, and that, too, out in the open woods with no protecting works, was something the hot Southern blood could not endure. Rushing among them, with information of how contemptible we were in numbers, appealing to the pride of boasted Southern chivalry, sneering in words of contempt at the plow boys of the North, the rebel officers at once rallied their men for another charge. On they came more fierce than before, blowing monstrous horns, pounding kettles, beating drums, screeching the harsh, shrill rebel yell. What possessed them? Did they think to scare the soldiers by whom they had been so severely punished a few minutes before by mere noise? So it seemed. With the most dismal racket that all of these things could make, added to by the less weird but more dangerous flash of rebel guns, the furious, overwhelming force was thrown upon us with all the insane zeal of maddened fury. This second charge took a more deadly and continued form than the first. As they came, in this headlong career, our trusty rifles were emptied into the dense mass with fearful results. Our deadly fire broke the rebel charge but they could not themselves fully stay the force of the onward rush. The fierce advance of the enemy carried many of them far beyond where our soldiers stood.

Now our guns as fast as loaded could be used upon rebels in our rear as well as in front. Rebels before us, rebels behind us, rebels each side of us, rebels, rebels everywhere. The enormous mass of rebels was strong enough to crush our ranks; to pass through and trample them down and to have captured or slaughtered us if they could have found our army lines—but we had none. Wherever the enemy were too thick to be driven back we would run in both directions and thus open a way for them to pass through while we looked for the protecting side of other trees. Noble trees they were. Many of them had firmly stood there loyal and sound to the core, since Washington's day. In a battle a good tree is often a soldier's bosom friend. Perhaps instead of recording that over five thousand Confederates fiercely fought less than four hundred Yankee boys we should count five or ten thousand trees as in line upon the Union side and thus in numbers make the contest equal. True it is that those staunch Arkansas trees right royally gave the strength of their side to the cause of loyalty upon that day, and in after years—far, far away—after the story is all forgotten, when those trees become brown and leafless with age and decay, and the wood man's ax lays them low, in the hearts of those old oak trees that stood for the grand old Union flag when misguided sons of the South would tear it down, will be found many a leaden ball which has rested there since that eventful day, when they stood within the fierce contest of July 7, 1862.

The fierce, unequal contest was raging still. Each of us was now virtually fighting upon his own hook. Each selected the best protection he could while loading his rifle and then sought for the largest band of rebels he could see to fire into, all of our officers did well their part, but all they could do was by example, and each officer was fighting side by side with the soldiers. Colonel Hovey went in on foot with the rest. During the most desperate part of the contest, as they were reloading their rifles, some of our soldiers raised a shout and laugh on seeing Colonel Hovey popping away toward the enemy with a little pocket revolver. A pop-gun would have been fully as dangerous at the distance he was attempting to shoot. "Boys," said he, "shooting is all that will do any good in this fight, you are doing better work than I." Soon, however, he borrowed a rifle from a wounded soldier, who was crawling to the rear, and from that time on he went right in with the soldiers wherever the fight was thickest, now and then borrowing a handful of cartridges from the cartridge box of the nearest soldier, and thus continued until the last gun was fired. All of our officers did the same, and long before the battle ended every officer in these woods, who was not himself wounded, had the rifle of some disabled soldier.

A charge of nearly spent small balls from a shot gun or musket struck Colonel Hovey in the breast. He stopped a moment, examined the wounds, picked out some of the balls that were buried in his flesh; said: "This does not amount to much," and paid no further attention to his wounds until the fight was over.

A round bullet hole, as it was supposed, was noticed in Colonel Lippincott's felt hat. "A pretty close call, Colonel," some one remarked. "Oh, no," said

Lippincott, with cool indifference, as the rebel bullets were whistling past his head, "I cut these holes this morning for the purpose of ventilation in this hot weather." He was too brave a man to be willing to accept any undue credit.

This second charge was soon broken by our accurate, telling fire. In a spasmodic form it continued. The fight became continuous. Heavy forces of the enemy were in front of us; some upon our flank, and often many were, by their fierce ride, carried through to our rear. It was fighting all around. Every few minutes a desperate band of rebel cavalry would rush upon us. During one of these fierce charges a powerful rebel, upon a superb horse, came dashing through our lines at the head of his band. The first man he reached was Sergeant Dutton of our Company. Dutton had just fired and was reloading his rifle. Seeing his advantage the athletic rebel drew his heavy saber and with a cry of desperate rage went fiercely on to strike and ride the Union soldier down. None of our boys within reach had at that critical moment a loaded gun so as to fire and save Dutton from his threatened doom, and besides, just about this time each of us had about a dozen rebels of his own to attend to and was kept mighty busy dodging out of reach of rebel balls while putting each fresh load in our rifles. Being just then near a fence which blocked his retreat with an open space of ground in front of him, giving the rider an unobstructed view, no escape seemed possible and Dutton's doom seemed at hand. Just as the fatal blow was about to fall, the little sergeant whipped a revolver from his belt, without moving a single step, and fired. The uplifted hand fell helpless, the bold rider dropped dead to the ground, and the riderless horse passed on through our lines and out of sight to our rear. Had Dutton's wonderful nerve for a second wavered, had he even given a single glance to look for a way of escape he would have been a dead man, and perhaps the result of the battle changed. Like incidents could be told of each soldier who stood in those woods at that hour. With the fearful odds against us the part of each was important, and had one failed, disaster to all would have been the result. Dismayed at the loss of their impetuous leader and terrified by seeing so many of their number fall from their saddles by the certain aim of the Union rifles, this band of rebel horsemen, like others, disappeared, only to be followed by others as desperate and reckless as those who had gone before.

The only military command I heard during that long contest after the battle was under way, was given by Captain Potter. A number of us were near him. He had been wounded, and with a handkerchief tied around the bleeding leg to stop the rapid flow of blood, as a little lull in the fierce storm occurred, he gave what was probably the only command given during those two desperate hours, in these words: "Boys, I believe that we can find some good shots over there," pointing to a clump of trees nearer to the rebels who were firing upon us. We advanced, and with the rifle he had been using for a cane, he came hobbling along after us.

Thus for two long hours this fearful contest continued. And only four small companies of the Thirty-third Regiment, with hardly fifty men each to meet the desperate onslaught. True, a like number of the Eleventh Wisconsin were with us, and right useful they were. Two companies, it will be remembered, were left at the road crossing. The other two companies upon the skirmish line, at the beginning of the battle, had been so hotly pressed that each man had all he could do to save himself. The companies upon the road formed in line. As the skirmishers came back they joined them. Our little cannon, after being saved from the enemy, had also gone back and taken place in the line. There was not much opportunity to use the cannon, but now and then, when our boys were clear from the road, a solid shot or shell would be sent through to greet the rebel hosts. Now and then some of the Illinois boys being entirely cut off from their comrades would run through the wood or field to the rear and form in line with the Wisconsin boys. Thus when the enemy came with such fierce force that we could not stay their headlong course but were compelled to fall to the right or left and let the heaviest columns through, as they passed by and looked down the road and saw the solid line still in front, raked as they were by the ceaseless side fire we were pouring upon them, they would in dismay rapidly pass off in the open woods to our right leaving us at liberty to turn and give our undivided attention to other rebels still advancing in our front. Standing there without a wavering man in their lines, that little band of Wisconsin men was of untold help to us. If Colonel Hovey left them there during all this time by design, it was a happy thought. If the fighting was so hot that he had no chance to send an order for them to advance, it was a most fortunate accident. Had the many rebels who, at different times, passed our lines in their mad career, been permitted unmolested to reform and reload and open fire in our rear, no protecting trees could have caught all of the rebel bullets, and we would have been swept off in a few brief moments.

A plan of the battle field would show the advantages which aided us in this desperate contest. Supposing that the main road we had advanced upon in the morning, was running east, that upon which the battle was fought would be running south. At the crossing of the two roads our reserve had been stationed. On the left of the cross road going south toward the enemy was a field connected with the frame farm house referred to, and all enclosed by a strong rail fence. This fence ran south along the road, about three quarters of a mile. The fence then turned east running in that direction until the heavy and almost impenetrable woods east of us were reached. The first part of the field near the farm house was quite free of trees, but the lower part ran into and included considerable of the woods in which we found the enemy. On the right of the cross road, which would be looking in the direction of our main army on Cache River, was a long stretch of ground thinly covered with large trees but free of underbrush. This, of course, ran back to and connected with the heavier woods where the enemy had made his rendezvous. For a short distance on the right side of the cross road there had formerly been an enclosure, and about a quarter of a mile from the main road the remains of a rail fence, running some little distance west, was still standing. When we first met the enemy we had passed beyond the farthest fence, but as the battle progressed we had fallen back to it, and many of our men were in the woods of the enclosure. Thus it will be seen that when the enemy's cavalry charged upon us, with the highway for his center, his right wing would strike the heavy fence and thus be thrown into confusion with his center upon the road, and this would naturally carry many of them into the woods to his left, our right, and those still advancing would soon strike the remains of the fence on that side causing many more to turn off into the open woods. Those who had kept in the open road would now suddenly come in sight of our reserve line; if near enough receive a leaden salute, and they, too, would then turn into the woods and disappear. Remembering that these desperate charges were mainly made by men on horseback in a mad headlong gallop; that they were first thrown into confusion by a fence on one side and then broken by the remains of one on the other side; that at every step and from each side they were severely suffering from the rifles of our sharpshooters, it will readily be seen that great advantages were open to us and that we improved them to the utmost.

The fight still goes on. The enemy became at last most desperately enraged. Their unobstructed access to the road between us and the rest of the Union army still gave them full knowledge that no aid had yet come to us. Why don't they come? We have been fighting on, on, expecting each moment to hear the dash of the Union cavalry coming to our aid. And then our own comrades of the Thirty-third and the brothers of the Wisconsin boys, why do they not come? Only four companies of each regiment are here. Six of each are there. Why do they dally in the woods? Are they playing by the wayside and we struggling here? Why don't they come? If all others become indifferent to our fate they can not. No, indeed! Too oft have they and we divided our scant rations with each other; suffered together; mourned at the same graves; mingled in the same joys and shared the same trials. A faintly whispered, dread suspicion passes among us. Can it be that the heavy rebel armies have come from east of the Mississippi or other fields in overwhelming force to destroy the Union army in these Arkansas wilds? Let it be remembered that we have long been cut off from communication with the outside world. We have no definite information from other fields. At the North it is reported that Curtis' army is lost in Arkansas. So little have we known of what has occurred in Kentucky and Tennessee and in the far East during the past months, that only wild imagination is our guide. Are the heavy forces so hotly pressing us, part of a monstrous, gigantic rebel army that has, unknown to us, crossed the Mississippi and come up the Arkansas and White Rivers? Has a still heavier force thrown itself between us and our army? Is the Union army we so lately left even now cut off from aiding us? With our eyes steadily fixed upon the enemy in front, our ears are turned anxiously toward our own army to hear if the murderous air shall bring to us the sound of their booming guns. But it matters little to us what the fate of others may be. It is now too late. Too well we know that the enraged rebels have already suffered too severely and that now no terms will be asked or given. It is now a fight to the death. The thought that life can be saved by a surrender is banished from every mind. To steal our way through the dark woods and deep swamps to our Northern homes is impossible. We begin to gather in more compact form. There is a feeling that in a few moments our last cartridge will be fired and then all that will be left is to fix bayonets and with the cold steel do all we can as we rush to our doom.

It is afterward learned that the Union troops have been so busily engaged and created such a continual racket in crossing Cache River that they did not hear anything of our fierce fight. It was supposed that we would only advance some two or at most three miles at which distance a stubborn contest could be easily traced by the sound of the firing guns. Thus it was supposed that we were quietly lying in the woods, waiting for the advance of the army. Instead of that we had gone some seven or eight miles and were so far away that the guns they now and then heard were thought to be only idle shots fired at random into the woods to see if any strolling bands of rebels were trying to creep upon us. The first information the Union army had of our hot engagement was given by one of our soldiers who had become completely demoralized at the first fire and ran back reporting us all killed. In quick time a force of Union cavalry was galloping to our rescue. Of this we were not advised.

Thus no reinforcements had reached us and the desperate rebels, chagrined, mortified, raving mad for the third time, with a fully organized force, came up on a desperate, sweeping, reckless charge. On they come with unbridled fury. We break into little bands among each thick cluster of trees and keep up a continued fire into the dense mass of advancing foes. All of the former scenes are reenacted now with redoubled force. We turn and fire at rebels in our rear as often as we do at those in front. Upon each occasion we had been obliged to fall further back. We were now so near that the rebel charge through our line carried some of them within range of the guns of the Wisconsin boys, who well and promptly improved their opportunity. Pressed by fire in front together with the shot we gave them in the rear those rebels who passed our line rushed with headlong speed into the woods on our right as those who came before had done. Grand confusion now reigns. The woods are full of riderless horses, running here and there, racing and tearing, hardly more reckless or aimless than those guided by their rebel riders. Our ammunition is now nearly exhausted. Those entirely out borrow two or three cartridges of others, but none have much. The store of our wounded has been greedily taken by those who still can use their guns. Straining every nerve, firing with the utmost care we watch the result with vivid interest. Too well we know the fatal result that threatens us. A few seconds of this vital anxiety and then the rebel lines begin to tremble, waver and then break, and those alive hasten away leaving the ground, even where we stand, strewn with their dead. Thus for the third time, a rebel charge in mass, has been repulsed and driven back. We now have to fire at long range, careful to do so only when we have a good shot. If they come on us again, in solid mass, we are helpless. Every movement is quickly noticed. The rebels who have crossed our lines in their headlong career and been driven into the woods on our right, toward our main army, are now seen to increase their hot speed toward the rear. Farther off, glimpses of the rebel cavalry, who have been watching upon the road, can be seen going fiercely toward their main command.

Beyond these, still further off, a cloud of dust is seen swelling up through and over the trees, and a moment more the glorious music of the rattling sabers of the Union cavalry is heard and then we see their foaming horses as they come to our aid. Closely following the cavalry, as they come to our relief, we soon see the gleaming guns and hear the glad hurrah of our infantry boys. The soldiers of the Thirty-third Illinois and Eleventh Wisconsin had run those seven long miles on a hot Southern July day to relieve us, their own comrades, and the battle is over.

CHAPTER VII.

AFTER THE BATTLE.

The Union loss in the battle of Cache River was seven killed and forty wounded. Company A had three wounded: Captain Potter, Sergeant Fyffe and Corporal Bigger. Seeing how lame Captain Potter was, one of the boys ran out as the battle ended, and captured a riderless horse which the Captain rode the balance of our journey to the Mississippi.

The loss of the enemy was large. How great is unknown. As we were continually obliged to fall back, it gave the enemy an opportunity to remove his wounded, which was zealously done. It is believed that the rebels also took away many of their dead. The Union soldiers were obliged to bury those left upon the field of whom they found over two hundred. This probably covered only a small fraction of their actual loss. But even that was fearfully large. For a small force that numbered all told three hundred and eighty two men to come out of a long contested fight in the open woods with only seven of their number killed and over two hundred of the enemy left dead upon the field is victory enough.

As to how many of the enemy were engaged is also unknown. By the best information we derived, gained from the rebel prisoners who fell into our hands, and from other sources, it is believed that there were at least ten thousand armed rebels in those woods and that nearly all of them were at one time or another in the fight before it ended. Large forces of both cavalry and infantry were certainly brought against us. The first heavy onslaught was led by heavy lines of infantry. The effective force of their charge was probably retarded instead of aided by the heavy columns of rebel cavalry that followed so close as to run upon them by the time they reached our first line after driving in our skirmishers. The following charges upon us were mainly by mounted cavalry. To this we were, undoubtedly, much indebted for the success we achieved. Mounted cavalry, in thick woods, can not successfully contend with well armed infantry. Another advantage we had was in our guns. We had trusty, far-reaching rifles that told with deadly effect at a distance the inferior rebel guns could not reach.

When our cavalry reinforcements first came up, believing that it must be an insignificant force that our little band could hold at bay so long, they at once decided to go in and take those who were left prisoners. On they went. They soon came up to the retreating rebels but found the enemy so strong they were exceedingly glad to come back to us on a right lively run.

Did we go over the battle field? No, indeed, I did not! Those who wished to do so did. But few of those who had been in the fight cared to review that gory field. Many a time our individual aim had been too distinct. By passing over the battle ground evidences could be found to tell whether the rebel aimed at had dropped to the ground only to escape from the whistling bullet or for a more fatal reason. Soldiers, even in the hottest fight, do not often care to know that their individual shot has proven fatal. For this reason most of us carefully kept from that bloody field, and the duty of gathering and burying the rebel dead was left to those who had not been in the battle.

ON TO CLARENDON.

After the battle of Cache River or Cotton Plant, as it was sometimes called, was ended, our troops came up rapidly and we were soon ready to push forward again. Our little force was highly complimented for its gallant action in the severe contest it had passed through and as a mark of honor we were to have the advance during the rest of our march. We went forward rapidly hoping that the entire force of the enemy would remain in our front and that we would be able to overtake them. A strong part of our army now kept near enough to our advance to be able to participate, and we would have made quick and thorough work of it if we could have caught the rebels. This we were not able to do. They took good care to keep out of our reach. What an ending of their great pretensions. They had been gathering a large force and loudly boasted that the Union army should never get out of the Arkansas woods. All of their available troops had been thrown in front of us to obstruct our advance. After a two-hours' fight with our little detached band, the grand rebel army that intended to capture the entire Union army that had come from Southwest Missouri under General Curtis and from Southeast Missouri under General Steele, was so completely demoralized that the smallest scouting party we could send out could hardly get sight of them before they would scamper away. They had not courage enough left to fire a single gun.

At Bayou DeView we found a good bridge. We came up so suddenly that the enemy had not time to burn it as they designed doing. The force left there by them for that purpose had hardly time to cross and save themselves before we were upon them and had possession of the bridge. It was now becoming quite dark and they had not expected us until the next morning. It was very important to save the bridge, and we at once charged across it, expecting a sharp contest with the enemy upon the other side, but they did not stop to trouble us. Throwing a sufficient force across the stream to guard the bridge we waited for our main army to come up.

At night on July eighth our army commenced crossing Bayou DeView, and with the Thirty-third on the advance, started forward. We expected to make an all night march of it, but the swamps we had now reached were so bad and the army mules so feeble for want of feed, that it took all night for the wagon train to be brought up.

The next morning we started at eight o'clock and pushed forward as rapidly as possible. The Southern July heat was terrific. The soldiers were faint and hungry. A lonely hard-tack and some miserable slough water was all we had for dinner. In this condition we marched over thirty miles before we found a resting place.

We reached Clarendon at ten o'clock A. M. on July tenth. After arriving there we went up the river two miles and selected a pretty camp ground. We did not know how long we should stay there. In truth, we were sadly disappointed. The Union steamboats with supplies had safely reached this place.[1] We had been able to hear of them, but they could not learn anything about us. We had made a forced march in this hot July weather so as to reach the boats. Some of our men fell upon the road with sunstroke. Arriving there we found that the Union fleet, despairing of reaching us and fearing capture by the rebels, had sailed back down the river. Our artillery were firing signal shots to advise them of our arrival, but we failed to hear the anxiously listened for reply of the gunboat cannon. Our condition was becoming critical, indeed. Our rations were exhausted. There was no supply in that forsaken, inhospitable land either to buy or confiscate. All the enemy needed to do to destroy this army was to block us in and prevent supplies from reaching us for a few days. Our condition was serious. What next?

FROM CLARENDON TO HELENA.

On July eleventh it became certain that the Union boats had left for good. Our cavalry scouts had pushed down the river as far as the worn-out condition of their horses would permit and returned with the information that the fleet had gone down the river with its utmost speed. The strength of the threatening enemy assured our sailors that departing speed was the only course of safety. Only the smallest kind of river steamers can navigate the treacherous water of this small river. They could not safely contend with land artillery. Had they only known that we were in reach their safest harbor would have been under the protection of our guns.

The boats had gone. There we were with nothing to eat. Only one thing was left for us to do. That was to attempt to reach the Mississippi River. We started and marched fifteen miles, most of the way through a pelting rain storm. But this was a luxury compared with the scorching sun and hot dust we had lately been marching through. Our wagons did not come up.

The next day we marched twenty-one miles. Our wagons were upon another road. They would not have been of much use if with us. There were no provisions on board. All the good they would have done would have been to bring our blankets for us to sleep on. As it was we had no blankets for the night, no food for the day, no decent water to drink. During the entire day the only water we could get was from one swamp we passed. In that, the thick green scum, from an eighth to a quarter of an inch thick had to be pushed away before we could get to the filthy, poisonous water beneath. We were tired and worn out, foot-sore, sick and hungry. That was soldiering in earnest.

On Sunday, July thirteenth, by marching, or rather crawling, twenty-five miles, we reached Helena, on the Mississippi River. Only a few were able to go in with us. Company A only had twenty-four men in line. The others still less. Some companies of our regiment did not have over half a dozen men to stack arms when our journey ended. Back for miles the sides of the road were strewn with our sick and exhausted soldiers. Full three fourths, if not more, of the entire command were thus lying upon the road side. The teams are bringing in the most exhausted. But now, thank Heaven, we had reached the shores of the Mississippi, which was in loyal hands, and we could rest and get something to eat.

Early the next morning the steamboat Acacia[2] arrived with provisions for us. Never was a vessel more thankfully received than this one bringing relief to us in our destitute and starving condition. It took two or three days after we arrived to bring in our worn-out and sick soldiers. The first thing being, of course, to send back food to distribute to them along the road. All were brought in and all were soon all right again. A few full meals of hard-tack, coffee and bacon soon put us in prime condition and we commenced to gleefully recount the incidents of our hard march out of the woods of Arkansas.

CHAPTER VIII.

FROM HELENA TO OLD TOWN—LIVELY TIMES–GATHERING COTTON AND FIGHTING REBELS.

We remained at Helena two weeks resting and eating, both of which we took to, as only tired out and starved soldiers can.

Friday, July twenty-fifth, we received orders "to be ready to march by land or water at an hour's notice."

The next day the Government paymaster arrived, the first paymaster we had seen for a long time, and our regiment was paid. Soldiers look with considerable interest for the army paymaster. The pay the soldiers receive, small as it is, thirteen to sixteen dollars per month, is to them quite an important matter. A little money to buy things not furnished by the Government, is at times much needed. Again, many of the soldiers have at home aged parents, a widowed mother, young sisters, or perhaps a wife and infant children to whom the small pittance of five or ten dollars a month is a matter of great importance. These things make the paymaster's visits of much interest to the soldiers. Of course there are sure to be some who put their money to such bad use that it would be better for them not to have any. This class of people will be found everywhere. Their number, however, is small with us. As a rule, the soldiers of the Thirty-third are men of good habits.

After we had been paid we went on board of a steamboat and sailed twenty-five miles down the Mississippi River. We then landed and camped on an old field a mile or so below "Old Town landing."

Sunday, July twenty-seventh, we moved up and camped at Old Town.[1] The "town" is so "old" that it has disappeared. All that is now left of it is part of an old log house. Vile and unhealthy swamps lay all around us except on the river side. The object to be gained by occupying this place, in any military point of view, is not apparent.

Tuesday afternoon our mission at this point became manifest: We are to guard the bringing in of the cotton that is confiscated by our Government.[2] We went down the river a few miles and got some cotton on the Arkansas side. We then crossed over and landed in Mississippi. This is the first time I was ever in the State. We went out one and a half miles to look around and then returned, and the steamer soon landed us at camp.

Just at dark Thursday night our company received orders from Colonel Hovey, who was over in Mississippi after cotton, to join him. It took us until eleven o'clock to get our teams and wagons together and load them on the steam boat. We then went down and stopped at Wilkinson's landing. Reaching that place we disembarked and remained upon the river bank until morning.

At day break, Friday morning, we went forward six miles and found Colonel Hovey and his force. They were all ready to start, so we at once went five miles farther out into the country. Our destination, this time, was McNeal's plantation. He had a large farm and we found over two hundred bales of cotton. The teams made two trips during the day, taking the cotton to the river.

During the afternoon we were awakened to the fact that we were in the enemy's country, by a lively firing from the heavy woods upon our picket guards. It lasted but a moment. The rebels fired upon our men and then ran away. One of our picket guard, a member of Company C, of our regiment, was badly wounded.[3]

Saturday morning we took the balance of the cotton at McNeal's to the river and loaded it on the steamer. After dinner we went out on another road. The rebels had preceded us. We found the cotton burning. The enemy was not far off and a sharp skirmish fight soon commenced. We chased the rebels until dark. Two men of the Eleventh Wisconsin were wounded. How many of the rebels were hit we did not learn. As it became too dark to chase rebels any further we stopped for the night. What a field for imagination to build upon. Here we were, a little handful of men, far out in the enemy's country. He could easily throw a large force upon us. Would he not do so before morning? Our situation suggested many desperate possibilities. But these things did not trouble us much. Soldier life has now become too real for us to waste much time fighting imaginary battles. Except those whose duty it was to stand on guard, the soldiers in those dark woods, with such an unknown destiny hanging over them, quietly wrapped their blankets around their tired bodies, and with the warm ground beneath and the summer sky above them, they slept as soundly as children in their mothers' arms.

The next morning, we started back toward the river. We did not know but that the rebels had cut us off. We approached each dark piece of woods with caution, holding our trusty rifles in our hands, not knowing at what moment we might run into a fatal ambush laid for us by the rebels. Relying greatly upon Company A, Colonel Hovey gave us the advance as skirmishers. We proceeded forward rapidly but found none of the enemy who would tarry long enough for us to get within gun shot of them.

The rebels in that vicinity appeared to be well mounted on good Mississippi horses so that it was idle for us to try to catch them when they wish to run away. We reached the river in safety and remained upon its banks all night.

The following morning, Monday, August fourth, our company went down the river one and a half miles to a place where there was a small amount of cotton. While it was being loaded into our army wagons, we were suddenly attacked by a band of one hundred and fifty bushwhackers. After a sharp skirmish we drove them off. When our quick victory was complete, and we looked over the field, every heart of our little band was crushed with grief. Alvin T. Lewis, one of our best and bravest boys, was dead. Sadly we placed his body in an army wagon and brought it back with us.

J. W. Straight was badly wounded. Bovee, Montgomery and Farwell were taken prisoners and carried away by the retreating rebels.

During the afternoon the steamboat took us back to Old Town. It was after dark before we could perform our last duty to our dead comrade. Lewis, the noble boy, was the first of Company A to fall before a rebel bullet. We went out in the dark evening hours, selected the prettiest piece of ground we could find, dug his grave in Arkansas soil, repeated the last prayer and fired the farewell shot over his grave as we thus in sorrow laid him away. The darkness of the hour, the deep gloom of the surrounding scene, the love of all for our dead comrade, the manner of his death, all of these combined, impressed us as nothing we had before passed through had done. As his spirit, during that dark and sacred hour, soared to its heavenly home, it carried above the renewed pledge of each stricken comrade heart, that those still left would always be true to the cause for which Lewis fought and died.

We lay in camp Tuesday. The three members of our company taken prisoners are with us. They were paroled and sent back. It turns out that Bovee and Montgomery were both badly wounded before they were taken by the rebels.[4]

On the eleventh of August we went down the river on another cotton expedition. We went nearly to the mouth of White River. Landed on the Arkansas side. Found some cotton. Our company did not leave the boat. Started back after dark. Reached camp at Old Town at nine o'clock the next morning.

Thursday, the fourteenth, went down the river five miles. We then landed in Mississippi and marched seven miles into the country. Got one hundred and thirty bales of cotton and returned to the river. At one o'clock P. M. the steamboat started and returned us to camp.

On Sunday another expedition went down the river after cotton. I had an interview with the ague and could not go. Thursday, the twenty-first, we moved our camp nearly a mile up the river, attempting to find a better camp ground. It is all bad enough here. Our new camp is right upon the river bank. Shaking with the ague so that I had to be moved in the ambulance.

By the time we had been in our new camp a week the river bank commenced caving in. By the last of August it was caving in so fast that we were obliged to move further back. The bank which is now about twenty feet above the river water, will suddenly commence settling down, and then we have to up and get or else swim for it. The water of the mighty river, to judge by appearances, first washes out the soft and yielding sand underneath and when a sufficient amount is undermined the more compact clay and soil above will suddenly, and with but little warning drop down into the deep waters underneath. By this time the sand is gone so as to create a large and deep underground lake. The only warning given that the ground upon which we stand is going down is that cracks begin to appear in the surface. When these cracks appear it is notice for all to at once hasten back beyond where the last crack appears. I do not know to what extent the same conditions existing elsewhere produce the same result. If the same results are usual elsewhere upon the banks of this river, the

Mississippi is a dangerous stream for those who venture to build upon its banks.

We commenced the month of September by sending a boat load of our sick up the river on September 1, 1862. A steamboat came down from Helena after them. One of our sick men who went away was Lieutenant Burnham who was down with the typhoid fever. Our wounded boys, Straight, Bovee and Montgomery, went with the rest.

At seven o'clock P. M., on September sixth, a force consisting of six companies of our regiment and six of the Eleventh Wisconsin, started down the river on another cotton trip.

On Sunday, the seventh, a large number of rebel prisoners, part of those taken at Donaldson, passed down the river on their way to be delivered to the enemy at Vicksburg. They have been exchanged, it is understood, and now they will have to be taken in another fight.

Various expeditions after cotton were sent out from time to time. One returned to camp on Saturday, September twentieth, that had an interesting trip to report. They went down the river some considerable distance. On the way down they were fired into by rebels upon the banks of the river. For a time it was lively work for our boys. They returned the fire as well as they could and the steamer soon carried them out of reach of the enemy. Two of our men were killed. On the return trip they passed through a still more severe fire. Four of our men were killed.

Captain Potter, of our company, had returned from the North, where he had been sent to recover, on the thirteenth of September, nearly well from the wound he got at Cache River. On Saturday, September twenty-seventh, our company and some other troops went to guard a train of wagons to Colonel Lippincott who had sent back word that he had taken lots of cotton. When five miles from the river the rebels made a fierce attack upon our guard and Captain Potter was again wounded—the only one of our company injured. One man of Company D was killed and four others wounded.

The next day Colonel Lippincott and his entire command returned back to our camp on the west side of the river. He brought in a large amount of cotton marked "C. S. A." which shows that it belonged to the Confederate Government.

We had, on September twenty-first, moved still nearer to Helena and were now camped at a place that at the time bore the name of "Cockle Burr."

By the last of September our force was much reduced. Many had been sent North too sick to longer walk, and many of those remaining were not in much better condition. The Old Town swamps had got in their work and as the result general sickness prevailed.

All we have or could hope to accomplish at this point is to pick up a few boat loads of cotton. All we have got is not worthy of a moment's consideration in comparison with the lives our stay here has cost us. A change is most earnestly desired. The soldiers think that they should be sent into an active field where they can have a fighting chance with the rebels—or else that a healthier camp should at once be found. To attempt to contend against these fever breeding swamps is useless.

CHAPTER IX.

NORTHWARD BOUND.

Sunday, October fifth, the good news, marching orders, came. We are ordered up the river. During the day we took a boat ride to Helena where we are to take a larger steamer for our northward trip. On the sixth, at the hour of five P. M., the good steamboat, Des Moines,[1] started with us on board from Helena and we were on our way northward. During the night we passed the mouth of St. Francis River and reached Memphis at seven o'clock the next morning. The boat lay at Memphis some hours which gave us an opportunity to see some of the city, which we improved.

At four P. M. we started north again. Passed Fort Pillow during the night.[2] During Wednesday night we passed New Madrid and Island No. 10.[3] Too dark to see much of them.

Thursday morning at ten o'clock we reached Cairo.[4] Hurrah for our noble prairie State. We gave Illinois three rousing cheers. A sight of even the least part of "God's country" is refreshing to our soldier boys. The name "God's country" became one in daily use in the army. There was no thought of profanity in its familiar use. It was the one name that clearly showed how the soldiers looked upon the land of their Northern homes compared with the Southern country in which their active soldiering was done. In their opinion a name having absolutely the opposite meaning would be the only one to describe the rebel country. Of course the feeling of dislike related more to the people of the South than to nature's handiwork. In the soldier's dictionary the name of "God's country" means the land of our Northern homes.

We took on a new supply of rations at Cairo and then proceeded up the river.

During Friday we passed Cape Giardue [*sic*] and Ste. Genevieve. Arrived at Sulphur Springs on Saturday, October eleventh.[5] Unloaded, pitched tents and slept in Missouri.

Thus we have returned from our first march to Dixie. It has been to us soldiers an eventful campaign. We have passed through many hard marches and although not participated in any extensive battles, have often had to meet the whistling rebel bullets. One thing is remarkable; although we have always been in near communication with and part of a large army, through some strange combination of circumstances the fighting has nearly all fallen to our lot. From the time we joined General Curtis at Batesville in May last, up to the end of our Southern campaign, a large share of his command have not been called upon to fire a single gun. But the Thirty-third seemed destined to have a hand in every fight. A reason for this can be found in the fact that we were usually the advance of the army where all the fighting was done. Another thing can also be said: It mattered not how small our numbers were, we never left the field of contest. In every case, when the battle was over, the flag of the Thirty- third was waving over the field.

Coming North now is undoubtedly a wise move for us. The broken health of the command demanded it. With restored health we will be ready for any active work. With the Mississippi River in the control of the Union forces so far south, we can, at short notice, be landed in the heart of the rebel country. What our part is to be we will wait and see.

IN PILOT KNOB AGAIN.

Sunday, October twelfth, we remained camped at Sulphur Springs.

On Monday we struck tents, got on the railroad cars and went to Pilot Knob. From there we went into camp at Arcadia. It was nine o'clock at night when we reached our destination.

October thirteenth we pitched tents for a permanent camp. Here we remained during the balance of the month. On the last day of October we received orders "to be ready to march with two days' rations."

THE THIRTY-THIRD STARTS SOUTH.

On November first our regiment started for Patterson.[6] Two large tents of each company were left for our sick soldiers. About two hundred men of our regiment remained here. This includes those who are still too unwell to march but not sick enough to be sent to the hospital. I was one of them.

On Monday, November third, our sick squad moved into Ironton and camped near the Hospital. On the twelfth those who had become strong enough started for Patterson under the command of Potter, who is now major of the regiment. Hovey has been appointed brigadier-general, Lippincott, colonel, and Roe, lieutenant colonel of the Thirty-Third. Before they started, those of Company A present took a vote for second lieutenant; the promotion of our captain, first and second lieutenants, creating the vacancy. There were twenty-four present, twenty voted for Dutton and four for Pike. It is understood that the main body of the company now with the regiment are taking a vote on the same matter at the same time.

On the twenty-third some more of our boys with Dr. Rex started to join the regiment.

WE REJOIN THE REGIMENT.

December 1, 1862, the balance of the Thirty-third boys who had been left at Ironton on account of sickness started to join the regiment. There were about eighty of us with Captain Morgan in command. We go with and as guard to an army train of seventy-five wagons. We marched seven miles.

The next morning, we started at six o'clock and marched fifteen miles. Found the roads in good condition.

Wednesday, December third, started at half past six and marched through to Patterson. After a short stop at this place we started forward for Black River where our regiment is now camped.

We started at half past six Thursday and reached our regimental camp at noon. We found the boys well and enjoying themselves finely.

IN CAMP ON BLACK RIVER—THE GUERRILLAS—A MOUNTAIN STORM—PRESENTING A SWORD.

We were now comfortably camped on the banks of Black River.

Drilling was now resumed. December seventh we had a battalion drill, the first since we left Reaves Station in April last. On December tenth a report came in that the rebel guerrilla, Tim Reaves,[7] with his band of thieves and murderers was within a short distance of us. The reputation of this Reaves, as it comes to us is that before the war he was some sort of a preacher in Southern Missouri and Northern Arkansas. He is said to be a member of the family from which Reaves Station took its name, they being landowners in that vicinity.

After the war commenced the Rev. Timothy Reaves developed into one of the meanest leaders of an irregular band of thieves and pretended rebels that the mountains of Missouri and Arkansas harbored.

These guerrilla bands are thieves and murderers by occupation, rebels by pretense, soldiers only in name, and cowards by nature. They terrorize over those they pretend to befriend and run from acknowledged enemies. They are hated by the rebel citizens of their own country and despised by the soldiers of the North and disowned by those of the South.

It being reported that Tim Reaves was near, a force consisting of our little cavalry force and some mounted infantry, was sent out to look for him. A few men were taken from each company. Wm. Pierce and John Wood, of Company A, went. After being gone two days the expedition returned, not having succeeded in catching the nimble-footed bushwhacker.

Those who were camped with us on Black River, in December, 1862, will never forget what it is to see a mountain stream on the rampage.[8]

A heavy rain storm came up on Saturday, the thirteenth, continuing all of that and most of the next day. Our camp was on a reasonably high piece of ground. The river at this point runs through a valley lying between the high hills and mountains on each side. On our side of the river they were some little distance back of us. The ground upon which we were camped was some feet higher than the rest of the valley between us and the high hills to our rear. By Sunday night the rain had ceased. The river had been rising rapidly and during the evening we had watched it with considerable interest. The rain storm being over, the river ceased to increase. Our camp being upon such high ground it was thought that we were above possible high water-mark. The "oldest inhabitants" of the neighborhood had assured us that such was the fact. By looking at the lay of the ground we could see that the volume of an entire river could pass between us and the high hills, and our camp ground still remain untouched. The river itself would have to rise many feet more before its waters would overrun its deep banks to take this course. We went to sleep apprehending no danger. We were not at the time fully advised as to the actual force of the fierce mad winter storm. It proved that the rain storm we had seen was only the slight outcropping of a most terrific one that was gathering and was to burst in its greatest fury on the mountains miles above us, and in which Black River has its source. Those of us whose lives have been passed in a level prairie country can not, until we once see it, comprehend the rapidity and fury with which water will rush down from the mountain sides. No matter how heavy the rainfall, it is all at once, hundreds of little mountain streams, thrown into the river outlet by which it is carried to the sea. Thus any river fed by mountain ranges will always be liable to sudden and severe overflows. We had contentedly gone to sleep Sunday night. At the hour of three o'clock in the morning, the attention of the guards was called to a fearful roar from up the river. The camp was at once aroused. What a fierce commotion met our ears! The mad, rushing waters, the sharp snap of breaking timbers, a continuous sound of roaring thunder could not excel it. The guards far up the river, loudly crying one to the other, passed the alarm down: Look out for the river! Instantaneously all comprehended the situation. Without ceremony or the loss of a moment of time, we at once started for the high hills. True to the soldier's instinct, each was sure to grab his gun and cartridge box before he ran. And yet with all this haste, before we could run that short distance, the water in its mad career was waist-deep as we waded through. In a brief moment more the swift and deep current between the hills upon which we had taken refuge and our deserted camp ground was impassable. Strong horses in attempting to swim it, were, by the swift current, thrown back to the side from which they started. A few of those soldiers who had been a moment too late found it impossible to escape. They were compelled to seek safety by climbing the trees that stood upon our high camp ground. For a wonder, no lives were lost.

High upon the side of a friendly hill we sat during those early morning hours and viewed the rushing fury of that mighty mountain stream. Strong timbers were broken as though they were but a mere twig. Deep rooted trees were torn up as though they were but a weed upon the road side. The effect may be seen, but none can fully comprehend the full power of the rushing waters of a mad mountain stream.

In the midst of all this, army plays and soldiers' jokes went on. Each, as usual, following the bent of his own mind. Here would be a circle telling stories; there others playing euchre. Daniels, the company student, instead of reading from the big book of nature open before him, was conning over the mass of wise maxims he had selected and was continually adding to. Weed, the flighty romancer, was mourning over the loss of the ten page letter he had finished writing the day before, to his imaginary sweetheart.

By noon, Monday, the waters commenced falling rapidly. Our camp ground was soon uncovered and yet when we returned at night, the water was still so deep over the lower part of the valley that we had to return over a pontoon bridge.

Without him being advised of our intention, our Company had sent to St. Louis and procured a splendid sword and belt to present to our old Captain, now Major Potter. At the close of the day on Thursday, December eighteenth, our company called him out and surprised him with the present. The presentation speech was made by Corporal S. M. Durflinger. Considering that it was prepared and delivered in the wild woods of Missouri by a soldier in the ranks, without any of the aid that a well filled library would give, Durflinger's speech is worthy of record. He said:

> MAJOR POTTER: For the past fifteen months you have been connected with us in one of the most endearing relations arising from the intercourse of men. That relation has been disturbed, yet we can not permit a separation without some expression of esteem, some testimonial of gratitude. United in this relation, we have mutually shared danger and adversity, health and prosperity. We have traversed together the mountains and fastnesses of Missouri, the long lanes and shady aisles of Arkansas, and the jungles of Mississippi darkened with all the wild untrained luxuriance of the primitive forest. We have drunk at the same springs, crossed the same streams, climbed the same hills, sustained each other in the same perils and rejoiced in the same triumphs. Though we have not been called to stand on the trophied field of Marathon and Arbela, of Austerlitz and Ulm, of Yorktown and Shiloh, yet the events of the past year furnish many circumstances of sad and pleasing memory —many incidents of "bitter and sweet" recollection.
>
> It is a sad thought that traitors would despoil the land we love. We love to visit the tomb of Washington, to linger around the shades of Ashland, and to think the Hermitage our own. It is an unpleasing thought that treason would shut us out from these sacred retreats.
>
> We love our homes, the oases in the desert of life, with all their tender associations and sweet influences. It is a sad recollection that we have gone from them, perhaps forever. It is a sorrowful thought that some of our companions are tenants of the "narrow house," sleeping in a stranger's land, with no marble to mark their last resting place. Their

memories are cherished by many a fond mother whose sighs are not loud but deep; whose tears are not many but consuming "heart's tears."

Let us, as we pass along, render the poor tribute of a sigh to the living, and mingle a tear with the dust of the dead.

It has been our lot to happen upon a momentous era, and to combat in the great contest of the ages. To our hands are entrusted the destiny of our country, and with us rest the highest hopes of a great republic.

Our pilgrim fathers are slumbering among the hills and pines of New England; the pioneers of our country are reposing in the valleys of the West in many an unmarked resting place. Washington has fallen and sunk uncensured to a peaceful tomb by which the traveler will pass remembering his many virtues and noble deeds; and as he drops a silent tear upon the sod that hides his noble form, he lifts his accents of praise to the God of freedom for the gifts of such a boon mingling a suppliant petition that Heaven would spare another such a man. Warren sleeps at the base of Bunker Hill, and upon the present age devolves the duty of perfecting what they had begun. Proud as were their achievements, prouder yet will be our place on the escutcheon of fame if we preserve the rich heritage they have bequeathed us. The interests of centuries are suspended on the efforts moments. Let us act in view of these great responsibilities.

Two parallels of civilization, the Atlantic and the Pacific, laden with all the rich results of art and invention, of science and industry, of learning and religion, are fast pushing their approaches toward the center of a mighty continent. When, like the tides in conjunction, these advancing waves shall roll over each other, let them close forever over the last vestige of despotism.

Let the happy millions of toiling freemen, who shall yet dwell along these streams, learn to chant the requiem of slavery and sing the high paean of truth and freedom. Let these high hills and voiceless solitudes, now the strongholds of treason, become the paradise of liberty.

The despots of Europe are looking on this struggle with jealous apprehension or scornful delight as the tide of success goes up or down. Every victory we win, every cannon we place in position, every trench we dig, we are pushing our lines nearer the sinking, wavering walls of European despotism, and sending a new ray of hope to the downtrodden sons of Gaul and Erin, of Athens and Rome. Let us not disappoint the hopes of expectant humanity.

Thus united with us by a common cause, bound together by kindred ties, sufferings and sympathies, you have shared with us whatever of "bitter and sweet" the past has afforded. That invisible tie uniting heart to heart and friend to friend, has, we little know where or when, sprung up between us. Though these pre-existing relations have been disturbed, we trust this bond of union may never be sundered. Though

> the events of the past year and the proceedings of this day may have no place on the historian's page, by ourselves they will be fondly cherished while memory holds her place, and when hoary age comes on, it will delight us to remember these things.
>
> In remembrance of past associations, in view of your many merits, and with feelings of sincerest regard, we offer you this token of our esteem, this memorial of our gratitude, knowing that it will never be dishonored; knowing that it will never be drawn but in the cause of justice and humanity; knowing that it will never be sheathed till the wrongs of our country are redressed. Accept it in the kindly spirit in which it is offered. (Uncovering and handing the sword to him.) And whenever in coming time you may chance to see it, either in the din of battle or the peaceful quietude of home, bestow a hasty thought on those who now stand about you, breathing a petition to the God of Heaven that your life may be spared and your arm nerved to strike long and valiantly in the battles of freedom.

The chaplain of our regiment, who happened to be present, reported the Major's acceptance thus: "Major Potter, who was taken entirely by surprise, made a brief reply in which he warmly referred to their pleasant relations which had been unbroken from the first; now while he had been their Captain they had never failed him in battle or the faithful performance of duty in any of the trying scenes through which they had passed; and that should they again go in to battle, he would hope to lead them still. He believed they would follow him wherever they should see the gleam of their elegant present. He thanked them for that beautiful token of their esteem and confidence."

"Major Potter has been twice wounded in battle, once at the Cache and once in one of the raids into the State of Mississippi. 'Boys,' said he, 'you know that I am lame; don't run till you see me run.'"

ON THE ROAD—GUARDING A SUPPLY TRAIN TO PILOT KNOB.

On the twentieth of December we received marching orders. The next morning we started and marched nine miles. We camped in a pretty little valley among the pines. Most of the country around here is very broken and worthless for cultivation. In the small valleys there is a limited amount of good land. We found the roads very bad. Our teams did not get in until the next morning. This compelled us to layover one day.

Tuesday, the twenty-third, we started at six o'clock and marched ten miles through to Current River and camped near to Van Buren.

At four o'clock the next morning our company were called up and ordered to prepare for an immediate march. We are to go to Patterson, or perhaps farther, as guard to a supply train. Marched ten miles and camped in the same pine grove we left yesterday morning.

During our day's march we were informed of a band of rebels who were lurking in the vicinity waiting for an opportunity to capture some of our supply trains. Captain Burnham sent back for reinforcements to strengthen our guard. Two more companies reached us Thursday morning and we pushed forward, going fifteen miles before we stopped for night, crossing Black River during the day.

We went forward and reached Patterson at three o'clock Friday. The late hard rains have made the roads very heavy, so that our teams can only make slow progress.

Saturday we remained at Patterson. A small fort and block house have been built here.[9] It is decided that we will go on to guard a supply train to Pilot Knob.

We started the next morning at eight o'clock and marched seventeen miles, half way from Patterson to Pilot Knob; camped for the night near a mill. A few of us took possession of a deserted log house and converted it in to soldiers' quarters for the night.

Monday, December twenty-ninth, we started at eight o'clock and reached Ironton at sundown. Came on and camped at Pilot Knob. Every thing looks natural here. Our boys are all well and in good spirits and having good times. This active life suits them.

On Tuesday we unloaded the ordnance stores our train had brought back from Patterson. Wednesday, the last day of the year, we passed in camp at Pilot Knob. At night we celebrated New Year's Eve in Ironton and Arcadia, and welcomed in the New Year with oysters, apples, cider, Roman candles, music, singing, etc. Ending the old and commencing the new year in a jolly, happy manner.

A REVIEW OF THE YEAR AS WRITTEN IN CAMP.

Thursday, January 1, 1863.[10] New Year's day. A happy New Year to all. We part with the old, and welcome the new year.

The year of 1862—the memorial year—is no more. It is now to be known only in the history of the past. We part with it sorrowfully, and yet are glad that it is past. It has brought us many, many sorrows, given us much to mourn over, and at the same time has taught us much and improved us much. It has been a year of stern, unrelenting reality, to our country, to us as a nation and to us as individuals. All have felt the harsh, iron hand of the past year.

Our country has been involved in all of the horrors of one of the most gigantic and desperate civil wars that has ever been waged upon the face of our world.

The year commenced; we then thought that surely we are in the midst of the war; that it had even then reached the highest point of its fury, and would soon subside; that at the end of the year 1862 at farthest, happy peace would look down upon a contented and reunited people.

The year ends and we are bewildered; instead of looked for peace we find the war and strife hardly yet fairly commenced; the mighty hosts are still marshaling, preparing for battle—for the bloody field.

We mourn the loss of many, many of the bravest, noblest ones who have died a willing sacrifice for their country's cause. Some fall by the enemy's hand; others push on, bravely bearing aloft their country's banner until camp fevers and army exposures sap their life's blood—then they die.

Others now come to fill the ranks of "brothers gone before." Time passes swiftly and their places are in turn left vacant for others to fill. This is war; war in reality. Such has been the history of the past year and such promises to be the history of the new. Parents, brothers, sisters, children and lovers mourn the untimely death of departed ones.

Thus closes the year. A year of momentous, eventful history. The most eventful in the history of our country. It is not strange that it should be so. Long have the elements of fierce strife been gathering. The mighty powers of freedom and slavery which for years and ages have been contending in desperate, savage strife—often overturning empires, crushing kingdoms, destroying and desolating countries, and even shaking the whole world to its very center by their tremendous and deadly conflicts, have at last concentrated them all—all the fierce hordes of slavery, all the mighty hosts of freedom—all concentrated in a final, last death struggle.

One year of desperate warfare and still the awful contest has hardly yet commenced. Some grow impatient and ask, when is the war to end? But why do they look thus early for the end? Who can reasonably expect a mighty, fierce contest like this, which has been growing for ages—a contest for life or death between freedom and slavery—to be ended in one short year? No, we need not, can not expect the end for a long, long time to come. No man can tell when or how loved peace will return to us. We must accept what comes to us. Let us not quarrel with our destiny, but quietly submit, knowing that we are but as mere instruments in the hands of a just God, who is working out his own will on earth. Let us willingly submit to Him, hoping, believing, praying and knowing that all will yet be well.

During the past year the armies of our country have gained many victories and suffered numerous defeats. Upon the whole we can boast of but little that we have gained and held, except the Mississippi River, and that is not yet entirely won. The rebels still hold Vicksburg which is so strongly fortified that as yet our gunboats have not been able to take it. Last summer our fleet exhausted its strength in the fruitless attempt and then withdrew. Now an army and fleet are moving down the river to make another attempt. If that does not succeed, try again. In the end we must win.

From the earlier days of the war the cry has been: "On to Richmond." Two splendid armies have made the attempt and failed. The first was under General McClellan, the last under General Burnside. McClellan was defeated; Burnside out-generaled. As the year closes we find the Eastern army holding nearly the same ground that it did a year ago. True, Yorktown and Manassas, two strong military points have been evacuated by the enemy, but our armies are still met by armies of the enemy holding other positions fully as strong. In the West the success of the Union armies has been more uniform. We can claim the glory of Fort Donaldson, Pittsburg Landing, Corinth, Hatche, Pea Ridge, Cache River and other battle fields. Why this striking difference between the Western and Eastern armies? They seem to fight as bravely, as earnestly—cowardice is certainly not the reason. Is the fault in their commanders? It can hardly be. We have sent them some of our best generals and still they fail. The reason is truly unaccountable; but let it pass. Perhaps the coming year—now present—will change this, and the Eastern troops win a series of glorious victories. We earnestly hope that it may be so.

A year ago we were quartered in the seminary here at Arcadia. The year passes and a few of us happen back here in time to serenade the seminary at the beginning of the new year, 1863. Here we are, with renewed health, buoyant spirits and unwavering hope, ready to go wherever duty calls, fully believing that the year 1863, like that of 1862, will fail to bring any enemy who can stand before us.

CHAPTER X.

FROM PILOT KNOB TO VAN BUREN—THE ARMY MULE, ETC.

We remained in Pilot Knob until the seventh of January and then started to guard a wagon train to our army camp. Bailey and I waited in Pilot Knob for the railroad train to arrive from St. Louis so as to get the mail for our boys and some newspapers. It was late before we got started. Had to wade the streams and were so much delayed that it became dark before we reached the command and were not able to get through. It was useless to attempt to proceed in those dark woods, liable at any moment to fall into some ditch of ice cold water. Just as we were looking for a dry piece of ground to stay over night upon we discovered a solitary camp fire just off from the road not far from us. We at once went up and found a Missourian and his wife who with their ox team were on their way to Ironton to barter their produce for goods. This is the way the people in the backwoods go to town. Men and women together, go as far as their slow teams will take them, during the day, and then camp for the night in the wild woods. They are usually from one to three weeks on the road going and coming before again reaching their wild woodland home. Those we met were very socially inclined and Bailey and I had a huge evening visit with them. We shared rations all round. They seemed to like a change, and relished our hard tack, while we took more kindly to the cornbread the woman had made. Of course, with other necessaries, they had a supply of home-made whisky which was offered as liberally as every thing else. It is strange, but it is undoubtedly a fact, that there is not a neighborhood anywhere in the wilds of Missouri, that does not have some way to make whisky. A little still to make a little whisky seems as necessary to the pioneer mountaineers of this wild country as a mill to grind their corn. And stranger yet, you will hardly ever find a drunkard among them. After the evening was well spent, we threw logs enough on the fire to keep it burning bright all night and then Bailey and I spread our blankets on one side and the Missourian and his wife theirs on the other and all hands were soon fast asleep. The only guard on deck that night being the mountaineer's two big dogs, sleeping and watching under the wagon. Now there was no disguise of the fact, which we knew full well, that in their own home, the man, and his wife, too, for that matter, were fierce rebels, and they at the same time knew that we were members of the hated Yankee army, yet there was no thought of suspicion on either side. It is only the cause we each believe in that is at war. Individually we have no quarrel to maintain. We met as would members of opposite political parties or members of different church organizations. In the early morning we bid our night-friends adieu and each went his own way.

We found our army comrades early in the morning and the entire force started at eight o'clock and went through to Patterson.

The train we came with from Pilot Knob this time is made up of raw mules that have never before been hitched to army wagons. It has been fun alive to see the teamsters attempt to drive the stubborn, unbroken animals. At first it was a continual runaway through the entire line. But being in the woods all the time, the only result would be that the ponderous army wagon would in a moment be caught upon a tree and then the mules would become tangled together and tumble in a heap. The thing to do now was to untangle the huge pile of mules. Let imagination picture the scene. Sometimes in a fierce run a small tree would be bent over by the force with which the mules would strike it and then regaining its strength would straighten up and thus frequently a team of the smaller mules would be found hanging up in a tree. An army team consists of six mules. The two largest mules being the wheel mules and the smallest two, the lead mules. The entire team is driven by a single line running up to the bridle of the right lead mule. A steady pull on the line means that the lead mule is to turn to the left, quick jerks tell him to turn to the right. It is wonderful how soon a raw mule can be taught to obey this awkward mode of indicating to him which way he is to go. With this single line the driver riding one of the wheel mules guides his team of six through many of the most difficult and dangerous places. The army mule occupies a place that no other animal could so well fill. His life in the army shows that the mule has never been fully appreciated. In reputation a mule is concentrated stubbornness and obstinacy. In reality he is generally docile, faithful and tireless. Even when running away a mule team never gets wildly crazy as horses often do. They never knock their own brains out against a tree or stone wall. Unless it is raw mules that have never learned to pull a wagon, like those we were driving on this trip, a runaway mule team will only go so far as it can have a safe place to run in. Of the hundreds of times that I have known of a team of six mules escaping from their drivers and starting on a run, I have not seen any that would run any farther than where they could find an open road.

Six horses in the same condition would become so frightened that the wagon would be broken to pieces and some of the horses killed. The mule as an army mule is a success.

Our wagons were run empty to Patterson. The two days' drive had broken in the raw mules so that they knew how to draw. During the forenoon of Friday, the ninth, we loaded up and started for Van Buren. Went five miles. At night camped by a vacant schoolhouse which some of us used for our night's sleeping room.

Saturday we went through to Black River, our raw mules drawing very well.

The next day we started at eight o'clock and went twelve miles. We have taken a new road, one a few miles north of the one we took before.

We started at eight o'clock Monday and drove within five miles of camp.

Tuesday, January thirteenth, we went to Van Buren in the forenoon, crossed the river in the afternoon and rejoined our regiment, which had crossed the day before.

As we were nearing camp a flock of hawks appeared in the high trees near us. We promptly shot some of them. Back came Captain Burnham in haste. It was against orders to fire guns near camp. He arrested half a dozen of us, that is, he said: "Boys, consider yourselves under arrest." They laughed and some of them offered their guns to him. Of course it is absurd to call a soldier under arrest while he has his gun in his hands. The captain turned and went forward to the advance of the command. We never heard any more about it. He did not even discharge the "arrest." Probably those soldiers are still under arrest. The object of the Captain was probably this: General Davidson, our army commander, was a very strict military officer and Burnham undoubtedly wished to be able to say, in case he was called to task for the firing, that it was not with his consent and that he had ordered those who did it under arrest. Except that he was responsible to those above him as captain, Burnham always considered himself as only one of the members of the company.

FORWARD TO WEST PLAINS.

The army started forward on Wednesday, January fourteenth, and marched only five miles. The weather is very bad, raining and snowing. The mud is almost knee deep. The roads are so fearfully bad that it took two days for the teams to come up the five miles we had advanced. It turned still colder Thursday and by night there were four inches of snow on the ground. This is unusual for this climate.

We went forward eight miles Friday. The roads are much better, the ground being now frozen hard enough to carry the wagons.

Marched nine miles Saturday and camped at Falling Springs. Visited some small caves in the mountain. As in all mountainous countries springs of good water are numerous here. One large spring at this place runs a mill. It is something of a curiosity. One side of the mountain is, for some distance up, a perpendicular rock. Up some distance from the ground of the valley below, there is a large opening right in the side of the rock from which there comes a large stream of water. Here a mill has been built. A wooden water-way from the opening in the mountain side carries the water to the wheel of the mill. Thus we have in effect a mill run by one spring.[1]

We started at seven o'clock, Sunday, and marched ten miles. Camped upon the banks of Eleven Points. For a wonder we found a wagon bridge here upon which we crossed the stream.

The next day we went nine miles reaching Alton, the county seat of Oregon County. It is a little town of no importance. The surrounding country is covered with worthless scrub oaks. The land is poor and never can be very valuable or productive.

On Thursday, January twenty-second, we started back again to guard the supply train on the road, which it is reported the rebels design capturing. Went as far as Eleven Points and camped for the night.

Crossed the river the next morning and camped near Falling Springs.

On Saturday went twelve miles reaching within three miles of the supply train. Here we waited for the train to pass.

The supply train having all come up we started back as its rear guard on Monday.

Tuesday we passed Falling Springs and then took the Thomasville road. We reached Thomasville Wednesday night.

We crossed the river at Thomasville Thursday morning and marched fourteen miles. Ed Pike's uncle from Illinois is with us. By some means he is in possession of an ox team and wagon, and he carries the knapsacks of our company in the ox wagon. The old gentleman seems to think that he is having a huge time soldiering with the boys. Friday, January thirtieth, we reached West

Plains. The entire army is fast coming in from Alton. A large force of rebels was expected to meet us in this vicinity, but they do not seem inclined to wait for us to get near them.

We camped a few days at West Plains. In coming and while here we took quite a number of prisoners. At one time we had nearly one hundred under guard, many of them belonging to the rebel army. It is not easy to always know whether the fellow you catch is a rebel soldier or not. Citizens and soldiers are all dressed in the same kind of home-made butternut clothing. When cornered the rebel soldiers throw their guns away and claim to be innocent citizens. General Davidson's[2] plan is severe but just. At least it is the only one we can safely follow in this country. He holds every suspicious butternut that is found away from where he ought to be, until the prisoner can show that he is not a rebel soldier.

General John W. Davidson. From http://www.generalsandbrevets.com/ngd/davidson.htm.

CHAPTER XI.

WE RETURN TO PILOT KNOB.

It being plainly evident that the enemy would not remain for us to get within striking distance of him, and the object of our winter's advance being accomplished by clearly demonstrating that the Union troops could at any time drive all rebel bands out of Southern Missouri and Northern Arkansas, we were ordered to march back "nearer to supplies."

We started at eight o'clock Sunday, February eighth, and marched twenty miles to Barnesville. The next day we went six miles. After seeing his army fairly under way General Davidson left us to go to Pilot Knob and thence to St. Louis.

Tuesday we marched fifteen miles and camped at Jack's Forks. We have now left the scrub oak country, and reached one where the soil is strong enough to produce fine large trees. They are oak with some very good pine. There is a combined carding, saw and grist mill at this place. It is a small affair. There is, however, a grand water power here which, with an enterprising people occupying the surrounding county, would be very valuable.

We layover at Jack's Forks until the thirteenth, on which day we broke camp at eight in the morning and marched twelve miles. The next day our company was sent to guard the ammunition train. We went back two miles, met the train and then came forward with it six miles.

Sunday, February fifteenth, we marched to within ten miles of Eminence. The rough and heavy roads have broken the mules up. A large number of oxen have been pressed into the service to help move our heavy wagons. The soldiers are in splendid health but many of them nearly barefooted. The rough mountain roads wear out shoe leather fast. A few days ago the raw hides of the beef cattle that were killed were ordered distributed for the soldiers to make something for them to walk in. But they are no good. The soldiers seem to succeed better in tying bark and pieces of wood to the bottom of their worn-out shoes.

We reached Eminence at two o'clock Monday. Crossed the river and went four miles farther, before we camped for the night. We helped to drive the ox teams over the mountains. Had lots of fun.

We now learned that we are to go to Pilot Knob. Company A of the Ninety-ninth Illinois is detailed to assist us in guarding the ammunition train and to help drive the Missouri oxen up and down the hills. The next day we marched sixteen miles.

The ammunition train being now safely out of reach of any strolling bands of the enemy we rejoined the regiment Wednesday morning and then marched twenty-one miles to Centerville.

The next day we went twelve miles and camped near Lesterville.

On Friday, February 20, 1863, we marched to our journey's end and camped at Belleview Valley, near Pilot Knob.

Lieutenant Norton, with his usual vim, had pushed ahead and when we camped he had the post commissary ready to issue us good rations including fresh bread instead of hard tack, so that we celebrated our arrival with a first-class soldier's supper which we were in condition to fully appreciate.

A FEW DESCRIPTIONS.

PILOT KNOB.—The greatest iron mountain in the world deserves a passing word. The first time I ever visited that mountain pile of iron ore known by the name of Pilot Knob was on Saturday, September 21, 1861, the day after the arrival of our regiment at the village of the same name.

Since then I have visited it, climbed to its top and roamed over its sides a number of times. It did not appear as I had expected it to. There is nothing that we become acquainted with by name before seeing, that does when met, agree with the picture that imagination had created. I do not know why, but for some reason I was surprised to see trees growing not only upon the sides but also upon top of the mountain. As I found it, trees were growing all over it except the highest peak, which is perfectly bare. I had not formed any definite idea of its appearance but from what I had read I rather expected to see a huge, gigantic and barren pile of iron ore. Yet, I must confess that it is much more interesting as it is than it would be otherwise. While new things when first seen are sure to do violence to our preconceived ideas, still there is a compensation in the fact that they will probably be found more beautiful than imagination had pictured them.

Pilot Knob might be described as resembling the noble bald eagle as he is sometimes seen sitting on the top of an old oak tree with his bald and naked head resting, with such marked and striking contrast, upon his huge body thickly covered with a heavy growth of feathers. Thus does Pilot Knob, with its huge body covered, with growing trees and creeping vines, above which its bald and naked head is extended, appear to us as we look at it from a distance. Its naked head is so marked, that it became customary when any of the soldiers were a long distance away, and wished to distinguish Pilot Knob from the mountains in its vicinity they always looked for the "bald head." "Old bald head" became its popular name with our soldiers.

Pilot Knob, with the exception of Shepherd Mountain, is the highest one of the cluster of mountains that lay in this part of Missouri. It is truly a gigantic mountain pile of iron ore. One to simply see it, gets but a faint idea of its actual size. To comprehend its magnitude one should pass a day or two in climbing over and examining it; and even then a person can hardly realize what a vast quantity of iron nature has here heaped into one mountain of solid ore. Standing on its top one can only view with amazement the mineral wealth that lies beneath him.

At the foot of the mountain stands a furnace for converting the raw ore into pig iron. The ore is taken from near the top of the mountain. All the work that has to be done in milling, is to break the ore up so that it can be loaded upon the cars which deposit it at the mouth of the furnace. The cars that bring down the ore run upon a double track built for the purpose. The cars are drawn by a wire cable fastened upon pulleys at the top and which are so arranged that the loaded cars coming down, by their weight draw up the unloaded ones on the other track. Thus the ore desired for use, not only lies conveniently at hand, but also furnishes the motive power to haul itself to the furnace. With all of its mineral wealth, its large amount of fertile lands, its superior commercial advantages, the State of Missouri, with an enterprising people for its citizens, will become one of the grandest States of our Nation!

FORT HOVEY.—Almost the next thing that claims our attention in point of interest in the vicinity of Ironton, after Pilot Knob Mountain, is Fort Hovey, which lays between Ironton and Arcadia.

First, as to the name of the fort. I have written it Fort Hovey, but that, we now find, is not the only name it has borne. The reasons for insisting upon its original name are good. In the first place, General Hovey, then Colonel of our regiment, did more than any other one man to push forward the building of it, and that in a time of danger. Colonel Carlin, then commander of the army here, though not exceedingly friendly to Colonel Hovey, was willing to acknowledge his services in the work and issued a general order in which he said: "The fort being built near Ironton will be named Fort Hovey and when finished will be garrisoned by the Thirty-third Regiment Illinois Volunteers."

This was considered as settling the matter at that time, and the fort was so called by those who built it and by the army that was here at that time. But now, over a year afterward, General Davidson,[1] the present commander of the district, in a general order refers to the fort as Fort Curtis.[2] For what reason no one knows. It may be said that Colonel Hovey did not desire his name to be given to the fort. The name he preferred was Fort Normal.

When we arrived at Ironton in September, 1861, the fort had hardly been built. The trees had been cut on the ground but none of the breastworks had been built. In fact the lines of the fort had not been fully established. At that time our condition looked dark in Southeast Missouri. The Union troops held Pilot Knob and a few places on the Mississippi River. With this meager exception the entire district was completely overrun by the rebels under Hardee, Thompson and Lowe. Pilot Knob was every hour in danger of being attacked. It was not safe to pass out of our army lines. Two men of Company C ventured out one day and were immediately gobbled up. Our force was small and undisciplined. Much was thought to depend upon the rapid building of the fort. The work was placed under charge of Colonel Hovey. The Thirty-third undertook to do the work and commenced at once. The work was pushed forward early and late. Many of our young soldiers in their earnestness overtaxed their strength. I doubt not but that the cause of the death of many of our soldier boys could be directly traced to overworking themselves on Fort Hovey.

The walls of the fort are built of heavy timbers. Two walls were in fact built, one inside of the other, of hewn logs pinned together. The center between them was then filled with timber and earth pounded solid. When finished it gave a solid wall of about twelve feet in thickness at the bottom and eight at the top.

The fort covers considerable ground, enough to accommodate quite a large force inside. Platforms are built around the sides for infantry to stand upon. It is arranged to contain four heavy cannon and so built that three of them can command a given point. In addition a number of pieces of field artillery can be used in it when necessary. It is situated upon a hill which seems to have been intended for the very purpose. It is almost the only high ground in Arcadia valley and the fort upon it commands the entire valley. It would be a very difficult place for an enemy to take. In case occasion should require, it may become important, but the present indications are that no rebel force will ever trouble this vicinity again.

PILOT KNOB village having been our head-quarters and base of action so long, and to which we have returned so often, is deserving a passing notice. It is a quiet little village lying snugly beneath the shade of the high mountains which surround it. It can never become a very large city for one good reason: there is not room in the little valley for a large city. There are only four outlets, through the mountains, from the place. One is occupied by the Iron Mountain Railroad which comes from St. Louis and terminates at this place. One is the Fredericktown road running east. One runs south through Ironton and on to Dixie's land. The other is a road running west through Belleview valley. For a military post a stronger natural position could not well be found.

IRONTON is the county seat of Iron County and situated almost a mile south of Pilot Knob, and just the other side of the iron mountain of that name. It is a very pleasantly located town and contains a brick court house, two church buildings, a number of fair stores and residence houses. In prosperous times it must have been quite a business center. It lies at the foot of Shepherd Mountain and Pilot Knob and upon the borders of the pleasant valley of Arcadia. An enterprising, pleasant city will some time in the future, no doubt, be found here.

ARCADIA is a pleasant little village a mile south of Ironton. The only building of note in the place is the Arcadia Seminary, where the good people of St. Louis used to send their children to school before the war and which furnished us such nice quarters during the winter of 1861–62. The beauties of the valley of Arcadia are often spoken of. Our regimental chaplain was so impressed with it when we first came here, that he wrote a long article for publication, describing its many beauties and attractions.

But for the mountains that break them into different parts, Pilot Knob, Ironton and Arcadia would probably have been in a more compact form and constituted but one city. As it is they may practically be considered as only different parts of the same town.

MIDDLEBROOK is a small place about two and a half miles north of Pilot Knob, and simply a small railroad station.

IRON MOUNTAIN is about three miles further north and is situated near the mountain of that name. The place is noted for the fine quality of its iron ore that is found in inexhaustible quantities. It also gives name to the railroad that runs through the town, the Iron Mountain Railroad. It contains an iron foundry and a number of good buildings.

BELLEVIEW, west of Pilot Knob, is a valley of wonderful fertility, and in beauty and pleasant scenery can well compete with the valley of Arcadia.

Such as these are the surroundings among which our lot has been so often cast during our soldier life. Upon the whole it has been to us a pleasant place, and when the war is over the memory of many soldiers will return to it with happy thoughts.

CHAPTER XII.

A PUBLIC MEETING.

All politics were ignored in the army. As to the political belief of our comrades, we cared not. It was a rare case when one learned his comrades' preference as between mere political parties. It would be a correct statement to say the soldiers of our army have no politics. The election of 1862 claimed but little of their attention, in fact, was not thought of. Believing that all at home were true Union men, the soldiers were indifferent as to who was elected or defeated in an election. But when the Legislature of Illinois, elected in the fall of 1862, began in the following winter to take such action as, whether so intended or not, was giving sympathy and encouragement to the rebels, its course was closely watched by the Illinois soldiers. The feeling became so deep that the soldiers, in conformity with the ways they had been accustomed to at home, concluded to hold a public meeting to give an expression of their sentiments. The meeting was called. It was in regular public meeting style; those came who wished, those present called upon such as they desired to hear, to speak; the floor was open to any who asked for it. Being the only public meeting our soldiers ever held, a record of its proceedings may properly be given. As written at that time, the following is the record:

CAMP MIDDLEBROOK,[1] NEAR PILOT KNOB, MO,

March 2, 1863.

At a meeting of the Thirty-third and Ninety-ninth Regiments Illinois Volunteer Infantry, held at the head-quarters of the Thirty-third Illinois, Dr. Rex, Surgeon of the Thirty-third Regiment, called the meeting to order and nominated Lieutenant-Colonel Roe, Thirty-third

Illinois, who was unanimously elected Chairman; Captain E. R. Smith, Ninety-ninth Illinois, Secretary. Colonel Roe (Democrat) addressed the meeting as follows:

"Ladies and Gentlemen: I suppose that this is an assembly that has met for the purpose of announcing opinions in regard to the action of the assembled, I had almost said wisdom, of the State of Illinois. I am glad I did not say wisdom; for wisdom and learning go hand in hand with loyalty. I know all Illinois soldiers read, and that you are posted in regard to the action of the Illinois Legislature. I need not rehearse that action before you. We do not love war; we abhor it. But are we now, in the midst of the thickening dangers that surround our banner, to ignobly desert it? I never expect to find an Illinois soldier who is willing to say to such men as have almost made the name of Springfield detestable, 'I agree with you in sentiment and sympathize with you in your legislative treason.' No such man can be found.[2]

"We will spend our last drop of blood in defense of the Constitution and the Union; and oh! how willingly would we see a few of the traitors at home immolated upon freedom's altar. We want to send home an expression of opinion; we, who have been for the time disfranchised—an opinion that may prove, in time, stronger than the ballot-box. In time we mean that the ballot-box at home shall tell what is now to us so apparent that men in high places have fallen! fallen!! fallen!!! never again to control public opinion."

Colonel Lippincott, of the Thirty-third Illinois (Democrat), came forward and announced that upon consultation with many officers and privates he had been induced to offer the following resolutions:

Whereas, Recent developments in our beloved State of Illinois seem to call for an expression of opinion and feeling among Illinoisans who belong to the volunteer army of the United States, therefore,

Resolved, That we took up arms in defense of the Constitution and the Union of these United States of America from a deep-seated loyalty to the Government established by our fathers; that we were not and are not actuated by any sectional prejudices or hostilities, but only by a strong sympathy with the declaration of Andrew Jackson: "The Federal Union—it must and shall be preserved."

Resolved, That the treason which has brought the existing civil war, with all its horrors, upon the country, owes no part of its enormity to the section which produced the original traitors, but is hateful for its own sake, and would have been equally odious had it originated in any other quarter of our indivisible Union.

Resolved. That as sworn soldiers of the United States, and as citizens of Illinois, we owe constant and earnest allegiance to the Government of our country, and that we will maintain our allegiance against all treason, whether coming from the armed and open rebels in the South, or from their abettors in Illinois, or elsewhere.

Resolved, That we, volunteer citizen soldiers from Illinois, temporarily deprived of our accustomed privileges at the ballot-box, esteem it a privilege to be able in this manner to express our scorn, abhorrence, and contempt of the display of disloyalty and sympathy with an armed and bolder treason recently made by a large part of the Illinois Legislature; and we pledge our duty as soldiers, and our honor as men, to free our glorious State from the disgrace with which it has been threatened.

These resolutions were enthusiastically cheered. The Colonel continued with characteristic and well-timed remarks:

"Mr. President and Fellow-Soldiers: I did not purpose to make a speech on this occasion, and in offering these resolutions as the index to my sentiments, I suppose I have said all I ought to say upon this subject. But a casual remark of Colonel Roe's, as to the political name of our Illinois traitors, leads me to say something more. He spoke of the men who have disgraced the State of Illinois as Democrats. We have not met here for any political, and, least of all partisan object. I am, and always have been a Democrat. I am proud of Democracy. I am proud of that Democracy whose principles are made manifest in the teachings of Thomas Jefferson, whose honor found an unflinching and devoted advocate in the lamented Stephen A. Douglas.

"I repudiate the Democracy of the Illinois Legislature which has repudiated all the teachings of Stephen A. Douglas. I denounce these men as false to Democracy and false to men.

"But it matters not whether they are Democrats or not, they were chosen to the Legislature by the people of Illinois, and they have betrayed their trust.

"While the oaths they had pronounced were still ringing in their ears, they were basely contriving means for the violation of those oaths, and for the subversion of the Constitution they had sworn to support. They have done all they could to assist the men, in contending against whom many of our men have fallen into patriot graves. Our foes have received aid and comfort from the Legislature of Illinois.

"I am glad you have met here with me today to denounce such men and the odious principles they represent. I am glad we have come here on an equal footing. No man came here under orders. Every man is privileged to openly declare his opinion. If there is one man among you who would defend the Illinois Legislature, he is invited to come forward and take the place which I now occupy.

"If we stand in the position now which we occupied in the beginning of this war, these resolutions will be fully vindicated.

"I went to visit the rebel officers who were in charge of the flag of truce which came into West Plains. I never was so humiliated since I was born as when one of the officers told me that the Legislatures of Illinois and Indiana were with them, and passed resolutions favorable to their cause. I told them that we could take care of rebels at home as well as those abroad."

Major Crandell, Ninety-ninth regiment Illinois infantry, said:

"Mr. Chairman and Fellow-Soldiers: I shall not attempt a speech on this occasion. Those of you who have left your homes and come here to fight for your country have read the proceedings of the Legislature of Illinois, and know what they are. While we are fighting the enemy, they are aiding and abetting treason. We have met here to tell them that we detest rebellion, that we are willing to go to our homes, and there put down traitors, as well as to put down traitors in the South. I know there is no soldier here but who is here from motives of loyalty. I know that you will indorse the resolutions which have been offered."

Dr. Rex, Surgeon 33d Ill: "Fellow-Soldiers: I cordially indorse every sentiment that has been read in your hearing, and I would that these words could be sent in tones of thunder to those traitors at home. We, as volunteers from the Prairie State, now say we are with our country.

"Our motto is: Our country—may she always be right, but our country, right or wrong. Our country forever! The Illinois Legislature have shaken hands with the stink-fingers of Davis, that we have already branded as traitors.

"In my opinion there never was a truer man, or a nobler patriot than Stephen A. Douglas. There is a little story of him I must relate. Fort Sumter was bombarded on Saturday. The next day, while Douglas was walking down the street of the capital, he heard a friend say that the President was about to issue his proclamation calling for troops. Douglas went to the White House, and calling upon the President, said: 'Mr. Lincoln, I hear that you have prepared your proclamation; if agreeable, I should like to hear It.' 'Certainly, judge,' said the President; and standing before Mr. Douglas and his friends he read the proclamation. Says the man who relates this story, never hawk eyed a chicken more closely than Douglas eyed the reader. When the reading was ended, he grasped Lincoln's hand and said: 'Mr. Lincoln, I indorse every sentiment in that proclamation. Such patriots let us be. Let us stand by our Government, and, right or wrong, sustain it. The man who gives aid and comfort to our enemy is a traitor, and the man who stands by his country is a true patriot.'

"I hope that these resolutions will be adopted; that those traitors at home may know that we are coming, and they had better get off the track."

Corporal Durflinger, 33d Illinois: "Fellow-Soldiers: We are here to-day to express our feelings upon questions of the highest moment in this hour of our country's danger and peril. As the mere automaton, and the unthinking agent, the private soldier must, in a measure, be amid the routine of camp and field. But as the thinking, intelligent patriot, as the disfranchised citizen of the State of Illinois, I but express your feelings by saying, that we indorse these resolutions, word by word. They are not the flashy rhetoric, or the empty soulless effusion of the partisan and politician, but the earnest, calm, unstudied expression of loyal men. Men who have more faith in actions than words; who are acting in the face of the impending storm, and we are aware of their danger, and are justly indignant at the authors of that danger.

"Can loyal men talk of peace, when all that we have so nobly contended for must be sacrificed to gain that peace? When every provision of the Constitution is violated by our foe in the field? When all the interests of our State, our country and humanity are suspended in the balance, and when our financial, commercial and national existence is dependent upon the success of our arms? Can loyal men propose peace in view of these facts, because emancipation, conscription or confiscation are contrary to our Constitution? These are but the weak subterfuges of traitors, and traitors base enough to avow their malignant, though restrained treason, in the hall of our National Capitol. Let us send home a voice of expostulation and warning. Let us bid our mothers, wives, sisters and daughters to spurn from their presence the cowards that have sent us into the thickest of the contest to gain political honor, and now disfranchise us at home, and mock our noblest efforts in the field."

Sergeant George S. Marks, Ninety-ninth Illinois: "Fellow-Soldiers of the State of Illinois: I feel at liberty to express my sentiment on the present occasion. I feel that the soldiers of Illinois have been slandered by those infernal traitors at home. We can see their mark in nearly all the press that have published the proceedings of the Legislature. Fellow-soldiers, I am a Douglas Democrat, and labored for his election at the last Presidential election; but the voice of the people was against my choice, and I said when Mr. Lincoln was elected, oh, people, thy will be done! I am willing to sacrifice my life for the Union and the Constitution as my fathers made them. I trust that the Illinois soldiers may return home and blast the hopes of those devilish Copperheads. May God grant that the enemies of our country, both in the front and rear, shall be brought to see their error, and lay down their arms upon the one side; upon the other, their sympathy. Then will peace be restored to our distracted and divided country."

Captain Elliott, Thirty-third Illinois: "Fellow Soldiers: I indorse and believe every word of the resolutions read in your hearing. I would like to introduce one other resolution, to the effect that those traitors in the Illinois Legislature should be hanged until they are dead."

Captain McKenzie, Thirty-third Illinois—Approved of the resolutions, and denounced traitors at home and abroad.

Captain Lawton, of the Thirty-third, also approved of the resolutions, and especially denounced traitors at home for writing treasonable letters to his boys.

Rev. N. Hawkins, of Perry, Illinois, made some timely remarks, which were well received by the soldiers.

Chaplain Eddy, of the Thirty-third, remarked that he hated snakes; but of all snakes, he hated the copperhead snake the most. He denounced the majority of the Illinois Legislature for the treasonable course they pursued; but complimented the manly course pursued by Isaac Funk, a member of the Legislature.

The speeches were well received and heartily cheered by the soldiers.

The Chairman arose and remarked that "it had become a one-sided affair," and so he put the question on the adoption of the resolutions, and they were unanimously adopted.

Colonel Lippincott proposed "three cheers for the Union as it was, and as it will be." They were given with a will.

Chaplain Eddy proposed "three cheers for Isaac Funk who bravely branded a portion of the Illinois Legislature as traitors." Given.

Colonel Lippincott proposed "three cheers for Richard Yates, the soldiers' friend." These were given as only soldiers can give them.

Lieutenant Lewis, Thirty-third Illinois, offered a resolution to the effect "that the resolutions of this meeting be published in the *Missouri Democrat* and *Republican,* the Chicago *Times* and *Tribune,* the Springfield (Illinois) *Register* and *Journal,* and the *Pike County Democrat.*"

The meeting then adjourned.

Lt. Col. Roe.

E. R. Smith, Capt., Co. F, 99th Ill.

OUR LAST CAMP AND TRAMP IN MISSOURI.

We remained in our Belleview camp a week and then moved to within half a mile of Middlebrook. On the third of March we moved our camp to the village.

General Carr,[3] our new commander, having arrived, he reviewed our division at Middlebrook on Wednesday, the fourth. The following Tuesday, March tenth, we broke camp and started for Ste. Genevieve, on the Mississippi River.

Marched sixteen miles, camped near the lead mines and within one mile of Farmington. We made a good march on Wednesday, passing through Farmington

Maj. Gen. Eugene A. Carr. From Johnson and Buel, *Battles and Leaders of the Civil War.*

in the morning and Valley Forge during, the day. The next day our march ended at Ste. Genevieve.

The boys were now in high spirits. We are now to go down the Mississippi River, join the army at Vicksburg and help to remove the last rebel obstacle upon our great river. Vicksburg must be taken. No stranger's flag shall be permitted to hold sway over the waters that flow from our Northern fields. The Mississippi can not be divided, the great river never can be broken. It is strange that any should think otherwise. The great Northwest will always insist upon their natural right to the free navigation of this great river. Until the water that flows from their fields is mingled with that of the deep sea and becomes free to all the world, it belongs to them and their right must be maintained. The people of the South by whose doors through nature's course it flows must not claim exclusive rights or ownership in the waters of our great river. They can, with us, freely use it, but no more. The water that flows from Eastern Alleghenies and Northern lakes and Western mountains must, for all time, be permitted to go unvexed to the sea.[4]

On Monday, March 16, 1863, we bid farewell to Missouri, broke camp, embarked on the steamship *Illinois,*[5] and with banners waving, music playing and soldiers hurrahing, we started down the Mississippi River.

Personally, I did not participate to any great extent in these parting scenes. I was still just a little too sick to be very lively. On the last day of our march to Ste. Genevieve I gave out and had to be carried in on an army wagon. Arriving in camp it was found that a very severe attack of pneumonia was well under way. In a couple of days its severity was broken, but I was fully aware of the fact that our army surgeon had tried on me his favorite remedy of severe blisters. If I had not been extra strong, I presume the doctor would have used me up with his harsh treatment, even if the pneumonia had not done so. Thus I was found in the regimental hospital when marching orders came, and remained there until after we had passed Memphis. A regimental hospital always goes with the army. If a disease threatens to be lengthy, sick soldiers are sent to the post hospital. It was proposed to send some of us to a post hospital, but all were so anxious to go with the regiment that the surgeon took his sick men on the steamboat, and we all went together. After leaving Memphis I became strong enough to rejoin the company.

CHAPTER XIII.

DOWN THE MISSISSIPPI.

We left Ste. Genevieve on Monday and reached Cairo at three o'clock Tuesday afternoon.[1] The steamboat started again at ten o'clock that night, reaching Memphis, Thursday, the nineteenth, where we stopped to take on a supply of coal. We were detained here the next two days. On Sunday Chaplain Eddy preached to us in the cabin of the boat. Shortly afterward the steamboat whistle sounded and in short order we were again under way. The result of our hasty departure was to leave a number of our soldiers to follow us as best they could on some other boat. Garrett, Ross, Smith, Bailey and Alderson, of our company, were among those left in Memphis.

We arrived at Helena, Monday. We find that the ground we camped upon when here last summer is now completely under water. Most of the town is also overflowed by the very high water now in the river.

On Tuesday afternoon we left Helena. Passed by where our camps at Cockle-burr and Old Town were last summer. It is not to be seen now. When we were here our camp was all of twenty feet above the water of the river. Now the water is a dozen feet or more above the ground. One of the largest river steamboats could now easily pass all over the ground we camped upon. During the day we passed what is called Yazoo Pass. Some of the steamboats were saving distance by taking a short cut through between the trees. It appears strange to see a steam boat going through the woods as easily as does the pioneer drive his ox wagon through the unbroken forest.

Wednesday, March twenty-fifth, we passed Lake Providence. Logan's and McArthur's divisions are here. After a short stop the boat went twenty miles further down the river to land us at our camping ground.

We landed Thursday morning, and had only got fairly on land when General Carr, with his boat, arrived, and ordered us to re-embark, and go further down. We went on and landed and camped at Millikin's Bend.[2]

We are now part of the thirteenth army corps, General McClernand commanding.[3] Among the first news we hear is that part of Farragut's fleet has passed Port Hudson and arrived at the foot of the canal, just below Vicksburg. We also hear that two of Porter's boats attempted to run past Vicksburg from this side. The Lancaster is reported sunk, the Switzerland through in safety.[4]

We camped at Millikin's Bend a few days. During the night of the twenty-eighth a fierce wind storm overturned our tents, blew away all light articles and raised the mischief for us generally.

On the thirty-first General Hovey, whose command is at Young's Point, called to make his old regiment a short visit. He did not forget to call upon Company A.[5]

On the first day of April, Captain Burnham left us. He has resigned and is going home.[6] His health is so bad in this Southern climate that he felt that he was becoming more of a burden than assistance to the company. He seemed to much regret his parting; as the boys surely did. His resignation had been sent forward before we had reached this important field. If it had been possible for him to have done so, he would to-day, no doubt, recall his commission and go with us until the important work that now appears to stand before us is completed.

About this time I began to be aware of the fact that I had not yet fully recovered. Although the pneumonia did not return to vex me, chills and fever did.

On the sixth of April the regiment drew six days' rations and went down the river to work on the canal that was being made so as to let the river take a short cut across the bend and leave Vicksburg out in the cold, two miles from the river.[7] Those of us who were too unwell to work were left in camp at Millikin's Bend.

OUR MARCH PAST VICKSBURG.

On Tuesday, the fourteenth, we found that the regiment was to go forward. All of us who could move immediately went down and joined the regiment and then all started on.

We are upon the west side of the river, and a march south will take us past Vicksburg, which is upon the other side of the Mississippi.

The next day we started at five o'clock in the morning. Crossed a bayou and then went through Richmond, camping for the night one and a half miles beyond the town. The land around Richmond appears to be very productive. The plantations are large and nearly all have good buildings. In time of peace this was evidently a rich and prosperous country.

Thursday, April sixteenth, we marched twelve miles, which brought us within five miles of Carthage, on the Mississippi and below Vicksburg. During the night we heard heavy firing toward Vicksburg, which we find was caused by our gunboats getting up a fight with the rebel forts so that some of our transport boats could run by under cover of the smoke of the battle. It is understood that they succeeded.

On the seventeenth heavy firing was heard below us all the afternoon, which was reported to us as an engagement with a force of rebels, which resulted in the capture of eighteen hundred prisoners. It is so far merely a report. We get definite news, however, that our tents and camp equipage have been run past Vicksburg on a flatboat. A flatboat is just the thing to run a blockade down stream. A hole through them does not do any harm. The rebel cannon can fire at them at pleasure. All that it is necessary to do is to get the flatboat in the right part of the current of the river and then let her go. After it has passed the rebel works, a Union steam boat is on the watch and takes the flatboat in tow. That is all there is in a flatboat running a blockade down stream on the Mississippi. For a steam boat to run by the strong rebel fort is another question.

Tuesday, April twenty-first, we received orders to march immediately, and on we went. Marched down the levee two and a half miles. This is the only ground we can find to walk on here now. Every thing except the high levees is under water. At the end of the two and a half miles' march we had to cross a bayou. As we were attempting to cross, our boat run aground on a sand bar where the water was about four feet deep. It was concluded that the quickest way to get off was for some of the men to go into the water and pry the boat off with handspikes. A number of them immediately volunteered to do so and commenced taking off their shoes, etc., so as to go into the water. To encourage them General Benton announced: "Five dollars reward for the one first in." The clothing began to fly lively. To win was more of an object than the money. It promised to be a pretty race. The enterprise of Biggerstaff of our company ended it. He was standing by the side of the boat not having made any move toward getting ready to go into the water, and the moment General Benton made the announcement Biggerstaff leaped over the side of the boat into the water. He was cheered upon his short cut to victory. Others followed his example and jumped into the water with their clothing all on. The boat was started, the boys pulled upon deck, and Biggerstaff called up by General Benton who at once gave him the promised reward in five brand new one dollar bills.

After crossing the bayou we went on to Carthage and then marched six miles farther down the river, and camped on a plantation known as "Perkins' Place." The next day we moved at four P. M. and took up our quarters on some reasonably dry ground, which but a few days ago was occupied by the rebel soldiers. During the night some of our transports with supplies ran past Vicksburg and it kept us busy next day unloading them.

GOVERNOR YATES.

On Sunday, April twenty-sixth, Governor Yates of our State made us a visit.8 He was in company with General McClernand.[9] Both made short speeches to the soldiers. The soldier boys think there is no one to excel "Uncle Dick Yates." Wherever he is seen by the Illinois soldiers a lively time commences. They do not stop for any ceremony, but at once cry out "Hurrah for Dick Yates." All who can get near him shake hands with him. Every Illinois boy knows him by sight. The reception he meets must be tiresome, but he seems to enjoy it hugely. It is plain that Governor Yates is popular with the soldier boys.

CHAPTER XIV.

CONFEDERATE NEWSPAPERS—ERRORS OF SOUTHERN OPINION.

During our advance we have met many things that show that the rebels are sadly at fault as to the real spirit and feeling of the Northern soldiers. Their newspapers show that they believe that the Union soldiers, if not in actual sympathy with them, at least are opposed to fighting the rebels upon Southern ground. As we advance we find copies of their late papers. They seem to fully believe that the Northern soldiers only enlisted to protect their own States from invasion. They believe that all the State troops are anxious and determined to return to their own States. This would only leave a few lonely soldiers of the regular army for the rebels to dispose of.

One of their late papers is a curiosity. It contains a strong, pleading appeal to the Northern volunteer soldiers to unite and demand that their officers immediately lead them back to their own States. The sanguine rebels evidently thought that it would create a wonderful effect upon the Union volunteer soldiers, and went to extreme lengths to be sure that copies of the paper should be placed in their hands. As we advanced, the papers containing the fatal appeal came to us in every conceivable way. They were upon the roadside cunningly placed in every place a soldier was apt to investigate. Even the secesh women were made useful. They, all at once, became extremely sociable, and every time an opportunity offered, they would slyly place some of the wonderful papers in the hands of our soldiers; acting as though they were doing such an awful act that their lives would be sacrificed if any of the Union officers should detect them. Judged from their own belief and standpoint these Southern women exhibited the highest bravery. For the Union soldiers it was huge fun. The absurdity of such oft repeated scenes was increased by our soldiers falling into the spirit of it. They would, apparently in just as sly a manner, instantly hide the paper until out of sight of the fair distributors. Never before had they been furnished with newspapers by such pretty newsboys. It was truly a comical scene; the rebels using their wives and daughters, dressed in their prettiest gowns and smiles, to place a fearful engine of destruction in the way of their enemies. Upon one side were the Southerners in dead earnest, on the other, the entire Union army laughing at the way in which they were receiving handfuls of harmless Southern newspapers. While it lasted it was one of the highest jokes of our army life. Growing out of it many a jest passed through the army lines.

Among other things it was reported, whether true or not no one stopped to inquire, that one timid officer of the regular army became so alarmed that he went to General Grant with the suggestion that an order ought to be issued to prevent rebel newspapers from falling into the hands of our soldiers. To which Grant is said to have replied: "Yes, yes, I understand all about it, and if it becomes necessary—I—will—appoint—you—(stopping to light a fresh cigar)—to be news agent to see that the Southern newspapers are promptly distributed to my soldiers."

AT PERKINS' PLACE.

The regiment remained at Perkins' Place a week. It rained much of the time. The ground and everything was wet and damp. It was a fearful time for all of us who were on the sick list. To add to all else, our supply of quinine gave out. Chills and fever in such a damp and unhealthy place and climate without any quinine to check them, are fearful. Then the dread of being left, when the advance was made. It is the daily talk that we are now to make a move upon Vicksburg. None doubt its success. All anticipate participating in a battle that will become historical. One who is sick two or three days now may miss the opportunity of participating in the great battle of the war.

Tuesday, April twenty-eighth, the regiment went upon a boat and went down the river nearly to Grand Gulf, and then landed upon the west bank of the Mississippi. It was a sad squad of us who were left in the hospital tent. As our doctor was leaving he called the attention of the one left in charge, to two of us who were lying, near together, saying: "These two men of Company A you must treat with care or they will not live." My sick comrade proved the prediction to be well taken. Poor fellow, he never carried his gun again, but was buried upon the banks of the Mississippi. I was bound to see Vicksburg and lived. The truth probably was that the fearful ague shakes, without any quinine to check them, had made me appear much sicker than I was. On Thursday morning a wagon with medical supplies came to our post. At my earnest request the young doctor left with us went and got a liberal supply of quinine for me. Either because he had not time to distribute it in doses or because he thought it made no great difference, he gave it to me in bulk to use as I wished. I commenced taking it freely and by afternoon called for something to eat. By night I could eat quite a moderate supper.

I not only got the quinine but during the day General Hovey came up the river and stopped at our camp. For some reason he leaves the army.[1] He brought the information that our troops are now below Grand Gulf and crossing the

Mississippi over to the Vicksburg side, the Thirty-third in advance. Now is the time to be there. The big battle is liable to be fought within a week.

FORWARD AGAIN.

Friday morning, May first, found me with sufficient strength to walk, and I determined to make an effort to go forward. A good-natured soldier who happened near carried my gun and knapsack on board a steamboat that was getting ready to go down the river. I went aboard, selected a good place on deck, spread my blankets, and thus the boat was bound to take me whenever it started. This was not as much an undertaking as people at home would suppose. If a soldier is sick in the army, one place is just as good as another for him. No worse camp ground can be found than the one I was leaving. As to going forward on my own hook, that was all right. Every one was in the midst of the commotion created by a moving army. There was no one to issue any orders, so I issued my own and went as I chose. I could have gone north or anywhere else, and no objections would have been made. The quinine held out and I gained strength rapidly all day. The boat was late in starting and did not reach the landing to which it was destined until night. As the boat was not to move again until the next day, I retained my quarters on board all night.

Saturday morning I went ashore. Our landing place was about four miles above Grand Gulf, and on the west side of the river. From here we march overland so as to pass Grand Gulf, which is occupied by some strong rebel batteries. The rebel fort is at the point of the river bend. By marching across two and one half miles we struck the river at a point over three miles below the rebel forts. Had we followed the course of the river the distance would have been some seven miles.

We find quite a fleet at this point. The transports are very busy carrying the army over the river. The gunboats standing guard. While waiting we were entertained by looking at the gunboat Lafayette, which went up and exchanged a few shots with the rebel forts. No apparent damage was done on either side.

One of our transports was soon ready to start. I took passage upon it and went down the river about twelve miles, and at three P. M. landed at Bruinsburg,[2] Mississippi. The first thing we saw upon landing was a lot of rebel prisoners who were taken in the hot fight at Magnolia Hills[3] the day before.

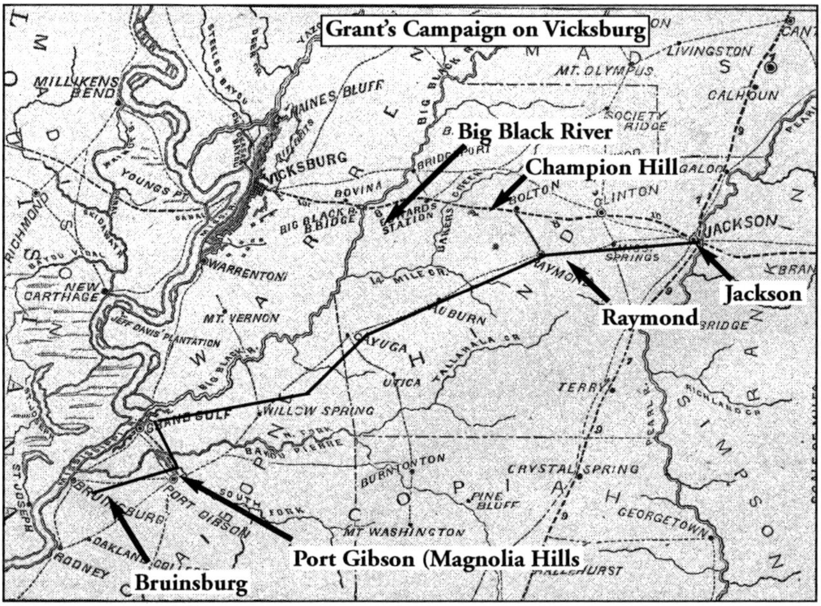

Vicksburg Campaign. From Guernsey and Alden, *Harper's Pictorial History of the Civil War.*

Having an independent command of my own—consisting of myself alone—I was not delayed by others, and immediately started forward. My quinine held out, its liberal use kept the chills off, and I was gaining strength rapidly. My gun and knapsack, however, made a load too heavy for me to carry, so I set about to find some transportation. I struck a good natured teamster who was driving a team and wagon belonging to a regiment of the regular army who agreed to carry my gun and knapsack. By the time he was ready to start forward we had become quite well acquainted, the result of which was that I paid for a ride for myself by telling army stories to the driver. When the wagon train reached the end of its day's journey, it still being early in the afternoon, I concluded to go forward. As I had done most of my day's march by riding, I concluded that a little evening walk would be beneficial. I went forward as far as the battle field of the day before, and took up quarters for the night with some soldiers who had been sent back to pick up the guns, etc., that were strewn upon the field.

CHAPTER XV.

MAGNOLIA HILLS.

Sunday morning I went forward and passed over much of the hard-fought battle field of Friday. The battle field presented a scene both grand and terrible. The dead had nearly all been buried and all of the wounded taken to the field hospitals. Enough remained, however, to plainly show how fierce the struggle had been. Horses, mules, wagons and guns, both large and small, lay strewn upon the field, often heaped together in a huge, misshapen mass, and the strong forest trees, the staunch old oaks, the beautiful magnolias, were torn and scattered as though fierce tornadoes had swept them down.

The ground that was fought over beggars description. The huge hills and deep gulleys running and counter-running in every direction created a wild and broken country. What a place for a battle field!

Taking position upon the top of the high hills the Confederates supposed it impossible for them to be dislodged. They were certain, they thought, that a successful charge could not be made against them. This belief was a natural one. It would naturally be supposed that a steep hill or mountain side, with an ascent so steep that soldiers could only with great difficulty climb it, would be the easiest defended and the most dangerous ground for an attempted charge. Our soldiers soon learned differently. They discovered that whenever the enemy held the top of a high hill a charge could be made up its steep sides much more safely than upon more level ground. Even when it was so steep that they had to support themselves by catching hold of the underbrush and limbs of trees and even actually climbing up on their hands and feet they could successfully charge the enemy who was holding the brow of the hill.

One reason why this is so arises from the fact that it is almost impossible for those on the top of a high elevation to fire low enough to harm those advancing up the elevation. In an open field fight a charge up the side of a high hill or mountain side is the safest one that can be made.

The Confederates upon the top always fired over the heads of the Union boys. Our soldiers found that they could safely run up hill, under the enemy's bullets without firing and when they reached the top they would, with loaded guns, meet the Confederates with unloaded guns in their hands. All the rebels could do under such circumstances was to seek safety in running down the other side of the hill.

Thus each Union charge up the steep sides of Magnolia Hills was successful.

When within two miles of Port Gibson, I stopped to eat breakfast, and had barely finished when some of our soldiers came up and said that we were on dangerous ground, as an attack was expected from the rear. Upon reaching the open road, I was surprised to find that, while I was eating breakfast, a line of battle had been formed within two hundred yards of and fronting toward us. My companions in the receipt of the cheerful information were an old colored man and his wife, living in a log cabin by the roadside, and at whose fire I had made some coffee. They were thoroughly alarmed, and without ceremony rushed through the Union line of battle, and sought safety in its rear. I went up and joined the Union line of battle. In a short time our scouts came back, with the information that rebels were running away instead of coming up for a fight. I then bid the Union soldiers farewell and pushed ahead.

GRAND GULF AND PORT GIBSON.

I soon reached Port Gibson.[1] Here I learned that Carr's division had started for Grand Gulf. I started forward and soon found the Thirty-third. They were slowly advancing with a skirmish line in front. When we got within four miles of Grand Gulf,[2] information was received that the forts at Grand Gulf had been evacuated by the rebels and were now in the hands of our soldiers. Thus our mission in that direction was ended. We now returned to Port Gibson, crossed the bayou and marched five miles toward Black River. At night we camped in line of battle, in a field of growing corn which the boys pulled and placed under their blankets to keep them out of the mud.

We lay still most of the day Monday. Toward night moved forward and crossed a small stream called Stone River.

On Tuesday our brigade had a sort of a mass meeting. General Benton[3] and other officers made speeches to the soldiers complimenting them upon their action in the late battle.

The next day Company A went out on a foraging trip. All we found was a little corn meal.

TO THE REAR OF VICKSBURG.

Thursday we started at three A. M. and marched fifteen miles, and camped near Rocky Springs. The advance drove the enemy as we advanced. General Grant informally reviewed our troops on Friday by passing in front of our lines in company with Generals McClernand, Logan, Carr, A. P. Hovey, Benton and others.[4]

We were called up at one o'clock Saturday morning, at three we started forward and marched nine miles.

Sunday, May tenth, we remained in camp. We hear that Sherman's corps is crossing the Mississippi at Grand Gulf.

The entire army will soon be on the ground and ready to advance on Vicksburg, which we are now within twenty miles of. The next day Sherman's men commenced coming up.

Tuesday we marched forward to within six miles of the railroad running into Vicksburg from the east. Our advance had a sharp skirmish with the enemy. We learn that the Confederates are in force upon the railroad in front of us, and in the neighborhood of Edwards' Station. Indications of an approaching battle are seen upon every hand.

Wednesday, May fifteenth, we started forward expecting to have a battle with the enemy in our front at Edwards' Station. After going two miles we turned toward the right and started east toward Raymond, at which place some of our troops were having an engagement with some of the enemy. The battle was over and our troops victorious before we got there.

The battle of Raymond[5] was an illustration of what odds a brilliant, determined effort can often overcome. The battle was fought by General Logan with a small force against an enemy three or four times as strong in numbers. Logan determined to hold his ground at all hazards until other Union troops could reach him. The Confederates, evidently posted as to the small number of Union troops engaged, pressed in determined to crush the small Union force. The battle had continued some considerable time and the heavy mass of rebels was pressing down upon the little band of Yankee boys with increased zeal. Seeing how his soldiers were suffering Logan became mad and with a number of strong words (when occasion requires, Logan, like Washington, sometimes swears in the army) he told his soldiers to "give the rebels hell," and started the work by himself leading a fierce charge upon the enemy's line. With a loud hurrah the entire command went forward on a fierce run and in less than five minutes the entire Confederate force was on a disorganized race to the rear, and the battle won by the Union boys.

Logan had learned one great secret of a battle field; in all sharply contested open field battles a time is sure to come when each side is so much in doubt as to the actual condition of affairs, and so uncertain as to what the result is to be, that if one side will press forward with sufficient rapidity and determination, the other is sure to give way. In other words in all sharply contested battles both sides are at times beaten and tenacity and vim win the day.

A small number of soldiers who have confidence in themselves, in each other, and in their officers, can any day take a field from thrice their number of timid souls. Confidence, tenacity, rapidity, determination and vim, with moderate skill always win upon a battle field.

Our entire army, it will be remembered, had turned to the east, leaving the main Confederate army at liberty to fall in our rear. Looking upon our action of this day with the light of later events it will be clearly seen that General Grant's action was one of the most audacious ever taken in the face of a strong enemy. The Confederates were known to be in force in front of us at Edwards' Station. To go on and attack them our army would be facing to the north, theirs to the south. In case of a repulse we could fall back to the protection of our gunboats on the Mississippi River. At the same time the enemy, if defeated, could fall back and then retreat to the interior of Mississippi. By going toward Jackson we left the large Confederate force in position where it could fall into our rear. Not only this, but by taking that route we would drive all of the rebels into one body and thus strengthen them for the great battle that was evidently near at hand. The course taken by General Grant was to go to Jackson, throw his entire army between the Confederates and their only route for retreat, thus producing this condition of affairs: If defeated, the enemy could only fall back and be penned in at Vicksburg, and on the other hand, the Union army, if defeated, would be entirely destroyed, because there would be no possible road for retreat left open. All of these things were well understood by the army, and as we turned toward the east all were elated with the audacity of the movement. No one doubted our ability to drive the enemy when the time came for the final blow to be struck. The confidence of the army in itself and in its commander was unbounded. The very audacity of our movement in turning to the east and leaving the enemy to fall into our rear if he chose, increased the enthusiasm of every soldier in the ranks. Each one felt as though he had said to the rebels: "You are not of much account, tumble into our rear if you like." Grant's movement in the rear of Vicksburg was like that of a farmer gathering up a flock of sheep. A few scattering ones are not worth trying to drive in. The object is to surround the entire flock and drive them all into the pen together.

On Thursday we passed through Raymond and continued our march toward Jackson, camping at night within five miles of that city, the capital of

Mississippi. A dispatch soon came informing us that our troops had taken the place and that General Grant's head-quarters for the night were established in the city.

Jackson being safely in our hands, and our army having now got outside of all of the Confederate soldiers connected with the Vicksburg army, we were ordered to "About face" and started upon our march to drive them in. On Friday we went through Raymond and then three miles farther on toward Vicksburg. Our advance under Osterhaus[6] had a sharp skirmish with the enemy. As we camped for the night, every thing assured us that a stubborn battle was now to be fought. We were now fronting west toward Vicksburg. All of the scattering bands of rebels had been driven in. Our cavalry scouts brought back word that the entire Confederate army had come up and were now in line of battle in our immediate front. On our side, we slept in line of battle with our guns by our sides and ready for any emergency.

CHAPTER XVI.

BATTLE OF CHAMPION HILLS.

At an early hour on Saturday morning, May 16, 1863, our entire army was aroused, a hasty breakfast consisting of some coffee and hard tack eaten, and every thing put in readiness for the coming contest.[1] The thick woods in our front covered the Confederate army lying there and waiting for us. The ground was broken and hilly as well as covered with a heavy growth of timber. Many capital positions could be selected by an army that chose to stand on the defensive. This was the course taken by the enemy. Between where we had camped for the night and the wooded hills where the rebels had taken their stand was some open ground.

Our army corps, the Thirteenth, was the left of the advancing Union army. At an early hour, between seven and eight o'clock, and before we were fairly under way, we heard the first guns of the day's contest. It was commenced by the advance of our corps and to our extreme left. This first firing being thus to the left of our army suggested the probability that the enemy was attempting to pass from the immediate front of our army and probably looking for a way to escape instead of maintaining his fighting ground. Our heavy infantry columns immediately went forward. As they did so the slight firing we had heard in front of our left passed along to our center and became somewhat heavier. It now became apparent that the rebels had determined to make a stubborn stand. Of course all the firing yet done had been only that of the advance skirmishers on both sides. The tell-tale stubbornness with which the rebel skirmishers stood their ground, in our front, plainly showed that heavy forces of the enemy were immediately behind them. A soldier, by observation, will learn so as to know when a strong force of the enemy is near at hand as plainly as an experienced sea captain, when upon the water, can tell when a fierce storm is approaching. As we neared the open woods in our front we formed in army line in the open fields and were all ready to march in and attack the waiting rebels.

Now a strange and wonderful day's experience opened before us. Although we were the first of the Union troops upon the ground, and within striking distance of the enemy, we lay still and made no forward move. A ten minutes' march would have brought us upon the main rebel line. The real battle had not yet commenced. We formed in line and waited. During the day all of the varied phases of the fierce battle could be noted by us.

Heavy firing soon told us that the real battle had commenced. Now a fierce artillery duel would be fought and then succeeded by the more desperate and stubborn conflict of small arms. Then a seeming lull in the contest would be again followed by the fierce roar of artillery, and this again followed by an infantry contest. Up and down the line the thunder roar of the battle would go; at one time fierce at one point, then to quiet there and rage with increased fury at another. The heavy cloud of battle smoke, as the dark mass arose above the trees, also told its story of the fierce contest. Now and then we would plainly hear the wild cheers of the Northern boys as some of our troops would charge upon and carry some point held by the enemy. During all this time we lay still. No order for us to go forward was given.

As the hours passed by some of our impatient soldiers would leave the ranks and go forward into the woods and then return with news of the battle. From them and other sources we had almost continual information from the front. This was hardly necessary, however, for we were so near that the smoke of battle, the firing guns and the varied sounds of the fierce struggle plainly told us of advances and retreats made. The progress of the battle was ever before us.

At last, after long waiting and much wondering why we were not permitted to go forward and share in the fierce conflict, the order to "Forward, march," was given. In a brief moment we were on the way. As we started the wild and advancing cheers that rose above the battle roar told us that the Union troops were making a fierce and successful charge upon the rebel lines. As we went in the battle was well-nigh over; we went into the woods and struck the right wing of the rebel army. It vanished before us like snow beneath the summer sun. Had we struck this wing of the rebel army an hour earlier it would have been thrown upon the enemy's center and the confusion that would then have overwhelmed them would have led to the destruction of the entire rebel army. As it was, at the time when we struck them, the Union troops under McPherson[2] had made their last charge and driven in the main rebel line, so that all were now upon a fierce run to escape. Had we been soon enough the confusion in the rebel lines would have been so great that they could not have seen any open way of escape and they would have been obliged to throw down their arms and surrender *en masse.*

We drove all before us and then rushed on to the main road where the fiercest contest of the battle had been fought. The hill upon which the enemy had made his most desperate contest was thickly covered with the dead of both sides. Broken guns and ruin covered the field. Rebel artillery with its horses and men were here and there all heaped together in a mountain of death and ruin. Over this gory field we rushed, and on into the woods beyond where we struck all that was left of the rebel army. It was the last shot of the day. The frightened enemy hardly having courage to return our first fire. We cut the remains of the rebel army apart. The largest force was driven toward Vicksburg. The other part ran over the hills and went to the east. The Thirty-third had been given the advance of the reserve force as it went upon the field. The last guns fired in the battle of Champion Hills was by our men and at the force of the enemy we drove to the rear.

Many pieces of rebel artillery fell to our hands. Hosts of rebels surrendered as we advanced. These were left for others to guard, as we pushed on, rapidly following the retreating rebels. Letting those who had gone to the east pursue their way to escape or be captured by other Union forces as their fate might be, we pushed toward the west after the rebels who were retreating toward Vicksburg. Darkness soon ended our pursuit and we stopped for the night at Edwards' Station.[3]

At night, as the full results of the battle became known it was found that a great victory had been won by our troops.

Having become historical, and its general results being open to all who choose to refer to the pages of written history, it is not necessary to here recount at large the scenes and results of the battle of Champion Hills.

CHAPTER XVII.

BATTLE OF BLACK RIVER.

Sunday morning, May 17, 1863, found us ready to move forward as soon as it was light enough to march.[1] We were now given the advance. A rapid march brought us within sight of the rebel works at Black River. The outside picket guards were driven in without difficulty.

The conditions for a stubborn defense were ample. The rebel position was a strong one. At this point Black River is a stream of considerable size. The wagon road to Vicksburg, as well as the railroad, here crosses the river. On the west side of Black River are some high bluffs. We were approaching from the east. Why the Confederates did not select these bluffs on the west side of the river as the place for their fortifications, it is hard to tell; they probably thought the position chosen preferable. It certainly was a mistake. Still, the place selected for their fortifications was by no means a weak one. Had not the west bank of Black River furnished stronger natural positions, that selected by the rebels would have been considered a wise selection. Some little distance from the east side of the main river was a channel of considerable width and depth. This virtually created an island, which lay between the main river and this channel or bayou. The island was the place selected by the enemy for his fortifications. The island was of sufficient size, and the ground being comparatively level and unbroken, it was probably selected by the rebels as a better place for the movement of troops than would have been the uneven hills upon the west side of the river. Again, east of the bayou was a smooth valley varying from half a mile to a mile in width. As the attacking force would have to pass over this level ground, the rebels doubtless thought that they could easily destroy all who attempted to approach, before their works could be reached.

A range of forts well supplied with heavy artillery had been built along the east side of the bayou. These had been connected with a complete chain of breastworks for the enemy's infantry. Thus an attacking force would have to first charge over a wide space of level ground; then pass a deep and wide stream of water, and then climb the rebel fortifications upon the bank of the channel before they could reach the well fortified rebels. What possessed the enemy to waste so much valuable strength in fighting in the open woods upon Champion Hills when Black River, so near at hand, afforded them such superior positions of defense, is, indeed, a marvel.

We were upon the skirmish line and consequently the first troops in sight of the enemy that morning. The position our company held was next to and upon the south side of the road running west toward Vicksburg. This brought us in front of the center and strongest part of the enemy's works. The valley between the rebel works and the small wood-covered hills was at this point a little over half of a mile in width. The valley at this point had been a cultivated corn or cane field. The previous year's furrows ran parallel with the rebel works. The small hills back of this field were covered with a thick growth of underbrush. Had the enemy been thoughtful and industrious enough to have cut and burned all of the small trees and brush upon these hills as far back as heavy artillery could reach, it would have been of untold advantage to him. To our right the valley lessened in width so that the ground covered with trees reached nearer to the rebel works. To our left it continued to widen so that the rebel works upon that part of the line had at least a mile of level ground over which to fire.

Our early morning call had evidently greatly surprised the indolent enemy. As we, upon the skirmish line, came out of the woods and upon the level field in front of their works, we beheld wild confusion in the rebel lines. Evidently they had not yet all got up and finished their breakfast, much less formed into line ready to meet us. All were aroused and called into line. If we had been supported by a solid column, at that moment, we could no doubt have rushed over and taken the works before the enemy was prepared to defend them. But just then the Union troops at hand were only those of a small skirmish line of barely sufficient strength to feel of the enemy.

From the ground we were upon, all of the movements of the enemy could be plainly noted. Officers mounted in hot haste and rushed among the rebel soldiers to arouse and hurry them into position. Every movement of the enemy

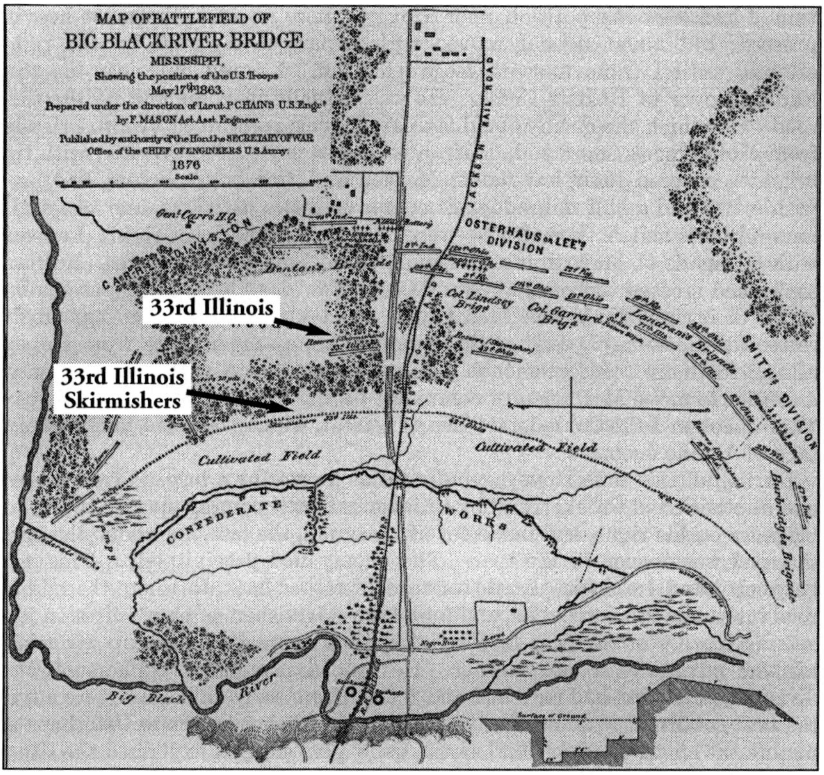

Big Black River Bridge. From Johnson and Buel, *Battles and Leaders of the Civil War.*

was plainly seen by us. We could note the strength of each rebel command and see to which part of the line it was sent. Probably no battle was ever before fought which was so completely seen from its commencement to its end as was the battle of Black River by those of us who were upon the advance skirmish line.

To get as near to the rebel works as we did upon such ground was wonderful. For any of us to live through the fight that ensued, holding the position we did, was a miracle. Our ability to advance so close to them was no doubt largely owing to the confusion in the enemy's ranks caused by our early approach. The first firing of the rebels was fearfully wild. They seemed only to put the muzzles of their guns over their breastworks and fire into the air at random. Such firing is more apt to bite those far in the rear as the bullets fall to the ground, than to trouble those who, like us, are near at hand. Now and then a gun in the hands of a cool-headed rebel would be fired with more judgment at our line. A few were hit. I supposed that I was one of the unfortunate ones. A rifle ball passed near enough to "burn" my face. I then knew by experience how it was with so many others who for a moment supposed they were hit, when they were not. I plainly felt a hole cut through my cheek. That the passing bullet had cut a deep, long gash through the side of my face I did not doubt. I immediately put up my hand to see how much of my cheek was left, and to my glad surprise found that the bullet had simply grazed and not cut me. Those who have experienced both, insist that at the first moment, a bullet that passes near enough to "burn" by the "hot wind" of a swift revolving bullet, produces a much sharper sting than that caused by a direct shot.

Our skirmish line pressed well forward, much further than prudence would have permitted, and then each selected the best place he could find and lay upon the ground and commenced to load and fire as opportunity offered. Amidst thickly flying bullets it is surprising how small an elevation of ground a soldier can make available as breastwork. The rough plowing of the previous year's crop had left deep furrows and corresponding ridges, the best of which served us well during the hot fight in which we were engaged. The success with which a soldier can, under such circumstances, apparently sink into the ground and out of sight while loading his gun, can not be realized by those who have never seen it done.

Some of our artillery were soon in place on the hills behind us and commenced their work upon the enemy. The artillery was supported by the infantry columns. This heavy force on the higher ground in our rear soon claimed the entire attention of the rebels in our front. They no doubt also believed that all who had advanced on the skirmish line had been killed. These things combined caused us to be neglected by the enemy so that we were at liberty to load and fire at pleasure and almost unmolested. While it, no doubt, did far more harm in the rebel ranks, still the few guns on the skirmish line attracted no attention when mingled with the fierce firing of the two contending armies. And then our nearness to the rebel line made it difficult for them to look over their works to take effective aim at us. Even when the conditions of the ground are favorable, the experience of war is that most of the firing done carries the balls high above the effective point. Situated as we were it was safe to calculate that the rebel bullets would pass above us. There being so much vacant space in the open air compared with the little space occupied by one individual, is the reason why so few are killed compared with the amount of lead shot in battle. The space occupied by a man is but a mere speck compared with all out doors and there are a thousand chances to miss, to one to hit him with the ball of a random shot.

Our artillery had a capital position. The hills upon which our cannon were placed were within easy range of the rebel works. Our gunners were much better marksmen than those handling the rebel artillery. The thick underbrush completely covered the movements of our men. An entire battery would be run into position under cover of the thick young trees, careful aim taken and then altogether commence a rapid fire upon the rebel works. As soon as the rebel artillery began to get their guns bearing on the spot our men would run their guns to another point and the first notice of the change the enemy would get was another well-aimed volley. With different batteries doing this and a fine range of favorable ground to stand upon our artillery did most effective work. With our sharp-shooters on the skirmish line so near at hand to annoy everyone who attempted to handle a rebel cannon, and our artillery-men so well improving their opportunities, the result of the artillery duel was favorable to the Union side. All things combined produced the strange result, that superior artillery protected by complete works was worsted by smaller guns in the open field. During the fight many of the protected rebel guns were dismounted, while our artillery out in the open field escaped with but little harm.

Thus the battle raged with our cannon in our rear, and the rebel guns in our front, both firing over us. We were fortunately low enough so that both sides fired their balls and shells above us. The smoke and confusion of the heavy contest also served to withdraw all attention from our skirmish line and left us free to use our trusty rifles to the best advantage. After the engagement had commenced in earnest, the greatest danger we were in was from imperfect shells which would burst on the way, and from faulty charges of powder or misdirected guns which now and then sent iron and lead to plow the ground where we lay.

It would be useless to attempt to describe the terrific scenes of this fierce contest as viewed from the position we held between the two contending forces. The heavy battle smoke rapidly rising continually opened the entire scene to our view. Even in the hottest of the fight every move of the enemy could be noted by us. One rebel officer, mounted upon a powerful white horse, attracted unusual attention. As he first started at the beginning of the fight he appeared to be supported by a numerous staff. His daring was so reckless that he often became the mark our riflemen aimed at. As time passed swiftly on, one by one of his assistants were seen to be disabled. He rode until the last of his staff had fallen or left the field, and still the rider upon the white horse, within range of our guns, continued to inspire the rebel soldiers. At last, as it became plain that the day was soon to be ours, a desire seemed to spring up to let the reckless rider live, and he was permitted to ride away at the last unharmed. As the artillery battle reached its height, all incidents and individual matters were absorbed by the fierce grandeur of the terrific storm raging around and above us. For a time the cannon in front of us, the cannon behind us, the cannon around us, thundered and roared and poured forth their fierce storm of fire and shot. Look to the front, look to the rear, look everywhere and the red-mouthed artillery seemed opened upon us. Above us was the black cloud of battle smoke, through which crashed and burst and screamed the murderous shell and ball. But few ever looked upon what we saw during that hour, and lived to tell the tale of the day's conflict. Imagination has often suggested that the grandest place from which to view a battle scene would be from a stationary balloon anchored high above the field of battle, and from thence to look down upon both contending forces. Even this would not prove equal to the position we held, because the rising smoke would then obscure the view, while with us, the dense cloud continually rose so that we could look beneath it and see the entire fury of the fierce conflict.

Although the gigantic grandeur of the conflict was created by the heavy artillery and the solid ranks of infantry in our rear, still the most effective work of the entire battle was done by the line of skirmishers, who, with their trusty rifles, had approached so near the rebel works. We held our ground during the entire battle. In fact it was better to do so than to have attempted to go back, while so plainly within range of the rebel guns. I had a little experience in this. Near to me was John Spradling of our company. A piece of bursting shell struck him in the side or top part of his hip inflicting a fearful wound. He supposed that it was fatal and told us that he would soon die. His wound bled badly but his strength remained so well that he soon thought that if he could get medical aid there might still be a chance for him to live. If death is inevitable a soldier will die without a single word of complaint. While there is hope of life he is anxious to improve it. Spradling became wildly anxious to get back where his wound could be attended to before be bled to death. He desired me to help him. It was a dangerous undertaking. The artillery on both sides was still firing rapidly. Standing up incurred more danger from the balls and shells swiftly flying from both front and rear over our heads. The worst, however, was to slowly walk over so much exposed ground, and that in plain sight and range of the solid line of rebel riflemen. The hope was that they would not care to waste any shots at a crippled soldier and his assistant, going to the rear. I got our wounded comrade up and started. With my gun fastened upon one shoulder—a soldier never abandons his gun—I lent my other shoulder and arm to the wounded man. He was so injured that practically he could use only one foot to assist in the walk. Going back in this condition was slow and tedious. The hope of magnanimity on the part of the rebels was misplaced. We had not gone far before the screeching rifle balls aimed at us commenced hissing by our ears. Spradling knew that he would die if he stayed upon the field. Another ball could do no more than kill him. He begged to go on. As a soldier who could yet be useful in front, I ought not to have taken the chance. But who could withstand the pleading of a wounded soldier. And then who could tell what the result would be. The chances were even that he would be hit as soon as I. Then my mission toward the rear would be ended. A soldier's life makes all reckless of danger. All places in the midst of a fierce battle are dangerous. What great difference did it make, for us to go or stay? I told Spradling to brace up and we would continue until one or the other of us fell. It is not wild to say that, during our tedious journey, at least a thousand rifle balls aimed at us passed near, and, strange to say, neither of us was touched. There must have been some special Providence that protected us. With much difficulty I managed to get back over the open ground, reached the woods, dragged our wounded comrade up over the hill and then back until we met a squad with their white badges and a stretcher in whose hands I placed the wounded soldier and who carried him back to the field hospital where his wounds could be dressed.

Relieved of our wounded soldier I turned and immediately went forward to rejoin my comrades. It is usual in such cases to remain with the main line and not hazard the attempt to reach the skirmish line in front. Probably it would be more correct to state the fact that it is always usual in all battles for the entire skirmish line to fall back out of the way when the actual engagement commences. It was only owing to the peculiar condition of the ground upon which it was fought that in this battle we upon the skirmish line retained our advanced position and allowed the heavy firing to be done over our heads.

Many indications told us that the battle would soon be ended. Most of the rebel cannon had been silenced. The rebel infantry began to exhibit evidences of uneasiness. I was anxious to be in at the end. To go forward was of course far different from what my retreat had been. Being alone I could skip along lively. There was a chance to select the ground and now and then dodge behind some protection. In short, going back was not by any manner of means a matter of recklessness.

My return had been none too soon. I had hardly reached our skirmish line when the last move in the battle of Black River was made. It was a brisk, sharp and successful charge upon the rebel works. This is how it happened: The woods to our right ran well down toward the rebel works. Colonel Bailey of the Ninety-ninth Illinois—"old rough and ready number two," General Benton had called him after the battle of Magnolia Hills—was with the advance. In their zeal the Union soldiers had pressed to the verge of the woods which brought them near to the rebel works. It became right hot for our boys so near to the enemy's lines. They had no orders to go farther; in fact, had already pushed on farther than orders had been given for them to go. The proper thing to have done was to have fallen back to a less exposed position. Colonel Bailey was one of those awkward officers who could never learn military rules. His only idea of war was to pitch in and whip the enemy whenever and wherever he could be found. By his impetuosity he became the hero of the day's battle. Had his unauthorized movement failed he would probably have been at least dismissed from the army. No, he would not. Had it failed and he come out of it alive, he might have been tried by a court-martial, but that never would have happened. His rash act was bound to succeed or Colonel Bailey would have been killed in the attempt.

Finding it disagreeable to be so near the rebel works and seeing the effective fire upon his soldiers, Colonel Bailey became fighting mad and yelled out in thundering tones that rang along the line: "Boys, it is getting too d—hot here. Let us go for the cussed rebels!" Before the last word was out of his mouth, with a drawn sword flashing in the air, he was on a fierce run toward the rebel works. With a wild hurrah his entire command joined him in the wild race. Others to the right and left, without a moments' delay or a single command, joined in the mad career, and thus with wild cheers the entire Union line joined in a charge upon the rebel works. The disheartened Confederates having already suffered so severely, and vividly remembering the fearful pounding they had received the day before at Champion Hills, at once gave up all hope of further defense and immediately abandoned their works, and were in a hot race to the rear before the Union troops had reached their lines. Crossing the bayou was no easy matter. In front of part of our line the water was only breast deep; through this the soldiers easily waded, holding their guns and cartridge boxes above the water. In some places the stagnant water was covered with drift-wood. Here some would jump from one log to another like rabbits. In places where the water was more open a soldier running up would jump on to a floating log and the momentum of the fierce run would carry both him and the log across so that he could jump dry shod upon the other side, before the log he thus used for a boat commenced to turn wrong side up. In front of us the water was deeper and wider, but as good fortune would have it, the rebels had only removed the planks from the bridge, leaving the narrow stringers still running over. Our company immediately jumped upon these stringers and ran across like squirrels. The rest of the skirmish line followed, and thus the Thirty-third was soon all inside of the rebel works, being the first troops inside the main part of the fort. Other troops came in hot haste. The rebels were gone. And the battle of Black River was ended.

A fine lot of rebel cannon was taken with the fort. Our boys had learned a little war experience from the fight of the day before. As we drove the enemy from some of his cannon at Champion Hills, we rushed forward without regard to the guns. When we afterward sent back for them we found that the troops who had followed us had taken possession of the captured cannon, and were thus entitled to the credit of their capture. The rule is, that if a command captures artillery it must retain possession of it, or else the next command coming up will have the right to claim it. Infantry troops can not always carry captured artillery along with them, nor stop in the midst of a fight to retain possession of it. To provide for these and other difficulties that might arise, the established rule has become for the troops who capture a cannon to have one of their men "straddle" it, that is, sit upon it as though on horseback. Then the command can go to any other work at hand, and the one soldier upon the gun will be recognized by the entire army as in full possession of it. Thus one man for each piece of artillery is all the regiment need leave to retain possession of captured cannon. Of course, should any of the enemy return, the straddling is ended, and it is again a fight for possession of the guns. We had profited by the Champion Hills lesson, and the result was that the captured rebel forts were full of Thirty-third boys "straddling" the captured cannon. Thus we were credited with the capture of cannon enough to supply a good sized army, and were more than made even for the loss of those we had neglected to "straddle" at Champion Hills. The captured guns came near being a burden to us, there were so many of them that they could not be disposed of at once, so an entire company of our regiment was detailed to take care of the captured guns until they could be properly disposed of. The rebels retreated across the river and went toward Vicksburg. One of their batteries took position upon the high bluffs on the west side of the river and fired a few rounds at us, but as soon as they saw one of our batteries getting into position to reply to them, they "limbered up" and scampered away. This was the last we saw of the rebels at Black River.

CHAPTER XVIII.

VICKSBURG.

We crossed Black River Monday morning May 18, 1863, and marched toward Vicksburg.[1] The rebels carefully kept out of our way. We camped for the night within a short distance of the noted city.

On Tuesday, May nineteenth, the battle of Vicksburg commenced. The first day's contest was mostly by the artillery. We drove the enemy to the inside of his fortifications.

The next day firing was kept up from morning till night. In many places our riflemen got near enough to annoy the rebel batteries. Toward night our division moved to the right, crossed the railroad and charged over a hill. Captain Kellogg of our regiment was killed.[2]

The ground here is broken into steep hills and deep ravines. Charging over this hill gave us possession of a ravine near the rebel works. In places the hills are very steep. In the charge, part of our line suddenly came to a place where there was a perpendicular fall of nearly twenty feet. They were going so fast that many fell over and a number were severely injured.

The ravine we had taken by our charge was of considerable width and length. It was of sufficient size to contain quite a large force. Situated so near to the rebel works its possession was an important gain to our side. It is surprising that we were able to pass the exposed hill, over which we charged, with so little loss. Our move was so sudden and unexpected that we were over the hill and in possession of the ravine before the Confederates had sufficiently recovered from their surprise to fire upon us with any accuracy.

The next day our regiment acted as sharp-shooters. A company would deploy as skirmishers and then work its way as far as possible upon the hills in our front and fire at the enemy. When the turn of Company A came we relieved Company D. They had been having a hot time with the enemy. Two men of the company had been killed.[3] We had a lively time ourselves, but came out of the contest more fortunately. Marion Deboice of our company was wounded, no one else was hurt.[4]

To soldiers there is no need to describe our movements while acting as advance sharp-shooters. It may aid those who never were in the army to explain a little. The high hill that protected our ravine from the enemy's guns was within easy rifle shot of the rebel forts and rifle pits. As soon as we reached the brow of the hill we were near enough to shoot them or be shot ourselves. The ground between the Union and rebel lines was everywhere badly broken by ravines and hills. When up out of the ravines a few scattered trees, once in awhile an old stump, now and then a little mound of earth or stone, and other things here and there served to give our sharp-shooters protection against the enemy's bullets. Without something to protect or some place to hide in, soldiers could live only a few brief moments that near to so many of the enemy's guns.

We advanced under such cover as we could find. After reaching the top of the main hill in our front each would select the best route he could find to advance. Then by dodging, running and creeping we would get as far forward as possible. Each of us would then select such cover as he could find, be it an old stump, a tree, or rock, or mound of earth, or best of all, a hole in the ground, and then lie there and watch and fire whenever an exposed enemy could be seen. Company A had hardly got upon the ground, when some of our sharp-eyed boys discovered that the most dangerous shots did not come from the continued and aimless firing from the rebel forts and rifle pits, but from a small band of rebels who had advanced in front of their works, and like us were acting as sharp-shooters. They had a position off to our right and at a point where the Union line was not advanced as near to the rebel works as with us. A small bunch of trees on high ground furnished them an excellent position. No doubt the shots from which Company D had suffered the most came from that quarter. As soon as discovered some of our boys slipped along a convenient ravine, ran off to the right far enough to uncover the hidden rebels, and with their trusty rifles ended all difficulty from that source. After this none of the enemy were seen outside of their fortified lines. The death of the two men of Company D was fully avenged by Company A.

Friday, May twenty-second, came to us as an ill-fated day. The day's early morning face was covered with blood. A rebel ball that had been fired high in air, probably an accidental discharge, in its downward fall, struck and killed a member of Company I while he was still asleep. He was lying beside his comrades who were awakened by the striking ball, but he who was struck never awoke again. As the morning sun cast its light over the field, our artillery, placed on the hill behind us, commenced a vigorous fire over our heads at the enemy. Through some fault in their manufacture or other cause, some of the shells burst on the way, resulting in wounding three men in our regiment and four in the Indiana Regiment which was beside us.

At nine o'clock official information was given, that in one hour the entire Union army would charge upon the rebel works. All necessary preparations were soon made. Each one carefully examined his gun to see that it was in proper condition. As a preliminary part of the contest the Union artillery along the entire line commenced firing upon the enemy's works. As the hour of ten came near to hand, every cannon upon our side was used to its utmost speed.

The rebel forts and breastworks were torn and riddled by the fierce cannonading. The rapid firing created a continuous roar of the terrific battle thunder. The fierce commotion shook the earth under our feet. Had the enemy been enclosed with solid walls of brick or stone, the fierce pounding they received would have torn such walls down and buried the inmates with the scattered fragments. Nothing but earthworks could have withstood such terrific firing. Thick walls of clay and sand will stand under a pounding that would knock those built of more solid material out of existence. Cannon balls penetrate and bury themselves in the soft walls made of earth, while if they strike those built of harder material, the parts displaced with each striking ball or bursting shell will be scattered far and wide.

At ten o'clock we started. The plan of the charge was for us to advance in solid column. That is, to march upon the armed enemy in the same form that a large procession on a peaceful parade would march up the street. This is a very awkward way for a large force to advance upon a strong and well fortified enemy. There is no chance to fire on our side while the enemy can all along the line direct his shots at the solid advancing column. Upon the other hand, if the attacking force is formed in line facing the enemy, each can, as he advances, fire at the enemy, whose fire must, on his side, be scattered along his entire front, and one ball can not hit more than one or two, while one properly directed into a solid column might disable twenty or more.

One reason why we advanced in solid column was because of the lay of the land. From the ravine held by us, an opening ran up between two hills on to the high ground immediately in front of one of the main rebel forts. The Thirty-third was given the advance. Company E was selected to head the regiment. Going up the ascent between the two hills not only brought us upon a level with and immediately in face of the rebel forts in our front, but also carried us across the main wagon road going through the rebel works and into the city of Vicksburg.

The plan of the attack is understood to have been: that the first troops up should cross this road and gain possession of the brow of the hill on the other side, and that the next regiment should turn to the right on the road and go in and take the rebel fort before the enemy could reload their guns. It must be remembered that the rebel works were not built upon a direct line, but made to conform with the crests of the chain of hills upon which they were built. Thus by going straight ahead in the direction we had taken, it would not only take us right past the front of the fort nearest to us but also bring us upon the brow of the same hill upon which the rebel works were built.

We went forward on the desperate charge. Company E nobly led the way. As the head of the column raised upon the brow of the hill and came in sight of the rebel line, the fearful storm, with all of its unbounded fury, burst upon our ranks. The first of the column was virtually swept away. Of all of Company E only one was left unharmed. All the rest of the company, who participated, were either killed or wounded.[5] Those who followed did not fare much better. It was a fearful storm. The enemy was well prepared for us. The heavy cannon were charged with monstrous loads of grape and canister and swept our lines with fearful effect. The enemy's infantry used their guns with all the vim of maddening fury. They not only used their rifles and muskets, but as we passed so near to them, the extra arms, consisting of double barreled shot guns heavily charged with buckshot were caught up and the contents poured into our ranks. How a single man ever went through that leaden storm and lived I do not know. At one point we passed a piece of ground that lay in such shape that the balls aimed at us from the top of the rebel works would strike the dusty ground of the well-trodden road over which we passed. The flying dust from each striking ball plainly told of the thickness of the leaden storm. I have seen many severe hail storms, and yet never passed through one where the frozen hail stones seemed to strike the ground thicker than did this leaden hail through which we were compelled to pass. It would seem to be impossible for a rabbit to run, or a bird to fly, through this fierce storm unharmed.

Many, many noble boys fell upon the deadly field. On we went, unheeding those who fell. I do not suppose that there was a single one in the advance of that fierce charge who expected to pass through it in safety. I did not. The only thing to do was to press on while we could. With others it was probably the same as with me. "I am not yet hit," was the thought that passed through my mind. With a fierce run, those of us who were not disabled reached the side of the hill to which we were going. Thus the rebel line was upon the inside and we in possession of the outside of the same range of hills.*

The following diagram will serve to give an idea of the situation under which the charge was made.

The advance had accomplished their share. We had passed across the road, drawn the enemy's fire, and gained the position which would enable us to at once jump over and into the rebel breastworks. Those who came after should have turned to the right as they struck the road in front of the nearest fort and rushed into it before the Confederates had time to reload. Instead of this they bore to the left, which carried them in our rear and away from instead of into the nearest part of the enemy's lines. A little farther on they, too, come up to another part of the enemy's fortifications, of which they took the outside the same as we had done. In truth, however, it was the entire division that did this. By the time our charge was ended all company and regimental organizations were destroyed. All were mingled together. No attempt to reform was thought of. Each held the ground they had taken. It made no difference to which regiment the soldiers by our side belonged. All mingled together. The Indiana and Illinois boys stood by each other like brothers.

*

NOTE—A further description of this charge will be given hereafter.

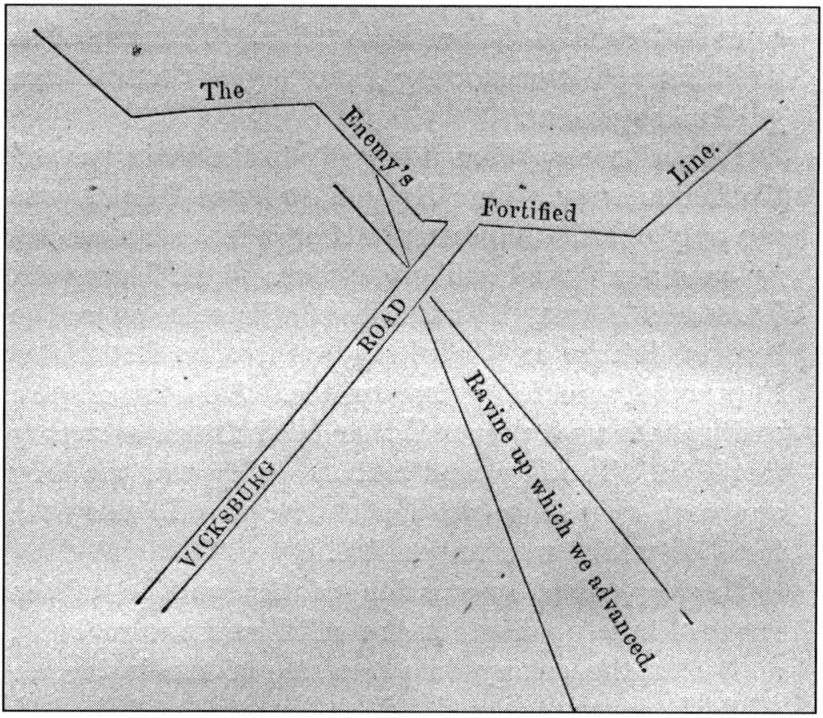

Attack route, Vicksburg. From Marshall, *Army Life.*

The golden opportunity, if there was one, was lost. My opinion is that there was no chance for us to have achieved a greater success than we did. We took the outside of the rebel works. We could not dislodge them; they could not drive us away. To make such a charge as we did in solid column out of a ravine never could be successful. We should have formed in line facing the enemy and then made a direct charge upon his works. A charge *en column* is always dangerous, having to advance up out of a ravine in the manner in which we did, and upon ground covered by a large part of the rebel lines made it doubly so. A better position for the slaughter of our entire command could not have been taken. That any of us lived through it was owing more to good fortune than good management.

This, of course, does not apply to the main part of the Union army. Our division, so far as I know, was the only one that entered the charge in such a cooped up manner. And still none were much better off. The trouble was, that the steep hills selected as the line of defense at Vicksburg, were, when fortified as they were, practically impassable. Soldiers can not easily climb up a perpendicular bank fifteen or twenty feet high. The deep and narrow valley was the only approach opened to the Union troops. To carry the fortified works was impossible.

Having gained possession of the outside of the range of hills upon which the rebel works were built, and with the enemy in possession of the inside, an all day's contest ensued. The depression of the hill upon our side made us nearly as good rifle pits as those the enemy had built on his side. Under such circumstances neither could fire with much effect upon the other. Our zealous marksmen with their trusty rifles were able to compel the enemy to continually seek safety by closely hiding in his works. While we held them thus closely, they could not greatly harm us. Had either side been supplied with hand grenades to throw over and burst in the other ranks the result would have been different. With such weapons we could, in fifteen minutes' time, have cleared the enemy's works. The trouble was we did not have any.

With all possible advantage, such a fierce hand to hand contest could not continue without considerable loss of life. Both sides suffered during the entire day.

At one time, for some unexplained reason, seemingly by mutual consent, all firing ceased in our immediate neighborhood. A number on each side rose up and looked over the dividing ground. In some cases words were exchanged between the opposing troops. Upon each side there were a number fully exposed, had the other desired to fire. I stood up with the others. At this moment I saw one rebel who, disregarding the open truce his comrades were so plainly maintaining, cowardly rose up behind his more honorable and braver comrades and took deliberate aim at us. He was not far away. Having been born in Illinois in the days when game was plenty, I was familiar enough with fire-arms to easily see where a gun was aimed. As I glanced over the barrel with a well-practiced eye I easily saw that it was correctly aimed at me. Quick as a flash I dropped to the ground, the murderous bullet passing over at the same time. There is no doubt but that when the bullet started I was directly in its path. Directly behind me, sitting on the ground, was Curtis of our company, who fell over insensible by the force of the bullet. Standing right behind him was a member of another regiment who was struck in the breast by the same bullet and badly wounded. Had I been the merest part of a second later in dropping out of its range the bullet, as intended, would have first struck me. In a moment Curtis revived. At first he placed his hand on the top of his head, saying: "I guess I am done for." In a short time more he was all right and then the most disgusted man in our army was Curtis when he found that he had been knocked insensible by a bullet that had not fairly touched him. It had passed just along the top of his head and the "wind jar" had struck him insensible, while the bullet had actually done no greater harm to him than to cut a few hairs off from the top of his head. But he was mad, nevertheless, and during the balance of the fight he was zealous in looking for good chances to fire at the enemy.

The sound of the first gun, of course, ended the spontaneous truce, and the soldiers on both sides at once dropped to cover and the fight continued as earnestly as before.

Colonel Lippincott, always the first to enter and the last to leave a fight, was beside us at this time. Now that there was nothing to be accomplished except to hold our ground, he became anxious to preserve all the soldiers possible, and exerted himself in having all keep under cover as much as they could. His wise counsel no doubt saved the lives of many of our soldiers. During the afternoon an unfortunate attempt was made to renew the charge with fresh troops. Mismanagement seemed to rule the day upon our part of the line. At first some officers came through bringing word that some fresh troops were coming up to assist us in a renewed attempt to take the rebel works. By passing through the winding ravines the orderlies who brought this information had no difficulty in reaching the ravine at the foot of the hill we were upon. It will be remembered that we held a place somewhat to the left of where we had advanced in the morning. Below us was a ravine of some considerable size. Back of the ravine—in front of it when looking toward the enemy—was another hill with high table ground at the top, of considerable width, the whole of which was easily swept by the guns of different parts of the enemy's fortified line.

We supposed that, of course, the new troops would pick their way under cover until they reached the valley held by us; then form, and at once run over into the rebel works. We were all ready to go with or even lead them if desired. To our great surprise, the first thing to claim our attention was the rebel artillery, which, from its different convenient forts, commenced a fierce firing toward the broad topped hill in our rear. Looking in that direction we saw the new troops advancing *on a walk* in solid line of battle. Not only were they within range of the enemy's artillery, but they were also within easy range of rebel rifles. The efforts of the officers seemed to be to keep the advancing troops in proper line. What they ought to have done, was to have come over the hill with a rush as soon as they came within range of the enemy's guns. The result can be easily imagined; in less time than it can be told, the Union line was broken to pieces and the scattered soldiers who were not shot, fell back to a place of safety.

Of all the sights I ever beheld, none were more heart-rending than to see those Union soldiers destroyed in such a useless and aimless manner. Many of our immediate comrades lay strewn upon the bloody field; ere the day's fight ends more of us will probably be sleeping with them the last sleep, and yet in the midst of all this, many exclamations of horror were heard among our thin ranks at the way the reserve force was brought up and shot down within our sight. As to who was responsible for the movement I did not know and have never cared to inquire. It is certain that there was not a private soldier with us who could not have gone back and more skillfully led up the troops that so vainly attempted to come to our aid. Had they been able to charge over the fatal hill from which they were driven back, they would then only have reached the valley or ravine already held by our troops. The place where they should have started from to make the proposed charge was never reached by them.

While it was difficult for us to gain this ravine in the first instance, still the command we had over some parts of the enemy's works and the possession of the advance ground we held gave us such advantage, that by some judicious movements between the numerous hills, this place could have been gained by the fresh troops without any great inconvenience or serious loss. With the aid of a brigade of fresh troops, it was the firm belief of our men who were holding the outside of the rebel hill, that they could, in a brief moment, have surmounted and taken the enemy's works in our front. With one part of the Confederate line in our possession, the whole would have at once fallen.

The reserve force was destroyed and driven back as stated, and we saw no more of them during the day. This left us to continue the battle alone. We continued, compelling the enemy to keep well under cover. We had no dinner during all of the long day, but no one thought of hunger. Many of us had been thoughtful enough to bring a canteen of water. This was valuable to moisten the parched lips of our wounded comrades. Those in command of soldiers should always see to it that their men are each provided with a canteen of water whenever a move of any kind is made. A canteen of water is not much to carry and no one can tell how valuable it may become.

All of our wounded who were not in a helpless condition were from time to time assisted back through the winding ravines. As night began to approach orders were passed along our lines for our troops to withdraw. As it grew dark we did so. Those in the most advanced and exposed conditions coming first. Sadly we wended our way back to the lines we had held before making our charge upon the rebel works of Vicksburg.

One of our most disgusted men was Lieutenant Dutton. He had been struck upon the leg by a small, nearly spent ball. The ball was not going with force enough to break the skin, but as it happened to strike upon a tender cord the injured part commenced to swell, and by the time we withdrew he could hardly use his foot, and was obliged to hobble along as best he could. To be so lame without any wound to show for it he thought disgusting.

The last one I was called upon to aid before leaving the bloody field, was Colonel Roe. He had been wounded in the early part of the charge and found protection from other rebel bullets in a deep ravine. He had not had a drop of water during all the long, tedious hours. My canteen, fortunately, still contained some, which refreshed him so that he was able to make his way back with us.

As the members of our little band, on our return, looked among its numbers—no formal roll-call was made—the strange fact appeared that after all we had gone through, Company A had lost only two men. Two of our noble boys, William Biggerstaff and Absalom Zartman, had made their last fight with us.[6] That more of us did not go with them on the journey to eternity is a wonder. How men could go through what we passed through this day and leave no more of their number on the field is one of the unexplained miracles of a battle field. How some live while others are killed in a battle, is something which no human reason can explain. While grateful to the Divine mercy by which our lives had been spared, we deeply mourned the loss of our noble boys who fell in the immortal charge upon Vicksburg on the 22d of May, 1863.

CHAPTER XIX.

THE SIEGE OF VICKSBURG.

May twenty-third, the day following the charge, we remained in support of our artillery, which kept up a slow fire on the rebel works.[1] During all of these lively times, since crossing the Mississippi, I had often been reminded that the ague was still staying with me. By the liberal use of quinine, and the exercise of some determination, I had gone with the company while there was so much active work to be done. Before the charge yesterday morning, two of us, as the least able to go, were designated by our company officers to remain with and guard the company knapsacks and effects we were obliged to leave in the ravine. Before ten o'clock arrived another of our boys became sick and I exchanged places with him and went while he stayed.

By Saturday afternoon it became apparent that no important move would be made for a few days, and Lieutenant Dutton, in command of the company, ordered me to the rear and into the doctor's care.

On Monday, May twenty-fifth, by agreement the firing ceased and both sides proceeded under a flag of truce to bury their dead who were killed during the assault of the twenty-second of May. The saddest part of all was to find some of our wounded boys still alive who had lain helpless upon the field since Friday noon. What they suffered during those three long days, helpless and uncared for, with the guns of both sides continually firing over them, can only be imagined; it never can be told.

The siege of Vicksburg may be said to have fairly commenced on Tuesday, May twenty-sixth. Our men commenced building rifle pits and to so fortify our line that the escape of the besieged enemy would be impossible. The day will never be forgotten by the members of Company A. The cooking, what little there is—is done in the rear and the food carried to the soldiers in the ravines held by them. When this day's box of cooked provisions for the company was brought in, Sergeant Besse went to it to take out and distribute the food. Just as he was bending over to do so, a large piece of artillery shell struck him, cutting off both his arms, one above, the other below, the elbow. This was one of the saddest things that ever happened in our company. He was a splendid young man and loved by the entire command. He was taken to the hospital in the rear.

Every thing possible was done for him. He lingered a week and died on Monday night and was buried, with soldier honors, on Tuesday, June second.

Each day work upon our line continued amidst the firing guns on both sides. It was a continued battle from day to day. While our loss was not large, still not a day passed without some of the Union soldiers being hit. Our experience in these ravines had shown that all places were alike dangerous. We had seen soldiers hit while asleep. Besse, when shot, was in what was thought to be the safest part of the ground occupied by our troops. Awake or asleep, it made no difference, the fatal bullet was liable to come at any moment.

With proper treatment I had checked the ague so as to feel fit for duty and rejoined the regiment on Wednesday, May twenty-seventh. The next morning our company went into the rifle pit to act as sharp-shooters. While there a rifle ball struck our brave comrade, Abram Myers, killing him instantly. He was standing beside me and fell over without saying a single word. The only mark upon him was a small bullet hole in his chin. It had probably glanced up into his brain or passed through and broken the spinal cord; at all events he fell over and never breathed again. His body was tenderly removed and given the honor of a soldier's burial.

Thursday evening I was detailed to act as provost guard for one week. Our duty was to guard the commissary stores just back of our army line. Those upon the sick list and not able to use a spade in the hard clay to advantage were selected for this duty. It became necessary for us to change quarters. In doing so we had to pass over a high hill on the top of which was the Vicksburg road bringing us in open view of the rebel fort in front and within range of their cannon. They opened fire upon us but did not do any damage. Our teamsters fully appreciated the position and after the first rebel gun was fired it was interesting to see how they would make full preparations and as the exposed place was reached whip the team into a dead run and thus cross the place of danger. With all their efforts the Confederates did not succeed in hitting a single team or wagon. Men on foot could, of course, skip across with even less danger.

On the fifth of June my week as provost guard expired. The regiment had come out of the works to rest and wash and I joined it before its return. In our works there is but little chance to wash, so that it becomes necessary to relieve the soldiers long enough at least once a week so that they can indulge in a bath. Much refreshed with the fresh water and a quiet rest under the trees, at night the regiment returned to its place in the front line.

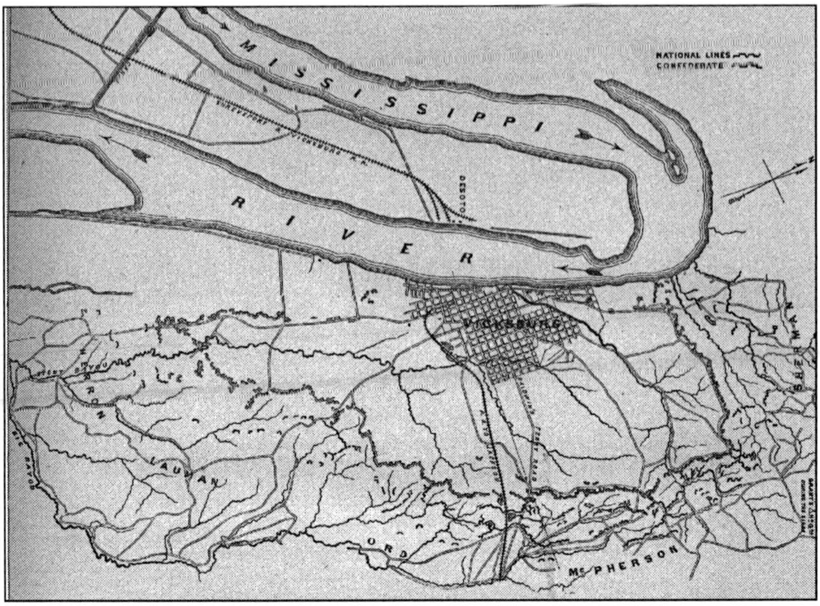

Map illustrating the Siege of Vicksburg. From Guernsey and Alden, *Harper's Pictorial History of the Civil War.*

Each succeeding day was now much like the preceding one. Work continued day and night on the rifle pits and the approaches to the enemy's lines. The first thing was to build a strong chain of rifle pits along our entire line around from the river above to the river below the rebel works of Vicksburg. This, with our gunboats to guard the river side, completely enclosed the entire Confederate army. After the rifle pits were built, including, of course, numerous places for our artillery, the approaches to the enemy's works were pushed forward with the utmost speed.

After the preliminary arrangements were completed our work was not seriously interrupted by the enemy. Our artillery, when properly placed, was too strong for the Confederate guns. In fact, the rebels soon learned to keep the artillery openings of their forts closed with bales of cotton. In such condition they could not fire at us. Now and then they would open some of the embrasures and commence firing. A few well-directed shots from our cannon would silence them. In the rifle pits we also had the advantage. The opposing lines were within easy rifle range of each other. Our riflemen were so alert that it was rare for a rebel gun to appear above their breastworks.

During the beginning of the siege the enemy got what satisfaction they could by firing during the night as a recompense for not being able to use their guns during the day. The result of this was that during the early part of the siege we were under fire day and night. Our rifle guards in front keeping up their work, and the rebel artillery in front and the Union artillery in our rear would both fire over us. Thus the thunder of the artillery would continue day and night. Men soon became accustomed to anything. With little practice, our soldiers learned to sleep right under the thundering cannon and just as soundly as though in their peaceful Northern homes.

As time wore on, by gradual process, without any formal agreement, we came to a mutual understanding with the Confederates in our front. After this, firing at night practically ceased on our part of the line. A sort of spontaneous truce would spring up each night. The way it worked was this:

As the sun went down the artillery would cease firing; after this the rifle firing would gradually grow less, and by the time daylight began to pass away it would cease entirely. A few minutes after the last shot was heard some one upon one side or the other would rise a little above his works for a second and then drop back out of sight. If no gun was fired upon either side, some soldier on the other side would repeat the action. If no gun was now heard, a soldier upon our side or the rebel side would openly stand up in sight of the opposite line, and his action would be replied to by one of his opponents. These two soldiers, Union and Confederate, would look across at each other a moment, and then, no firing being heard, one after another on each side would get up, and then we would have a line of Union sharp-shooters sitting upon the top of their works looking over at a line of Confederate soldiers sitting upon theirs, each within easy rifle range of the other. When this was done it was understood that all firing was over for the day. As it began to grow dark, each side would send a line of guards over in front of their works to remain during the night. These lines were often within a short distance of each other. As we had much work to do upon our new lines, the enemy was usually first ready, and it would be on his side that the movement for the night's truce was made. Thus, the first man to rise was usually on the rebel side. If for any reason we were not ready, the soldier who exposed himself for this purpose would not be fired at, but a gun would be fired in the air, which was notice for all to again seek protection. In the morning it was the same. If the guards who had advanced upon the open ground between the two opposing lines tarried longer than the other side desired, a warning gun would be fired in the air above them, but no one would be fired at until ample time had been given for all to return to their own works. Without any formal agreement, all of the Confederate soldiers in our front and all of ours seemed to fully understand the mutual arrangement. One of the strangest things connected with these nightly truces was that they were confined to different parts of the line. No agreement having been formally made, such a cessation of hostilities could only occur where each side had confidence in the enemy in his front. The Union troops at our immediate left and the rebel troops in their front never had any such understanding, and with them it was a continual fight, day and night. Thus a visitor, passing along the line in the evening, would see the strange contrast of Union and Confederate soldiers peacefully looking at each other at one point, and as he came to the next division, would find a fierce contest still raging.

The reason of this was found to be in the rebel soldiers in that part of the line. The Union soldiers at our left never had any confidence in the rebels in front of them. It was found that they were the most inferior and worthless soldiers in the rebel army. Only brave soldiers can be safely trusted. The rebel who fired the cowardly shot during the charge of the twenty-second of May, we learned, was one of the command that our comrades at our left would never trust. They were despised by the braver men of their own army as well as by us.

After the night guards of both sides returned to their own works each morning, firing would commence and continue all day. We were so well fortified that we suffered but little loss, but occasionally some would get hit. Lieutenant Higgins of Company K was shot through the face by a rifle bullet, while in our rifle pit, during the afternoon of June eighteenth, making an ugly wound.

During all of this time work had gone on swimmingly. The soil was most favorable for our plans. The clay was so firm that it could be safely mined through without the necessity of building any supporting walls. The deep ravines carried off all surface water, so that we were not troubled any from that source. As stated, our first work was to build a complete chain of forts and rifle pits. This done we commenced digging the approaches toward the enemy's works. These were governed by the lay of the land. The general plan was to run open ways as far toward the Confederate line as possible. These were run in such a direction that soldiers could pass along them and not be exposed to fire from the enemy's guns. By gradual approaches we were at last able to strike the foot of each hill upon which a rebel fort had been built. This point gained, we started straight in digging a tunnel directly under each fort.

A strange war incident is connected with our gaining possession of the desired ground, facing the main fort in front of our command. During the day, while the firing was going on, all of the rebels were back of their lines. Our men had, during the day, continued digging in the trenches. The work to do was so situated that the enemy could not well reach our workmen, besides, our men were so low down that the rebels could not see them without getting up and looking down over their best works. If a rebel attempted this during fighting hours, he was a dead man. The trenches we were making were approaching the objective point diagonally from each direction, and in such a manner that they would meet at a sharp angle, directly in front of the main rebel fort; that is, the two trenches would meet in a V shape with the point resting on the rebel hill. On Monday, June twenty-second, toward night, firing ceased in the manner before described and our night guards were sent out. Company A had often been sent out for this purpose. For some reason we were selected again at this time. The Confederates came out of their works at the same time. Our approaches had taken up so much of the space between the two lines that they had but a short distance to come and had their line in place before we got to our ground. Of course our guards were always thrown out far enough to enclose all of our works. Now there was some trouble. We went up in the advance, an engineer in charge of building the trenches came with us, and it was found that the line of rebel guards covered the ground upon which our two trenches were to unite. Their line cut off the point of our proposed trenches. We went up and formed a line right along with the rebel pickets. Still we were not advanced far enough. The Confederates were notified of the difficulty. The trenches had to be dug that night or else have a fight over the ground. If we could not do otherwise, each would return to his own lines, and then see what the result would be. That would, of course, mean a stubborn night fight. The rebels consulted over the matter, then called for our engineer, who went over the ground with them and marked the course our trenches would take. After this was done the Confederates called in their guards and placed them in such positions that our work could go on. It certainly was a strange war scene, for the opposing men of a desperate contest to meet and talk over the disputed ground just as though it was adjoining neighbors who had met in a friendly way to establish their line fence. For the Confederates to kindly withdraw their guards so as to give us room to build our approaches to a vital point of their line of defense was indeed remarkable. It certainly is entitled to record in the history of the great events of which it was an incident.

They fell back, and as we were to keep outside of our workmen we went with them. The plan of our guard was to form a chain by placing three men at each post, thus to prevent the necessity of relieving the guard during the night. One of the three must be on guard all the time so as to fully note every thing between him and the next post, which was only a short distance away. The enemy posted his guard the same way. There were six of us together, three Union and three Confederate guards. Instead of standing guard it was more of an evening's visit with them. Another amusing thing connected with our ditch occurred. The Confederate guard we were with remained near to the line marked for our trenches. The excavated earth had to be thrown toward them and us, too, as we were with them. It proved that they were just in the place where the loose dirt would be thrown. Either the Confederates and we must move farther over on the enemy's ground, or be buried up, or stop the work. We suggested that we move back. "Oh, that don't make any difference. You Yanks will soon have the place anyway," one of them said, and without bothering their officers, they and we moved forward far enough to give the men in the trenches room to finish their work.

Some of our boys who had tobacco shared with the rebel guards. Jack-knives and such things were traded and the situation talked over. So far as the condition of the Vicksburg armies was concerned, there was not much chance to speculate. The Confederate soldiers knew as well as we, that it was only a question of time when they would have to surrender. Consequently there was not much ground for discussion.

Although actually on the same ground we did not mix up with the rebels. Oh, no! That would not do. We were soldiers of opposing armies. Both sides were armed. We were part of opposing armies, still fighting. An imaginary line passed between us. They kept on their side, we remained on ours. Even when the pickets were moved back this order was not changed. The imaginary dividing line was, so to speak, taken up and carried farther on. In other words, as they moved back at our request, the ground over which the Union flag floated was extended and that under the Confederate flag lessened. If at any time a Confederate had been seen upon our side of the line he would have been captured and taken in as a prisoner of war. Had one of our boys strayed over to their side the enemy would have promptly disarmed and taken him inside of the rebel forts. The various phases of war are strange, indeed. Personally we had not the least feeling against the opposite guards with whom we were apparently simply having a pleasant evening visit. As representatives of causes at war with each other we were deadly enemies. We could smoke, and visit, and trade jack-knives with them to-night, and when tomorrow's sun arose be engaged in a deadly contest.

When my turn came I selected a good place, wrapped my blanket around me, leaving my comrades on guard and thus slept soundly with the armed rebel guards within ten feet of where I lay and slept.

For our guards to meet the enemy's guards on the picket line was a common occurrence during a part of the siege of Vicksburg. Toward the last, however, a change was made. Our approaches had been advanced so as to cover most of the open ground between the two fortified lines. There was no available space between our advanced trenches and the rebel works for night pickets to occupy. The condition of affairs suggested that the Confederate night guards should remain within their own works and ours within our advanced trenches. After this, there was no occasion for the night pickets to meet.

The work now to be accomplished was to undermine the rebel forts. Starting from our trenches which had been completed to the foot of the hill, upon which the fort was situated, we commenced to dig directly towards the enemy's works. Some protection against rebel bullets was now necessary. For this purpose huge rollers of sufficient length and from twelve to fifteen feet in diameter were made. These were made with wild cane stalks, such as are shipped from the South and used by the Northern boys for fishing poles. When the huge rollers were completed, a cannon ball could not pass through them. With hand spikes they would be slowly turned forward in advance of the work in the trench. After advancing a short distance into the hill, the thickness of the clay overhead became sufficient and then the open trench would be changed into a. tunnel. The object was to run the tunnel under the enemy's fort and then when all were ready, a wagon load of powder could be taken in and the fort blown out of existence. That is the idea. Time will tell how it succeeds.[2]

While the land forces, on our part of the line, ceased from firing during the night, the gun-boats and mortars upon the river side were the most active during the darkest hours. The mortars were used to fire huge shells high in the air at such an angle as to drop within the enclosed rebel lines. Many an evening hour, after our day's duties were performed, we would pass in our protected quarters telling stories, talking of home and watching the course of the huge shells our river sailors fired up over the city. The burning fuse would plainly mark its course. In clear moonlight nights we could sometimes see the dark body of the shell itself. Often a brilliant flash would tell us that the huge shell had burst in the air, throwing its scattered fragments far and wide, and bound to strike in a hundred different places as the pieces of iron fell to the ground. These bursting shells created brilliant fireworks for us to look at.

The firing, day after day, by the land forces became monotonous from its sameness. One would serve as descriptive of each day's proceedings. The record for the entire month runs about like this: Tuesday, June twenty-third. As soon as the night guards returned this morning, the enemy sent a few artillery shots at us. They were at once silenced. During the day our riflemen kept up a slow fire; the only return the enemy attempted was to occasionally fire a rifle in the air. It is not safe for them to raise up in their breastworks high enough to aim at us.

The next day our artillery commenced the day's work by opening a heavy fire upon the enemy's works. He attempted a reply, but after a few feeble efforts subsided.

At one o'clock on Thursday we were ordered to be ready to fall in. The occasion of this was that Logan was ready to blow up one of the rebel forts in his front. At three o'clock we fell into line to be ready to take advantage of any opportunity that offered. The fort, a small one, was blown up. The powder charge had not been large enough to have much effect upon the earth fort. The real purpose of the experiment, which was to ascertain the effect and determine the amount of powder needed for such a purpose in such ground, was accomplished. The next day there was some firing along the army line on our side. The Confederates seem to be completely discouraged. They can not open with a single gun but that half a dozen or more on our side will immediately reply. They keep their port-holes closed with bales of cotton most of the time.

Our mines and tunnels under the rebel forts are now nearly completed, reaching up to and under the rebel forts. We meet with but little difficulty. Why the enemy did not counter-mine against us by digging trenches and tunnels to cut us off is a wonder. We expected, of course, to meet some such difficulties. We have not, and everything is approaching completion in fine shape.

It is understood that General Grant has consented that the soldiers who first complete the excavations under an important rebel fort may try the experiment of blowing it up. As it is doubtful whether the besieged enemy will hold out until all are ready and the general blowup occurs, the soldiers are anxious to win in this race to be first.

Sunday, June twenty-eighth, it was announced that Logan's boys, who were just to our right, had won and were ready to blow up the large rebel fort in their front, which we called by the name of Fort Hill. We went into the rifle pits to be ready for any thing that might turn up. At the appointed time Logan blew the large fort into the air. Being so near to it we had a full view of the gigantic exhibition. The entire hill seemed to rise in the air. The more compact pieces of earth and all solid bodies in the fort, such as magazine timbers and artillery, and even men, were shot up into the air like rockets. The ground beneath our feet trembled as though a fierce earthquake was passing beneath us. As the force of the explosion ended, the loose earth and broken fragments of the destroyed fort fell back, into the opening made, a shapeless mass. Had it been so desired our soldiers could easily have gone upon the broken remains. Such was not the design, as other rebel works covered the ground of this one. The true course was to wait until all were ready, blow them all up and then the enemy would be powerless in our hands.

The first of July found every thing almost finished. We not only dug a tunnel under the rebel forts, but when there cut run-ways and side tunnels in every direction. This would enable us to place large quantities of powder under all parts of the works to be blown up. With pick and shovel, day and night, the work was pushed to completion. Every thing was to be ready by July fourth. It was. If our plans are consummated, we will witness the grandest explosion the world ever knew. But—

On Friday, July third, a flag of truce came out of the rebel lines. It was at once understood that it was brought by Confederate officers who came to treat for terms of surrender. At night we had no definite information as to what the result of the rebel mission had been, but it was generally thought that Pemberton had or would agree to terms of surrender.

A bright, pleasant and grand summer day opened to us on the morning of July 4, 1863. The first information that passed along our lines was, that terms of surrender had been given to the enemy. His acceptance was to be indicated by the Confederate soldiers coming out in front of their works, and stacking their arms and colors and returning unarmed to their own lines. They had been given until the hour of ten to do this. We were to hold our lines without firing until that hour.

No formal order was issued as to what our reception of them should be if they came out to surrender. But word was passed along the line to this effect: General Grant desires his soldiers not to make any loud demonstrations when the enemy surrenders.

Between nine and ten o'clock the Confederate soldiers came out, laid down their arms and colors and returned unarmed into their own lines as prisoners of war, and Vicksburg was ours.

The wonderful regard the Union soldiers had for their commander was shown in a manner never more vividly illustrated in the world's history. In response to Grant's simple request, the entire Union line looked on in silence, and saw the entire rebel army lay down its arms and surrender, without raising a single cheer of triumph over the famous victory they had achieved.

CHAPTER XX.

CHARGE UPON VICKSBURG.

The charge upon Vicksburg was described in an address delivered in Lockport on July 4, 1866.[1] As the journal from which this record is taken was drawn upon for part of that description, it can properly be given here:

Some of my friends have expressed a wish—perhaps most of you desire—that upon this occasion I should, as a soldier, give a brief picture of a battle scene. Such request I can not well disregard, yet I would prefer some more pleasant theme.

Standing here as I do today, and remembering that this is not only the anniversary of our National birth, but also that of a later event, how can I forget that three years ago I saw the surrender of Vicksburg. Those of us who were there can never forget the time when we stood upon the immortal hills of Vicksburg. We can never forget the trying hours, the dreary days of that long, desperate, eventful and bloody conflict. And the desperate charge of the twenty-second of May! It can never be forgotten. How can it be portrayed? Words would fail to describe the scene. One might as well try to paint on canvas the fearful sound of roaring thunder, as to at attempt to fully describe a battle.

Opposing armies lay confronting each other. The enemy was entrenched behind his seemingly invincible works. Nature's strongest fortifications had been improved, if improvement was possible, by the most elaborate engineering skill. The high and steep hills made most directions of approach impossible. Through deep and narrow defiles converging toward the city were the only possible roads; and at the end of each of these an absolute guard seemed to have been placed in the shape of some stubborn hill from the heights of which frowned the red-mouthed artillery of the rebel battlements. Where can a comparison be found? Could you, my friends, by soaring off on fairy wings to other worlds, imagine a scene where the arch fiend of evil having been defeated had retreated to the high realms of his own domains, and there, with all the skill of his destroying genius, had invented a castle, the only approach to which was through long, deep and narrow defiles, in which only a narrow column could advance; the whole length of which was swept by the most destroying machines that satanic ingenuity could invent, you will then have some impression of what we met on our attack upon Vicksburg.

Such as these were the conditions opposed to us upon that eventful morn of the twenty-second of May, when word was passed along the line that in one hour we would charge the enemy's works.

The emotions caused by this announcement can not be explained by any natural passion of the human heart. No fear nor dread seemed to be coursing through the soldier's veins. It was not false indifference nor wild, consuming, enthusiasm; all spoke calmly or thought quietly of the desperate contest in which they were soon to mingle, perhaps to die. Love tokens and short messages were left with the simple and seemingly almost indifferent request. "If I do not come back, send them home." Perhaps some of you, my friends, have some of those last tokens of remembrance; and all, yes, upon every heart throughout the land, there is, I know, impressed the token of kindest remembrance for some noble soldier who did not come back from the war. Neither could vaulting ambition nor lofty patriotism, nor wild, consuming religious zeal fully explain those strange emotions. It was as though some all-powerful spirit, like the ancient god of war, had come down and consumed the human hearts of those who once were men. Not brutalized them—no! no, indeed! All were tenderly kind to each other. And yet the fiery god had changed them so that all would march quietly on to death as though it was a higher aim to contribute to the fame of fiery Mars than to simply live a human life. A clear and pretty stream, clothed by imagination with human life and thoughts courses sweetly, quietly on its way; leaping down the rugged hills, playing across the fertile valleys, laughing over the blooming meadows and passing through the golden fields; running on, on toward the grand and beautiful lake, or boundless ocean, by which it will soon be swallowed up and consumed. It approaches the end with a quiet dread and solemn regret that its individuality is to be lost; yet it would not stay if it could, because it will soon form part of that greater and more magnificent grandeur beyond. Is it some strange, undefined emotion like this, that actuates the soldier when he so willingly marches on to death, and which the world, that through ages past, carelessly named the soldier's love of glory? Perhaps it is so; yet to those who judge according to the dictates of reason how strange it is. Although I once, to some extent, felt this strange spirit of war, yet as I am here today, in this pretty grove, surrounded by the cool, peaceful and pleasant influences of this hour, it all seems but as a dream, and I can understand it no more than those who never saw a battle field.

The fated hour of ten arrived. Officers of high rank seemed to have forgotten the usual words of military command. No formal commands of "Forward, march" were given. With drawn swords they started I forth, simply saying, "Boys, come on, follow me." A moment more, and the hurricane of ruin burst upon us, as with but one stroke of a sweeping, crushing tornado. Within, what a rapid seething sea of death were we now mingled. Even at this late day, I hardly dare, even in thought, to review that gory scene; nor could I do so if I would, for the terrible grandeur of that terrific conflict so completely drowned us with its sweeping fury, that we were not able to appreciate its destructive powers. The thunder roar of ponderous artillery; the fiery flash of bursting shell and powder blast; the singing, screeching rifle balls; the heavy sulphurous clouds of battle smoke that enveloped those murderous hills and deep valleys of the dead in one great, dark and mysterious sea of fire, and death, and ruin—all this combined was a scene of reality which could not be equaled except by transforming the scene of the first great battle refought, not beneath heaven's shining light, but amidst those clouds of darkness—darkness so dense that it could be felt—that reigns throughout the realms of eternal night; combine these two most graphic of human imaginations; combine the fury of heaven's battle with the darkness of eternal death, and you will then have a picture of the realities of a battle scene.

Deep ravines were filled with the bodies of fallen heroes, over which passed succeeding ranks. Still on, on pressed rank after rank until the rebel works were reached. Our comrades lay strewn upon the field behind us. Those left had not strength to surmount and hold the works upon which we were now contending. Both friend and foe were now upon the same range of hills, only separated by the narrow breastworks; and there, through all the hours of that livelong day, the terrible conflict continued, in a bitter hand-to-hand contest. Thus the fury raged until night mercifully threw its mantle of darkness over the gory scene and then each of the contending parties returned to the lines from which they advanced to commence that unparalleled conflict.

Such as these were the scenes through which we passed during our desperate charge upon Vicksburg. Then during those long hours of night, as I stood, watching upon the borders of that gory field from which we had returned, and where so many loved comrades lay in those dark hours of night, as the truth passed before me in thought, I could but almost doubt the realities of our own existence. Do we live in a world of truth, or within the dark realms of despair? Is this earth, or is it the place of eternal death? Were these beings before me men and brothers, or were they demons? Does God reign and are such things as these real? After many long and tedious days the glorious anniversary of our National birth returned, bringing with it, as it ever does, the glorious shout of victory. On the fourth of July, Vicksburg fell. Then the feeling of joy in every heart, could be equaled in depth only by the anguish of those former days. Then throughout our lines every soldier's heart rose up in praise to heaven in thanks, that the cause of justice and right had triumphed, and that we could once more believe in the reign of a just God.

A FEW INCIDENTS.

During the siege of Vicksburg many amusing incidents occurred.[2] A few will be recounted: One of our soldiers, an Irishman, was on guard one night in the front trenches. These advanced trenches ran so near to the enemy's line that the picket guards could at night, when it was still, talk across from their rifle pits. Discovering that Pat was easily annoyed, the rebel guards commenced blackguarding him. After plaguing him about other matters they began to tease him about the worthlessness of the shells fired from the Union mortars on the gun-boats. As a rule it must be admitted that these shells did no great damage. Among other things the rebels told Pat "that the only harm the shells have yet done is to kill two mules and lame one old woman." Just then through some strange accident a shell happened to come from the river dropping and bursting among Pat's tormentors, injuring two or three and causing the balance to scamper for dear life. Ere the sound of the bursting shell had died away the shrill voice of Pat was heard crying "There, ye infernal cusses, put that in ye haversack and chew it, will ye, ye blathering black guards."

Another about the mortar shells is this: When General Bowine [Bowen],[3] the Confederate officer, first came out under a flag of truce, on the third of July, to treat for terms of surrender, he suggested that hostilities cease during the negotiations. The Union officers readily acquiesced, but mentioned the difficulty of getting orders to the gun-boats in time. "Oh, well," he replied, "that is of no consequence; never mind the gun-boats; they never harm us any."

One day toward the end of the siege, one of the Confederates cried out to our soldiers, saying: "We are going to have a new General." "Ah, indeed," was the reply, "and who is he?" "General Starvation," coolly replied the comical

Maj. Gen. J. S. Bowen. From Johnson and Buel, *Battles and Leaders of the Civil War.*

Confederate soldier. To appreciate this it should be remembered that the rebel soldier was at the time almost starved; with him it was an empty stomach joke.

One of the incidents that was often repeated with lively jest and caused many an evening laugh to ring among those stubborn hills even during the darkest, dreariest and hardest days that we passed in trenches during the siege of Vicksburg, ran thus:

One night after Logan's men had worked their approach up to the foot of the rebel works in front of them, they discovered the Confederates at work inside bringing up bales of cotton to repair the damage our artillery had done to their works. Among the Union soldiers was a Yankee sailor who had been, as he claimed, "all over creation and the rest of the world," and who "could do a little of every thing, and a thing or two besides." He suggested the plan, which was quickly indorsed by his merry comrades, of trying to steal the cotton away from the rebels. The suggestion was promptly acted upon. Some grappling hooks with a long rope attached were procured. Placing the rope in the hands of his comrades so that they would be ready to give a sudden pull at the right time, the sailor boy soldier gave the grappling hooks the proper swing and cast them over the walls of the rebel fort. As the hooks struck inside he cried to the boys who had hold of the rope to "pull like h—ll" which of course they did with lively zeal. The first pull showed that the merry experiment had succeeded, a result they had hardly expected. The hook had evidently, actually caught a firm hold of a bale of cotton. The wild cry that arose from the bewildered and astonished rebels, and the tenacity with which they hung to their end of the line, showed that they were not well pleased to see their cotton climb over into the Union lines in that manner. Those nearest at hand had caught hold and were doing their best, but a band of terror stricken rebels made but poor show when pulling on a rope against twenty wild, enthusiastic Yankee boys. With a cry of triumph the Union soldiers brought the rope, grappling hooks, cotton and all over the walls of the rebel fort and down into the Union trench. Their surprise was now unbounded, to find that instead of a bale of cotton, as they supposed, they had actually caught and brought over a rebel lieutenant. The grappling hooks had firmly caught in his clothing and he was obliged to come over. He was hurt considerably, but with good and proper care at the hands of his captors soon recovered, but insists that he can not understand how he happens to be on our side of the line. This incident is insisted upon so strongly that we are almost compelled to believe that in the main it is true. There is only one matter of doubt:

It is well known that Logan's soldiers are not only famous fighters but also capital story tellers. It would be hard to find boys that do more fighting and have more fun than they. They also had a little story they told about Logan himself: When Vicksburg surrendered Logan was placed in charge of the city as post commander. Many of the citizens were in a starving condition, and were supported by our Government. Among the first to apply for aid was one of those haughty Southern ladies, who had not yet discovered that any one from the North deserved any other treatment than such as she had been accustomed to extend to her negro slaves. When her mission was told she was directed to the commissary quarters as the proper place to apply. But no, it was beneath her dignity to talk with any one of lower rank than a major-general. So she went to General Logan. She commenced by demanding, "Are you the man Logan?" Like all good fighting soldiers Logan is slow to anger, especially toward a woman, and although considerably surprised at the unladylike form of her question, assented. "Then," said she, "I want you to give me some provisions to pay for what your dirty soldiers have stolen." "The h— you do," the General replied. The sharp answer of the Northern commander seemed to penetrate her mind as a revelation. The new dispensation was beginning to open before her. For the first time in her life the idea penetrated her brain that all Northern men were not mud-sills to be treated as on a par with mere chattels. With an humble apology she withdrew and meekly went to the sergeant in charge of the commissary and received, as a donation, the necessary food to keep her and her family from starving. Logan's sharp, four word reply was repeated far and wide, and no doubt did more to educate the people hereabouts as to the respect due to Northern soldiers, than many more elaborate lessons would have done.

A slaveholder received his lesson at the hands of one of his own late slaves. The former slave had become a contraband, and had been enlisted in a colored regiment that had been formed since we came to the neighborhood of Vicksburg. He was on guard with orders not to let any citizen pass his line. Who should happen to be the first one to come up and attempt to pass but his old master. He was at the head of a little procession, consisting of himself and family, and remaining slaves. He came boldly up, walking as though the dignity of the entire world was upon his shoulders; and he feared, if a single unmeasured step was made, that some of it would drop off. "Halt, there! Halt, I say!" cried the colored soldier as his former master approached his beat. The haughty Southerner did not intend to be checked in his career by one of his own slaves, but continued to advance, and with a haughty wave of his hand, majestically exclaimed: "What do you mean by such impudence, Jim? Out of the way and let me pass." "But stop there," said soldier Jim. "I hab orders, massey, and you can no pass ober me now." The master continued as though determined not to further notice the obstruction. Jim became desperate, and with fixed bayonet started toward and would no doubt have run his former proud master through had he not appreciated the real condition of affairs in time and beat a hasty and inglorious retreat, leaving soldier Jim master of the situation. The owner may well have been astonished at Jim's course. There is something in these cases that is puzzling to us all. As a matter of fact the master is still the owner of Jim. Jim is as much his property as the other slaves he has under his control. The only difference is this: They are good, Jim is bad. His other slaves were kind and docile and remained with their master. Jim was naughty, ran away and became a contraband. For a man to be stopped upon the road by his own property, with a gun in its hands, and compelled to obey the orders given, is strange indeed. When and where will all of these puzzling things end?

While the prisoners were being paroled we frequently met and talked with some of them. I talked with one who was in New Orleans at the time General Butler was there and in command. Knowing the extreme bitterness existing against Butler among the Southern people, I suggested that it was probable that General Banks, who had succeeded General Butler, would prove more acceptable to people of New Orleans. The Confederate, who belonged to the laboring class, and who was a well-informed and intelligent one of their number, replied: "No, that is all a mistake. General Butler is the best man that ever ruled in New Orleans." I expressed surprise at this view from a Southern man, and asked: "Do not the people of the city complain that he ruled them with unnecessary severity?" He replied: "The rich complain, but the poor people do not. If he had not fed the poor people many of them would have starved." This Confederate was in New Orleans when it was taken by the Union troops, and left to join the Southern army during the time when Butler was there. Said he, with much earnestness: "I wish to God, I was back in New Orleans, and that General Butler was in command of the city." In reference to the rich class who so loudly complained, he said: "Butler is not as harsh as they are ugly." Such views as these from one who had fought us through all of the campaign and siege of Vicksburg, and who was now going to the interior of the Confederacy under parole to be afterward exchanged and then fight against us, seemed peculiar. If an opportunity had been given to all who wished to enter into an obligation not to again enter the rebel army, and they allowed to go to some part of the country within control of the Union army, no doubt but that many of the rank and file would gladly have embraced it. It seems that this should have been done.

Sometimes we meet some of the extreme class, those who talk of "fighting until the last dog is eaten and then dying in the last ditch." A squad of Confederates were talking with a number of Union soldiers. One of these extreme rebels became the prominent talker. The difficulty of a harmonious settlement at the end of the war was being discussed, during which the following dialogue occurred:

Confederate—"And what does it signify if you are successful and take all of our most important cities, what do you propose to do then?"

Union—"We simply purpose to do this; put down the rebellion; defeat your armies; and conquer the entire South if necessary to restore the Union."

Confederate—"But if we will not submit what can you do? You may burn our cities, desolate our land, yet we will never submit to be ruled by the Northern Yankees." Growing warmer: "No, never; we will die first. I would die a thousand times first. Yes, sir, I tell you I will die first. Die before I will yield an inch."

Union—In a pleasant good-natured tone it was replied: "My good fellow, are you not a little too fast? You have just taken an obligation not to fight again until duly exchanged. Do you not know that with a few surrenders like Vicksburg, the entire South will be under our control. If you wished to die for your cause what better place than this do you ever expect to find? Why did you not die in Vicksburg instead of surrendering before you were even wounded?" This was bringing the point a little too near home. For some reason his Confederate comrades commenced laughing loudly at his confusion, which caused him to beat a hasty retreat. As he departed, his Confederate comrades said: "Oh, yes, that is the way he always talked when there were no bullets flying near him. When actual danger came he dug a hole in the clay bank, crawled into it and never came out only when he was pulled out."

We will now bid farewell to all Vicksburg scenes by a brief reference to our commander. Grant is a wonderful man. He does not make mistakes. The volunteer soldiers of our army are not mere machines. The perceptions of the soldiers in the ranks, as to the correctness of military movements, are often equal if not superior to those of the officers in command. The actions of other officers are often criticized, and justly so. Every thing that Grant directs is right. His soldiers believe in him. In our private talk, among ourselves, I have never heard a single soldier speak in doubt of Grant.

He is one of the most modest and unpretending officers we have served under. His usual course is to ride along the line unattended save by one or two orderlies. These are necessary to carry orders if occasion arises. Officers of less rank often appear in grand style attended by a full staff and cavalry body-guard. By the careless way he goes among them, Grant evidently thinks that every Union soldier he meets is part of his body-guard. The soldiers seem to look upon him as a friendly partner of theirs; not as an arbitrary commander. As he passes by, the private soldiers feel as free to greet him as they would to address one of their neighbors when meeting him at home. "Good morning, General," "Pleasant day, General," and like expressions are the greetings he meets everywhere. The soldiers when meeting him are never embarrassed by the thought that they are talking to a great general. Upon the other hand the soldiers do not become as wildly enthusiastic when Grant passes the lines as they sometimes do with others. When General Grant passes, the entire line is not impelled to throw up their hats and greet him with thundering cheers. A pleasant salute to, and a good-natured nod from him, in return, seems more appropriate.

General Grant evidently has a wonderful memory. He seems to always know merely by memory where every part of his entire army, even down to the: smallest detachment or company, is or ought to be. He will ride along the long line of the army, apparently as an indifferent observer; yet he sees and notices everything. He seems to know and remember every regiment, and in fact every cannon, in his large army. If a single gun or regiment is out of position or can be better placed he sees it at once. An expert chess-player will look over a game and at once detect the weakness of even a pawn out of proper position. Grant seems to look over and comprehend all the complications of a battle field as easily as an expert player looks upon and comprehends a game of chess. But the great thing can be briefly told. One thing is the key to military success. It can be stated in a word. It is: Confidence. Grant's soldiers have full confidence in their commander.[4]

CHAPTER XXI.

AFTER THE SURRENDER.

The regiment started for Black River on Monday, July sixth.[1] I was not able to keep up, but reached the night camp after sundown.

At noon the next day the command started forward. Doctor Rex came along and ordered me to the hospital. I stayed and the regiment went on its journey. Not caring to stay at the over-crowded hospital at Black River, I took passage with a wagon train going back for supplies, and went to the convalescent camp at Vicksburg. With plenty of quinine and proper care of myself, and avoiding the army doctors, I soon had the ague again broken.

On the twenty-fourth of July the regiment returned and went into camp on the banks of the Mississippi River, two miles below the city of Vicksburg.

On the first day of August one division of our corps started down the river. On Sunday the chaplain of our regiment preached his farewell sermon.

WE JOIN THE ARMY OF THE GULF.

We received marching orders on August eighteenth. We are to go to New Orleans and join the Army of the Gulf. The next day we went on board the steamboat Gladiator,[2] and started toward our destination. We reached Natchez after dark and remained there until the next morning. At day-break on the twentieth we started again and arrived at Carrollton, near New Orleans, during the following night.

Friday, the twenty-first, we landed and camped at Carrollton. The next day we had a review by General Banks,[3] our new commander.

Carrollton, at this time of the year, is a pretty place.[4] We had a fine camp ground. In front of our camp was the famous shell road, much patronized by the people who have a good team to drive. People from New Orleans often show their horses upon it.

The orange and lemon trees, now full of fruit, are a pretty sight. These and other convenient trees, with a soft bed of grass underneath, furnish us elegant places to rest during the heat of the day.

Lake Pontchartrain, a few miles back of us, and to which accommodation trains on a narrow gauge railroad run, give us a splendid place for saltwater bathing.

Maj. Gen. Nathaniel P. Banks. Courtesy of the Library of Congress.

On the twenty-fourth we commenced, what is very unusual with us Western soldiers, a change guard around the camp ground.

Tuesday, the twenty-fifth, I went down to see the city of New Orleans. Looked at the St. Charles, City Hall, Clay's Monument, Jackson Square and monument, and other buildings and places of interest. The cleanliness of the city was notable. Along the gutters between the sidewalk and wagon track, on many of the streets, there was a running stream of fresh water. All filth is kept well swept off the streets. It is said that General Butler is the one who taught the people here how to keep their city clean and healthy.

On August twenty-ninth there was a general review of the Thirteenth Army Corps by General Banks and other officers. General Banks is one of the finest appearing and best looking officers in the army.

The first of September found us again under marching orders. We are to cross the river at New Orleans and go west on the railroad. On the third, we commenced shipping our supplies. With some others, I went in advance to guard the goods. We rode down to New Orleans and then crossed over to Algiers.

September fourth—Grant, Banks and other officers had a grand review of the troops at Carrollton. After the morning review was over, our regiment came down and crossed the Mississippi and went forward on the railroad. It took all of the next day to ship all of our supplies. After this was done, we who were guarding them, took the train and joined our command at Bayou Bouef at midnight.

We have a disagreeable camp ground at this place. The ground is low, wet and marshy. The tents we now have are what the soldiers call "dog tents." They consist simply of two pieces of canvas about seven feet in length by five or six in width. The two pieces are buttoned together, thrown over a center pole and the bottom sides fastened to the ground. Each soldier has half a tent. When put together and erected there is just about room enough for the two soldiers to crawl into them. All they are good for is to sleep in, and a poor excuse for even that.

Our mission at this place is to guard the railroad bridge over the bayou. It is a new bridge. The old one was burned by the rebels during a late raid made by them.

Wednesday, September ninth. Once more we are in the near neighborhood of strong enemy. They are a large force about twenty miles from us. It is

Lt. Gen. Richard Taylor. From Johnson and Buel, *Battles and Leaders of the Civil War.*

Dick Taylor's[5] band and said to be about fifteen thousand strong. Some things indicate that we have a good prospect for an early fight. Other reports say that Taylor has already commenced to retreat. Yesterday, five deserters from the rebel army came into our lines. They report that Taylor's force, many of whom are conscripts, are discouraged and tired of the war. This seems to be the feeling of the Southern citizens and soldiers upon this side of the Mississippi River. If free to act no doubt but that a large majority of them would now gladly come back into the Union.

CHAPTER XXII.

AT BRASHEAR CITY.

The enemy began to show a very threatening spirit toward our troops at Brashear City, nine miles further west.[1] On September eleventh we started at four o'clock in the morning and marched to that place. Brashear City is a small place of no great importance except as a military post. The river at this place is the dividing line between the Union and rebel armies. The enemy holds the west side and our troops the eastern side of the river. The river itself may be said to be entirely in our control. The enemy taking good care to keep out of range of our gunboats. Two small gunboats came up from Sabin Pass[2] this morning. They bring us news of a severe engagement between our boats and the rebel forts. Our side was whipped. Two boats were lost and others disabled.

Troops continued to arrive until quite a large force was assembled at Brashear City. General C. C. Washburne [Washburn],[3] who is to command, came in from New Orleans on September fifteenth. The prospect is good for an early forward movement.

While we were camped at Brashear City, with our lines on the east side of the river, and the enemy in possession of the country on the west side, a little band of five boys belonging to our brigade had an adventure that at the time attracted much attention. The five Union soldiers got possession of a skiff and crossed over to the enemy's side of the river. The object of this raid, it must be confessed, was to forage some chickens and pigs; everything in that line being very scarce on our side. Of course they had no right to thus venture into the

Southern Louisiana operations, 1863. From Guernsey and Alden, *Harper's Pictorial History of the Civil War.*

enemy's country. Considerable time had passed without success, and the prospect of leaving the rebel land as hungry as they came began staring them in the face. At last they discovered the smoke curling up from a fire in the woods near at hand. As they approached they were surprised to see that they had run upon a camp of some thirty Confederate cavalrymen. The rebels were evidently on a scouting expedition, and at the time when discovered by our boys, were busily engaged in cooking their dinner. The discovery brought the Union boys to a halt. What to do was the question. Should they retreat? No. The boys of the Thirteenth Army Corps never retreat. As for fighting that was equally out of the question. They only had one gun among them, and besides the odds were six to one against them. In this dilemma they decided that the only thing to do was to frighten the Confederates out of their position. It must be remembered that the little band was composed of five of the most reckless and daring men of our brigade. If they had not been so, they would not have thus ventured so far, merely for the chances of finding some fat chickens. The plan was no sooner suggested than acted upon. With a whoop and a yell like wild savages they dashed through the thick brush and right into the midst of the astonished rebels. The alarmed Confederates thought that Old Nick himself had come, and ran for dear life, leaving guns and sabers and even part of their horses in the possession of the wild Yankee boys. The reckless Union soldiers grabbed up the abandoned guns and fired rapidly, thus completing the Confederates' delusion that they were being attacked by a large force, and they continued their rapid retreat without once looking back, glad to escape with their lives. The dinner, consisting of some fat chickens and plump pigs about ready for eating, was also left by the departing rebels. With cool impudence the five reckless boys sat down and ate the dinner. After the dinner was disposed of, they gathered up the things they had captured and returned to camp. The large amount of plunder they brought in was conclusive evidence that their report of the adventure had not been exaggerated. But from the fact that in crossing the river in the first instance, they had violated positive military orders, they would no doubt have been highly commended and rewarded for their brilliant action.

On the twenty-first of September, recommendations favoring the promotion of Colonel Washburn of the Eighteenth Indiana Volunteers were circulated and largely signed by the men of our brigade. The boys signed freely saying that they "wanted to see one man promoted who did not get drunk."

Our rations since we came here have been very poor. For dinner we had baked beans, bread and coffee. An extra good meal for these times. Most of the time all the bread we have had is wormy and buggy hard tack, and the meat issued to us was actually rotten. This with some coffee is all we have had for days at a time. The soldiers think that this is rather severe while we are near ample means of transportation.

Our knapsacks were brought to us from New Orleans on September twenty-second. Since we have left Carrollton up to this time, all I have had with me consisted of one woolen blanket, one rubber blanket, one half of dog tent, one pair of trousers, one hat, one shirt, one pair of shoes and stockings—all in constant use—my canteen, haversack, gun and accoutrements and one small memorandum book. Many of my comrades are worse off than I, for the reason that their clothing has more holes in it than mine has. Now my knapsack has come, adding one coat, one shirt and one pair of socks to my list of clothing. Although yet limited it is about as much as I wish to carry on a march in this warm Southern climate.

Soldiers manage to be reasonably comfortable with a very limited amount of clothing to wear and bedding to sleep in. Two will join together. The moist ground they are often compelled to sleep upon is more dangerous to their health than storms from above. An experienced soldier will never lay down without first spreading his rubber blanket on the ground. At night two soldiers fasten their pieces of tents together, erect it, and then spread on the ground inside, one of the rubber blankets and upon this a woolen blanket and the bed is complete. With the other woolen and rubber blanket for a cover they sleep as snug as a bug in a rug.

Thursday, September twenty-fourth. We are now ordered to cross to the west side of the river, there to be ready to start forward on a foot march.[4] Some of the troops have already crossed. The transportation train of our brigade was sent over to-day.

The next morning we broke camp at six o'clock and crossed the river and camped upon the river bank.

Quite a lively excitement was created in part of the camp during our last night in Brashear City. About ten o'clock, after we had gone to sleep, we were awakened by a lively racket in the vicinity of a brigade camp next to ours. A large number engaged in shouting, yelling, screeching, running, commanding, halting and defying, all combined, created a scene and commotion that can be more easily imagined than described. Knowing that it was some of our soldiers, probably on a spree, I did not get up to see what the trouble was. This morning we learned the cause of the disturbance last night. There is, as is well known, considerable jealousy between the Western and Eastern soldiers. It is not deep enough to cause any serious anxiety, only extending far enough for each to wish to make the others the butt of any merry joke that may be devised. As soldiers are apt to do, the boys often carry their jokes to an extreme length. Since we have joined General Banks' army, a month ago, is the only time we have had Eastern soldiers for neighbors. Getting acquainted with them and becoming accustomed to their ways, is almost like the beginning of new camp life. The boys seem to be almost as much given to wild pranks now as when they first met in camp life at Camp Butler two years ago.

Last night a number of the wildest boys of our brigade determined to celebrate the last night in camp at this place with a spree at the "Yorkers'" expense. They easily ran our brigade guard as the night was dark and the weeds high. Each brigade has its own guard around its camp. Arming themselves with fire-brands, clods of dirt and other harmless weapons, our wild boys made a charge upon, and drove in the entire guard of the Eastern brigade camped near by. As was to be expected the officers of the brigade were much vexed at this proceeding. They soon had a number of companies in line and by quiet move in the dark night had the disturbers surrounded before they were aware of the movement. The boys, who had only come out for a wild spree, did not relish the idea of being captured, and thus raised a wild commotion, in the confusion of which most of them made good their escape. This was the first racket we heard last night.

The affair did not end here. The Eastern men were holding a few of the wild jokers under guard. Another plan was formed. Just as quiet was again restored and the Eastern soldiers retired to their night quarters their entire camp was thrown into the wildest confusion. They were alarmed in earnest this time. In wild dismay they broke from their tents, running fiercely and wildly, crying to their comrades to run for their lives. "They are going to shoot!" "There they come, run, run!" "They are going to fire upon us; see their cannon, run, run!" were the wild exclamations that came from the now thoroughly alarmed camp. Above the din could be heard, as was supposed, a battery of artillery as it went thundering at a fearful rate over the rough ground of an old cane-field. Added to this, a deep strong voice could be heard in the night air giving the commands: "To the right!" "Unlimber to the rear!" "Aim to the center of the camp" all of which were given in quick succession and with a master's decision. The Eastern soldiers fully believed that the wild Western boys had become maddened to absolute recklessness and had stolen some cannon and come to take revenge for the capture of their comrades

The New York boys are not cowards, and as soon as fully awake they charged upon and captured the cannon. The wild raiders, as was expected, dispersed without going to the extreme length of firing. When the Eastern boys came to look their capture over they were surprised and could not refrain from smiling at their needless alarm, when they found instead of deadly cannon, the boys of the First Brigade had only stolen the wheels of some old army wagons.

Such wild night pranks as these ought not to be indulged in. It seems impossible, however, to ever tame some of our wild boys. The only thing that will keep them within proper bounds is hard marches and heavy duty.

BRASHEAR CITY AND VICINITY.

Brashear City is situated on the Atchafalaya River and lies about seventy-five miles west of New Orleans, with which it is connected by a railroad.

It is a city of no great pretensions save as a military post. Such at least is its condition in these war times. Perhaps in times of peace it may be different. I think it is. To judge by its situation as connected with the surrounding country it ought to become, with prosperous times of peace, an important commercial town. It lies at the foot of the rich Teche Valley; is within easy communication with the Gulf of Mexico by water and with New Orleans by rail.

Only a small part of the land lying east of here is under cultivation. It is mostly wild, low, swampy land generally covered with a heavy growth of timber. In many places every tree is buried beneath an enormous load of Spanish moss. Why it is so called I do not know. It grows upon the limbs of the trees. It often covers the trees from the bottom to the top. It grows like small vines and hangs down from the limbs in thick clusters. It becomes so thick as to often smother large forest trees to death. Where it is the thickest it creates a "dismal swamp" indeed. It seems to thrive upon those trees that stand in the lowest ground and in swamps where water stands on the ground nearly the entire year. When a thick grove of large forest trees becomes thoroughly covered with this moss even the light of the sun can not penetrate the dense mass. At mid-day it is dark and dismal beneath such a grove. No one ever ventures far within them. They are full of vile reptiles. As for mosquitoes they are thick enough to darken the sun even were it upon an open prairie. The mosquitoes are night birds and as it is always night in these dark swamps, they are ready for business at all hours. Unless your delight is mosquitoes keep out of the Louisiana swamps.

Brashear City will have its little share to claim in the history of this war. After having remained under Federal control for a long time, and being made a depot for a large amount of military stores, it was recaptured by the Confederates. Thus it is one of the very few places that have been under the Confederate rule the second time. The recapture by the rebels was in June last.[5]

General Banks had withdrawn most of the Union troops to have them operate on the Mississippi. After the fall of Vicksburg and Port Hudson this place was speedily re-occupied by our troops. The enemy promptly withdrew without a battle. A strong fort is being built here by our troops. It is an easy city to strongly fortify. It is surrounded on three sides by water. The Achafalaya River bends around the north and west sides of the city. A deep bayou runs along the south side of the city, emptying into the river. The only open ground upon which to approach the city is on the east side. The fort is being built so as to fully cover this ground. When the fortifications are completed the place

Bayou Teche Campaign. From Guernsey and Alden, *Harper's Pictorial History of the Civil War.*

will be absolutely impregnable so far as any rebel force in this vicinity is concerned. Had the fort been built in time it would have saved our Government the heavy loss of property and the deep mortification it suffered last June when the Confederates came in and captured the city and a large amount of Government stores.

After our arrival here I was in a building that had been occupied by our Government prior to the rebel capture. In one room a mark on the wall showed that it had been used for "ordinance stores." This the rebels had completed so as to make it read: "Ordinance stores captured from the Yankee army June 27, 1863." Beneath this, at a later date, some one, evidently a young collegian, a sophomore at least, for want of something better to write, had added: "Avaunt, Old Jeff, Louisiana is redeemed." In other places less esthetic hands had covered the walls with such notes as this: "Vicksburg captured, July 4, 1863. Old Jeff, you are going to the devil."

CHAPTER XXIII.

MARCH UP THE TECHE VALLEY.

We remained in camp at West Brashear City, or as it is otherwise called, Berwick City, a week.

Saturday, October 3, 1863, saw us again on the road. We started at six o'clock in the morning and marched fifteen miles. Our present course is up the Teche River. The next day we marched ten miles. On Monday we started at six o'clock, and marched thirteen miles. Passed through Franklin during the forenoon. We started at seven o'clock, Tuesday, and marched thirteen miles and camped for the night on a prairie within four miles of New Ibeary.[1]

Our trip this far has been through a splendid country. We have passed rich prairie lands and some fine plantations. Most of the cultivated farms are, however, at present in a sorry condition, plainly showing the sad effects of war. The natural fertility of the soil is unequaled; cotton and sugar cane grow finely. The Teche Valley will some day be the home of a rich and prosperous people.

Our rations have improved very much. The rich prairies have furnished feed to fatten the cattle which are numerous enough to furnish us with fresh beef. In addition to this the country furnishes us with a liberal supply of chickens, green corn and beans, sweet potatoes and other vegetables. With these, added to the rations we brought with us, our soldiers are living high at this time.

We lay in camp Wednesday and started forward again at three P. M. Thursday, October eighth. We marched through New Ibeary and four miles farther and camped. The next morning we made arrangements to establish a permanent camp for a few days. News then came of trouble ahead and we immediately started forward and marched eleven miles. During the early part of the day we heard some artillery firing in our front. It is evidently considerable distance ahead. Had chicken and sweet potatoes, hard tack and coffee for breakfast, a cold lunch for dinner, and fresh beef, hard tack and coffee for supper. Boys are growing fat.

Saturday, October tenth.—We started at seven and marched twelve miles and camped in line of battle near Vermillionville[2] on the Vermillion bayou. The bridge across the stream at this place had been burned by the enemy and we crossed on a pontoon. It was at this place that the firing took place that we heard yesterday.

Our wagon trains started back for supplies on Sunday. We are to remain in camp a few days. Some of the boys of our brigade are becoming rather lawless. It is impossible to keep them in camp. This fine country is too tempting for them. They seem bound to get out of camp and roam at large over it. That the Confederates do not capture many of them is a wonder.

Monday, October twelfth.—We have a new experience to-day. This afternoon a regiment from Lawler's brigade was sent to guard our brigade, because, it is said, of the lawless action of some of our soldiers who persist in running at large all over the country.[3] During the next day the guard around our brigade was continued. A chain guard is placed entirely around our camp. The Fifty-fourth Indiana is performing the duty. The guard is more a matter of form than anything else. Our wild lads are on too good terms with the Indiana boys to have any trouble in running the guard whenever they wish. The Illinois and Indiana soldiers are always on friendly terms. And then half of our brigade are Indiana soldiers. Colonel Shunk[4] commanding our brigade, is ordered to report to New Orleans under arrest. As to just what the real cause of the trouble is about no one seems to know or care.

We remained in field camp at Vermillion bayou nine days. We drilled nearly every day. The open, smooth prairie makes it a splendid drill ground. Colonel Lippincott, while a good soldier in a battle, is not the most proficient drill-master. He usually makes some awkward blunders. One day during a brigade drill he got our regiment so badly mixed up, that he was obliged to have the regiment reform on the colors. Such blunders remind us of the days of Lockwood.

Tuesday, October twentieth.—We started forward again and marched twenty miles, and camped on the banks of the Teche River. The soil here is wonderful. We dug some sweet potatoes that had grown so large and solid that we had to cut them with an ax, a butcher's knife not being heavy enough for that purpose.

The next day we marched forward eight miles and then back three and stayed overnight at Leonville[5] on the Teche. On Thursday we marched twelve miles, camped on the east side of the Teche near Barr's Landing. Here we found General Burbridge[6] with his command, who had come on another road.

We remained at Barr's Landing until Tuesday, October twenty-seventh, and then started on a march back toward New Ibeary, to which place it is thought we are to return. Marched fifteen miles. The next day we marched fourteen miles, keeping on the east side of the Teche. We have found a better road than that taken during our advance. We save considerable in distance. On Thursday we marched twelve miles and crossed the river at St. Martinsville. The next day we marched through to New Ibeary.

We received two months' pay on November first. This time we settled for our second year's clothing. We are allowed a certain amount for clothing and all we draw is charged to us. The advantage of a warm climate where but little clothing is needed, was shown in our accounts. Although the amount allowed to us is not large, I found that my allowance exceeded the amount drawn by the sum of six dollars and ninety cents. This I received in money in addition to the two months' pay.

We made quite a stay in New Ibeary. Early on, Friday morning, November sixth, we were called out to meet an expected attack. We went out and formed in line of battle, and remained in that condition all day and night. The expected enemy did not arrive. The next day we heard of an engagement near Oppelonas.[7] One brigade of our troops was surprised and cut to pieces.

Sunday, November eighth.—We started at seven o'clock and marched twenty-five or twenty-eight miles. It was a hard day's march. We stopped for the night within three miles of Franklin. This looks some as though we were running away from the rebels. It would suit the boys better to stay and fight.

The next morning we started expecting to march all day, but when we got to Franklin we found a boat waiting for us. Embarked and sailed down to Berwick City. This ended our march up and down the Teche River valley.

CHAPTER XXIV.

TO TEXAS.

We soon learned that the reason for our hasty return from the Teche Valley, was to go to Texas by water.[1] The overland route was too long and difficult. Part of our brigade started on November twelfth. On the fourteenth we crossed over to Brashear City and took the cars and went to Algiers. General Washburn,[2] commander of our division, came with us.

The morning of November 15, 1863, was actively occupied by us in embarking in the steamship Clinton.[3]

General Washburn was with us directing and watching the work. This prevented much of the delay often incident to such occasions. In such times we are often much delayed by the confusion that always exists when there is no clear-headed person in control to direct the work.

Our wagons and mules had been brought along with the intention of taking them with us. After the wagons had been taken to pieces for the purpose of loading them, it was found that there was not room enough on the boat and we were obliged to leave them. This we much regret, as we have always found insufficient transportation for supplies the greatest drawback we have to contend with.

General Washburn and staff, and part of the Eighteenth Indiana sailed with us on the Clinton. Most of the field and staff officers brought their horses with them. These with the few mules we brought crowded all of the space that was available for animals on the boat.

After every thing else was loaded the men went on board. The boat was badly crowded. The rule seemed to be to crowd the soldiers in the odd places where nothing else could be put. There was hardly standing room. In fact General Washburn and Colonel Bailey, the ranking officer of our brigade present, had to use every effort to find room to crowd the men in even standing. "Crowd up, crowd up a little more, boys," said Washburn. "There will be plenty of room when we get started." The boys liked Washburn's plain, blunt, Western ways and did the best they could to comply. At the same time some of them seemed to doubt the boat being any larger when at sea than it is when lying at the wharf at Algiers. At last it was announced that the last man had walked the plank and that all were on board. In a moment more we heard a sudden, stentorian voice commanding: "Stand by there, my hearties," "Heave off." Looking up, we saw that the fat, jolly, old sea captain of the Clinton had mounted the top of the wheel house, and was giving the necessary commands to start us on our journey to Texas.

Our voyage from Algiers and New Orleans down the lower Mississippi was pleasant and interesting; considering our crowded condition it was as delightful a ride as we could expect. As we leave New Orleans, the country along the shore of the river appears to have a rich, fertile and productive soil. Many pleasant and cheerful residences could be seen upon the banks of the river, surrounded with many evidences that they were the homes of a contented and prosperous people. Having been under the protection of a strong Government ever since the capture of New Orleans by General Butler the country along the lower Mississippi shows evidence of thrift and industry that contrasts happily with most of which we have seen since we came to this Southern clime.

As we were sailing down the river notice was given for the men to fill all their canteens, camp kettles, coffee-pots and every thing else that would answer for the purpose, with fresh water. All of the water casks were carefully refilled. This was done, so that when we came upon the briny water of the gulf, we should start across the salt water with the fullest supply possible of fresh water. With the large number of soldiers on board this was a wise forethought. The time has often been when careful anticipation like this would have prevented some of the severest hardships of our soldier life. Provident attention to such things as these, by a commanding officer, does more to win the confidence and respect of his soldiers than the most imposing reviews or grandest exhibitions of military style. Washburn's strong point is in the care he takes of his soldiers. After he arrived at Brashear City there was not any more rotten provisions issued to us. General Washburn is extremely popular with his soldiers.

It was a lively, jolly crowd of soldier boys that went down the Mississippi on this trip. The general health was never better. To see the healthy, fat, jolly crowd now sailing down the Mississippi in the Clinton no one would have believed that they were the same tired, worn-out and sick men that were a few months ago seen in the trenches in front of Vicksburg. Most of our soldiers are between eighteen and twenty-three years of age. Boys of that age with good health and plenty to eat recuperate with wonderful rapidity. We start for Texas in the best of health and spirits.

As night came on, we commenced to think of how we were to sleep. Many laughable scenes ensued. Room to lie down in was out of the question. It had been found difficult to get the men all on board even when all were standing. The boys doubled and twisted themselves up into the smallest possible compass. They supported each other sitting thick together. In places they were even piled on the top of each other. Thus crowded most of them slept part of the night. A hungry soldier can eat and a tired one can sleep under almost any circumstances and with little regard to the fitness of things. Mere propriety and beauty are at a discount with a soldier when he is at dinner, asleep or in a fight.

As we neared the mouth of the river it was thought that, owing to the darkness of the night, the crowded condition of our boat, and the shallow water, that it would be unsafe to attempt to pass the bars at the mouth of the river; so we anchored at midnight and lay still until the next morning.

At early daylight on the morning of the sixteenth, we hove anchor and sailed through one of the narrow channels that form the Delta of the Mississippi. To our right, as we passed out, was a lighthouse standing upon a forlorn sand bar. The only building near it was one little hut, intended, I suppose, for the use of those whose duty it was to take care of the lighthouse.

The deep, rich and fertile soil, with its smiling foliage that greeted us from each bank of the river as we came down from New Orleans has here given place to barren tracts of sand.

I found that the mouth of the river was different from the idea I had formed of it. I had supposed, from the descriptions I had read, that the Mississippi at the mouth was broken by two or three large islands, and that the water ran into the gulf through about three large channels. But as it appeared to me this morning, from the deck of the steamer where I was standing, the river is broken by a host of little islands and sand bars, and runs into the gulf through a large number of narrow and crooked courses.

Passing through one of the numerous channels at the mouth of the Mississippi, we were soon sailing quickly and pleasantly upon the broad waters of the Gulf of Mexico. With interest we watched the receding shores, as one after another, this and then that particular point was lost to us until the last, boldest point, in its turn, also became enveloped and finally lost in the undefined mist of the distant shore. We looked again, carefully and long, but all is lost. The water around us and the sky above is all that can now be seen. For the first time in my life I am out of sight of land, sailing upon the deep, deep sea. Most of the young soldiers, my comrades, being farmer boys like myself, were also taking their first ride over deep and boundless waters.

A strange and weird feeling comes over one, as he, for the first time in his life, realizes that he is out of sight of land and upon the waters of the deep sea, with nothing to cling to but the frail craft that carries him above the rolling deep. All there is near him is the thin air above and the hardly less yielding water beneath him. In case of danger he might as well attempt to cling to a handful of one as the other. A handful of water, like that of air, would melt in his grasp. Cast adrift here how helpless one would be. A feeling of man's insignificance, compared with nature's greatness, comes over us. Many unbidden thoughts will come to him, who, thus for the first time, realizes that he is upon the deep sea and out of sight of land.

After the young soldiers became accustomed to the situation many queer questions were asked and wild speculations indulged in. The chances of a jolly fit of seasickness received a fair share of consideration. The sea was calm and smooth, the ship ran as even as does a boat upon the smooth waters of a placid river. When night came only a very few had experienced any symptoms of seasickness, and many of the boys seemed disappointed in not being as sick as they had expected to be. Many of them became convinced that the stories of seasickness, deep waves and plunging boats, were merely sailor yarns, and protested that sailing upon the deep waters of the gulf was fully as pleasant as riding upon the smooth water of the land protected rivers. Those of experience smiled to themselves and kept their peace. They could well wait for time, and the treacherous gulf, to answer the objection; that sailing upon the deep waters was too smooth and monotonous to be pleasant.

During the night a sharp wind sprung up. In a short time the waves were running high. The boat plunged up and down over them. Many of the soldiers were soon sick enough to satisfy old ocean for the fun they had laughing at him during the day, because he could not make them sick. Seasickness is peculiar. It shakes some up lively, others it leaves alone. Never having been seasick myself I will not attempt to explain what it is.

As the sun rose the next morning and smiled down upon the sea, the stormy elements quieted down, and in a few hours the ship was again running as smooth as though we were sailing along the shores of some pleasant river. Thus passed our second day at sea. During the night following the wind came up again, but not as strong as during the preceding night. We had a pleasant all night sail.

At an early hour on the morning of the eighteenth we came in sight of the rough sand bars of the Texas coast. We kept within a few miles of land during the remainder of our voyage. The wind that had come up during the night had continued to increase and gave us a rough sea during the entire day. Many of the boys were quite seasick.

Just an hour before sundown we arrived at the Pass of Point Isabel, at the mouth of the Rio Grande River. We attempted to go through the pass into the harbor but failed. We ran aground on a sand bar. Signals were given for some of the boats in the harbor to come and help us through. None came, and the attempt to get through was abandoned. With much difficulty the ship was backed off the sand bar, and we considered ourselves fortunate in being once more on the open sea, and safely away from the dangerous shores. When daylight came the next morning it found us sailing up and down the shore off Point Isabel. We were also within sight of the shores of Mexico. Along the coast of Mexico, just below the mouth of the Rio Grande, we saw a large fleet of steam and sail vessels, all flying the French flag. We were informed that it was part of Louis Napoleon's French fleet, sent over by him to capture and subjugate unhappy and sad-fated Mexico. The American soldiers do not look with pleasure upon the French flag, floating in American waters for such a purpose. The views of all were expressed by one of our soldiers, in a manner more forcible than elegant. Shaking his fist at the French fleet, he exclaimed: "When Uncle Sam and his old woman get over their little family difficulty, you French rascals want to be right lively in getting out of that melon patch."

Returning as near as possible to Point Isabel, we fired signal guns in hopes of receiving some assistance from the harbor, but the sea was so rough that none would venture out to us. Toward night, when the tide was at its highest, we again attempted to enter the harbor. In doing so we ran aground twice. It was a critical time for us. The huge breakers were tearing fiercely. I have read graphic accounts of the huge wave breakers of the Texas coast, but none gave me more than a faint idea of such fierce ones as those by which we were now surrounded. Lying in the fierce waves in front of us, as stern evidence of what our fate might be, were the broken wrecks of the fated vessels that had a few days previously attempted to pass through those terrible breakers. It was plain that no boat could live long in such a fearful place. The staunchest boat ever made would soon be pounded to pieces if aground among those fierce waves. The first sand bar upon which we were caught was a small one and we got off from it in a short time. We hardly had time, however, to take a free breath when we struck again. This time it seemed certain that we caught for keeps; it was a serious affair. The vessel ran aground hard and fast. We worked hard and earnestly. Still we stuck fast. The tide had turned. Soon it would run down and then we would be left helpless, and by morning nothing but the broken pieces of our staunch boat would be left. The front half of the boat was fast on the bar. Every thing movable was carried to the back part of the vessel. The plan was to lighten the front half of the ship so that it would raise while the rear half settled down in the deeper water. After every thing of weight that could be moved had been carried back, and just at the critical moment the soldiers on the boat were asked to move to the rear. They did so effectively. How the large crowd of soldiers hung on to the stern of the boat as they did without some falling overboard is a mystery. The last effort was made, the boat trembled for a moment, and then commenced to move, and then after once getting a start continued with increased speed and slid back with a huge splash into the deep water. We were fortunate, indeed. In ten minutes more the tide would have receded enough to have made our escape impossible.

At one time the captain of the boat almost gave up all hope of being able to save his ship. He earnestly declared that he "would never be caught in such a place again." When the darkest moment came he sadly commenced a remark which if ended as intended when he commenced speaking, would have shown the boat of but little value at that moment. Said he, "I would not give one hundred-thousand dollars for this boat." The amount mentioned was more than it was worth standing at the wharf at New Orleans. At first he only intended to say one hundred dollars. Even, although badly alarmed, the old fellow could not withstand the sailor's propensity to joke a little. It was second nature with him. We were fast and in critical danger for about two hours. During all of this time the boys remained cool and unexcited. They bantered each other on the prospect of attempting to swim ashore when the vessel broke to pieces, bargained with the little ship boys for lemons, invented practical jokes upon each other, and in many ways showed an indifference to danger that was hardly allowable even in soldiers. A load of citizen passengers on the boat under such circumstances would have been well-nigh frantic with fear. I sometimes think that the greatest difficulty in dealing with soldiers who have been in much service would be to convince them of actual danger. A few were somewhat alarmed. I noticed one who was of the class called "no account soldiers." They are usually drunk while in camp and hiding when there is a fight on hand. He became so frightened that he would have thrown himself overboard in the mad attempt to swim ashore, had he not been caught by some of his comrades.

The reckless indifference of the soldiers proved of great advantage to us. The captain of the boat afterward declared that he had never seen such coolness in time of danger, and that it was owing to the promptness with which the soldiers complied with every request made, that enabled him to save the ship. When at last the announcement was made "She moves, we are now safe," a loud and hearty cheer arose from the entire command. This plainly showed that beneath the seeming indifference the soldiers really had a deep sense of the danger they were in, and were truly delighted when it was past.

As soon as we were free from the dangerous sand bar we ran out into the deep water to remain overnight. We had barely time to get fairly anchored and make some arrangements to sleep when the weather-wise sea captain gave us notice to secure everything, as "in a few minutes it will be blowing about four points." What a "four points" wind was we did not know but took the captain's advice and proceeded to secure our guns, knapsacks and other soldier's fixings. We were none too soon. In a few moments a hard wind storm with some rain burst upon us. It was impossible for the boat to lay at anchor. The only course of safety was to run out into the deep sea. This we did. During the night the storm raged with tremendous fury. The water of the deep sea was whipped into rolling mountains of white foam. The angry waves raged as though they would tear asunder the bottom of the mighty deep. The ship careened and rocked from side to side until at times the bottom seemed uppermost; and then jump and plunge headlong, up and down over the huge mountain waves as though it would turn a somersault and dive down to the bottom of the unfathomable sea. Huge waves often threw great sheets of water over the highest part of the deck. The mad sea covered the entire boat with the white foam it spit forth in its fearful rage. Each deep opening between the gigantic waves resembled a mouth of boundless width and unmeasured depths opened to swallow us. It appeared as though some monster of gigantic size had come that could devour our entire boat and its contents at one effort as easily as a huge ox swallows a mouthful of corn. A fierce, wild animal foaming with rage is a fearful sight to behold. An angry sea like this can well be compared with an angry wild beast of gigantic size. It seemed as though the entire gulf had been changed into some fierce animal of destruction as large as the entire sea and with unnumbered mouths of monstrous size, each foaming with rage and opened to devour us. Such as this is a storm at sea on the Gulf of Mexico. After passing through one we never questioned the wildest story the most gifted sailor could relate.

By the next morning the fury of the wild storm had abated and we again returned as near as possible to Pass Isabel, anchored, raised the flag, Union down, in signal of distress, and fired signal guns to those in the harbor. These are the sailors' signals of distress. The intention was to try by every means to get some assistance, at least a pilot from the harbor. If not successful in doing so before night the conclusion was that it would be necessary to start back for New Orleans. This we would have to do to save the horses and mules we had on board. We have not fresh water enough to keep them alive much longer. In fact they have had but little water since we left the Mississippi. This and the rough sea we have had has almost ruined the horses and mules. A rough sea is a hard place for live animals. During the fierce storm they were, by the plunging of the boat, thrown against the sides of the vessel with a crash that seemed as though it would break every bone in their bodies. They were badly injured. Some were killed. During the forenoon the dead horses were drawn up and thrown overboard. One horse was thrown over which became revived by the salt water of the sea, and for a while struggled with the waves and kept swimming around the ship. Of course it was impossible to fish him out and some of the boys out of pity shot him.

No assistance came from Point Isabel, but during the afternoon a small messenger boat arrived from some other quarter, bringing us orders to effect a landing at some other point. We hove anchor and sailed up the coast of Texas, and the next morning found us anchored off Aransas Inlet.

Our rations upon this voyage, as they usually are upon such occasions, were very poor. About all we have had to live upon was hard tack and some coffee. One reason why we did not fare better was because there were no conveniences on board to cook for our large number. For the first part of our trip the boat cooks charged us at the rate of about ten cents per quart for hot water to make our coffee. The objection to this was the well known fact that the Government paid for all the fuel, and liberal wages to everyone connected with the boat. Even at the rate charged we could not get more than half enough. When hardships are unavoidable our soldiers pass through them without a murmur. In this case they could see neither necessity nor justice. The matter was soon settled. Some of the soldiers, without consulting their company officers, went into the cabin and reported the facts to General Washburne. He took the matter in hand at once. The trade in warm water immediately ceased. During the balance of our cruise upon the gulf we had an opportunity of making all the coffee we wanted twice a day. Soldiers can live very well with plenty of coffee and hard tack. Still it is not a very rich diet. The reaction of the first seasickness had given the boys huge appetites. Before our voyage upon the gulf was ended they were hungry as wolves.

After an understanding was had with the boat officials, by closing the money making part of their business, and, no doubt, a little plain talk from

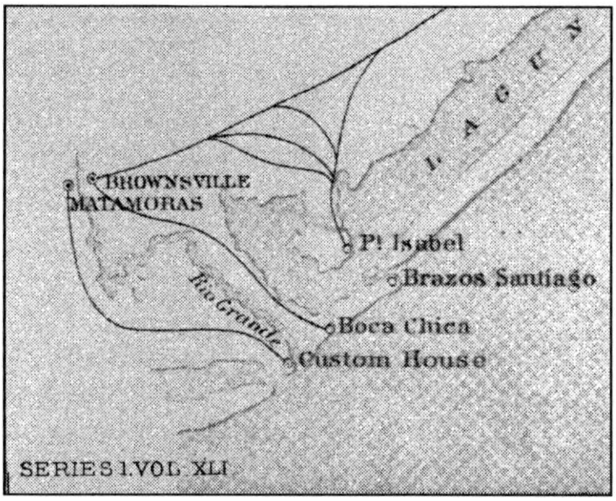

Banks's Expedition to the Texas Gulf Coast. From *War of the Rebellion: Official Records.*

General Washburne, they became quite clever and we managed to get some meat cooked now and then. The commissary, with the assistance of the boat cooks, one day cooked a full barrel of pork. Some of the boys met the commissary before the cooked meat was issued. When he was asked to explain why he had let some of it go before it was regularly issued, he declared that the "hungry soldiers were determined to eat either the pork or the commissary sergeant and I preferred to let them eat the pork." The explanation was accepted as satisfactory.

During the forenoon of Saturday, November twenty-first, the steamboat Warren[4] came along-side and part of the men and horses were transferred to her from the Clinton. This was done to lighten the latter boat so that she could pass up the channel. Our company went on board the Warren. We then sailed up the inlet. At first we stopped a short time at Mustang Island. Here we found part of our brigade. Those who came on the St. Mary[5] from Algiers. When they first landed, they had a short engagement with a force of rebels they found entrenched here. Our boys captured their entire force and their fortifications and arms. These consisted of two small forts mounting three heavy guns, and its garrison of one hundred men and all of their camp equipage, small arms, ammunition and supplies. We stopped a short time without landing and then sailed up and landed upon the southwestern end of St. Joseph's Island.

We had considerable difficulty in landing. The pier and wharf had been destroyed. The water was so shallow that we could not reach the shore with the Warren. The only way for us to land was to use the ship's small rowboats. They were put to work and the men were soon ashore. Then came the horses and mules. How shall we manage them? Anyone can easily see that it will be quite a difficult matter to carry heavy horses and nimble legged mules ashore in small rowboats. Apparently the only way is to lay them on their backs, in the little boat, with their feet tied as the countrywoman ties her chicken's legs when moving. Then only one animal could be taken at a time. Should a mule's legs get loose, look out. He would have a boat all to himself in short order. Evidently there is lots of fun ahead. But in the army, things very difficult in theory become exceedingly simple in practice. In this case the soldiers promptly solved all difficulty by drawing the horses and mules up out of the ship and throwing them overboard without ceremony. They struck the water in every shape. Some would strike head first. Others would turn a complete somersault in going down. The fall from the place on the boat where they were thrown off to the water was some twenty feet. Each would be plunged out of sight in the deep water. Although they were somewhat stunned and confused, none were seriously disabled. After floating around the ship awhile some of the men in rowboats would lead them to the land and they would swim ashore. All except one were saved. One horse became bewildered, or else disgusted with such treatment, and concluded to desert from Uncle Sam's service, and started up the bay swimming toward the land of rebeldom. The last I saw of him he was a mile or more distant. Some of the men started after him in a small rowboat. I do not know whether he was captured or not.

More difficulty was found in getting the artillery ashore than anything else. The cannon could not be thrown overboard as the horses had been. This difficulty was also soon solved. We lashed some of the small boats together, laid some planks across, and in this manner made a flat boat of sufficient strength, and soon run all of our artillery on shore. Then came our supplies and ammunition, all of which required much hard work to land. Even the small boats could only reach within several rods of the shore. The water ran very shallow and we carried every thing over water from two to six inches deep for considerable distance. The artillery wheels could run without injury to the gun in water of that depth, but nearly every thing else had to be carried by hand. We all took hold and worked until midnight, when our task was finished, and during the balance of the night for the first time we slept upon the land of Texas.

CHAPTER XXV.

FIRST MARCH IN TEXAS.

The southern or southwestern end of St. Joseph's Island, where we landed, consists mainly of rough ridges of sand.[1] While the rough, wild scenery could hardly be called beautiful, still it was quite interesting to us who were not accustomed to see the moving hills of drifting sand. When I looked upon the white sand rolling and drifting up into huge piles I thought of the grand old times we used to sometimes have in our Northern clime as we went dancing with the merry bells over the huge drifts and through the flying snow. Sweet remembrances of the past! When will those happy times be ours again?

There is some level land on the island, upon which considerable wild grass grows. Although the soil is light, some of it might repay cultivation. It is evidently better adapted for grazing purposes than any other. The coast along the gulf is very rough. The breakers run very high with a never-ending roar, sounding, sounding, day after day and night after night as though old ocean was determined at all hours to remind us of his unbounded power. It would be madness to attempt to land anywhere upon the gulf shore. The only way is to sail up some channel or inlet before attempting to land. The large bay between the island and the main land furnishes a safe harbor for any number of vessels. The only difficulty is in reaching it. The channel running from the gulf to the bay is narrow and its water shallow. It is not deep enough to admit large gulf steamers.

Sunday, November twenty-second, was fully occupied by the balance of our troops in landing on St. Joseph's Island.

By Monday morning we were in marching and fighting condition. The entire command were safely on shore. Our artillery and every thing had been landed in good shape. More ammunition was issued so that each soldier now had eighty rounds. Three days' rations of hard tack and coffee were issued. This was all the rations we had on shore. Having no transportation we will have to carry every thing and thus march heavily loaded.

The water of the bay is warm and the bathing splendid. At our Northern homes we would look for ice instead of outdoor bathing at this season of the year.

At Monday noon the order to "Fall in" was given and we at once started for the northern end of the island. We kept along the gulf shore all day. Upon the beach were many rare and curious shells. The boys would pick them up, admire them and then throw them away again. Cartridges instead of things of mere beauty are carried by soldiers in time of war, with an armed enemy near at hand.

By keeping upon the wet sand near the water of the gulf, we had a smooth, hard and splendid road the entire distance. We reached the northern end of the island at a late hour of the night, pretty well tired out by our heavy loads and rapid marching.

When our advance first reached the extreme end of the island they overtook a band of Confederates who were rapidly crossing the channel over to Matagorda Island.[2] A slight skirmish ensued but the enemy soon passed out of range of our guns upon the other shore. One rebel officer was shot. None of our men were hit.

A chain of islands ran along the entire gulf coast of this part of Texas. Evidently the gulf shore was, ages ago, along what is now the mainland. Some sudden convulsion of nature probably produced such an effect that the subsequent accretions of sand and earth washed up was deposited along the shore some distance in the gulf from the former water-line. These accretions in time formed into solid land, leaving a space for water, between it and the former shore. At different points the action of the waves and water has kept a channel open through the later-formed land. This leaves the new land in the form of long islands, running parallel with the mainland, from which they are separated by the water lying between them. Thus there is a chain of long islands running along the shore and a chain of bays running along between the islands and the mainland. These inland waters are convenient to the light boats that run through them, along the Texas shore. None but large ocean steamers or ships can venture far upon the waters of the gulf. Small sail and row-boats can run through the inland waters with as much safety as if in the best protected harbor.

We lay in camp on the northern part of St. Joseph's Island, during the following day. We found oysters in the bay and gathered what we wanted to eat. We are also feasting on venison. The island is well stocked with deer. They have been troubled so little lately that they have increased to a large number and are quite easily approached to within good rifle distance. As we marched up the island many deer were seen on our route. Some even came near enough to fall

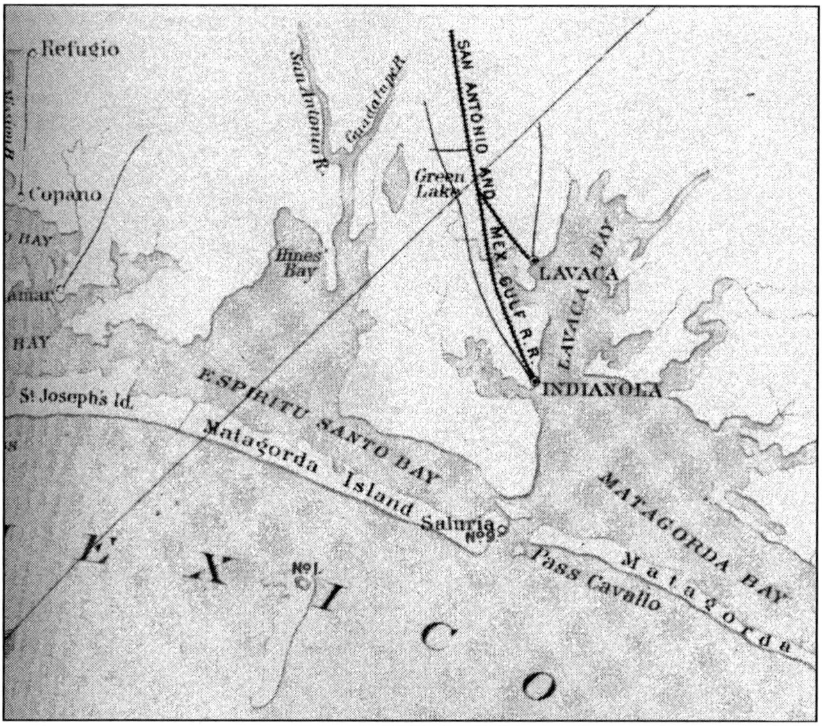

The Thirty-third Illinois operations in Texas. From *War of the Rebellion: Official Records.*

a victim to the soldiers' rifles. As we remained in camp all day our hunters went over the island and had a grand time hunting. Nearly a hundred deer were brought in to our brigade during the day.

During the daytime of Wednesday our regiment remained at the same place. Other troops were busy crossing over to Matagorda Island. During our stay here we had a tedious time. We had our first experience of a Texas "norther." A steady wind will commence coming down from the far-off snow-covered mountains in the north and northwest, and the result is a fierce, cold, penetrating storm. We were exposed to the full blast of the severe storm for nearly two full days. Our little skeleton tents furnished but little protection against the fierce driving storm of cold wind, freezing rain and frozen sleet. To make our exposed condition worse, there was no wood within reach upon the island. It was with much difficulty that we found fuel enough to cook a little meat and make some coffee. Our only resource for fuel was to gather "buffalo chips." (A large number of cattle had at one time fed upon the island.) The boys used their rubber blankets as baskets to bring in the fuel. The best we could do was to make a fire to half cook our rations; fire enough to keep warm was out of the question. A roaring camp-fire, such as we used to have in the woods of Missouri would have been a rare luxury to us.

The fury of the storm had somewhat abated by the night of November twenty-fifth. At sundown we put every thing in readiness to cross over to the other island. Two small boats were the only means we had of crossing. Our regiment waited for its turn, and it was nearly ten o'clock at night when we got over.

We marched forward immediately. For the first two miles we kept along the gulf shore, and then turned off so as to pass through the sand hills to the prairie back of them. The boys supposed that this was a signal for camping, and commenced picking up drift wood, of which there happened to be a reasonable supply on the beach. After we had passed through the sand hills to the open prairie, instead of camping, as was expected, we again turned to the right and continued marching up toward the northern end of the island. Still thinking this was only to find a better place to camp, the soldiers continued to carry their backloads of wood in hopes that a halt would soon be made. As we continued our onward course they soon became tired of such an addition to their previously heavy load, and first one, then another, with an exclamation of disgust, threw away their load of wood amidst the laughter of their more plucky comrades, who declared that they "would never pick up anything that they could not carry." Each quarter of a mile was expected to end our march, but we went on, on, tramping along our night's march, and others in turn became still more disgusted and threw down their extra loads amidst the still louder laughter of their merry comrades. Some, more stubborn still, disdained to throw theirs away, and the wood they had picked up was actually carried full eight miles during a night march, and the plucky soldiers used the fuel they had carried so far to make some coffee with when we finally camped.

At last, toward one o'clock, we stopped for the balance of the night. Forming in line of battle, knowing that there was an armed force of the enemy somewhere in our front, we wrapped our blankets around us, lay down upon the prairie grass and were soon sleeping as soundly and happily as though we had never heard of war, nor ever learned what hardship was. Many a one who never saw a line of battle formed, tired and exhausted with business affairs or disease, as he lies sleepless upon his warm and soft bed at home, would willingly make almost any sacrifice if he could sleep as soundly as we did this night, and have upon many a more critical occasion.

At an early hour Thursday, November twenty-sixth, we were awakened from our quiet slumbers by the drum's earnest and sudden reveille. Ere the echoing sound had passed away, the command, "Fall in," was given. Without stopping for a mouthful of breakfast the lines were formed and the column put in motion. We marched forward as rapidly as possible. At eleven o'clock we came to a halt, long enough to make some coffee. We carry coffee boilers and other light cooking utensils with us. Some ground coffee, ready for the coffee-pot, will always be found in the prudent soldier's haversack. Dry drift-wood was convenient, and some coffee was soon made. A combined breakfast and dinner, consisting of coffee and hard tack was soon disposed of and we pushed forward again.

Matagorda Island seems to be the home of large droves of cattle. We saw a number of droves during our day's march. They were extremely wild. Every little while we would come near to a drove that were quietly grazing, or resting upon the rich grass. At our approach they would spring up and raise their shaggy heads, crowned with the huge, unsightly horns of the Texas cattle, look upon us in wonder, and then gallop away in grand disorder for half a mile or more. Moved by some strange and unexplained cause, the entire drove, in a body, like a company of soldiers, would at once wheel around, stop and gaze upon us as though inclined to come back and get acquainted, and then, as if suddenly repenting of such folly, again turn and scamper away faster than before, and thus continue until they disappeared from sight behind some distant and friendly knoll.

We also started up many droves of beautiful deer. They would scamper and circle around us, gazing in innocent bewilderment and strange surprise at the moving column of soldiers, until some horseman would dash among and fire at them. The little deer would then, terror-stricken, scamper away in wild dismay, to join the drove of cattle that was by this time fast disappearing beyond the distant hills. The deer upon this island seemed to have learned to keep near a drove of the almost equally wild cattle for protection. Probably many generations of deer have been accustomed to run among a drove of cattle to escape from wolves and other animals of prey, until it has become natural for them to run to a drove of cattle when they are alarmed.

During the afternoon a few Confederate soldiers occasionally appeared in view, for a brief moment, and then suddenly disappeared beyond the distant sand hills. But little attention was paid to them. A brief announcement that "some rebels are in sight" was passed along the line, and no further notice given them. But few of our soldiers took any pains to even look at them. A nice flock of deer, capering over the sand hills attracted more attention. It appears natural for old soldiers to think that scattering bands of an enemy are beneath their notice. Besides this, experience had told us that whenever we were approaching an armed enemy, we would frequently see a band of his scouts who would always take good care to run away before our advance came within gunshot of them. The occasional appearance of a band of rebels in our front simply meant, as we knew to be the fact, that an armed force of the enemy was still in our front and upon the same island with us. Their brief appearance to view, and promptness in running away also assured us that we had not yet reached the place they had selected to stand and contest our further advance. Thus seeing a few of the armed enemy now and then, instead of indicating danger, was an assurance that for the present there was none.

At night we stopped within ten miles of the northern end of the island. The northern end of the island is at the entrance to Matagorda Bay. That is the place where we expect to find the enemy in force and probably strongly fortified. If strong enough they may venture out to meet us. Thus it is important for us to be well on guard from this time on.

This day's march can be classed among the hardest marches we have in our varied career ever made. Many of our toughest soldiers became exhausted and were compelled to dropout of the ranks and lie down upon the sand, unable to proceed farther. As they revived they would resume their wearied step and follow after us. During the entire night the tired soldiers continued straggling into camp, one after another. Some were so completely exhausted that they had to seek the warm side of some friendly sand hill for an all night's rest, and were unable to reach their regiments until the next morning.

I think that we here reached the climax of bad drinking water. How it would be possible to find any worse drinking water than that we were obliged to use at this place, I can not imagine. Two small sink holes contained all the fresh water we could find. The supply was small and it soon became so muddy that by dipping up a cupful and letting it settle, there would be a full quarter of an inch of mud and filth at the bottom. The water was fairly alive. Unless the cup was held very still the active insects caught in it would never let the water settle. The two places that were the only source of our supply were in the center of a piece of low, marshy ground. Having been the place where large droves of thirsty cattle had, during many years, concentrated when attempting to quench their thirst, it had all of the advantages of an old barnyard, coloring and scenting the water in a beautiful manner. Straining this water was of but little use. That only removed the larger kind of insects and the solid pieces of filth. Boiling the water improved it very much, and when the coffee was made pretty strong, it was considered quite passable. As much as we could, we boiled the water and let it settle and cool over night. When impure water must be used, it should be first boiled. A wise commander will always teach his soldiers to boil impure water before drinking it. If all would do this, an army could pass through a country infected with malaria without the entire command being laid low with fever. With our large force and limited conveniences, it was on this hurried occasion impossible to boil enough water to go round. When it came to filling canteens with the water just as it could be dipped up, muck, insects and filth altogether, without time enough to let it settle, even the veterans of the Thirteenth Army Corps admitted that it was "rather tough."

CHAPTER XXVI.

ADVANCE UPON, AND CAPTURE OF FORT ESPARENZA.

On the morning of Friday, November 27, 1863, after a light breakfast, consisting of coffee and hard tack, in heavy marching condition and in complete fighting order, we moved forward.[1] We had some expectations of seeing an armed enemy ere the sun went down. We knew that they were yet upon the same island with us, and that only ten short miles were left between us and its northern end, which we were now approaching. Our real expectations, however, were to find that the enemy had evacuated. The morning was so dark and foggy that the most prominent objects could be discovered only with the greatest difficulty.

Our brigade marched upon the beach along the gulf, and under cover of the sand hills. Had occasion arisen, these sand hills could, at once, have been extemporized into splendid breastworks. Another brigade, under command of General Ransom,[2] moved forward upon the opposite side of the island.

Our mounted men, consisting mostly of staff and artillery officers, displayed commendable energy in examining the neighboring hills, to guard against a surprise by the enemy. General Washburne, with field glass in hand, was foremost in scrutinizing every suspicious place.

We went forward in this manner until we reached the light-house at Pass Cavallo, without meeting anything of greater interest than a brief view of a few mounted Confederates, who quickly passed out of sight. The heavy fog still made it difficult to see far in advance. The lighthouse is at the northeast corner of Matagorda Island. Having reached this point, we made a halt to rest, and also in order to give Ransom time to come up and join us.

Among other things we found here, worthy of note, was an old fort, said to have been built by the soldiers under General Taylor, during the Mexican War. It had been built of sand and earth, and was now nearly beaten down by the wind and storms that have year after year passed over it; still the walls retained their form enough to plainly show the plan of the fort. Whether or not any guns were ever mounted in it, I can not say.

Having reached Pass Cavallo,[3] at the northern part of the island, and finding no enemy in sight, our previous impression that the Confederates would evacuate before we could reach them was apparently realized.

When we started forward we were soon convinced of our error. Instead of having reached the end of the island, as it appeared when we struck Pass Cavallo, we now found that the long, narrow island, which had thus far continued with so much uniformity in a direct course, here turned suddenly to the west, forming almost a direct angle to our left. It is one of the strange freaks that nature sometimes delights to surprise us with. A little observation shows us how nature's work at this place was done. When the new land of the long island lying parallel with the shore of the main land was formed by the sand washed from the deep gulf, it left at this point a bay of considerable width between the island and main shore. The wind and tide then carried more sand through the opening now known as Pass Cavallo and deposited it so as to build up and leave Matagorda Island with an L shaped end as we now find it.

After waiting for Ransom's brigade to come up and join our left we moved forward and soon found ourselves in front of the still occupied rebel works. A lively little skirmish now ensued. Our skirmishers advanced near enough to exchange rifle shots with the rebels in their outer works. A few shots of heavy

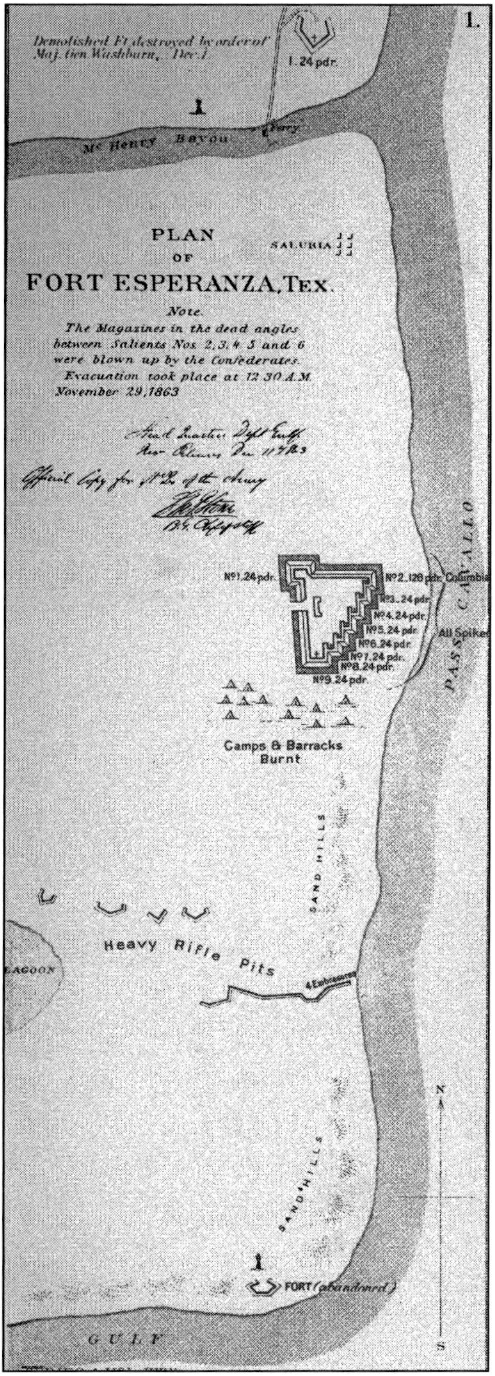

Fort Esperanza on the Texas Gulf Coast. From *War of the Rebellion: Official Records.*

artillery coming from beyond, claimed our attention and we soon distinguished the elaborate walls of a strong and complete rebel fort. The foggy mist had now commenced to raise and we soon saw that we were in front of more complete and much stronger fortifications than we had expected to find. Not being ready to commence a general engagement we moved back out of range of the cannon on the rebel fort and camped for the night. Company G of our regiment being in advance as skirmishers were the most exposed part of our force. Some of their men were wounded. Lieutenant Fifer,[4] of our regiment, who, acting as aid for General Washburne, was shot, a rifle ball striking him in the breast. He had gone to the front with orders for the skirmishers to retreat. Thus fell a young, brave and accomplished officer, nobly doing his duty.

It was nearly sundown when we fell back. By this time the atmosphere had cleared. When there are no cloudy mists or fogs around, the atmosphere here is much clearer than that to which we Northern soldiers have been accustomed. It now became so clear that we could easily see the balls as they were fired toward us from the largest cannon in the rebel fort. Even the smaller cannon balls and shell could often be seen as they flew through the air. It was an interesting sight. Looking at the rebel gun, we could see the smoke that told of a discharge, before the vibrating sound reached us. Coming toward us, we could see and watch the course of the eleven and thirteen inch shell and ball. The trained eyes of our Western soldiers easily determined the exact course of the approaching missile, and quickly running to the right and left, gave them a good wide and unobstructed way of passage. The time from its discharge until it reached our line was sufficient for us to run a safe distance. This was the first battle we were ever in where we could easily watch and dodge the cannon balls fired at us. The shell fired from the fort fell short or burst on the way. It was only solid shot that they could easily send far enough to reach our line. The balls that came generally were so well spent that they would commence striking the level prairie as they came in our neighborhood. At the first strike the ball would bound high in air, again to strike and then go on striking and bounding to the end of its career. Some coming with less force, would have passed through the striking and leaping play before reaching our line, and then continue rolling easily and slowly along on the ground. Apparently one of these slowly rolling balls could easily have been stopped with a touch of a soldier's boot, but no one attempted it. All of our soldiers well knew of the deceptive, hidden force in a heavy rolling cannon ball. Near us were pieces of light wood,

George H. Fifer. From Elliott and Way, *History of the Thirty-Third Regiment Illinois Veteran Volunteer Infantry in the Civil War.*

washed up long ago by the waves, and seasoned through many a Southern summer's sun. The soldiers took pieces of this light wood ten or twenty feet in length and over a foot in thickness, and watching an opportunity, threw them in front of some of the balls that moved so slowly that apparently a touch of the hand would stop them. The seemingly dead ball would strike with fierce force, sending the timber far out of the way, and the ball itself bound high in air, and then go bounding on its way with renewed life. A few such examples were sufficient to warn the soldiers not to touch a live cannon ball, no matter how slowly it was moving. The hidden force of an almost dead cannon ball is supposed to consist in this: while moving forward slowly it is also spinning around rapidly. An obstruction brings into action the force of the unnoticed rotary motion. If the obstruction struck is of sufficient resisting power, the ball will fly rapidly in some other direction than that of its direct course.

During our little engagement we had an opportunity to witness the difference between experienced and raw troops. Most of the soldiers with us were those who had seen hard service. Among them, however, were two Maine regiments, and this was the first time they were ever under fire. One of the regiments, fresh from the pine tree State, was immediately to the left of ours. As the skirmish line only was engaged, all we had to do was to remain in line of battle behind our skirmishers and watch the progress of the slight and irregular contest. The fresh soldiers had been so eager to see what was going on that it was with difficulty that their line had been called to a halt at the desired place. In fact their part of the line was pressed rather farther ahead than ours. When the heavy rebel cannon first opened, the balls were directed to their part of the line. The Maine boys now skipped back right lively. They did not even stop when in line with us but fell back a few rods further where a raise in the ground gave them good protection. The heavy guns were now turned so as to bear on our part of the line. The old soldiers who had become familiar to the fire of artillery during the siege of Vicksburg and elsewhere, remained coolly within sight of the rebel works, trying to ascertain their exact position and strength, and to judge of their distance by watching the fire of their guns, promptly stepping to one side or the other when a ball came directly toward them. With a time-piece in hand one watched the smoke that told of the discharge, and another the ball and thus determined the number of seconds after it left the gun before it struck. As the enemy had only two guns bearing on us of sufficient caliber to send a ball thus far, it was quite easy to notice their fire and evade the balls when necessary. Loading and firing such large cannon is a slow and tedious proceeding. Old soldiers, in an open field, do not much fear heavy artillery. In fact our men kept their eyes wide open watching, and had more fear that some of the enemy's sharp-shooters might creep along the sand hills and up within rifle range, than they had of the eleven inch cannon in the rebel fort.

Mention of the action of the Maine boys is given only as an illustration, not to censure them. They were not demoralized, but fell back in good order and reformed with their line of battle intact. I have no reason to doubt their bravery. A number of balls came near to them, and a shell struck a building, in their immediate neighborhood, bursting with a terrific explosion. As they were not engaged at the time it was the wiser course to fall back out of range of the rebel cannon. In fact, it was but a short time afterward, when Major Elliott, chief of out brigade staff, came up and ordered our regiment to also fall back out of range of the strongest rebel guns. We did so. The day was now spent, and all there was now to do was to pass the night as best we could.

The engagement for the day was over. After our skirmish line was withdrawn no one was hurt. After that the enemy turned his entire attention to our line. It was a funny fight. The rebels would fire away and our boys would play. We could plainly see them and every move they made; and they could just as plainly see us and every motion we made. All kinds of bantering motions were made by our soldiers toward the enemy. The most absurd was to mimic their firing. While the Confederates were loading, our boys would, apparently, become impatient, and by vigorously motioning with hats and hands and loud yelling, hurry them up. When the rebel cannon was fired, loud cheers showed the rebels that their efforts to amuse our boys were appreciated. Some of our wildest boys would also run out with their hats in hand as though, like small schoolboys playing ball, they would catch the flying ball in their hats. Then one would take his rifle, step plainly in front, and hold it in a horizontal position, while three or four of his merry comrades came up and went through all the motions of loading an eleven inch cannon. The gun would then be fired and our soldiers would loudly cheer, as though they believed the shot had dismounted the rebel cannon. Part of those running the gun would fall as though the discharge had done more execution in the rear than front. The rebels seemed to fully appreciate the pantomime and eased up on their firing toward us. They even became good-natured, and, as if wishing to amuse us, turned their heaviest gun away from us and toward the water and fired a few shots in that direction. It was a splendid sight. The huge balls would strike the water opposite us, throwing up a huge volume that sparkled brilliantly in the bright rays of the setting sun. Glancing up, the ball would again fly through the air, strike and bound again, and thus for a long distance go skipping and playing across the smooth water. Our boys were not slow in showing the enemy that they appreciated the entertainment.

The night of the twenty-seventh of November was one of the severest I ever passed. It fell to my lot to be on picket guard. My post was between our line and the enemy's works. About two o'clock during the night, a fearful storm of wind, rain and sleet burst upon us from the north. The fierce sharp northern wind seemed as though it would pierce our vitals. Each blast seemed to be a piece of sharp frozen steel that cut us through and through. Thus it continued all night. The following day was but little better. No doubt the storm was felt by us more keenly owing to our long exposure to the warm Southern sun, which had tempered us to its warm and penetrating rays. The warm marching we had done and the short rations we had lived upon had also served to unfit us for the exposure of a severe, cold storm like this. An empty stomach gives but little warmth to a freezing man. The penetrating force of these "northers" is beyond description. No comparison with the severest storms of our Northern States would portray the fierceness of this Texas storm as experienced by us. As well attempt to compare the fierce and driving March tornado, with the mild and gentle June zephyrs, as to compare a Texas "norther" with any Illinois storms.

Having finished my turn on guard I joined with my comrades in fighting the fierce storm. The officers, for once, were in a worse condition than the men. No tents had been brought with us except little "dog tents" the soldiers had carried in their knapsacks. By joining our little shelter tents together in a long row, and sodding up the sides and ends, they made something of a protection against the severest part of the storm. When the soldiers offered the officers a place in their tents the favor was gladly accepted. The only hesitancy soldiers in the ranks ever have in sharing rations and shelter with their officers arises from a fear that the officers may view the offer as a bid for official favors. An independent volunteer soldier disdains to be judged as acting from such motives. Thus it is that the best soldiers sometimes neglect to extend their friendly services to the officers, which they would freely extend to them as men and brothers. This is different in the case of those officers who have risen from the ranks with the approval of their comrades. Such officers can share with their men without stopping to insist upon the dignity due to their official position.

The severity of the storm is shown by the fact that the rain turned to snow and covered the ground with a heavy coat of snow before the storm was over. In still water, on land, ice of considerable thickness formed. Cold of this severity is said to be almost unknown in this climate.

The severe storm continued with unabated fury all day Saturday. Every effort was necessary to keep from freezing and we were thus prevented from making any move upon the enemy. When night again came upon us, the storm was not yet over, but had modified so that the sharp sting of the raw, cutting wind had lost its keenest edge. We were bound to press the enemy as soon as possible. After dark a night force was sent forward to plant a battery, and build some rifle pits near to the rebel works. With many willing hands, plenty of shovels, and soft, pliable sand, complete works were soon erected.

Early on the morning of the twenty-ninth of November, our artillery, that had been placed in position during the preceding night, opened fire upon the enemy. He was, no doubt, greatly surprised to receive a morning salute from works built within such easy range of the heavy guns of his fort. The Southern rebels would as soon expected to see us flying in the air above them as to believe it possible for the Northern soldiers to go out in such a cold storm, and in the dark hours of night, build elaborate works right in their teeth as we had done.

During the forenoon our infantry went forward to feel of the enemy. The Eighth Indiana went first and was soon followed by our regiment. The enemy made but a feeble resistance to us. As we pressed them, they promptly abandoned all of their advance lines and fell back under cover of Fort Esparenza, leaving us in possession of all their outside works.[5]

Our artillery did splendid work, proving the benefit our gunners have derived from much practice in many more desperately contested fields than this. As we advanced, we brought other batteries with us. In coming up they had to pass in open view and within easy range of the guns on the rebel fort. They moved up grandly and gained their position without accident. With accurate firing our unprotected guns have the advantage of the cannon in the enemy's fortifications. We trouble them so that they fire but little and that at random.

At night our blankets were brought up and we slept in the captured rifle pits. The boys are delighted with their success thus far. With but little loss we have gained every position we have attempted to take. The prospect is bright for us. We will soon have entire possession of the rebel works. If the Confederates do not evacuate before the investment is complete we will have them, too. But for the delay the fierce storm has caused, we would before this have had the enemy completely boxed up. We lay down in the captured rifle pits and slept soundly right under the rebel cannon, our only anxiety being, for an early return of daylight so that we can proceed with the work at hand. Up to this time, this contest seems more like a picnic than a battle.

We were sleeping, as only soldiers sleep, when, nearly an hour after midnight, the entire command was suddenly aroused by a terrific explosion near us. We at once knew that it was a magazine in the rebel works.[6] This told us, in the plainest tones, that the enemy had evacuated and fired the fort. We were immediately upon our feet and went forward without delay. As expected we found the fort abandoned and the magazines burning. The second magazine blew up just as we reached the fort, the third soon afterward. Before the fire was subdued two more blew up, leaving only two of the seven magazines that were not destroyed. The enemy seemed to have calculated on the fire burning through the woodwork of each magazine until the powder was reached. To some extent, as is seen, the plan succeeded. But why did they take any such foolish chances? A mere schoolboy could have told them that it was easy to lay powder trains to each magazine and thus made it certain that all should be blown up and the fort destroyed to the fullest possible extent.

Some of our boys were hurt by the falling debris. The wonder is that a large number were not seriously injured. When the second explosion occurred we were up to the walls of the fort. Large masses of earth, together with timber of all shapes and sizes, from pieces of thin boards to heavy logs, were thrown high in the air. All that goes up must come down. The ground where the falling fragments struck was the place of danger. The first explosion showed us where the place of safety was. It was to remain near to the burning fort. The night was still, cold and clear. Every thing was plainly seen. All the debris that was sent directly up fell straight down and struck inside of the walls of the fort. Every thing that went into the air diagonally from the zenith, in its fall kept the same angle and in the same direction, and consequently struck the ground a long distance away. The thick and strong wall of the fort prevented every thing thrown sideways from passing. Thus there was a zone of entire safety just outside of the walls of the fort. While the danger lasted we remained within the place of safety. As to how far the line of danger extended to the rear it would be hard to say. The magazines had been built with heavy hewn timber. Pieces twenty to thirty feet long and eighteen inches or more in width and thickness were thrown far out of sight in the air and fell, some of them, more than half a mile away.

No place can be dangerous enough to deter some soldiers from its investigation. We had "stacked arms" and were leisurely waiting for the burning fort to exhaust itself. Some of our soldiers must, of course, look inside. Captain Lyons of Company I, and Sergeant Pike of Company A, among others, slipped away without orders, went around to the further end of the fort and then inside. They came near being buried by one of the explosions. Fortunately, they happened, at the moment, to be near the walls of the fort and escaped harm. Pike, true to his nature, as the best orderly sergeant in the army, always looking for rations for his company had discovered the store-house and secured a large sack of flour and other eatables, an old fashioned "Dutch bake oven" and a frying pan. As the explosion occurred he dropped down by the fort wall and placed the sack of flour over his head as a protection from the falling *debris.* He presented a comical picture, when be returned to us, covered with flour and loaded with his captured provisions and cooking utensils. Captain Lyons, appreciating what he needed most, our officers having none at this time, brought out an officer's tent. They were the first Union soldiers inside the rebel fort. It is fortunate they were not killed. A soldier should never be killed except when in line of duty. They had no business inside the fort at that time.

Inside of the walls of the fort were some dry frame buildings. They were on fire. They burned like cotton. The strange scene we were witnessing was made doubly grand by the bright light of the fast burning pine buildings. The darkness of night and the brightness of day were combined and added to the effect of the grand exhibition. Standing where we did, we had an unequaled view of the terrific explosions and the sights they presented. It was a wonderful display. A mountain of earth, iron and timber all mingled together darkened with immense clouds of smoke and brightened with the fierce flame of fire was, with one huge burst, thrown high above us by the powerful power blast, creating one of the wildest and grandest scenes mortal man ever witnessed. It was a fire-work exhibition never excelled and one, those of us who stood beneath the imposing sight, will never forget.

The first thing done, without waiting for the hour of danger to pass, was to place the emblem of victory—the Union flag upon the conquered walls. The flag of the Thirty-third was the first to wave over the captured fort.

The result of our victory was a few prisoners, some provisions, ammunition and small arms, eight heavy guns and Fort Esparanza. It gave us the entire command of Pass Cavallo and Matagorda Bay, one of the best harbors upon the coast of Texas.

The fort was a very strong one in many respects, but built more with reference to an attack by water than by land. The walls, especially towards the gulf, had been built with care. They were thick and heavy. Being built with sand and earth, cannon balls could not have had much effect upon them. Judging, however, by the ease with which our field artillery silenced them, it is probable that a careful gunner, aiming at the fort's embrasures, with a good ship cannon could easily have silenced the fort. Not only this; but there were the frame buildings in the fort. They were built of Southern pine, full of rosin, and thoroughly seasoned with the heat of many Southern summers and ready to burn as fiercely as though soaked with tar. A most indifferent gun-boat could have fired them almost at the beginning of an engagement. These buildings once on fire, the ruin of the fort was certain. Even the powder magazines were largely built with the same inflammable wood. A child ought to have been able to have made valuable suggestions to those who left the fort in such a condition. One of the Confederate officers, whom we captured, when asked why the dangerous frame buildings had been left in the fort, replied, that the highest ground had been selected as the location of the fort, and the buildings happened to be in its centre, and thus were left standing; that they had made convenient quarters for the soldiers, and the intention was, if a fleet ever attacked them and the buildings were found dangerous, to tear them down and throw the lumber out of the fort.

They must have been the most simple class of home guards who pretended to practice soldiering in this fort. The idea, that if a fleet attack them, they could stop in the midst of the fight and tear down and remove the dangerous tinder boxes, was absurd in the extreme. Every thing would have been burning and they driven out of the fort by the flames and exploding magazines long before they could have removed the shingles from the smallest house. They evidently thought that war was merely some sort of a friendly parade and if the first part of the exhibition did not pass satisfactorily they could commence over again and thus continue until the show ran all right. The strangest part of all was, that the rebels of the country round about thought that they had a second Gibraltar. They had come from far and near to look at and admire it, and actually believed that Fort Esparenza never could be taken.

There is but little doubt but that our field artillery could have driven the Confederates out of the fort, had they been turned loose to do their best for an hour, during Sunday afternoon. But it was a sort of free and easy fight. Our men would silence the rebel guns and then stop and look at them. If a move was made by the enemy to reload their cannon another well-directed shot would drive them under cover. The object on our part was, not to be in too much haste in driving them out, but to bring up enough force and advance far enough to first cut off their retreat. But for the fierce "norther" that burst and raged upon us we would have done so. It is probably fortunate that we did not. We gained the position and full command of the bay and harbor which was all there was worth taking. The prisoners, if we had captured them all, would not have been worth guarding. It is not probable that any of the rebels that ran away from Fort Esparenza will ever be within reach of another Union gun. As prisoners they would not have been worth their feed. It is just as well they ran away.

A CONFEDERATE ACCOUNT OF THE CAPTURE OF FORT ESPARENZA.

I have before me at this time (1883) a copy of a paper published by our soldiers while in Texas. It contains an account of our capture of Fort Esparenza from the Confederate standpoint. It can appropriately be inserted here. In the little soldier paper it is preceded by a short editorial note.

At the urgent request of many friends we republish the following account of the Fort Esperenza affair, communicated to the Houston (Tex.) *Telegraph* by one of the chivalry:

> Port Lavaca, Dec. 3, 1863.
>
> *Dear Sir:*—After what I wrote you the other day, when I was about to start down to the fort, you will naturally expect me to say something of the finale of that affair, especially as it created quite a sensation in the State, and is really a very unfortunate affair for our cause. Those who are guilty are the very ones that will escape in the whole matter, and those brave officers and men who periled their lives in that "man trap" called Fort Esparenza are the victims, of course, to whatever odium is attached to its evacuation.
>
> You have, no doubt, heard that the work was splendid, and so it was; for a prettier thing to look at no man would wish to see and, until I saw it tried I thought it the best thing in the world. But it only shows that a man may know very well how to dig a trench, or grade a street, and yet know nothing about military matters or preaching. I therefore infer that a man may go to school "a heap" and learn to make a beautiful drawing on paper, and then by aid of the bone and sinew of the country can construct a pretty thing to look at, and yet, after all, not know the first thing about military matters or preaching. This is the idea that occurred to my unmilitary cranium. In other words, the fort was built with the sole view to an attack by water, and if they had made it that way they might have hammered away till doomsday, and we would have been there yet, and I have not the slightest doubt but we could have demolished the whole ten vessels that were off the bar. But, unfortunately for us, the enemy knew our weak points and the "lay of the land," just as well as we did; hence they landed at the west end of the island, in Cedar Bayou, where they found no opposition, and took their time to get everything on shore in good order, with their two thousand five hundred veterans and five hundred horses, and, with all their appliances came upon us in our rear, picked their locations and went to work on us with their rifled guns, and, in short, got our range to such a nicety that almost every shell dropped into the fort—everyone

of which was liable and perfectly able to penetrate one or all of our seven magazines, which were adjoining our bomb-proofs, that were intended for the protection of our men; thereby making them the most unsafe places in the fort; in fact, the only safe place about it was the parapet.

Some may say that it is the business of a soldier to die, and that we ought to have stayed there till at least half of us were killed and then surrender to a merciless enemy, whose motto is: "No more exchange of prisoners till the war ends." This is very pretty talk for those who are at a safe distance; but I would suggest a change of place for the time being. Let them imagine themselves cooped up in a pen like sheep for the slaughter, and this, too, with little or no means to hurt the enemy, while they had all the means to hurt us they could ask. Let them also imagine their number to be only six hundred, a large majority of whom had never been in a battle, and about half the number State troops, who, although they were good and true men, yet knew very little about the drill of a soldier, and consequently were not near so effective as they otherwise would be, and that the guns of our fort were located with strict reference to a water attack, and were of very little use for a rear attack from a force of two thousand five hundred veterans, with rifled guns that could throw with as much precision, almost, as an old deer hunter could shoot a buck at a hundred yards. I say, let those who are disposed to criticize our evacuation at a safe distance place themselves in our position for a moment, and then let them say what they would do, otherwise, "let him who is without sin, cast the first stone."

But I have not told all the trouble we had, for the fort was on an island, bounded on the east by Pass Cavallo, where the gunboats would have been up as soon as the norther ended, which proved to be the next morning; on the west and southwest by the enemy, in full possession of the prairie, with their teams and sixteen horses to a gun, dashing about at a full gallop, and taking position wherever they pleased, as we had no cavalry to oppose them, and the little harm we could do them with our smooth bore guns did not seem to trouble them at all. In fact the whole three days' fight seemed to be a sort of a holiday for them, and reminded me of a cat at play with a mouse that she knew to be perfectly in her power.[7]

On the north we were bounded by Saluria Bayou, nearly two miles from the fort, and it is a deep and wide one, with only one tolerable ferry-boat, the rope of which was old and rotten. Then two miles this side is another called Big Bayou, and is, like Big River, also crossed by one frail ferry-boat. Then, before we get to Powder Horn, there are two other smaller ones, with a bridge over one and a ferry over the other.

Now, then, with all of these bayous to cross, and by such frail means, with a wily foe that we knew could certainly surround us at their leisure with batteries, I would like to know what else we could do but evacuate the place while we could?

I regret this sad affair as much as any one possibly can, but we had the alternative placed before us to evacuate and destroy everything, or wait a day or two and surrender with what men we might have left, thereby giving to the enemy the full possession of the fort and all our munitions of war. Now, if we could have had a regiment of well-drilled cavalry, to have skirmished with them and kept them at bay when they first began to come in sight, until our reinforcements could have got to us the case would have been very different. Yet with such field batteries as they have got, while we have none, we have got to be pretty strong to fight them, even in the open field.

They will, no doubt, make raids up here among us and do us a heap of damage, but unless they are very largely reinforced, and that soon, we will soon pick them up—although it would be considered contraband for me to say why I think so.

We have news from below this morning that the whole fleet (Union) is inside the bar; also that two or three hundred heavy guns were heard today near the gulf shore off Guadalupe, and we hope that Seemes[8] has got among them. Our fight at the fort occurred on Friday, Saturday and Sunday, November twenty-seventh, twenty-eighth and twenty-ninth. For particulars see official report.

Yours truly, Texas.

The careful observer will readily notice that the Confederates, at least their anonymous correspondent, profited to some extent and discovered some of the weak points of their defense. In other respects the delusions seem still to exist. As to their strength against an attack by water their confidence remained unshaken. Two or three shells from a gun-boat, bursting among the frame buildings, would have corrected them of that error. The delusion in relation to "a regiment of well drilled cavalry" to keep us back is still worse. With our trusty rifles, and the convenient sand hills among which we could skip along, a regiment of cavalry would have been more useless than their "smooth bore guns" proved to be. Our regiment alone could have disposed of half a dozen regiments of Texas cavalry in that locality. They needed many things to have "kept them at bay when they first began to come in sight," but cavalry was not one of them. Cavalry was just what they did not need, on that narrow island. But, it is not our purpose to review the enemy's report. Let it be read as written. It speaks for itself.

CHAPTER XXVII.

IN WINTER QUARTERS AT INDIANOLA.

The first of December, 1863, found us camped upon the shore near to the captured Fort Esparenza.[1] As we now had possession of Pass Cavallo and the harbor of Matagorda Bay, other troops coming to act with us had a good and easy landing place. The third brigade of our division came December first, and landed at Dederoo's Point,[2] on the opposite side of the channel. For the next few days boats continued to arrive, bringing in more troops and army supplies. Our time was passed pleasantly. A little guard duty and some drilling upon the prairie was all the soldier duties we had to perform.

On December twentieth our regiment went on board a steamboat and sailed up the bay to Indianola. We landed and caught a few stray Confederate soldiers, who were visiting in the town. We tore up part of the pier and carried the material on board and took it back with us, to build a pier at Pass Cavallo. We returned to camp after dark. The plan is to make a winter camp here.

Three days afterward the plan for us to camp on Pass Cavallo at Fort Esparenza was changed and we left Matagorda Island and went to Indianola[3] and took up quarters in that town. We are in the part of Indianola known as New Town, or Powder Horn, as it is sometimes called. Four companies of our regiment were given quarters in a large building that had formerly been used for business purposes by a "Runge & Co." Our company had one room, which was the front half of the main floor. Company B had the rear half. C and D had the rooms above. In the condition in which we put the building we soon had splendid winter quarters.[4]

General Warren[5] was the officer in command of our troops at this time, he was rather strict in his ways; the boys at first thought more so than necessary. When we came into the town it had been hastily deserted by many of its inhabitants. They supposed that their former activity in behalf of the Confederacy would subject them to arrest and punishment. Stores were abandoned with goods in them. Some of the boys would insist upon looking them through General Warren had properly given strict orders against their doing so. One evening as he was walking along the street he found some of the lawless soldiers who had found a way through a back window into one of the deserted stores and were taking a look at the tobacco and other like goods. Instead of having them arrested General Warren dismissed them in his own prompt and energetic way. One of them was the eccentric Weed, of Company A.[6] He was always sure to be caught if anyone was. Weed soon returned to our company quarters. He had been suddenly converted. General Warren was now his ideal of a thorough soldier. He rushed into the company quarters with wild enthusiasm—"I tell you, boys," he exclaimed, "General Warren is just one of the staving best officers we ever had! He means business! He is the kind of officer we want!" Such unexpected commendation for General Warren brought all the boys around him, asking for explanation. Weed explained: "I just now saw the General catch some of the boys who had broken into a store and were stealing the tobacco and sugar. He did not fool about it a bit. He caught one fellow and kicked him lively—kicked him clear into the middle of the street. I tell you, boys, he is a splendid officer! He is a staving fellow! He is the boss!" As soon as this eloquent praise could be broken into, the boys asked: "Weed, who was it that got the kicking?" With increased enthusiasm Weed answered: "Oh, I tell you, boys, General Warren is a staving fellow—a good officer—chock full of energy! I got the kicking."

And it was true. Weed, in his awkward way, had stumbled in after some of the other soldiers; they had skipped lively out of sight, and Weed, the most innocent one of the crowd, was left to be caught and booted into the middle of the street by the angry and energetic Fitz Henry Warren.

Early on the morning of the twenty-sixth of December, a large portion of our brigade, under the command of General Warren, started out to make a reconnaissance in force up the country, to learn, if possible, something of the number, whereabouts and intentions of the enemy in our vicinity.

We went as far as Port Lavaca before returning. When fairly out upon the open prairie, every now and then we would see a small band of rebels, sometimes only two or three and then other squads of a dozen or more, start up from some distant hiding place, look at us a moment like a frightened deer when awakened from its quiet slumbers by the near approach of the dreaded hunter, then mount their horses in hot haste and scamper away until lost to sight in the far distance. As it was impossible for us to overtake them, we made no effort to do so, but marched quietly forward without paying any further attention to them.

Within four miles of Port Lavaca we came to the Chocolate River. The river here is crossed by a very fair bridge. We found the bridge in the possession of a small band of the enemy. They had set it on fire and attempted to hold it until it should burn enough to prevent us from crossing. This plan of theirs did not suit us in the least, as, had it been executed, it would have detained us considerably, if not actually prevented us from crossing. Our artillery was wheeled into line and opened on the enemy. Under cover of the fire of our cannon, some of our soldiers ran up, and using their hats for buckets carried water from the stream and put the fire out, almost in the face of the furious Texas rangers who had attempted to burn the bridge. Seeing that they were defeated, our opponents mounted their horses and rode away and were soon out of our reach. As we were unfortunate in not having any cavalry with us, they easily escaped. With a couple of companies of good cavalry we could have captured them.

To throw a few planks in place of those burned was the work of but a few moments. We then crossed over and continued our march into the town without further obstruction.

Lavaca, situated at the head of Lavaca Bay, is an interesting little town, and to judge by appearances was once quite a lively business place. Of course, nothing to amount to anything in a business line is done here during these war times. Some future day it will become a very important commercial town if its opportunities are improved.

Many of the people at this place appeared glad to see us, and welcomed us with demonstrations of joy. Men and women at their open doors and windows greeted us with such kind words and earnest applause as could not be mistaken. Numerous little incidents served to show that most of these protestations of friendship to the Union cause were their genuine sentiments. The varied and extensive experience we have had in soldiering from Northern Illinois through to Southern Texas has taught us to easily read the true sentiments of the people among whom we pass. In the beginning, a strong Union sentiment existed in many of the towns of Texas along the gulf. Ruin and decay have been their share since the war commenced. They have no hope for the return of prosperity until peace returns. The unbroken success of the Western Union army convinces most of them that the end can only be when the National flag waves over the entire land. This revives the original Union spirit of such towns as this, and they gladly welcome the arrival of the Union troops.

We took up quarters for the night in some of the vacant houses.

At eight o'clock the next morning we started toward Indianola, where we arrived at an early hour during the afternoon.[7]

The country over which we passed was one continuous prairie, unbroken save by an occasional stream or bayou. It is well covered with wild grass upon which cattle feed and keep in good order during the entire year. We often came across droves that contained many fit for beef. What grand pastures these prairies of Texas will be in some future day!

We had some little excitement on Wednesday, December thirtieth. In the morning our company went up to Old Town, as outpost pickets. Two companies are sent out together, and they are relieved each morning by others. We relieved a company of the Eighteenth Indiana. They had had a hard guard during the night. An alarm on picket had caused them all to stand on guard all night. The usual rule is for part to stand on guard while the others sleep. The provost-marshal, or post commander of Old Town, was in hot water. He was a Texas officer. A captain in the Second Texas (Union) Cavalry.[8] He was undoubtedly much more anxious than a Northern soldier would have been in his place. Our arrival seemed to reassure him and we were quietly assigned to our places. Toward noon, some of the roving bands of rebels that run wild upon these prairies appeared in sight. Word was sent to the provost-marshal. He immediately mounted his horse and came out to the picket post. To his excited imagination, a few horsemen were magnified into the advance guard of an immense army, moving in line of battle, and coming down to destroy the Yankee army in this part of Texas. Every soldier in Old Town was ordered out to reinforce the pickets. A messenger was dispatched, in hot haste, to General Warren, with the information, "that the enemy is advancing upon us in force." We soon heard the drums beating the long roll, and soon horsemen commenced coming up from Indianola, and in a short time more, Colonel Bailey, at the head of the Ninety-ninth Illinois, appeared. This made us a good strong picket line. We also learned that the entire force at Indianola, artillery and all, had formed in line of battle with the full certainty that a hard battle was at hand. During all of this time our sharp-eyed pickets, who were watching the open prairie over which they could see for miles, insisted that it was merely a small band of horsemen moving upon the prairie. A few of our horsemen soon started out, and the Texas rangers skedaddled right lively. At night the Thirty-third came up and the Ninety-ninth went back to their quarters at Indianola.

The next morning all of the troops except our company went back to quarters. During the afternoon, we also went, leaving Old Indianola unguarded. It was not thought advisable to keep a mere picket post so far from the army quarters. We performed what soldier duties there were to do and returned to our quarters for the night. This is Thursday night, December 31, 1863, the last day of the year. Thus closes the year of 1863,—an eventful year—one that has witnessed many great, strange and bewildering events. Who can fully comprehend the magnitude of such momentous events? Already many of the scenes through which we have passed seem impossible; seem to me more the remembrances of a strange dream, than of reality. I would that it were so, but it is not. Ah, no! The absence of so many loved comrades that we have laid in their soldier graves, only too vividly reminds us that we are in the midst of scenes of sad reality. As I shall have but little of soldier duties to occupy my attention on New Year's Day, it may afford me some satisfaction to indulge in and write here, a few reminiscences of the year that has gone; for to-night, to the year 1863,—farewell.

CHAPTER XXVIII.

THE YEAR 1863 AS VIEWED BY A SOLDIER—AN ARMY NEWSPAPER—SHORT RATIONS.

Indianola, Texas, January 1, 1864—New Year's day.[1] Another year has come and passed. An eventful, historic year; one that history will ever remember; a year that we, the actors in its scenes, can never forget. It is a year that has witnessed many strange, great and important events. No one can tell how far-reaching the results of the past year's work will be.

A year ago, the objects, the aims, the purposes and the intentions of this great struggle could hardly be said to be more than fairly determined. Prior to that time, it seemed as though both sides were slowly feeling their way to determine what great principles were involved in the gigantic war that had burst upon us. Since then, it has been a contest for the principles then acknowledged to be involved. During the year, neither party has suggested any new principles to sustain or justify its side of the contest. It has been an undisguised conflict between freedom and slavery.

The strife has been desperate and earnest. The desperate, passionate and madly insane struggles of slavery have been met by the earnest, patient, cool but determined zeal with which freedom has reluctantly, yet thoroughly, learned to fight in defense of its cause.

The cause we advocate and fight for, the cause of liberty and justice to all men, the cause of our country, has, during the year, been successful enough to warrant us in the belief that a just God fights our battles with us. We need not write down the battles which have been fought in 1863 to remember them. No American will ever forget the names of Vicksburg, Gettysburg, Chattanooga and hosts of others that have been made historic during the year 1863.

To me, personally, the year has been, by far, the most eventful one I have yet or ever expect to pass. A year ago to-day we were at Ironton, Missouri, with one of General Davidson's supply trains. We soon rejoined the army at Van Buren, Mo., and then went through last winter's campaign to Alton and West Plains and thence back again to Ironton. From there we marched to the Mississippi and came down the river. Then came the important Vicksburg campaign. Being sick I was not at the battle of Magnolia Hills, in which the regiment took part, but rejoined it soon afterward at Port Gibson. Then followed the battles of Champion Hills and Black River, charges of twentieth and twenty-second of May, and siege of Vicksburg, all of which, owing to the protecting care of a kind Providence I passed through in safety.

Next came our short campaign in Western Louisiana and lately our operations in Texas, the capture of Fort Esparenza and Matagorda Bay. And now New Year's day finds us enjoying comfortable quarters in Indianola where with a consciousness of being engaged in a just and holy cause, and with every promise of an early, successful and honorable termination of this unhappy civil war, we are as happy and contented as soldiers in active service and far away from home and friends could expect to be. Gladly we greet the new year of 1864.

The first of January found us quartered in Indianola with but few soldier duties to perform. We were soon quite well supplied with reading matter, and the time was largely passed in reading books and papers, playing chess and other games, and some of us resumed our interrupted school studies.

Among other things we found in an abandoned condition was a printing office. Some of our soldiers who understood the printing business took possession and printed a little army paper. They do very well considering the disadvantages under which they labor.

I will take the liberty of interrupting the history of the journal to describe one of the papers issued at that time. As before stated, I have at this time, 1883, a copy of one of those papers. It is dated: Indianola, Texas, January 5, 1864: Vol. I, No.4. The name is "*The Horn Extra,* W. M. Berry, Editor."[2] It is printed on a sheet of letter writing paper, opened out to its full size, making a two page paper, nine inches in width by fourteen in length. The printed matter is three newspaper columns in width by one foot in length.

It is "published semi-occasionally on the first full moon before hog-killing time, by W. M. Berry & Co."

No sign having been painted, "persons looking for our office will observe a large horn hanging to our door knob."

Fair warning is given to the soldiers given to gallantry, in the following editorial: "We learn that several of our soldier boys have contracted matrimonial alliances with some of the fair ladies of Indianola and Old Town. One wedding has already taken place. We give fair notice to those already married, and those contemplating a consummation of the happy event, that cake or no cake, we shall give publicity through the medium of the *Horn* of their marriage, giving names, company and regiment to which they belong, as their friends at home will be anxious to hear from them."

Two advertisements are copied from the Galveston *News* of October 3, 1863, as showing the "value of Confederate money, and also the scarcity of fighting material among our misguided brethren." The first is the announcement by "an able-bodied man" of his willingness to go as a substitute "for $2,000 in specie."

The second states "that a substitute can be had for $10,000."

On the same page is the "roster of the Thirty-third Illinois Infantry Volunteers, field and staff," giving a full list of all of the officers of the regiment. Then follows the Confederate account of the capture of Fort Esparenza, heretofore given. A few unimportant matters complete the page.

The opposite page commences with brief mention of news gleaned from late New Orleans papers. A complimentary mention of Colonel H. D. Washburn follows.

The Chaplain heads the second column with the following card: "Mr. Editor—In compliance with your kind invitation the following items are furnished for your spirited and loyal sheet. We are enjoying a refreshing time of religions ingathering. Between one and two hundred are already banded together for good. The temperance organization for the first brigade, first division, Thirteenth Army Corps, now numbers one hundred and twelve members. Come, see, hear and act to-night in this good work. —J. S. DONALDSON."

Then follows the announcement of the staff of Brigadier General Warren, which is headed by Major J. H. Elliott as chief of staff.

Obligations are acknowledged to Captain S. H. Dunbar "for late New Orleans papers"; to Sutler Boas of the Thirty-third "for part of the paper on which this issue is printed"; and to Lieutenant E. B. Chambers of the Thirty-third "for valuable assistance in getting up this number." Each in country newspaper style being referred to in a separate editorial note.

Two or three editorial notes tell where "Washingtonian cigars and fine fruits can be found."

The card of an Indiana attorney is the only matter appearing in regular advertising form and it closes as follows: "Particular attention paid to procuring divorces—especially soldiers recently married or those who have done so just for a joke. Charges moderate." In an editorial note the attorney is indorsed by the editor on his personal knowledge.

Other small editorial notes complete this page. That the publishers were about out of ink is shown by the following appeal: "Will some of our friends in New Orleans, send us a small quantity of printer's ink? If this paragraph meets the eye of Lieutenant Colonel Charles or Captain J. B. Tyler, we are confident that it will be attended to."

For some reason supplies have failed to reach us. We commenced to live on short rations. By running in cattle off of the adjoining prairies we have plenty of Texas beef. There is something peculiar in the atmosphere here. At nearly all seasons of the year, dressed beef can be hung up in the open air and it will keep in good condition for a number of days. By the sixth day of January, all of our rations were exhausted so that all we had was coffee and beef. This is a light diet, but as our work is also light we can stand this living for a short time.

On January seventh enough meal to make mush twice was issued to our company. The boys ground the corn in one of the little Texas wind-mills they have here. These wind-mills, only suitable for grinding corn, are not of much account. It took two days and one night steady running to grind the small amount we had to distribute to the company.

THE THIRTY-THIRD RE-ENLISTS FOR THREE YEARS MORE.

A regimental meeting was held at our company's quarters on Friday, January eighth, to consider the matter of re-enlisting for three years more.[3] The orders from Washington, offering a bounty of some $402, were read. Lieutenant-Colonel Potter and Major Elliott made some remarks in favor of the soldiers re-enlisting and showing the advantages to be gained by accepting the propositions made by the Government. Enlistment papers were afterward circulated and the boys joined quite freely. The next day Colonel Potter came over in the evening and talked to the members of Company A about re-enlisting. He is very anxious to have enough of the boys re-enlist to hold the regimental organization. Colonel Lippincott has gone home to Illinois. Lippincott is peculiar. Sometimes he is popular and at other times unpopular with the regiment. He had got into one of his unpopular streaks just before he started for home. Potter at the time was the favorite. Potter did not hesitate to tell us that Lippincott had gone home to strive for a brigadiership and that if he could not get promoted, he would resign and not return to the regiment. With some of the boys this was an inducement, with others it was not. A large share of those present with us have signed the re-enlistment papers, but not quite the full three fourths desired. There is no doubt but that the required number will join.

The Chaplain held what he calls "an interesting meeting" on Sunday. Meetings are held nearly every evening. Quite a religious revival is in progress.

A few pounds of shelled corn were issued today. The boys are parching and eating it. Except this, all they have lately is beef and water.

On Monday we received a supply of rations. The boys have lived through the period of starvation, as it can almost be called, without complaint. They even enlisted for three years more when the hungriest.

The next day while on brigade drill with simply our guns with us, news came of an approaching force of the enemy. We made quick time to quarters for our cartridge boxes and then marched to the northern end of town to meet their attack. The enemy approached within firing distance and our artillery opened upon them. A few shots caused them to beat a hasty retreat. We followed them a short distance and let them go; they were mounted and we were not.

January thirteenth, the Third brigade came up from the camp at Fort Esparenza. General Dana[4] has arrived and relieved General Washburne who has started for New Orleans.

On Thursday, the fourteenth, our brigade was reviewed by our commander, General Warren. He came out in full dress, with gold fringed epaulets, a big feather in his hat and all of the other fixings that go to make up a full dressed brigadier. In fact, Fitz Henry Warren came out a little ahead of anything I have yet seen in this line.

On the seventeenth our men commenced work on the fortifications north of town.

New officers are always thinking of something new. The new military duty added this time is for one regiment of the brigade to fallout at daylight and remain on the parade ground under arms every morning. This is claimed to be to prevent the enemy from surprising us. Extra zeal was also used in other ways. With two drills each day and dress parade every afternoon, our time was quite fully occupied, rather more so than the soldiers really enjoyed.

The question of re-enlisting claimed the attention of our regiment during these days. The time set by the War Department for the re-enlistment of our regiment had expired and Major Elliott went to New Orleans to get an extension. He returned with permission from General Banks for the Thirty-third to complete its re-enlistment and to go home on furlough. The order of the War Department is to be evaded by ante-dating the muster rolls to January first.

After inspection Sunday morning, January twenty-fourth, our regiment went out upon the prairie and held a mass-meeting, to consider the question of re-enlisting—or rather for the purpose of persuading the boys to re-enlist. Colonel Potter, Major Elliott and others made speeches. The boys responded nobly. Full three fourths of the regiment will re-enlist.

The next morning, Colonel Potter requested those of Company A who had not re-enlisted to meet him at his quarters. There were twelve of us besides two others not present with the company. Potter had got the strange crotchet into his head that it would be a big thing for him if he could persuade all of his old company to re-enlist. Of course we all complied with his request and met him at his room as invited to do. When there he used his best endeavors to persuade us to reenlist. Spoke of it as a plain case of duty and mentioned the history that would be published, in which he should give those re-enlisting the highest honor. After talking in this manner for a while, he put the question to each individually: "Provided every man will go if you do, will you go with them?" This was a severe test to refuse. Potter possesses a powerful will and in this case he chose to exert it to the utmost. Most of the boys assured him that in such a case they would not refuse. When he came to me, I replied that I was in full sympathy with the movement, but that owing to many reasons and other duties it was impossible for me to re-enlist for three years more. Two or three more also feeling that other duties called upon them stronger than those which would induce them to re-enlist, refused. Finding it impossible to persuade us all to re-enlist, he dismissed us with the assurance that he still expected many of us to go and would probably speak to some if not all individually. During the day a deep and exciting interest continued upon this question, and before 9 P. M. nearly all of those who had not done so, changed their minds and were sworn into the veteran service. All honor to those brave boys who after passing through all the trials of the severest soldier life, while in far-off Texas, and far away from home and friends, went up so nobly and re-enlisted for three years more. And yet under all of these adverse circumstances, all were anxious to do so. Those of us who could not had the hardest struggle. To refuse was harder than to go.

Tuesday evening Colonel Potter requested those of the regiment who had not re-enlisted to meet him, so that he could inform us what our future fate would be. We met him at his quarters, Major Elliott being present. Potter read the orders from General Banks transferring us to the Ninety-ninth Illinois.[5] This was pleasing news to us. We had been with the Ninety-ninth so much that the ties of comradeship existing between us and them were almost the same as those existing among members of our own regiment. Major Elliott evidently thought that Colonel Potter was treating the boys in a crusty, if not harsh manner. With tears in his eyes the major bid the boys an affectionate farewell, said that he "should always hold each in grateful remembrance" and wished us "a happy future, and may God bless you wherever you go."

The Major was evidently somewhat mistaken in his estimate of the Colonel's feelings. Potter did not intend to be severe. It was his natural way. In my own case, he was fully aware that by far the best way was for me to remain through the winter in Texas. For fully two thirds of my army life I had been troubled with the ague. I had passed through a severe case of typhoid fever and another of pneumonia. As captain of our company he had at different times deemed it best for me to go to a Northern hospital or receive a discharge. Knowing that I was bound to see the three years through, if possible, he had acquiesced and assisted me whenever he could. I was doing nicely in the bracing air of the gulf and the best opinion was, that to remain the entire winter on the Texas shore would be more beneficial than anything else. When he talked with me, even when most anxious to have all re-enlist, his suggestion was that if I commenced shaking with the ague again on our return to the Southern swamps, I should then go home. Even this he did not insist upon when I informed him that it was not my purpose to agree to do a thing and then not do it. If I reenlisted, well or sick, I should, as I had done, remain at the front. At the end, as he saw, that enough had rejoined to preserve the regimental organization, he was undoubtedly glad that those who could not consistently do so, had not re-enlisted. Potter's natural way was blunt and harsh and those not well acquainted with him would think him severe, when in reality, none but the kindest feelings existed in his heart. As it appeared to him we were to remain with our friends of the Ninety-ninth and have a jolly, happy winter, upon the warm and healthy shores of Southern Texas. To Major Elliott it looked like banishment. Potter's cool reason led him to the correct view. Elliott's warm and sympathetic heart led him into error.

The regiment started for New Orleans, on the way north, on January twenty-seventh. When the regiment returns we will probably rejoin and serve with it until our three years expire. We wished them a happy journey and a pleasant time.

CHAPTER XXIX.

WITH THE NINETY-NINTH ILLINOIS.

Thursday afternoon, January twenty-eighth, we moved into our new quarters with Company B of the Ninety-ninth Illinois.[1] They treat us royally. The old Company A boys, four of us,[2] J. D. King, C. A. Bailey, S. Smith and myself were given a nice room by ourselves. The non-veterans of Companies B and I of the Thirty-third were also assigned to the same company. The next day we made writing-tables and other things, and fixed up our new quarters in nice shape.

With reading, studying and playing and light military duties, our time passed pleasantly. Rations were now plenty. On February third our little squad of four made capital arrangements about our food. The captain of Company B kindly directed our rations to be issued to us. A citizen by the name of Smith living near had a neat housekeeper for his wife, and a good cook by the name of Theresa for his hired girl. We made arrangements to board with them. By giving them our rations and the sum of fifty cents each per week they felt well repaid. It certainly suited us nicely. Our food was now much better cooked, and of more variety than ever had been our fortune to have since we joined the army. Our jolly first winter camp at Arcadia was now duplicated with the one exception, that it was farther away and more difficult to hear from home; and on the other hand, two important advantages: our food was prepared in a more wholesome shape and the health of all was much better than when at Arcadia during the first winter of our soldier life.[3]

Friday morning, February fifth, a force consisting of six regiments of infantry, some cavalry and artillery, all under command of General Warren,[4] started out to make a reconnaissance and to get some lumber. We marched fifteen miles, keeping west of Lavaca. We found a good supply of lumber, loaded the wagons and camped upon the prairie for the night. The next morning we started back at eight o'clock and arrived at our quarters at half past three P. M. When coming back some of the boys thought that they must have the fun of seeing the prairie grass burn and started some lively prairie fires. This made the General hopping mad.

Sunday, February seventh, there was a grand review of the troops at Indianola. Generals Ord[5] and Dana came up from Pass Cavallo and joined our officers in making the review.

The Eleventh Wisconsin,[6] Colonel Harris, started home on February fourteenth, they having re-enlisted for three years more or for the war. We have been with and near them so much during the past three years that we have become well acquainted with them. They are a fine body of men and splendid soldiers. Colonel Harris would not part with any of his boys and took them all home with him; those who did not as well as those who did re-enlist.

On February twenty-second, a force of the enemy came down toward us. The Ninety-ninth went out under arms and worked all day upon the fort and breastworks. The enemy appeared within sight upon the prairie but did not come near enough to disturb us.

A skirmish took place between the enemy and some of our mounted men some distance away. Fourteen of our men were captured. The next day a flag of truce came in from Port Lavaca bringing letters from our captured men. One was badly wounded. The rest reported that they were all right and being fairly treated by their captors.

With these few exceptions the month of February passed quietly. Our duties were light and every thing passed pleasantly. With the exception of the "northers" the weather was delightful. These cold wind storms come occasionally and last from one to three days. As we were now in comfortable quarters all the trouble they were to us, was, it required a little more attention to keep our fire going. None of these winter "northers" equaled in severity the one that first welcomed us to Texas while we were advancing upon Fort Esparenza.

INDIANOLA EVACUATED.

On March first, orders came for us to evacuate Indianola and rejoin the Union army on Matagorda Island. The next day some boats came up and we commenced loading our army stores upon them. In a short time we suspended the moving work. The citizens of this place are wildly anxious for the Union troops to remain. They do not wish to again come under the control of their Southern brethren. If we leave the place the Texas rangers will at once return to town. A short delay was granted and a delegation of the citizens started for New Orleans to petition General Banks to countermand the order to evacuate. As a military point the place is of no importance. All we need do is to hold Matagorda Island and retain control of Pass Cavallo. Unless an advance up into the interior is to be made, Indianola is of no particular importance. Should the Confederate soldiers come down we could return and drive them out any day. The only thing to be considered is the citizens of the place. They are heartily tired of the rebellion and do not wish to again see the Confederates in town. Should we go and they come back they could not do any harm unless they burned their neighbors' houses over their heads. The only thing I can see in the citizens of Indianola going across the gulf to New Orleans to beg for the retention of the Union troops, is a mere matter of sentiment. They are so completely converted to the cause of loyalty that they do not wish to see another Confederate flag waving in the town.

General McClernand[7] has been restored to the command of our army corps. He came up to Indianola on March eighth. His old soldiers were well pleased to see him.

The efforts to have our troops retained at Indianola failed. We evacuated on March thirteenth. All of the troops except our brigade started in the morning.

During the day all of the army stores were loaded on the boats and we started at one P.M. The soldiers marched down to the island. The Ninety-ninth was the last regiment to leave Indianola. Colonel Bailey is a good officer to leave in charge of the line most exposed to attack. He would rather fight than eat his dinner any time. We camped for the night near the place where the town of Lasala is said to have once been located. The city has gone away.

We started early the next morning, and soon reached Big Bayou. We had an all day's job of it to cross Big Bayou, and Saluria Bayou, two miles apart, both of which we were obliged to cross before reaching the island. We had to cross on very poor ferry boats.

The troops in our advance had a sad accident yesterday. While they were crossing one of the ferries heavily loaded with soldiers sunk in the deepest part of the water. About forty men were lost. Twenty-five of those who met this sad fate were members of the Sixty-ninth Indiana Volunteers. The others were some of the colored troops who were working the ferry. Such a serious loss of life in such a manner is far sadder than to see our comrades fall in battle. A feeling of deep sadness was felt by the entire army.

We succeeded in crossing in safety and camped for the night upon Matagorda Island at the place where General Washburne's headquarters were established during the battle of Fort Esparenza.

COLONEL BAILEY AND THE NINETY-NINTH ESTABLISH A JOLLY CAMP ALL ALONE.

Tuesday, March fifteenth, we procured some lumber which we loaded on the army wagons, with our tents and camp equipage, and marched down the gulf shore to find a good camp ground for ourselves. At night we camped upon the same ground where we spent the second night when first upon the island in November last.

The next morning it was concluded that a more desirable camp ground could be selected about two miles nearer the northern end of the island, and we returned to that place and established the camp of "Bailey's Pasture." The name arose from this: Once while drilling his regiment when at Indianola, Colonel Bailey used the expression, "Hold your heads up like fat cattle!" From this arose the nick-name, "Bailey's fat steers." When we got back to the island with the rest of the army, Colonel Bailey got permission to camp his regiment by itself. Our camp was upon a pretty piece of grassy prairie six miles away from any other troops, and under the sole command of Colonel Bailey. The boys claimed that he had brought his "fat steers" out to recruit on better pastures than any others had, and insisted upon calling our new camp by the name of "Bailey's Pasture." Thus it goes into history that for one full month we camped at "Bailey's Pasture." A jolly camping ground it was, too. In front of us was the sandy shore of the Gulf of Mexico. It was soon warm enough to enjoy bathing in its waters. There was no possible chance for the enemy to reach us. All soldier duties were of the lightest kind. Colonel Bailey and his men had a fine and easy time together. If the boys wished to drill, Bailey would take them out and after a short time would any, "Boys, guess you can have more fun in camp," and back to camp we would go. We had about one such drill as this per week. Bathing in the gulf, gathering shells upon the shore, roving and playing upon the island, reading and writing, lying around resting and having fun, with plenty of rations, was the way our time was passed. At the end of our camp at "Bailey's Pasture," there was not a sick man in the regiment. To give each day in detail would only be to quote such as these:

"Wrote letters today. Weather fine." "Read some in Washington Irving's Sketch Book, and went bathing."

"A short skirmish drill this afternoon. Grand weather."

"Bathing and rambling along the shore. A fine, grand day."

"Lying around, doing nothing. Weather too nice to think of anything else."

"Reading and writing letters,—Sunday.—As the Ninety-ninth has no chaplain, there were no religious services with us to-day." This shows that our ease was not disturbed even on the Sabbath.

Our pleasant camp at "Bailey's Pasture" was established on the middle of March. On the seventeenth of April Colonel Bailey left us to rejoin the camp of the army near Fort Esparanza, known as Camp of Matagorda Island. By the absence of all officers ranking him, Colonel Bailey had to take command of our brigade, and of course he had to go to brigade headquarters. The old fellow seemed to at once become lonesome when out of sight of the boys of his regiment; at least he soon sent for us and, on April nineteenth, we moved up and joined the brigade camp.

Our new camp was also a pleasant one. We still had fine opportunities for salt water bathing, and nearly all the advantages we had enjoyed during the past month. On April twenty-second, Smith, the man with whom we boarded in Indianola, came to camp and made us a visit. General Roberts came on April twenty-eighth to take command of the post, relieving General Warren, who goes to New Orleans. Three days after his arrival General Roberts[8] declared that we did not need so many men on guard at the same time and ordered them reduced one half. This pleased the boys, as standing guard is the only hard duty they have to perform now, and our situation is so well protected that the reduction can as well be made as not.

On Thursday night, May third, the Ninety-ninth, with Colonel Bailey in command, started off for a night trip. After dark we embarked on some small boats to take a run up the bay. Those present of two companies, A and B, were united as one company, in all forty men, and we went upon the tug Perry.[9] The balance of the regiment went on the steamship Sufficks.[10] In attempting to pass up the channel we ran aground and did not succeed in getting over the sand bars until morning. Thus our night expedition failed. After we were safely past the sand bars in the morning Colonel Bailey decided to go up the bay a short distance, any how. He did not wish to return without passing out of sight of the fort, and report "nothing accomplished." On we went, sailing up the bay. As it was now daylight we would have to move carefully in order to succeed. The main object was to slip in somewhere and pick up a few of the enemy's soldiers and learn something of the Confederate force up in the interior. The plan adopted was for the small tug to run ahead some four miles so as to be able to run in on them. Running with as little smoke and steam as possible so as not to attract attention, we passed the landing at Indianola, keeping off as though running toward Port Lavaca until we came to the further side of Old Town. The tug was now suddenly run toward the shore. Striking the shallow water we jumped into the small boats and rowed ashore. Then came an interesting foot race. As expected some of the enemy's soldiers were in town on a visit. They attempted to save themselves by flight. They had nearly a mile the start of us and made lively time across the prairies. But we had some fleet runners. With a lively run they would get near enough so that by firing high the balls would pass within whistling distance of the running Confederates. The sound of one bullet was enough. They would instantly stop. As our good rifles could send a ball nearly a mile, we soon had the runaways sitting upon the prairie as evidence of their surrender. We brought them in, came back through Indianola, found our boat at the landing and re-embarked at three P. M. and returned to the fort with our prisoners, reaching there after dark. Colonel Bailey had one captain, one sergeant and four private soldiers to turn over as prisoners of war and was consequently, reasonably happy.

The boys found a deserted library from which they selected and brought down a few choice books.

Friday, May twelfth.—By some means our commanding general has got into the belief that the Confederates want this place bad enough to fight for it. Today all hands are busy upon the new line of works near Fort Esparenza. When completed these works will be very strong. They will be harder to take than were the rebel works of Vicksburg. In short, we would be willing to lay behind them and defy all the armies the Confederates choose to bring against us.

The next day I was off duty and finished my first reading of Bunyan's Pilgrim's Progress. This was one of the books our boys confiscated on our trip to Old Town. Through some unexplainable reasons I had never thoroughly read it till now. It is a strange, ingenious and instructive work. At one moment we are completely bewildered; the next we smile at our own confusion and say that it is so plain and simple that a child could understand it. From beginning to end the same strange ingenuity is found. Aptly has the poet said of him:

Ingenious dreamer, in whose well-told tale,
Sweet fiction and sweet truth alike prevail.

CHAPTER XXX.

NATIONAL QUESTIONS—ABOLISHING SLAVERY—HONEST VOTING—THE PRESIDENCY—VIEWS OF A PRIVATE SOLDIER.

Among other things with which we occupied our time and amused ourselves was that of writing, schoolboy like, upon different subjects.[1] After being read for our entertainment, such writing was, of course, usually thrown away. One of these essays having, however, by many curious incidents, escaped destruction, to appear to us nearly twenty years after it was written, will now be permitted to join the journal as part of the history of our army life. It is not given for the matter it contains, but as an illustration of the thoughts of our private soldiers. As then written it is as follows:

MATAGORDA ISLAND, Texas, May, 1864.

As this terrific storm of treason begins to abate; as this black cloud of rebellion begins to break; as we begin to see through this dark night of strife and conflict, through which our country is now passing, and discover the morning light of the coming day; as this terrible war is nearing its end, does it not become us to earnestly and carefully review the position we, as a people, occupy; the principles upon which our Government rests and by which it is controlled, that errors, if any there be, may be rectified, and the true principle of human rights strengthened and perpetuated, so that when bounteous peace once more returns to our loved country, she may reign unshaken and unvexed by the jarring of any false theories in the organic law of our land? The great, the divine principles of human rights voiced in the Constitution of our forefathers, will, we trust, long remain the fundamental law of a great, contented, prosperous and happy people. And yet, perfect as it is, we can not doubt, but that even in this Constitution, there are some errors that can be rectified. To deny this, would be to deny its human origin. To be entirely perfect it would have to pass beyond the influences of this world of human error, to one of divine purity. And then, in such times as these, none can say that there is no error in the theory of our Government; that there is in our country no conflict of false principles with those of right; ah, no, too vividly has this war convinced us of such a conflict. Still, I doubt whether all the wisdom of this age combined with all our dear bought experience could better our grand old Constitution, further than with a few brief amendments; I would suggest only these:

I. A constitutional amendment immediately abolishing and forever prohibiting slavery in this Republic.

II. A constitutional or statute law determining the qualifications of electors and guarding the purity of the ballot box.

III. An amendment to the Constitution, changing the term of office of our President from four to ten years, and making the occupant ineligible for a second term.

Is it proper to consider these matters at the present time? This is the first question that meets us. There are undoubtedly many good and thoughtful men who are opposed to any change during the continuance of our present troubles. They wish first to re-establish the Union as it was under our fathers, and then under the quiet reign of peace, to calmly and dispassionately review our position, and make what changes reason may dictate, unbiased by the high excitement that always exists during the continuance of a bitter civil war. They argue, and with a show of reason, that during the existence of such unnatural excitement, it is both unwise and unsafe to depart from old and well tried landmarks; that we are not, in such times, qualified to reason with the cool and impartial judgment necessary to fairly understand all of the varied and complicated questions that will arise, and that if we attempt to adopt and establish new precedents and rules under such circumstances, we not only are liable to infringe upon the rights and liberties of others, but also liable to neglect and endanger our own.

Thoughtful men admit the force of such suggestions. But is there not another light in which we can view this matter? May we not think, may we not hope, that such trials as these are given for the purpose of purifying us? Is it not a duty, as well as a privilege, for a people, as it would be of an individual, to rise to a higher, truer state, whenever the furnace of trials has fitted them to fill it? Most certainly, the time of the greatest trials is the time to call forth the greatest excellences; the time of trial is the one that develops the noblest, truest virtues. Does the smith, when he takes the iron from the furnace, stand still and let it return to its cold and untempered state, still harder, more brittle and unyielding than before? No, indeed! He strikes with quick and heavy blows, tempers it aright, and forms it into the useful implement.

It is the same with man, with communities, with peoples. When the fire of adversity has made them wiser they must rise to a higher state—then or never. If they wait for a return of prosperity, they will become harder and more unyielding than before. Through evil and vile habits a man falls into misfortune. A friend wishes to reclaim him. "When I am again prosperous I will reform and not till then," is the savage response. Leave such a man alone. He never will reform. So, too, with nations. In every case in history where great reformations have been made, it has been during the heat of the greatest excitement and often also amidst the deepest of bitter experience and trials. The inspired Declaration of Independence is not an exception to this general rule. The noble Warren's blood had been shed upon Bunker Hill, and many, many immortal patriots had died a willing sacrifice for their country before the Independence of America was earnestly advocated by our forefathers. It will be admitted that great wrongs have sometimes been committed during the heat of great excitement, such as occurred during the French Revolution. But this rule will always hold good: No great wrong was ever committed by the party or people that followed the principles of right. We need never fear doing injustice to others so long as we follow the dictates of justice and right

I.

The proposition to abolish slavery in our country by an amendment to the Constitution is now receiving the earnest consideration of our ablest statesmen; at least we judge so by what meager news we receive from the North. As soldiers we have had many opportunities to become acquainted with the institution of slavery. The slaves early learned to confide in the Union soldiers, and would freely tell us of their hopes, desires and ambitions, such as the most observing slave owner would never have thought could possibly have found a home in the breasts of the patient and apparently unthinking negroes. Large volumes could be filled with incidents and anecdotes illustrating this. Every colored man that comes into the Union camp proves it. I confess that my experience proves the black man different and of greater capabilities than I had supposed. With many others I had serious misgivings for the result, when it was proposed to let him at once step from the depths of slavery to the high position of a freeman. I feared that a change so sudden, so great, would so intoxicate him that he would be dissatisfied with his natural condition as a member of an inferior race and would refuse to fill such position unless big extravagant and impossible demands were allowed. Becoming acquainted with the natural traits of the race has convinced me of the error of such views. As a race they make the fewest demands and are the easiest satisfied of any people in the world. To "be my own man" seems to be their greatest expectation. Only let them know that they are free and they will work willingly and faithfully, and be fully contented with a position that the proud Anglo Saxon race would never long endure. * * *

It is not necessary to argue, at length, the question of slavery in the abstract. That it is an evil to be regretted and that ought to be abolished as soon as practicable, is now conceded by the whole civilized world. * * * The only question now seems to be, when shall it be done? Many who are in favor of abolishing slavery, ask that it may be done by some gradual process, so that the bondman may become accustomed to the new position and learn to fulfill its duties. Perhaps the time was, when such would have been the wisest course; but it is now past. After reviewing their present qualifications I am convinced that the present is the best time, we can hope to ever see, for the success of the black race. The colored people are better qualified, today, to commence life as free men than they probably ever will be again. This war has taught a deeper lesson to them than to us. It has awakened every better impulse of their nature and developed their every trait of true manhood to a high degree. * * * If we honestly wish to improve the colored race we should not fail to improve the time when their enthusiasm is raised to the highest degree by the grand excitement of this gigantic war between freedom and slavery. Now is the most favorable time America will ever have to assist the colored race to a nobler, higher position. Does it become a great and wise people to endanger the loss of this auspicious opportunity by procrastination?

As far as the feelings of the white people of the South are concerned, we are still more emphatically called upon to abolish slavery within this Republic. I am convinced of this more from actual experience and a knowledge of their sentiments, than from any theory of reason or logic. With slavery abolished they can think of the Union restored without mortification. In such case they will look at it as slavery, not themselves, that is defeated. If the Union should be restored with slavery, the only explanation that could then be made would be that the people of the South had been defeated in a military contest. Any one acquainted with the strange pride of our Southern brethren can well understand how much they would prefer to lose all they ever had or claimed in the institution of slavery rather to be shorn of their military glory.

It is claimed, by some, that the re-establishment of fraternal relations between the North and South will be impracticable if not absolutely impossible owing to the bitter feelings that have been created by this war. A portion of the remaining rebel leaders lay emphatic stress upon this argument. In fact it is the only tangible one they now have to support their falling Confederacy. To some extent these Southern leaders are right. It may be possible for people of other countries that have once fought as enemies, to unite as fraternally as may be required under a despotic form of government, without the cause of the contest being removed. But I do not believe it possible for the North to unite with the South in as fraternal, trusting and brotherly union as should exist between the people of the same republic so long as one part of our country upholds the institution of slavery. Destroy slavery and then it will not be necessary to re-unite our people, for the simple reason that they will not then be divided. Slavery is all that ever divided the people of our country. Take it away and there will be nothing to separate us. With slavery abolished the South will have stronger interests and more pride in the preservation of the Union than the

North. The quiet sons of the North could content themselves with a mild and unpretending government, but the ambitious sons of the South will never be happy unless they have a share in a nation of sufficient strength and power to demand the respect of the entire world. Forgetting all differences, union with the North will appear to the South as only so much additional strength to the common government.

I have yet to see or hear of the first Southern Abolitionist who was not an enthusiastic Union man. It is invariably the rule, that whenever those fighting against us signify their willingness to abandon the rebel cause, and it is a frequent occurrence, it is always because they believed that slavery is defeated. They never say the South is defeated, but always, slavery is destroyed. The impetuous sons of the South can not endure the thought of being themselves defeated. They can easily look upon defeat with the thought, as I have heard it expressly that, "perhaps, after all, slavery is not right, if so we can never succeed in its defense; but with a just cause the South can never be subdued." This characteristic spirit is frequently plainly manifested. A case like this will often occur:

Confederate—"But what can you hope to accomplish in the end? You can not expect to conquer the whole of the Southern people and then hold them in subjection."

Union—"Oh, no! We only expect to subdue the rebellion and destroy slavery; and then, as there will then be nothing to divide us, we will be united together again as brothers, with stronger ties of kindred and interests than ever before." "Well, well," the proud Southerner thoughtfully replies, "I don't know about that. We always thought that slavery was a divine institution; if so it will exist forever. But," he adds with enthusiasm, "if our people are united again under one flag and government they can whip the world." This is no fancy sketch but one of actual occurrence. We meet with this spirit everywhere. They will admit that a wrong cause may be defeated, and yet curious as it is, maintain that they never can be subdued. Nor is it strange that they should be governed by such feelings. Were we placed in a like position we would easily understand how an unjust cause which we had, through error, been led to support, could be overthrown, and yet be loath to admit that we, ourselves, had been defeated. This is, no doubt, a new theory and one that would not be accepted by those who judge of people only by what they know of the arbitrary governments of the old world. Being accustomed, as they are, in all contests, to see error pitted against error, they have never learned that a cause can be defeated without the power of those who supported it being broken. But in a Government like ours, where all the people have a right to participate, we have learned that a bad cause can be defeated and yet those who sustain it remain as before. The very like principle of a free republic is to permit the united wisdom of all to decide which shall be adopted and for the defeated party to submit without being themselves defeated further than the one question in issue is concerned. Many of our hardest fought political contests prove this. Parties have often seen this cause fail, but its members, as men and as citizens would never admit that they had been defeated, or their individual rights impaired. It is the cause, not the individual, that has been overthrown.

With slavery destroyed, what would remain that need mortify the proudest Southern heart? In anticipation I can look forward and see our country returned to more than its former prosperity; with peace regained, the Union restored, slavery abolished, and a free and happy people, brothers of the same republic, only striving to see which shall be the most zealous in advocating human rights and in adding to the renown and glory of our common country. Hand in hand the people of the South will then join with those of the North in pushing forward every good work. What would then be found in the history of our country that need give shame to the proudest of an illustrious race? Going back to its first commencement as a feeble Government, and tracing up the course of our nation's various contests, it will be found that the sons of the South have had their share in every great and noble event. On every battle field they were represented. In civil and political matters they were leaders more often than followers. Down to our present contest the South has always nobly done its share. With slavery abolished they will regret that they ever attempted to maintain a wrong cause, but need not feel chagrined at their want of valor in its behalf. While we of the North regret some of the strange fanaticisms and great wrongs committed by our pilgrim fathers, still we proudly trace back to our New England ancestry. There is a deep and earnest religious faith firmly implanted in the hearts of the Southern people, and as soon as they plainly see the sin of slavery they will look upon its defeat as a decree of Heaven. But for the great mistake made by ministers of the gospel who claimed to prove that slavery was justified by the teachings of the Bible, not a single regiment could ever have been organized to fight for the Southern Confederacy.

Emancipation is also necessary to give us the confidence and trust that ought to exist between the brothers of the same republic. No matter how extremely Southern a man is in his views and interests we are willing to trust his loyalty to the fullest extent when we know that he is opposed to slavery. As a son of Illinois I fought long and hard to re-open the Mississippi, and now I frankly admit that with slavery destroyed and the Union re-established upon the true principles of universal freedom, I know of none in whose hands I would sooner trust the immortal hills and works of Vicksburg and the guarding of our great river than those of the sons of Mississippi.

Believing that the slaves are better prepared now than they ever can again be, that the interests and especially the feelings of the white people of the South will not be in harmony with those of the North until slavery is abolished; that the North will never have full confidence in the South while it sustains slavery; and that procrastination will only be to continue the errors of the past, I am convinced that immediate emancipation is the true policy.

II.

The proposition to place better guards around our ballot boxes will be passed over briefly. Not having witnessed an election during the three years past, and when I did, not being old enough to cast a ballot, I do not feel at liberty to say much about voting. Confessing that I know but little about the subject, I will say that I have a strong belief that some attention should be given to the qualifications of voters and to prevent illegal voting and false returns.

Although not old enough before the war to vote, I did occasionally "look on" at an election. I well remember how disgusted I then felt to see some of the poor, ignorant beings who did not or could not think for themselves, led up to the ballot box by some political leader and vote the ticket he had, already folded, perhaps, placed in their hands. As far as giving an intelligent ballot is concerned it would have been just as well to have given the party leaders the right to vote the same number of wooden men. Allowing totally ignorant and irresponsible men to vote has the effect to destroy the equality it strives to give to each citizen. In the end it amounts to the same as giving half a dozen or more votes to a sharp wire-worker while an honest and quiet citizen has but one. There ought to be some plan devised by which a voter would go to the ballot box untrammeled by hangers-on, and where he does not know enough to designate for whom he wishes to vote, let his vote go without being counted. Just what plan would be the best I will not attempt to decide. If it was arranged so that a ticket with the names of all the candidates upon it could be given to a voter by the election officers, and the voter required to step into a private box and mark the names of those he wishes to vote for, and no one allowed to see or know how he was making his ticket, nor to approach or speak to the voter from the time the ticket was given to him until it was placed in the ballot box, it would do away with the ticket peddler's occupation.

In cases where the voter could not read the language in which the ticket was printed it might be provided that a sworn officer should read the names and mark it as the voter dictates. Some would, with much force, argue that if a man could not read enough to mark the names upon a ticket he ought not to be permitted to vote. Probably a more simple and efficient mode than the one here suggested can be devised. The idea is to require every voter to vote his own ticket and do away with electioneering and cat-hauling at the polls.

The more graver question is that of fraud at elections. Illegal voting ought to be prevented. With the slavery question disposed of the next great danger to our country will arise from illegal voting or false returns. In a republican government confidence must be maintained or the nation can not long exist. The only basis upon which a republican government can exist is that the majority shall rule. Where the elections are tinctured with fraud none can know what the true expression of the majority is. The ballot box should be guarded by such strict laws and governed by such absolute rules that all will have confidence in its purity. A family will soon break to pieces if there is a want of confidence therein. A republic is but a large family. Want of confidence will soon destroy it. A moment's thought will plainly show this. To start with, we will take a people who are agreed that the majority shall govern. The majority believe that they have been out-counted by illegal votes. How long will the majority be content that the minority shall rule, by illegal votes? Whether fraud actually exists is not so much the question, but does a large portion of the people believe that they have been defeated by fraud? Want of confidence is where the danger lies. Thus the importance of having such rules and laws that all will know that no illegal votes are cast and that the ballots are honestly counted. I believe that some plan of keeping a permanent record of the voters of each district should be established so that the right of anyone to a vote could be investigated prior to the day of election. Much could be said upon this, our second proposition, but for the reasons stated, inexperience as to details, we will pass it with these brief suggestions and proceed to the consideration of the third proposition.

III.

There are, I think, many reasons why the presidential term of office should be increased, and the occupant prohibited from being a candidate for re-election. There are many vexations connected with frequent changes of administration that would be avoided by less frequent elections. It is worthy of consideration, whether much of the bitter partisan spirit that sometimes threatens to endanger our wisest institutions and dearest liberties, is not created more by the frequency of our elections than by the elections themselves. If a longer period was allowed to elapse from one political contest to another, the excitement and bitterness caused by one campaign would pass away and the people would enter upon a new election as men rather than as partisans. They would vote for principles and not for a mere party name.

Our elections are now so frequent that one political contest can hardly be decided before another presidential campaign is commenced. The whole country is kept in a continual fever heat by these frequent contests. Who will be our next President, is the question that meets us in every society, every place and every day in the year? The baneful effects of such unhealthy excitement are felt in every branch of our Government. If a true statesman suggests a wise measure or policy the chances are that it will be defeated by the opposition of rivals to him, with but little reference to claims of the principles involved.

Reforms have often been defeated by selfish jealousy. The suggestions of the wisest statesmanship have often been ignored or opposed because the contemporaries of him who introduced the measures were afraid, that if successful it would make the originator President instead of one of his rivals. During this war how many hard fought battles have been turned from victory into disaster by the detestable spirit of rivalry? When a man gets it into his head that he "may be the next President" he is of no further use at the head of an army nor as a leader in Congress. When a farmer gets the idea into his head that he owns a fast horse that will win the next race, that horse is of no further use upon the farm. It will not plow any more. Such horse is at once put into training upon the race track. Neither horse nor driver will now earn their feed. All is wagered upon the result of the coming race.

It is so with the presidential race. When once thoughts of the presidency possess a man he may, like the supposed race-horse, just as well abandon everything else and go into training at once. Presidential candidates and race-horses, while in training, are of no use in the every-day affairs of life. If the race is won, all right; if it is lost, "all is vanity." It would have been better if all but the winning horse had been kept at the plow, and for all but the successful candidate to have given attention to other duties. When the end is reached, even the owner of the winning horse is usually out of pocket in money and totally bankrupt in morals. It would be well for farmers and statesmen and others to learn the golden lesson: Stick to the plow.

Less frequent elections would diminish their supposed chances for the presidency, and thus the only hope our statesmen would have of seeing their names high upon the roll of fame would be to gain the lasting gratitude of their fellow-men by noble works of patriotism and earnest labors for the cause of humanity. Then, perhaps, the vaulting ambition of some of our leaders would be turned from their own selfish ends, to work for the glory of their country and the happiness of their fellow-men.

One thing in which a republic is far superior to any other form of government is in being able to choose from among its ablest and best men for its administrative officers. This advantage is seriously impaired when our elections are so frequent that every man of moderate abilities and medium talents is led to think that the presidency is within his reach if he can succeed in destroying the influence of some of his brother statesmen. This is, undoubtedly, one of the reasons why our ablest statesmen are the most bitterly opposed by professional politicians. This jealousy often leads the crowd of weaker men to oppose the true, earliest teachings of the wisest statesmanship. Because of such opposition, such men as Webster, Clay and Seward are never elected president. John Quincy Adams never would have been, only that he was so fortunate as to live in an age before politicians learned their trade.

If our Presidents were elected for a term of eight or ten years we could look for an improvement in this respect. Political leaders would then devote their talents and abilities to the best interests and improvement of their country. Wire-working and political knavery would not pay. Congress would then look to the good of the country instead of the next presidency. The people being free from bitter party spirit and extreme political excitement would learn to view matters of government with cool judgment and careful reason; and as they learned to think for themselves the baneful influence of political tricksters would diminish. The election of a President for a long period would be viewed as a serious matter and the people would insist upon choosing from among our best and wisest men. An able statesman would then be looked for and chosen.

As it is now, it seems impossible for us to elect a great and able man unless by accident, we find one in disguise like "Honest Old Abe." Such frequent elections only tend to bewilder the people and create an intense political excitement, and then some one is chosen more by luck or chance than upon merit or from deliberate choice. In such a scrub race the one who promises to be the most pliable in the hands of "his friends" is the favorite.

Changing our chief magistrate so often has a tendency to weaken and destroy the esteem and reverence that the people should feel and extend toward the head of their government. Retaining good men in office tends to increase the people's confidence. The different branches of our Government emphatically prove this. Look, for a moment; make a comparison; mark the contrast and note the degree of respect given to each. There is the House of Representatives, whose members are only elected for two years, the Senate, whose members are elected for six years, and the Supreme Court, whose members continue in office during good behavior, which, with honest judges, means for life. The confidence of the people that is felt in each, as a body, increases in about the same ratio. For stability in public affairs, the people turn with much greater confidence to the Senate than to the House of Representatives. Any military man would highly prize a resolution of commendation by the Senate. He would feel that such an endorsement was one that would command the respect of all. The same resolution, indorsed only by the House, would not be as highly prized. Whether right or wrong, the popular opinion is, that the favor of the lower house and the passage of measures therein is generally to some extent aided by shrewd maneuvering, while the action of the Senate is more apt to be governed by merit.

Great as is the respect and confidence of the American people in the Senate as a body, it is in turn eclipsed by the higher regard for the Supreme Court of the United States. This regard is so great that the people will faithfully obey the rulings of the court, although they believe it wrong in principle, until it is reversed by the same high authority.

It seems to be an inherent principle of human nature, that the longer we are obliged to trust others, the greater will be our care in the selections made, and the greater will be the confidence we will feel in those chosen to fill the position. When a man enters into a brief business partnership he respects the honesty of the one chosen; when he chooses a partner whom he thinks worthy of sharing the "joys and sorrows of life with him," he esteems and cherishes her;

when his heart tells him that he has found one who will be united with him through all eternity, he loves her with wild devotion. None would expect to see a college of learning establish an enviable reputation, whose president and professors were frequently changed. Where efficiency is demanded frequent changes are never allowed. None would attempt to maintain an efficient army where the officers were appointed for brief terms, and the successors chosen by frequent elections. Prior to the war it is plain that the South often exerted more than her due share of influence in national affairs because of its custom to re-elect members of Congress, while in the North, frequent changes is the rule.

It is conceded that many things can be said against a long presidential term. There are two sides to almost every question, especially to one like this which involves only matters of policy. Upon questions of principle, like that of slavery, the only possible division is between right and wrong. Questions of mere policy are always open for discussion. Most of the objections against a long presidential term will be obviated by providing that no President shall succeed himself. Even without reference to the length of the term there are many reasons in favor of prohibiting an occupant of the presidential office from being his own successor. With a term of increased length these reasons would be multiplied. Let us suppose that a man is elected President for ten or even eight years. At the age he must have reached before he would be selected to this high position he would look upon the work before him as practically the end of his life's duties. The only ambition that could actuate him would be to have the best possible administration, to serve the people well, and leave an honored name in his country's history. He would be above all mere matters of party politics. In fact, in this rapid age of change and progress, when all great questions like that of slavery and secession are disposed of, it is probable that parties would so mingle and change that at the end of such a presidential term the President, looking only to the best interests of all, would not know to which political party his leanings were. Like a true army officer he would forget all mere party divisions among the people and be zealous only in the performance of his actual duties. It is a question worthy of consideration whether all of the administrative branches of the Government should not be, as is confessed the army and navy should be, managed solely with reference to efficiency, and confine all political questions to Congress. The peculiar manner provided by the Constitution for the election of a President and appointment of other officers would indicate that the fathers designed that the administrative officers should be selected for efficiency and not for political reasons. In practice the plan has been changed so that in effect the name of the party candidate for President heads the party ticket at each so-called presidential election.

As now practiced the cumbersome electoral college might as well be abolished, and allow the candidates named for President and Vice-President to be directly voted for. At the last election I witnessed, all were voting for Lincoln or Douglas. No one seemed to understand that he was voting only for electors, and probably not one in twenty could have repeated from memory the names of the list upon his ticket. A long presidential term, it is believed, would, to a large extent, remove the office from mere party politics.

With the changes purposed, the ratio of the terms of the different branches of our Government would be gradual and natural. The lower house of Congress would be renewed every two years; the terms of the senators six years, and the executive eight or ten years. The confidence of the people in the conservatism of each would run in about the same proportion. Then the President of the United States being certain of the support of the people in all just measures, could at home and abroad claim the respect that ought to be shown to the representative head of a great people. Thus we suggest that the immediate prohibition of slavery, the protection of the ballot box and an increase of the presidential term are matters deserving the earnest consideration of the American people.

CHAPTER XXXI.

WE LEAVE TEXAS AND RETURN TO LOUISIANA.

By the middle of May there began to be considerable talk of Matagorda Island being evacuated.[1] We were loath to believe this. With the fortifications in the shape they are a small force could successfully hold this place and thus command the entrance to the only available harbor upon this part of the Texas coast.

On May eighteenth we moved up and camped beside the fort on the beach of Pass Cavallo. The next day positive orders came to commence the evacuation. We worked all day dismounting the heavy guns upon the fort and in loading ordnance stores upon the gulf steamboats. From this time on we continued to load our boats as fast as they came.

On the twenty-seventh of May while strolling along the beach of Pass Cavallo, I stopped to look at the grave of one of the soldiers who fought in the Mexican War. The grave has been sadly neglected. A short time ago a little mound of earth over which horses and cattle roamed at leisure, was all that showed that here was the last resting place of one who was once a noted officer in our army. General Roberts, whose head-quarters are near by, has remedied this neglect to some extent. He has caused some posts to be set around the grave and a rope fastened upon them, which serves to keep the horses and cattle from treading over the remains of the dead. A plain plank head board has also been erected to mark the grave. Upon one side in large, awkward letters are the words:

> Drowned, near
> Salura, about
> 1852.

Upon the other side is the name:

> General
> Alexander
> Summerville,[2]
> One of the heroes of
> San Jacinto.

If General Roberts superintended the marking of the head board, the work is not very flattering to him as an artist, yet we can not refrain from giving him due praise for the respectful regard he has shown for the remains of one who once fought in defense of our country's noble flag.

By the last of May most of the troops had sailed for New Orleans.

General Roberts and all the higher officers had gone and the month ended with Colonel Bailey, the commanding officer, at this post.

He is the right man to leave to guard a retreat. About all he knows or can learn of military matters, is to fight if he sees a chance. If he only had two hundred men left on shore and five thousand rebels were approaching, while he had only a single wagon to take on board, the chances are that he would stop and fight before he would allow it to be said that the rebels had captured even an old army wagon from him.

During the last of May and first half of June we had jolly, easy times upon the Island. Our rations were abundant and excellent. As the large supply was being reshipped to New Orleans we selected the best for our own use. In shipping we retained the barrels containing the hams and shipped those filled with army bacon. Other things we served the same way. The rest of our Army go and leave us all the chances of fighting; we select the best rations and send them the balance.

The climate surprises us. The weather is delightful. Cool and refreshing sea breezes come to us nearly all the time. We were somewhat afraid that the hot summer sun in this Southern land would be too severe for us Northern soldiers. The cool, refreshing breezes from the gulf have thus far made it otherwise. None are sick.

Tuesday, June fourteenth, the last of every thing movable was loaded on the boat, or burned; Fort Esparenza was blown up and the rear guard, consisting of part of the Twenty-first Iowa and the Ninety-ninth Illinois, went on board the steamship St. Mary.[3] With the Thirty-third we had been the first to enter, and with the Ninety-ninth the last to leave Fort Esparenza. It was so dark by the time every thing was on board that we could not pass the sand bar at the entrance to the harbor. The next morning we passed out of the harbor and started for New Orleans. Just as we entered upon the gulf the steamship Clinton[4] met us with our mail from New Orleans. After giving it to us she went on her way to the Rio Grande and we went on our way to the Mississippi.

We had a quiet and slow trip across the gulf and reached the mouth of the Mississippi late in the afternoon of June seventeenth. We found the river very high, so much so, that we found fresh water while yet a long distance from the mouth of the river. We entered the river through what is known as the "Southwest Pass."

We reached New Orleans and disembarked early the next forenoon. We marched toward Carrollton and camped for the night.

On Sunday, June nineteenth, the Ninety-ninth was favored by the arrival of a new chaplain—an officer we have not had for a long time, and also by receiving news that the resignation of Lieutenant Colonel Parks had been accepted.[5] His resignation was probably a matter of necessity. Whisky had ruined him. He is a total wreck. Naturally Colonel Parks was a man of fine abilities and should have been a good soldier in the field and a useful man at home. He has held the office of Lieutenant-Colonel ever since the Ninety-ninth took the field, but been such a drunkard as to be entirely worthless. His entire pay has been squandered in riotous living and his family at home have been entirely neglected. He will either reform or die soon.

On Monday, Demp King[6] and I went to New Orleans. When we got back, we found that the regiment had moved camp. At last we found them near Carrollton.[7]

The next morning we broke camp at four o'clock and marched up the river and camped at Kenderville. We lay in camp here three days. At two o'clock on the morning of the twenty-fourth, we were called up and at once commenced to load our camp equipage on a steamer. When this was done, we went on board a steamer and sailed up the river and landed at Donaldsonville.[8] We established a pleasant camp a quarter of a mile from the river.

Fort Butler,[9] a strong work, mounting nine heavy guns, is here located at the junction of Bayou La Fourche and the Mississippi River. One regiment is required as a regular garrison. During the past season it has been garrisoned by the Ninetieth New York. By some mistake the Twenty-sixth Indiana and our

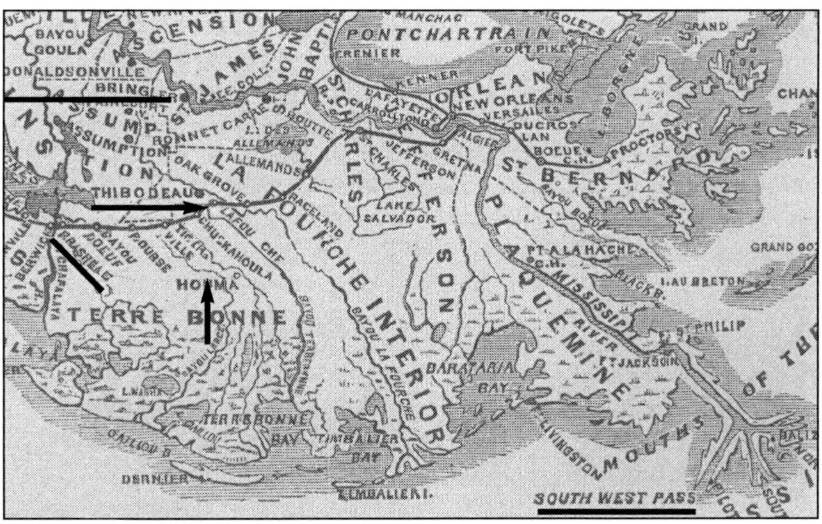

Southern Louisiana operations, 1864. From Guernsey and Alden, *Harper's Pictorial History of the Civil War.*

regiment have both been sent here. As to which will remain has not yet been decided.

Donaldsonville appears to have been quite a thriving town in former times, but it is now in a sorry condition. The best part of the town has been burned, and of course, it will not be rebuilt during these war times.

We reached Donaldsonville on Saturday, June 25, 1864. I remained in camp on Sunday. On Monday went through the town. Tuesday I went out into the country. The soil is very rich and productive in this vicinity. This will some day be the home of a prosperous people. Spent part of the day gathering wild blackberries. They are very plenty here. Blackberries seem to be adapted to nearly every climate. Everywhere from the far North to New Orleans, I have seen them growing in great profusion. As a general thing, as the wild berries are crowded out by cultivation, that is the last we see of them. I wonder why more attention is not given to their protection and cultivation.

WE REJOIN THE THIRTY-THIRD.

On Sunday, July third, we, the Thirty-third boys, bid farewell to our comrades of the Ninety-ninth, and started to rejoin our own regiment, which is now camped at Brashear City.[10] We have had jolly good times with the Ninety-ninth boys and were sorry to part with them. We had been in hopes that the Ninety-ninth and Thirty-third would again meet in brigade together. In that case we would all still be together. Instead of going down to New Orleans and then out on the railroad, we took a small steamboat that runs down one of the bayous that here branches off from the Mississippi. We rode down to a place by the name of Thibodeaux, and landed and remained there over night. We saw a number of fine plantations on the way down. Among others we passed the one that had formerly belonged to the Confederate Gen. Bragg. They have a peculiar mail delivery along the bayou. A young man upon the steamer is provided with some small pieces of wood and string. As he comes to a residence he ties the papers and letters to a stick of wood and throws it ashore. Should he miss in throwing, all the difference it makes, in this still water, is that the people have to take a small canoe, and all have them, row out and get their mail and then wait until it dries before reading it.

The next morning July fourth, we marched from Thibodeaux down to the railroad. At one o'clock we took the cars and went to Brashear, where we met and joined our old comrades of the Thirty-third. We had a right jolly greeting from them. We found them doing well and enjoying themselves. The boys had been having quite a jolly time celebrating the Fourth of July and the first anniversary of the surrender of Vicksburg. We were in time to join in the evening pastime.

We remained at Brashear until the twentieth of July. In this short time an old acquaintance of mine, whose home is in these swamps, made me one of his unwelcome visits. He greeted me most cordially, shook both hands and in fact shook me all over. I was not a bit glad. It was the ague.

On the twentieth of July, Company A took the cars and went to Tigerville Station; a small railroad station fourteen miles east of Brashear. Our duty at this point will be to guard the railroad. We relieved a company of the Eleventh Wisconsin. This is the first time our company was quartered in a place by themselves. Captain Dutton will be in command of the post. We were soon nicely quartered in the buildings at this place.

Our time now passed rapidly and in many respects pleasantly. Occasionally there was a report of the enemy approaching to make a raid upon us. We were sometimes called up in the night to prepare to meet the Confederates, but none ever came within gun-shot distance of our lines. Our guard duty was quite severe. Usually each of us would have to be on guard as often as every second night. With this exception our soldier duties were light, and these days can be classed among the most pleasant of our soldier life.

The big man among the citizens of this place is a very wealthy planter by the name of Gibson. He is a large slave holder and is recognized as a loyal man. This district, it seems, is also considered as loyal and was excepted by the Emancipation Proclamation. Gibson's property in his slaves is thus still respected. He remained loyal, after the Union troops came, for the double reason that he is too old to join the rebel army and because he has so much property to protect. His son is said to be a general in the Confederate army,[11] and his daughter is being educated in Europe. These things show how the Gibson family actually stand, better than the old man's oath of loyalty that he has taken. Waiving these things he is a fine, pleasant old man. He is frequently in visiting with the soldiers and they are much pleased with him. His large plantation is now in cultivation and it has been found desirable for one of our soldiers to be quartered at his place. The soldier is supposed to be a sort of referee between the colored people and the overseers. In case of difficulty the negroes are told that they must do their proper work and that they will be protected from abuse.[12] The moral effect of a Union soldier being present seems to settle everything. The plan is for one or two soldiers to go there and remain one or two weeks at a time. Mr. Gibson provided for them in his own house and practically all they have to do is to visit, hunt, fish and have a jolly time. The old gentleman makes it exceedingly pleasant for those who stay with him. In the middle of August when the guard at Gibson's was being changed, Captain Dutton proposed that I should go there for two weeks. This was for my benefit as it would be much easier for one with broken health than to stand guard at our post. The Captain was much surprised when I told him that I preferred to remain with the company and perform my share of the more severe camp duties. I explained to him that I had been born upon the line of what was known in early abolition times as the "underground railroad." That my grandfather while he lived was always a zealous Abolitionist. That in those early days, before he had a following of any size, Owen Lovejoy, when making his country school-house speeches, was a frequent visitor at my father's house.[13] Thus by birth, education and belief I was opposed to slavery and did not wish to take a place where it could even have the appearance of assisting a slave-holder to make his slaves work for him. Captain Dutton said that such views had not occurred to him and good-naturedly asked, "Suppose you were sent out, what would you do when there?" "Probably get his negroes all to run away within two weeks." "I believe you would," he laughingly replied, "and I guess for fear of further difficulties, I had better let some one else go." Which was done and I remained in camp taking quinine for the ague each day and standing guard every other night.

On August eighteenth, some conscripting officers came up from New Orleans and conscripted some of the colored men. Only a few were taken from this vicinity. Some of the colored women appeared nearly frantic when they were parted from their men.

Crocker's[14] discharge papers came on August twentieth. He was one of those who reenlisted. He was so broken in health at that time, that he should have been discharged then. He was permitted to re-enlist, examined and passed. When the regiment was re-enlisting, it was an inducement held out, by some of the officers, to those who were too unwell to re-enlist, that they would thus get the extra bounty and then be discharged for disability. Such things look to me like dishonesty. Some cases in the regiment were so palpable that they have been sent North so that they can be discharged at some military hospital and thus relieve those who were responsible for their wrongful re-enlistment from responsibility.

The early part of the summer here is very wet and disagreeable. For a long time we had a rain-storm every day, and often as many as from three to five in one day. By the last of August, this wet season seems to be about over. We now have fair weather most of the time.

By the first of September, the planters have commenced gathering their cotton.

Youngman,[15] a recruit brought to the company, was discharged on September second. He enlisted, received a large bounty and drew pay for six months and during all of that time all he ever did was to answer to his name twice. He was a poor, helpless imbecile, who had always been subject to fits. He should have been sent to a charity hospital or poor-house instead of having been enlisted as a soldier. An army surgeon who would pass such a helpless being ought to be cashiered at once.

On the eleventh day of September an order came for the muster-out papers for those whose three years expires, to be made out. According to date of enlistment papers the three years expired on August twenty-first; according to date of muster rolls on September fourth. As it will be some little time before all the necessary papers are made out and we reach Illinois to be discharged, we will probably make a good start into the fourth year before we reach home.

CHAPTER XXXII.

FROM NEW ORLEANS TO NEW YORK AND THENCE TO ILLINOIS.

Saturday, September seventeenth, we were surprised by the sudden and unexpected orders to start at once for the North.[1] A special train at once took us to Algiers. We immediately crossed the river to New Orleans. The reason for this sudden haste was this: a large number of Confederate prisoners were on hand and it was desired that we should guard them on the way to the North. We are to take the prisoners to New York and then go to our own State to be discharged. There are over one hundred soldiers of the Thirty-third whose time has now expired, who will go with us.

On Sunday, September eighteenth, we embarked on the steam propeller, Cassandra.[2] We had some three hundred prisoners. They were part of those captured at Fort Morgan. They were very well clothed and the best looking set of Confederate soldiers I have yet seen. As we took them through the streets from the prison to the ship, the Southern women came out to smile upon and wish the Confederate prisoners good-bye. This pleased the prisoners. We took the prisoners on board at three P. M. At five o'clock everything was ready and we steamed down the river.

At sunrise Monday morning we passed from the river to the gulf through the Southwest Pass and then turned southeast and sailed toward Key West. We had a pleasant sail Monday and Tuesday. Toward night on Tuesday the wind began to rise and through the night and the next day we had a rough sea. Many of the boys became seasick. We reached Key West after dark Wednesday. We had one passenger and some mail to land. As the yellow fever is raging in Key West we did not wish to run into port and laid outside until Thursday morning. A small boat then took our passengers and the mail and we went on our way. At night we passed the last lighthouse we will see on the southern coast of Florida and turned to the north. The boys were greatly pleased when the boat commenced running to the north. It seems like going home when we can see the north star in our front. During our three years' sojourn in the south, with danger and death for our daily companions, often, in the dark night march, and still more frequently during the lonely night guard, the only steadfast guide we could see and know was the ever faithful north star, always shining like a beacon light over our Northern homes. Thus the north star, always reminding us of Northern liberty and the land of our birth, has become to us soldiers of the North, a well-known friend and faithful guide, and with glad hearts we follow in the path it marks, knowing that every step taken, with its light in front, takes us nearer home. Glorious star of the north; glorious land of liberty, gladly do your sons follow the light of the one that guides them to the bosom of the other.

Saturday and Sunday we had a splendid sea with a good brisk wind in our rear which aided us to sail nicely. During part of the time enormous shoals of fishes followed us. It was a wonderful sight. Where could so many fish come from? Some of the boys declared that all the fish in the sea had assembled and come up to greet us on our happy journey home. We passed Cape Hatteras during Sunday night and ran within sight of the Atlantic shore most of the day Monday. As we began to near the busy cities of the North we met with evidences of their busy commerce by seeing many sails upon the water.

On this trip I heard more politics than is usual with us in the army. The services were very short. It consisted of this: Some of our soldiers had newspapers, part of which were given to the rebel prisoners, whom we kept guarded in their part of the boat. Among the papers given to them was one that supported the Democratic candidate for President, General McClellan, and contained a positive prediction of his election.[3] This was read aloud by one of the Confederate prisoners to the others, and thereupon they all joined in loud cheers for General McClellan. Upon hearing the rebels cheer for McClellan the few Union soldiers who had intended to vote for him announced that they should vote for Lincoln. It was the shortest and most effective political address I ever heard. A speech without words—simply three rebel yells—changed all the McClellan voters into Lincoln men.

The weather remained fine and we had a pleasant run the rest of the way to New York. Reaching that place the first thing to do was to turn our prisoners over to the proper authorities. This done we landed in New York City. Wednesday afternoon and evening we had a little time to run around the city, which we improved.

Thursday, September twenty-ninth, we took the cars for the west at Jersey City. Passed through some fine towns and country. Paterson, as we saw it, appears to be a very pretty place. Goshen is the center of a splendid farming country. We passed through Elmira during the night and ran on to Hornellsville where we changed cars. We took the forenoon train Friday, from this place, and ran through to Dunkirk.[4] We arrived too late to make connection with the west bound train, and had to lay over and take the evening train for Cleveland. We rode all night and reached Cleveland at a late hour Saturday morning. We were again too late to make connection and had to layover in Cleveland for the afternoon train. Ran around and looked at the town a little. Visited the waterworks and a few other places. Cleveland is one of the prettiest cities I ever visited. At half-past two we started again and passed through Oberlin and other thriving Ohio towns and reached Toledo at a late hour at night.[5] Our afternoon ride gave us a fine view of some of the finest farming country in the world. We stopped at Toledo, sleeping in the depot buildings over night. We remained in the city over Sunday. As it was our first opportunity for three long years, a number of us attended church, in a peaceful land, Sunday forenoon. At night we got upon the cars and just before midnight started for Illinois.[6] We passed through Fort Wayne during the night and reached Peru in time for breakfast. At the

State Line we found the train of the Great Western waiting for us. Our cars were attached and we started forward and reached Camp Butler shortly after dark, Monday, October 3, 1864.

Thus after three years' absence once again our feet are upon the soil of our own noble State. All hail to Illinois! Proud and noble State, your sons are as proud of you as you are justly proud of them. The land of our birth; the home of our youth; the hope of our future, gladly do we greet thee, our own prairie State. If the returning soldier boys stood erect, if they walked with a proud step, if their eyes beamed with glad satisfaction as they returned the cheers that greeted them on their return to Illinois, who can blame them? In every battle from Missouri and Kentucky to the Southern gulf and even on to the borders of Mexico the soldiers of Illinois have been in the thickest of the fight. On every occasion the Illinois soldiers have added to the proud fame of the grand prairie State. No matter how thickly came the iron and leaden hail from the rebel guns, the volunteer soldiers from sister States never wavered when by their side they could see the regimental banners with Illinois written thereon. All knew that the Illinois part of the line would be maintained.

With all of the long distance over which we have marched and desperate fields upon which we have fought with the gallant Western army we have never left our wounded nor our dead to be handled or buried by rebel hands. Upon all occasions we have taken care of our own. We have never left a contested field except as victors. Fortune has been exceedingly kind to us, and we return to our own State at her capital, to lay down unsullied the proud commission she gave us to serve as part of her volunteer soldiery. Grand and noble State of Illinois! May her sons through all time sustain the record made in the years of 1861–62–63 and '64. All hail to the State of Illinois!

CHAPTER XXXIII.

THE END OF MY SOLDIER LIFE—HOME AGAIN.

There was some delay in the making out of our discharge papers, which gave us an opportunity to visit the city of Springfield and other points of interest in the vicinity of Camp Butler.[1]

On Wednesday, October fifth, some of us attended a great mass meeting of those who favor the re-election of Lincoln. I saw Governor Yates, Judge Trumbull, Senator Doolittle, Generals Logan, Palmer and Oglesby, Deacon Bross, Colonel Ingersoll and other speakers. Met Lieutenant Fyffe[2] of Company A, and M. J. Nye,[3] a former member of our company.

Edward Pike,[4] the orderly sergeant of Company A, whose term expires and who came home with us, became so unwell that he had to be taken to the camp hospital. Sunday, October ninth, the One Hundred and Thirty-eighth Illinois came into Camp Butler, having just returned from Western Missouri. My brother Griffin was with them. This was the first time I had seen him, or any of my relatives, for over three years. He had grown considerable since I saw him last. Then he was a little boy, now he is a young soldier.

Monday, October eleventh, the mustering officer called the roll of our detachment, and then in formal manner pronounced the words: "You are now honorably discharged from the service of the army of the United States of America."

The only thing now to do was to wait for the paymaster and then go home. Those who lived near enough to Springfield went to their homes immediately; those of us whose homes were too far away remained. The paymaster was slow in coming, causing us to wait longer than we expected.

I spent most of the day, the following Wednesday, in Springfield, and in the afternoon returned to Camp Butler. I was much surprised to there meet two more of my brothers in camp, Ralph and Webb. They had lately enlisted in a new company that was organizing to join the old Twentieth Illinois. The first had served for a time in the One Hundredth Illinois and was now returning to the army. The latter, who was younger, had grown up, so as to be large enough to be a soldier since I left home in 1861. Both were buoyant and happy.

A few months afterward a sadder page was here inserted: Of us four brothers who had thus happened to meet as soldiers in Camp Butler, Webb, the poor boy, was the only one who was destined to fill a soldier's grave. He was stricken down, while in Camp Butler, with that fearful scourge of the army, typhoid fever. He was brought home sick but all assistance was in vain. He died and was buried in the little country grave-yard near our farm home. He was the pride of the family. His strength of mind was never excelled by one of his years. Knowing him as I did, and fully appreciating how such mental activity as he possessed, unfitted one of his tender years for the physical hardships of soldier life, I had often written to dissuade him from joining the army. He ought to have remained at school. But the spirit of soldier ancestors was too strong and he, like the rest, was bound to be a soldier before the war ended. He joined the army and was mustered out by death, and all that is left of our brightest hopes is to revere the memory of our young soldier brother, Edwin Webb Marshall, who died on January 24, 1865.

On Monday, October seventeenth, I went into the city, and, at headquarters, found that the United States paymaster would be on hand the next day. I telegraphed to Bloomington and Carlinville, for the Thirty-third boys to return. This was my last opportunity to serve my old comrades as soldiers. I went to Camp Butler, packed up my personal traps and then went to Springfield and stayed at the hotel over night. This was the first time I had slept in a bed, other than one made out of my soldier blankets, since I left home in 1861.

On Tuesday we met at Camp Butler: the Government paymaster paid us the balance our due, we bid farewell to our comrades, and each started for his own home. I took the night train on the Chicago & Alton going north and reached Joliet at an early hour the next morning. Here I took the morning train on the Chicago & Rock Island railroad, and ran up to Mokena. From there I walked across the fields to the township of New Lenox and was soon upon the old home farm, upon which I was born and thus I reached home on Wednesday, October 19, 1864. The first one I met was little sister Mary—how she had grown while I was away. The little girl was out in the field trying to do what she could, attending to the farm stock, as her big brothers were all away soldiering. It is not strange that it was difficult for me to recognize her. I had never thought of the little puss only as for her brothers to tease and play with—just big enough for us to throw up and catch, as a ball, when playing with her.

The youngest of the family, little George, he, too, had grown and now was quite a large boy, had his team in the field, commencing to gather the fall crop of corn. Having come on the first train, my early arrival was taking those at home somewhat by surprise. At the house, both busily engaged, I found sister Sarah—our oldest sister, whose frequent home letters had so often gladdened me during the past, three long years—and our mother—a mother, who, many, many long years ago, had been left a widow, with two little girls and five small boys to care for. All of her boys who were old enough had taken a part as soldiers, and now the prospect was fair that the end would come and she not be called upon to make her sacrifice. Upon this day a happy mother was she. Her greeting, to me, will not be described.

Wednesday, the day of my arrival, was a home visit. The next day the neighbors, hearing of my return, dropped in, one after another, to talk with and ask a thousand questions of army life. I was glad to meet and greet them all. And yet, sad greetings some of them were. Now and then, when the honest old farmer, his white-haired wife, or other kind neighbors grasped my hand, I could see tears mingled with the joyous words. The tale the tears told did not need to be explained in words. Too well I knew, that in the neighbor's home there was a vacant chair that never would again be filled. Many of the boys with whom I had joined in many a wild play at the little old log school house, in the edge of the woods, with whom I had worked, and rambled over the prairie land, with whom I had passed many a long, jolly night in the wild woods, lunching upon roasted, green corn and ripe apples gathered by the way, while hunting wild raccoons and other game, with whom I had robbed my own melon patch as well as theirs in turn, many of these boys had gone to the war never to return.

Thus was sorrow mixed with joy. Could I have said to each honest old father, to each fond mother, to each devoted wife, to each loving sister, brother, child and sweetheart: "Your soldier has lived to return from the war," these hours of my return home would have been the happiest of my life.

But for the sorrow it brings, every young man could well commence his worldly career by spending three years in army life.

THE END.

Appendix A

The Normal Picket

The *Normal Picket* was a newspaper "published weekly by the boys of the 33d Illinois Volunteers." Eight issues were produced between December 24, 1861, and February 12, 1862, in Ironton, Missouri. The story of the two Company C men captured by rebels appeared in the first issue (December 24). The complete set of eight issues were found on the Internet at http://history.alliancelibrarysystem.com/IllinoisAlive/files/is/htm2/ispicket.cfm, but they have since been removed.

It is rather amazing that no mention of this publication is made by Marshall in his narrative, especially when one considers the depth he goes into describing the amusements of the Normal Regiment over the winter in Arcadia and the information he gives about the newspaper produced at Indianola, Texas.

It seems to the editor that there can be only one reason for this—modesty. Nowhere is any authorship noted in the publications, but when the style of Marshall's book and the style of the *Normal Picket* are compared, there is a great similarity. It is entirely possible that Albert O. Marshall was—at the very least—a contributing author, if not the editor!

THE NORMAL PICKET.

We cannot at the same time extend to Rebels the rights of peace and enforce against them the penalties of war. Gen. Halleck.

VOL. I. IRONTON, MO., DECEMBER 24, 1861 NO. 1.

The Normal Picket. Vol. I, No. 1, Ironton, Missouri, December 24, 1861.

The Normal Picket

Vol. I. Ironton, MO., December 24, 1861. No. 1

Narrative of an Escaped Prisoner

On Friday, the 4th of October last, Messrs Levin A. Moore and David McWilliams, privates of Company C, Normal Regiment, left Camp Hovey, Arcadia, for the purpose of enjoying a day's hunting. Not returning to evening roll call, it was suspected they had fallen into the hands of the enemy, and on the following day, in a pouring rain, a number of searching parties scoured the surrounding country for some miles, without finding any trace of the missing men. Searches were made at subsequent times, but with similar ill success, and the fate of the absentees remained long a mystery.

The supposition that they were captured was correct. They had gone as they supposed, some three miles from camp in a southwest direction, outside of the pickets as then stationed, and were helping themselves to fruit in an apple orchard, when they suddenly found themselves surrounded by six armed rebels, and were obliged to lay down their arms and surrender. Their captors searched and plundered the prisoners and then took them into the woods where they (the rebels) had left their horses, and immediately mounted with the prisoners behind them, and struck out for the main camp of their roving party on Black River, which they reached before nightfall.

The whole gang, when united at this place, numbered forty men.

They were a hard looking set, ragged and rough, without any pretence of uniform and with shot guns and old rifles for arms; and were all mounted.

They claimed to belong to Col. Freeman's force. After spending the night on Black River, they took up their line of march down the river for some miles, and thence across the country by local roads, in a general course nearly West, until they had put sixty or seventy miles of distance between them and the Union camp.

The prisoners were usually mounted behind some of the party, but were sometimes allowed to walk, which they greatly preferred, the riding being usually rapid and anything but agreeable.

On reaching a point some fifteen miles southeast of Houston, Texas County, Mr. Moore fell sick, and was declared by a doctor who was summoned to see him, to be unable to travel.

He was accordingly left, in charge of a family, friends to some of the rebel squad; his captors promising to return for him in a week or so. The party then moved on, taking McWilliams with them. It seems they afterwards swore the latter and let him go; but he was again captured by another squad, from whom he made his escape, "borrowing" a horse to help him along, and at last arrived at Fort Scott, Kansas, much broken in health.

We learn that he has within a few days returned to his home in McLean County, Ills.

To return to Mr. Moore. His traveling companions did not keep their appointment, but allowed him to remain for about four weeks without coming to see him again. He was well treated by the family and slowly recovered his health and strength. As soon as he was able to walk, he got in the habit of wandering off into the woods in search of nuts, for some hours at a time, and one fine day he neglected to come back at all. After getting some miles away, (having first thrown away his blue uniform jacket) he made interest with an old lady and her son by representing himself as a deserter on his way to join the rebel army, and got his blue pants dyed the regular butternut color, and such other changes made in his apparel as would better suit his assumed character. Thus, he made his way through Houston, and to a point some ten miles northeast. His intention was to go to Springfield, but learning that that place was again in Price's hands, and hearing also that Pilot Knob had been taken(!) he stopped and spent some three weeks in working for a "secesh" farmer. During this time, a body of Union troops visited Houston and raised a flag on the Court House, but Mr. Moore did not hear of it until after they had left.

Mr. M. finally determined to try to reach Rolla. He accordingly left his employer without saying good bye. Being ignorant of the roads, and afraid to inquire, he wandered back nearly to Houston, and then asked the way to "The Lick" a point on the main road from Houston to Rolla.—He was told the only way was to go through Houston; and, putting a bold face on the matter, he went through the town, unmolested, though at one point he was considerably startled by a loud summons to "halt," accompanied by the crack of an ox whip which sounded for the moment very much like *something else.* The challenge was probably not addressed to him, as he kept straight on and it was not repeated. The Union flag raised by our men on the courthouse had blown down, and lay on the roof, a corner of it flapping over the edge in the wind.

Stopping for the night with a resident some four miles south of the "Lick," Mr. M., (still professing to be a "secesh" and on the way to visit his "folks" near Rolla) managed to learn of some Union families on the road. Next day he arrived at the residence of one of these, some nine miles north of the

Lick. The head of the family was in the Union army at Rolla, and some of the household were just starting thither with an ox team. Here our wanderer told his story without hesitation, and was made welcome to a seat in the wagon and a share of the provisions for the journey. Thus he reached Rolla without further trouble and was there taken care of by the Quartermaster, and furnished with a pass to St. Louis. In that city, being without money and without friends to testify to the truth of his story, he had some trouble, the authorities at headquarters refusing to give him a pass to his regiment. Luckily, he met at the Marshal's office, Captain Lowe of Company E, 21st Ills. Regiment, who took hold of his case like a brother, provided for his wants, and, backed by the newspaper report of Mr. Moore's arrival in Rolla, succeeded in obtaining for him a pass to Pilot Knob. Through his kind aid, Mr. M. was soon on his way rejoicing and on Sunday evening, December 1st, he rejoined his company at Arcadia, and was received with a welcome which went far to compensate for the hardships of his captivity. All he wants now is a chance to meet the rebels on fair terms, and square old accounts.

The Normal Picket
January 8, 1862
Another Prisoner's Narrative

We published in our first number the narrative of L. A. Moore of Co. C, 33rd Regt., who with David McWilliams of the same company, was captured on Oct. 4th, by six armed rebels in an apple orchard just outside our pickets near this post, carried that night to a camp on Black River where a rebel gang of forty had their rendezvous, and from thence, during the next two days, taken as far westward as the neighborhood of Houston, Texas county, where Moore fell sick and was left in charge of a secesh family, from whom he afterwards escaped. McWilliams returned here on the 31st ult., and we are now able to add to the above a brief sketch of his adventures after parting from Moore.

His captors continued their march southwest, and presently united with a larger party, the whole then numbering some two hundred and sixty men, said to be of Freeman's force. They continued to move southwest and passed through Springfield. They were continually sending off scouting and roving parties, so that the number left in the main body was often quite small. McW. was with them two or three weeks. They had plundered him of pretty much all his clothes when he was first taken, and he had supplied the place of some of them with old garments which were given him. He was often cursed and blackguarded, and his fare was usually corn bread when his keepers had considerably better for themselves, but beyond this he does not seem to have been abused. At Springfield, he was shown what was said to be the jaw bone of a Union man who was killed at Wilson's Creek battle, and was told to be thankful that his jaw was not in the same fix.

Soon after passing through Springfield, there was a stir in the camp about joining Price's advance to the north, and one Capt. White administered to McW an oath not to serve against the South, gave him a pass and released him. He started for home, but had not gone far when he stumbled upon another party of some five or six hundred, said to be Col. Talbot's men. Their officer refused to recognize White's discharge, and took McW into custody again. With this party McW continued some days, he does not exactly know how long. He says whisky was plenty, and he drank "to drown sorrow" so that he was fuddled a good part of the time. In this condition he used to sing and "carry on" until his keepers began to have so much of a fellow feeling for him that they did not watch him closely. So one dark night he crawled out under the edge of his tent, made his way through the pickets (there being no chain guard) and escaped.

He now bore away for Kansas, but was stopped almost immediately by a regiment, posted a few miles north of Carthage. But this time he did not show his pass, professed to be a secesh and was released. There were said to be twelve thousand rebel troops at Carthage, and some two thousand in the vicinity where McW was. McW now hired with a secesh farmer near by, but on the very same day came tidings that Fremont had crossed the Osage with seventy thousand men; and all the rebel force began to retreat southward, and the rebel citizens packed up to go with them, McW's employer among the rest.

McW. helped him pack, then borrowed a horse in the evening for an errand to a neighbor's and—started for Fort Scott. After riding some twelve miles, he heard a party of half a dozen horsemen in rapid pursuit of him (as he supposed) but by hiding in the timber he escaped them. For three days, he continued riding northwestward as cautiously as possible, sometimes hiding from apprehended pursuit, and sleeping on the open prairie at night; suffering much from cold, and also from hunger, as he had nothing to eat except a small piece of bread he had brought along, and a raw cabbage he found at a deserted house on the way. At the end of the three days, he found a settler's house where he obtained supper, and the next day he reached Fort Scott. This seems to have been late in October.

From this point he traveled northward to Nebraska City, thence across Iowa, disposing of his horse on the way; and finally, by railroad from Eddyville, reached his home in McLean county, Illinois, where he staid [*sic*] some time to recruit his health, and then came down here again as already stated. Whether his "swear" will be regarded as of any account here, after being repudiated by the rebels themselves, we are not authorized to say.

Appendix B

A Soldier's Letter

Soldier's letters from the Trans-Mississippi theater are not common. Those that use a "Patriotic Cover," that is, an envelope with flags, portraits, slogans, etc., are still less common. Finally, those that have a regimental and/or company notation are quite rare. The example shown above is one of these rarities, from Company B of the Thirty-third Illinois Infantry Regiment. On the reverse of this envelope is noted that "this letter is add to my mother written by myself." The cancellation bears no year date, but must be from 1862. Finally, the name of the writer is not given, but there was only one soldier in Company B that came from Minonk, Illinois, and that was Joseph B. Smilie. Elliott and Way note that Smilie was "discharged for disability at Ironton, 6 Dec., '62" (*History of the Thirty-Third Regiment Illinois*, 100). This rare cover is the property of Mike Nichols of St. Louis, to whom the editor gives thanks for permission to illustrate it.

The envelope for a letter written by a soldier from Company B of the Thirty-Third Illinois Infantry Regiment. Courtesy of Mike Nichols.

Appendix C

The Thirty-third in Print

In February 1862, the St. Louis *Missouri Democrat* published two letters from an anonymous correspondent from the Thirty-third Illinois from Ironton. They are transcribed below.

St. Louis Missouri Democrat
Feb. 13, 1862.
From Ironton

THE THIRTY-THIRDERS—CAPT ELLIOTT EXCHANGED—
ONE THOUSAND FIGHTING MEN

Fort Hovey, Ironton, Mo.,
Feb, 10, 1862

Editors Missouri Democrat:

All the world is agog with the excitement of the "onward movement" now fairly begun. It has reached even the quiet village of Arcadia, where since the stirring events of last fall at Big River Bridge and Fredericktown, the Normal Regiment has peacefully been drilling and toughening.

We are, as you know, nearly all young, unmarried men, and though students and teachers, and men of that "ilk," are none of your lean, sickly sort.

We belong to the "sound body" wing of the "brain" tribe, and believe ourselves able to do just so much marching and just so vigorous fighting as the General commanding shall order. We await the order. Our ranks are full and hospital empty.

The gallant Capt. Elliott and two dozen comrades, who fought at Big River bridge, against over six hundred rebels, and at last, after having slain twenty-two men, were compelled to surrender, have just been exchanged. Isaac is himself again. He will join his regiment in a few days, together with his boys, who will swell our number to a round thousand fighting men.

The Twenty-onesters, the bloody, have already, as you know, taken up their line of march for Greenville. Colonel Baker and his Hoosiers profess an entire willingness to visit various objects of interest in Dixie, while the Thirty-eighth is in excellent trim, and Capt. Manter, who everybody knows, or ought to, is exactly the man to introduce his "Pet Lambs" to our friends over the border—they would bleat, under his promptings, to the point and in time, and all the time, if needed. I will give the "personnel" of our officers, or some of them in my next.

Thirty-Third.

St. Louis Missouri Democrat
Feb. 21, 1862.
The Normal Regiment

PROFESSORS IN EPAULETTS—DIPLOMAS EXCHANGED FOR COMMISSIONS AND GOWNS FOR UNIFORMS

Fort Hovey, Arcadia, Mo.,
February 18, 1862

In my first note, I promised in a second some account of the *personnel* of our regiment. The rank and file are an intelligent body of men, who, like the balance of the grand Union army, enlisted, not from any love of courage, but of country. They are not so much soldiers of fortune as soldiers of principle, though dreams of honor may have been dreampt [*sic*] in our camp as well as elsewhere. The controlling idea is that the Republic shall live—shall live to thwart the predictions and hopes of tyrants, cis-Atlantic and trans-Atlantic.

I will not deny that there exists among us a strong desire to test the boasted powers of the chivalry. From infancy up, we have observed an affected superiority by them both ungentlemanly and insulting.

Now let us meet us man to man in a fair field and settle the question, or, if they prefer strategy, we will oppose our Halleck and McClellan to their Beauregard and Johnson [*sic*], or "any other man." Let them build their forts and their marked batteries or navigate their steam rams. A few well-constructed gunboats and well planned flank movements will furnish explanations entirely satisfactory. I say there is a feeling of this sort, hardly confessed, but yet well defined and strong. We do not swear much—we students—but I would not like to go security for the morals of the camp, should this war terminate without fully testing the vaunted powers of Southern chivalry.

Colonel Hovey is a Green Mountain boy, a graduate of Dartmouth, where, while a student, he was by common consent accorded the post of leader, and received the highest honors of the college. Since then he has rapidly risen till now he is the most influential man of the great common school interest in Illinois. At the time of entering the service, though a young man, hardly thirty-four, he was at the head of the State University. As the superintendent of schools in Peoria, he made a host of friends, in fact, wherever he has been, he has succeeded. Whatever enterprise he touched, at once assumed importance and commanded confidence. Lieut. Col. Lockwood, I know less about.

Major Roe is a man of varied attainments as a surgeon, editor, and politician. He was the late Douglas candidate for Superintendent of Public Instruction, and is widely know and respected. Surgeons Rex and Abbot are skillful men, the former a graduate of Jefferson Medical College, where old Dr. McClellan, father of Gen. McClellan, was at the head of it, the latter, a graduate of Berkshire Medical College, under Drs. Childs, Dewey, and Clark. Captains Potter and Moore, late Professors in the Illinois University, are graduates of Yale. Captain Lippincott, of Illinois College; Captain McKenzie of Knox College; Captain Kellogg of Amherst College; Captain Elliott of Michigan University; Captains Morgan and Pope, of Illinois University, while Captains Lawton and Roberts were educated at academies.

Of the Lieutenants, eight are college graduates, and the remainder either students who have not completed their studies or teachers who have not been liberally educated.

Our only West-Pointer is Adjutant Crandal, a young Pennsylvanian of great promise and popularity.

Quartermaster Wright is the most unique man among us. He is an old bachelor, and yet he prides himself on his knack of managing youngsters and their mothers. It is no use to undertake to describe him—it can't be done.

And Chaplain Eddy is of the same sort. Long study has not squeezed the humanity out of him. He does not believe that religion is wrapped up in "solemn faces" and "blessed tones." "The bloody old Twentysters" are still at Greenville, wooing by their isolated position, a visit from the brigand Jeff Thompson.

They are in great hope that the charm will work. The Indiana Cavalry have got their battery of mountain howitzers. All else remains the same here.

We are anxious to know what part we are to take in the "forward movement."

Is it true, as rumored, that we are to have a Brigadier sent us?

Thirty-Third.

Appendix D

Problems with Cotton

When General Curtis's army, including the Thirty-third Illinois, arrived at Helena, they were, unbeknownst to themselves, embarking into new territory, both physically and politically. They were the first Union troops in Helena on July 12, 1862, and also some of the first to encounter significant quantities of baled cotton that was available for the taking. However, the system of permits, licenses, and regulations for cotton gathering did not begin until December 10, 1862 (*Official Records of the Union and Confederate Navies*, series 1, 23:620), and mechanisms described elsewhere were not in effect (see Surdam, "Traders or Traitors," 301; and Johnson, *Red River Campaign*). In the interim, July to December 1862, the system for gathering cotton was haphazard at best. Regulations were promulgated in Memphis and Helena, and many of them were ignored. The chaos that resulted has been well described by Hess in his article "Confiscation and the Northern War Effort: The Army of the Southwest at Helena." The men of the Thirty-third and the other units of Curtis's army were essentially on their own.

It was not long before complaints about Curtis's policies surfaced, and on August 10 he wrote to General Halleck, saying, "I see the cotton lords are down on me. I at first let everybody trade in cotton, but soon found my camp infested with Jews, secessionists, and spies, and had to issue an order confining the business to a few, whom I restrain as sutlers under military law. Your order on the subject does not seem to suit necessities that exist in a country where cotton is the only available means of subsistence. A few bales have been retained by families to buy the necessaries of life, and such persons have nothing else to buy with. They must, therefore, have some payment in hand to prevent actual suffering for the necessaries of life. I must therefore ask to modify your order to such emergencies" (*War of the Rebellion: Official Records*, series 1, 13:553). On September 18, 1862, Curtis was promoted to command the Department of Missouri (made up of Arkansas, Missouri, Kansas, Indian Territory, and northern and western territories). On October 1, 1862, Curtis issued General Orders No. 5, which included this: "To prevent the transmission of supplies, and especially articles contraband of war, into the enemy's lines, no public trade or commercial business shall be carried on within the department except by persons strictly loyal. No license shall be given to disloyal persons, and any license or authority to such person which has been or may be given by any officer, civil or military, within this command is rescinded and void" (*War of the Rebellion: Official Records*, series 1, 13:698). In addition, he quoted similar and more specific wording from General Orders No. 119, War Department current series on the same subject.

On October 5, the Thirty-third was one of several units ordered north, to return, ultimately, to Pilot Knob. Cotton confiscation continued with the remaining units down the river.

Cotton textile mills in the North were desperately short of cotton, and pressure was put upon the military to "find" some as they moved south. In addition, the lure of rapid and large profits was too tempting for some in the military to resist. Both General Curtis and Colonel Hovey were accused of acquiring cotton for their own profit ("The Cotton Court of Inquiry," *New York Times,* May 24, 1863, 2). Charles Wilcox, another member of the Thirty-third, noted on August 2, "Got the remainder of McNeil's cotton. This planter is very wealthy, owning over a hundred slaves. His negroes loaded and unloaded the cotton. Col. Hovey gave him a claim on U. S. for the cotton, to be paid after the war closes, provided the latter proves himself loyal" (Erickson, "Hunting Cotton in Dixie," 499).

Another man, John S. Phelps (1814–1886), also protested the excesses of cotton acquisition. Phelps, a lawyer, Democrat U.S. congressman from Missouri, and Unionist, raised an infantry regiment, fought at Pea Ridge, and was mustered out in May 1862. In July 1862, he was appointed military governor of Arkansas by Abraham Lincoln ("Military Governor of Arkansas," *New York Times,* July 21, 1862, 5).

In a letter to Gen. Halleck, datelined "St. Louis, Mo., August 17, 1862," Phelps stated:

> GENERAL: It is reported by both officers and men who have arrived in this city from the army in Arkansas that large quantities of cotton have been seized by individuals and shipped on their own account to Cairo and to this city. In some instances the cotton has been obtained from negroes by purchase; in some cases purchased of citizens.
>
> I am also informed some of the cotton has been sold on Government account at Helena at 14 cents per pound and the same cotton has afterward been sold in this city at from 40 to 46 cents per pound.
>
> I have the honor to suggest all cotton, as well as mules and horses, should be seized on government account; that the cotton shall be shipped to this city for sale; that accounts shall be kept of the persons from whom and where taken, leaving to loyal citizens, if any there be, an opportunity hereafter to apply for the proceeds of the cotton. It appears to me there is no other course but the one I have suggested. If speculators, hangers-on of the army, or others are permitted, under the protection of the army, to seize and carry away cotton, the Government bears all the odium, if any there shall be, arising from the transaction, without deriving the least benefit therefrom. Again, this speculation tends to demoralize the army. (*War of the Rebellion: Official Records,* series 1, 13:577)

Then, on September 28, 1862, from Helena, Arkansas, Phelps wrote to Halleck:

> From Saint Louis, under date of August 17, I wrote you, stating the rumors in relation to the seizure of cotton and the speculations in that article, in which it was said officers of high rank were engaged. Such rumors are current here in relation to the conduct of some of the officers, and the late commander of this Army of the Southwest is not exempt from such charges. I have not investigated these rumors. The army was much demoralized in its march from Batesville to this point and whilst lying here. In my letter I suggested the course I deemed expedient in relation to cotton, and time has satisfied me I was right in those suggestions. (*War of the Rebellion: Official Records*, series 1, 13:683)

And yet again, on October 20, 1862, Phelps wrote to E. M. Stanton, secretary of war:

> It is also reported that Colonel (now General) Hovey, of Illinois, who had some "contrabands" in his camp belonging to some persons in the State of Mississippi, exchanged them for cotton, giving two "niggers"

> for a bale of cotton. This I suppose is not returning negroes to their masters, but fair and legitimate trade, in the opinion of that colonel. (*War of the Rebellion: Official Records*, series 1, 13:751)

Colonel Hovey had received a promotion to brigadier general as a reward for valor at the battle of Cache River. But Hovey's promotion was never confirmed by Congress and was allowed to lapse. As a result, Hovey resigned from the army. One must wonder if the publicity raised about cotton transactions might be the cause for lack of confirmation.

However, trade (confiscation, purchasing, etc.) continued unabated. Surprisingly, little appears in the *War of the Rebellion: Official Records of the Union and Confederate Armies* about cotton acquisition. On the other hand, the *Official Records of the Union and Confederate Navies in the War of the Rebellion* is a much richer source of information since naval vessels (or contracted civilian vessels) were needed for the transportation of baled cotton. Memphis was occupied on June 6, 1862, and shortly thereafter (June 18) the capture of the *Clara Dolsen* with one hundred bales of cotton was reported (*Official Records of the Union and Confederate Navies*, series 1, 23:217). Other reports on cotton movement are found (*Official Records of the Union and Confederate Navies*, series 1, 23:255, 257, 358, 451, 455, 465, 476). On November 14, Admiral Porter ordered Lieutenant Commander Shirk of the U.S.S. *Lexington:*

> SIR: You will proceed down river and give protection to such vessels as may desire to obtain cotton below Helena. I have placed the Signal under your orders, and you will direct the commander which vessels to protect. You are not required to undertake any loading operations. The persons going down must meet the consequences if they have undertaken a thing they can not carry out and get into a scrape in the interior and out of reach of your cannon.
>
> Very respectfully,
>
> DAVID D. PORTER (*Official Records of the Union and Confederate Navies,* series 1, 23:481)

On November 27, Lieutenant Commander Shirk reported to Porter on the success of the expedition. In part, he stated,

> I find that the wish and desire of almost every planter on the river is to save their cotton, but the authorities are burning it wherever it can be found. The smoke is seen from the river at all times and in all direc-

tions. There will be no use in sending persons down below [Helena, ed.] for cotton unless some arrangement has been previously made with the planters, so that it may be concealed and ready to be produced at the proper time. (*Official Records of the Union and Confederate Navies,* series 1, 23:509)

On December 18, 1862, General Sherman also issued orders related to cotton in which he laid out procedures and penalties, with all cotton to be turned over to the army chief quartermaster at Memphis (*Official Records of the Union and Confederate Navies,* series 1, 23:557). Finally, on December 10, Admiral Porter promulgated detailed orders on cotton gathering:

CAIRO, ILL., December 10, 1862.

Mr. Yeatman is the recognized agent of the Treasury, and is about to appoint persons in accordance with law to grant permits, etc.

You will recognize all such permits except in cases where they are in direct violation of law, in which event you will bring the matter to the notice of Mr. Yeatman, who, it is presumed, is not cognizant of the violation of the law.

Boats will be permitted to trade with the legal permits at such points on the river as are mentioned, and the gunboats, as heretofore, will protect vessels while so engaged.

No vessel will be considered as legally cleared unless she has a permit from the collector, surveyor of the port, or board of trade appointed by the Treasury Department. She must also carry a manifest, containing an accurate list of her cargo, signed by the proper authority, the collector, surveyor, or board of trade.

Salt is contraband, but will be permitted to pass on proper permit. The present object of trade is to permit steamboat captains to carry small quantities of family stores, to be exchanged for cotton, and officers are called on to assist in every way to carry out this plan by giving protection whenever they can do so.

No boats will for the present be permitted to go within 10 miles of the mouth of White River. This restriction to be modified by order as our forces advance.

Commanding naval officers at Hickman, Columbus, Memphis, Helena, and other trading places on the river will require boats leaving to show their permits and manifest before they depart.

When vessels are seized by a naval officer for a violation of the laws of war, a prize crew must be put on board, and the vessel delivered over to the district attorney for adjudication; but when they carry legal permits for contraband (except munitions of war) they are to be allowed to pass, and the facts reported to me.

> The following extract from the order of the Secretary of the Navy will be complied with. See regulations concerning internal and coastwise intercourse:
>
> There will be no interference with trade in, or shipments of, cotton or other merchandise conducted in pursuance of said regulations within any of the waters controlled by the naval forces of the United States, unless absolutely necessary to the successful execution of military or naval plans or movements. But in case of the violation of the condition of any clearance or permit granted under said regulations, and in cases of unlawful traffic, the guilty party or parties will be arrested, and the facts promptly reported.
>
> No officer of the Navy will seize cotton or other property of individuals within the territory opened to traffic, and subject to the regulations of the Secretary of the Treasury, unless the same is exposed to destruction by the enemy or needed for naval purposes or for confiscation under the act of Congress, and in all such cases the facts, with all attendant circumstances, shall be promptly reported to the Department.
> DAVID D. PORTER,
>
> Acting Rear Admiral (*Official Records of the Union and Confederate Navies,* series 1, 23:620)

One final area needs to be considered. What were the opinions of cotton gathering held by the enlisted men doing the gathering? The best source for information on their feelings is to be found in their letters home. Marshall ends his chapter VIII with these words: "All we have or could hope to accomplish at this point is to pick up a few boat loads of cotton. All we have got is not worth of a moment's consideration in comparison with the lives our stay here have cost us."

Thomas Rescum Stearns of the Twenty-seventh Regiment, Wisconsin Infantry, wrote to his wife on December 14, 1862, from Camp Salomon, Mississippi:

> We are lying still and doing nothing except guarding cotton that is brought in and sold by the officers for speculation and to line their pockets with. The only thing that (in my opinion) is the prolongation of this war but soon that will be played in this part for I should think they had got about all the cotton there was to be got within reach here. (McCown, "Thomas Rescum Sterns")

Floyd Thurman of Company F, First Indiana Cavalry (Twenty-eighth Regiment), wrote on October 9, 1862,

Cotton speculators are not quite so plenty some of our officers had monopolized the trade to some extent in picking and guarding gins till the men was getting tired of it, getting none of the profits so the last relief refused, they told them if they would go they should have one dollar per day, one Lieutenant and fifteen privates went, was there till next morning when a hundred secesh dashed in and picked them up. They have not been heard of since. No more speculations in the Ind. Cav. (Thurman Family Papers)

Notes

Editor's Introduction

1. For a more complete history and roster of the Thirty-third Illinois see Isaac H. Elliott and Virgil G. Way, *History of the Thirty-Third Regiment Illinois Veteran Volunteer Infantry in the Civil War* (Gibson City, IL, 1902; repr., Salem, MA: Higginson Book Co., 1998).
2. Biographical information on Albert O. Marshall was obtained from the Joliet Historical Society, Illinois.
3. The books used are Robert U. Johnson and Clarence C. Buel, eds., *Battles and Leaders of the Civil War,* 4 vols. (New York: The Century Co., 1887); Alfred H. Guernsey and Henry M. Alden, *Harper's Pictorial History of the Civil War* (New York: McDonnell Bros., 1894); Marcus J. Wright, *Official and Illustrated War Record* (Washington, DC: n.p., 1899); Louis S. Moat, *Frank Leslie's Illustrated Famous Leaders and Battle Scenes of the Civil War* (New York: Mrs. Frank Leslie, n.d.); and The Official Atlas of the Civil War (New York: Thomas Yoseloff, 1958).
4. Gottfried Duden, *Report on a Journey to the Western States of North America.* (Columbia, MO: State Historical Society and University of Missouri Press, 1980).
5. In the census listing of the one hundred largest cities from the 1860 census, New Orleans ranked sixth with 168,675 people. Cincinnati ranked seventh (161,044), St. Louis ranked eighth (160,773), and Chicago ranked ninth (112,172). Louisville, Kentucky, ranked twelfth (68,033), and no other trans-Appalachian city had reached 50,000 in population. See http://www.census.gov/population/documentation/twps0027/tab09.txt (accessed July 2006).
6. The St. Louis ethnic population in 1860 was mainly German and Irish. In the 1860 U.S. Census, more than half the population was listed as "foreign born." The total population of St. Louis, city and county, was 190,524. Of this number there were only 1, 156 slaveholders and 3,346 slaves. Walter Ryle, *Missouri: Union or Secession* (Nashville, TN: George Peabody College for Teachers, 1931).
7. See http://www.civilwarhome.com/population1860.htm (accessed July 2006).
8. The Republican Party was formed in 1854 in Ripon, Wisconsin. It ran its first presidential candidate, John C. Fremont, in 1856.
9. Ryle, *Missouri: Union or Secession,* 153, 167.
10. Claiborne Fox Jackson, quoted in Sceva Bright Laughlin, *Missouri Politics during the Civil War* (Salem, OR: n.p., n.d.), 28–29.
11. Laughlin, *Missouri Politics,* 28.

12. Ibid., 25.
13. Ibid., 34, 36.
14. Ibid., 39; *Journal and Proceedings of the Missouri State Convention Held at Jefferson City and St. Louis, March, 1861* (St. Louis, MO: George Knapp & Co., 1861), 36.
15. William C. Winter, *The Civil War in St. Louis* (St. Louis: Missouri Historical Society Press, 1994), 38–40
16. Ibid., 38–48.
17. Christopher Phillips, *Damned Yankee: The Life of General Nathaniel Lyon* (Columbia: University of Missouri Press, 1990). Nathaniel Lyon was born in Connecticut in 1818, entered West Point in 1837, and graduated in 1841, eleventh in the class of fifty-two. He served in the Seminole War and the Mexican War and rose to the rank of captain. He had red hair and a legendary short temper.
18. *The War of the Rebellion: Official Records of the Union and Confederate Armies* (Washington, DC: U.S. Government Printing Office, 1880–1901), series 3, 1:68–69. Hereafter cited as *War of the Rebellion: Official Records.*
19. *War of the Rebellion: Official Records*, series 3, 1:82–83.
20. *War of the Rebellion: Official Records*, series 1, 1:649.
21. The arsenal was located on the Mississippi River and steamboats could be loaded directly from a wharf at the arsenal. The arms were first taken upriver to Alton and then shipped to Springfield, Illinois.
22. Laughlin, *Missouri Politics,* 48.
23. James Peckham, *Nathaniel Lyon and Missouri in 1861* (New York: American News Company, 1866), 114.
24. Ezra J. Warner, *Generals in Gray* (Baton Rouge: Louisiana State University Press, 1987), 94. Daniel M. Frost (1823–1900), Brigadier General of the Ninth Missouri Militia District, graduated from the U.S. Military Academy in 1844 and won a brevet for gallantry in the Mexican War. He resigned from the army in 1853, engaged in business in St. Louis, and was active in the Missouri Militia organization. After his capture at Camp Jackson and exchange, he served as brigadier general in the Confederate army until resigning in 1863. After the war, he farmed in St. Louis County.
25. Winter, *Civil War in St. Louis,* 52.
26. Uriel Wright, quoted in J. Thomas Scharf, *History of St. Louis City and County* (Philadelphia, PA: Louis H. Everts & Co., 1883), 1485.
27. Frank Moore, *Rebellion Record* (New York: G. P. Putnam, 1861; repr., New York: Arno Press, 1977), 1:363–364.
28. Peckham, *Nathaniel Lyon,* 256 ff.
29. Ibid., 268–275.
30. Stephen D. Engel, *Yankee Dutchman: The Life of Franz Sigel* (Fayetteville: University of Arkansas Press, 1993). Franz Sigel (1834–1911) was among the most prominent of the German officers who had fled Europe after the failed revolutions. During the Civil War he rose to major general, more for his popularity with the German population than for his military ability. A popular ditty early in the war was "I goes to fight mit Sigel."

31. Peckham, *Nathaniel Lyon,* 294–297; David C. Hinze and Karen Farnham, *The Battle of Carthage* (Campbell, CA: Savas Publishing Co., 1997).
32. Warner, *Generals in Gray,* 200. Ben McCulloch (1811–1862) fought in the Mexican War, was an Indian fighter in Texas, became a brigadier general in the Confederate army, and was assigned command of Arkansas troops. He was killed at the battle of Pea Ridge (Elkhorn Tavern) on March 7, 1862.
33. William Garrett Piston and Richard W. Hatcher III, *Wilson's Creek: The Second Battle of the Civil War and the Men Who Fought It* (Chapel Hill: University of North Carolina Press, 2000).
34. *Journal and Proceedings of the Missouri State Convention Held at Jefferson City, July, 1861* (St. Louis, MO: George Knapp & Co., 1861).
35. Lawrence O. Christensen, William E. Foley, Gary R. Kremer, and Kenneth H. Winn, *Dictionary of Missouri Biography* (Columbia: University of Missouri Press, 1999), 329. Hamilton Rowan Gamble (1798–1864) served as Missouri secretary of state (1824–1826), practiced law, and was elected to the Missouri Supreme Court (1851–1854), where his most famous decision was his dissent in the Dred Scott case. He retired because of ill health in 1854 and left the state in 1858. He returned to Missouri in 1861 for the February session of the constitutional convention and was named governor of Missouri at the July session. He died of pneumonia in January 1864.
36. Fremont's arrival on July 25 was criticized for a delay of three weeks from appointment to arrival. Others have noted the problems of staffing and supplies that were tackled in New York and Washington prior to his departure.
37. Winter, *Civil War in St. Louis,* 70–73.

Chapter I

1. Camp Butler was located east of Springfield at the location of today's Camp Butler National Cemetery.
2. The Prairie State or State Normal University was founded in 1857 in Bloomington, Illinois. The original bill stipulated that the school's location would be at the place offering the most financial backing. Bloomington won. Classes were held in Bloomington until the first building opened north of Bloomington in 1861. Charles E. Hovey was the first president, taught many classes, and superintended construction.
3. Marshall's swearing in on September 14 was one of the last in the regiment. While Marshall had been a college student, but only for a short time, he probably considered himself a farmer.
4. While Marshall does not give the names of these men, they were probably James Alcorn of Company I and Thomas J. Stone of Company K. Elliott and Way (*History of the Thirty-Third Regiment Illinois*) list their deaths on September 12, 1861, and September 15, 1861, respectively.
5. Ezra J. Warner, *Generals in Blue* (Baton Rouge: Louisiana State University Press, 1992), 236. Colonel Charles E. Hovey was born in Thetford, Vermont, in 1827. He graduated from Dartmouth College in 1852. He served in several

schools in the East and became principal of the Peoria, Illinois, Boys High School and superintendent of schools in Peoria. He served as president of the state teachers' association, was a member of the first state board of education, and founded the original state teachers' university at Normal, Illinois (just north of Bloomington). In 1861, at the outbreak of the Civil War, Hovey organized the Thirty-third Illinois Infantry, made up largely of teachers and students, many from the Normal school. He was commissioned colonel of the Thirty-third on August 15, 1862, and led his regiment through the early years of the war. After the war he received a brevet promotion to major general and practiced pension lobbying in Washington, D.C., where he died in 1897. He is buried in Arlington National Cemetery.

6. The travel orders for the untrained Thirty-third reflect the concern for the status of Missouri. The Union had retreated to Rolla, leaving most of western Missouri open to the rebels. Price and his Missourians moved northward toward Lexington. The Lexington bank was said to hold almost a million dollars in gold and currency, money desperately needed by the Missouri State Guard. But Lexington also had been fortified by Colonel James Mulligan and his Twenty-third Illinois Regiment along with several other loyal Missouri units totaling about 3,500 men. The Union units began fortifying a hilltop position just east of the main part of Lexington. By Sunday, September 15, the position was surrounded and the siege began. By Wednesday, September 18, the situation was growing dire for Mulligan. The Union troops were cut off and supplies, food, water, and ammunition were dwindling. By September 20, it was over. Mulligan and his men surrendered and accepted parole, all except Mulligan. Price then retreated southward and took Mulligan with him. Mulligan was exchanged on October 26 and returned to Federal lines. News of the siege and surrender reached St. Louis, and Fremont was blamed for not sending reinforcements. Michael L. Gillespie, *The Battle of Lexington, 1861* (n.p., 1995).
7. Jimtown was located northeast of Springfield and today is called Riverton.
8. The town that grew up around the ferry to St. Louis run by Samuel Wiggins was originally called Illinoistown. Later the name was changed to East St. Louis.

Chapter II

1. Here are problems: There was no Seventh Nebraska according to Frederick Dyer. The Seventh Indiana Cavalry was not formed until 1863. Dyer notes that the First Indiana Cavalry was at Pilot Knob at this time in 1861 and participated in the battle of Fredericktown. The First Nebraska served at Pilot Knob but was transferred to Syracuse, Missouri, on August 19, 1861. It is possible that in Marshall's notes, he mistook "1" for "7." He notes that "part of the 7th Indiana" was found at Pilot Knob. Twenty-first Illinois was originally Grant's regiment. Frederick H. Dyer, *A Compendium of the War of the Rebellion*, 2 vols. (Dayton, OH: Morningside Books, 1994).

2. Twenty-first Illinois was Grant's original regiment. He received his promotion to brigadier general in early August and moved to Pilot Knob. A monument was later erected there to commemorate the event. Originally, Grant had brought his regiment into Missouri and was assigned to guard the railroads in northern Missouri. His promotion brought him the command of the District of Southeast Missouri, which included all of Missouri south of St. Louis and southern Illinois districts. After a few days at Cape Girardeau, he moved his base to Cairo, Illinois. on September 4.
3. The rifles mentioned may have been of Austrian or Belgian manufacture. Fremont had purchased 25,000 guns, 13,000 of them new, 12,000 used; $6.50 was paid for each with an additional $4.50 paid for alterations. There were reports that many of these rifles could not be fired (in one case, 80 percent were unusable). Fremont was said to have profited in this purchase—made via the New York firm of Kruse, Drexel and Schmidt—in the amount of $30,000. *War of the Rebellion: Official Records*, series 1, 3:544; Marion Hixon, "Fremont's Hundred Days" (Master of Arts thesis, Washington University, St. Louis, MO, 1926), 74; *Senate Report No. 180,* Part 3, 37th Congress, 3rd Session, 37. While the opinion of Marshall and many of the Thirty-third Illinois was that these rifles were nearly worthless, others thought differently. J. R. Purvis, assistant adjutant-general serving under Jeff Thompson, reported, "We captured, among other things, 50 muskets, 15 overcoats, and a number of blankets. . . . The captured guns belonged to the Fremont purchase of Belgian guns, and are much prized by the men, who used them in the battle of the 21st." *War of the Rebellion: Official Records*, series 1, 3:231–232.
4. First Nebraska. See note 1, this chapter.
5. Elliott and Way, *History of the Thirty-Third Regiment Illinois,* 89: "Johnson, Henry E. Bloomington. 21 Aug., '61 to 19 Sept., '61. Drowned in Clear Lake, near Camp Butler, Ill."
6. The position of the Union troops at Pilot Knob and Ironton could certainly be considered an outpost. Their main link for support from the outside world was the St. Louis and Iron Mountain Railroad, a thin reed for support. Otherwise, transport would be by wagon over poor roads north, nearly paralleling the railroad, or east to Farmington and Ste. Genevieve. The area was heavily forested, making ambush and attack quite possible. In this section, "Warlike Times," some of the first real action for the Thirty-third, is described.
7. The capture of Captain Isaac Elliott and his subsequent efforts to be exchanged are detailed in *War of the Rebellion: Official Records*, series 2, 1:139, 173, 287, 534, 535, 537–540. The capture of the Big River Bridge by M. Jeff Thompson and his men can be found in *War of the Rebellion: Official Records*, series 1, 3:202, 231.This action at the Black River Bridge presents an arithmetic problem. The *War of the Rebellion: Official Records* reports a total of fifty-four captured, including Captain Elliott, three lieutenants and fifty-four men with four dead and seven wounded among the Union forces. However, Elliott and Way write that Company E (Elliott's command) lists only seventeen of the company as having been captured, three of whom were wounded. Only one man, Sergeant Foster, was listed as killed. The officers were exchanged and the

enlisted men were discharged upon release, according to Elliott and Way, *History of the Thirty-Third Regiment Illinois.*

8. The story of these two men was told in the December 24, 1861, issue of the *Normal Picket,* a weekly newspaper "published weekly by the boys of the 33rd Illinois Volunteers" while stationed in Ironton. Eight issues were published between December 24, 1861, and February 12, 1862. The complete story of their adventures can be found in Appendix A. The originals can be found at http://history.alliancelibrarysystem.com/IllinoisAlive/files/is/htm2/ispicket.cfm.
9. Thirty-eighth Illinois. Information on this unit can be found in Dyer, *A Compendium of the War of the Rebellion,* 2:1062. Their colonel, William P. Carlin, was born in 1829 and graduated from West Point in 1850. He remained in the army and at the beginning of the war he ranked as captain. August 15, 1861, he was commissioned colonel of the Thirty-eighth Illinois. After service in Missouri and Arkansas he went on to serve with distinction east of the Mississippi River. He was brevetted brigadier general and then major general and led the First Division of the XIV Corps in the Carolinas campaign. After the war he returned to the rank of major and served in occupation posts in the South and on the frontier West. He was promoted to lieutenant colonel in 1872 and colonel in 1882. He was promoted to brigadier general and retired in 1893. He died in 1903 and is buried in Carrollton, Illinois. Warner, *Generals in Blue,* 69.
10. There are several sources that tell the story of the battle of Fredericktown, Missouri. *War of the Rebellion: Official Records*, series 1, 3:201–236; Jay Monaghan, *Swamp Fox of the Confederacy: The Life and Military Services of M. Jeff Thompson* (Tuscaloosa, AL: Confederate Publishing Co., 1956), 41–44; Elmo Ingenthron, *Borderland Rebellion.*(Forsyth, MO: Ozark Mountaineer Press, 1980), 118–122; Harry Carl Koelling, "The Civil War in Missouri during 1861" (Master of Arts thesis, Washington University, St. Louis, MO, 1937), 154–158; Donal J. Stanton, Goodwin F. Berquist, and Paul C. Bowers, eds., *The Civil War Reminiscences of General M. Jeff Thompson* (Dayton, OH: Morningside Press, 1988), 106–117; John G. Westover, "The Civil War Experiences of General M. Jeff Thompson in 1861" (Master of Arts thesis, University of Missouri, Columbia, 1941), 160–182; and Jerry Ponder, *The Civil War Battle of Fredericktown, Missouri* (Mason, TX: Ponder Books, 1996). This last source is highly biased toward the Confederacy; and several of the others, biographies of M. Jeff Thompson, may not tell the complete Union story. Several Web sites also cover the battle but add little. Marshall's account of the battle is in agreement with most of the sources consulted. Meriwether Jeff Thompson was born at Harpers Ferry, Virginia, in 1826. He moved to Missouri in 1847 and to St. Joseph, Missouri in 1848. He became mayor of St. Joseph and was a rabid secessionist. He was named brigadier general of the Missouri State Guard, First Division (located in southeast Missouri), and raised troops. He was noted for "hit and run" actions and became known as the "Swamp Fox"—an allusion to Francis Marion of the Revolutionary War. (Union supporters had another name for him, the "Swamp Rat.") During Price's expedition into Missouri in 1864, he led part of Shelby's Brigade with

excellent results. After the war he tried his hand at business in Memphis and New Orleans, but returned to St. Joseph in ruined health in 1876, where he died. He petitioned Jefferson Davis for regular army brigadier general rank but was repeatedly turned down. Bruce S. Allardice, *More Generals in Gray,* Baton Rouge: Louisiana State University Press, 1995), 219.

11. The name "Sanger" given by Marshall does not agree with that given in the *War of the Rebellion: Official Records*, where Sergeant Goodsell is named. *War of the Rebellion: Official Records*, series 1 3:215.

Chapter III

1. The "academy" noted by Marshall was the Arcadia High School, a private school founded in 1849 by Rev. J. C. Berryman under the auspices of the Methodist Episcopal Church, South. Berryman was forced to abandon the school in 1861. The sponsoring Methodist Episcopal Church, South, was greatly persecuted by Union authorities as subversive in Missouri, so its closing was not remarkable. After the war, the school sputtered along in several incarnations, becoming Arcadia College in 1869. In the late 1870s, the college was transferred to the Ursuline Sisters and was run as a finishing school. The last class was graduated in 1970 and the school was closed. The building described by Marshall was replaced by a four-story brick building in 1869. Today (2007) the grounds house a restaurant, antique mall, and bed and breakfast inn. *Goodspeed's History of Southeast Missouri* (1888; repr., indexed ed., Cape Girardeau, MO: Ramfre Press, 1978), 454.
2. See Appendix B for an example of a patriotic envelope of a soldier's letter.
3. Crandall was Frederick M. Crandall. He was promoted to adjutant upon organization of the regiment. He resigned November 23, 1862, to become captain of the Forty-eighth U.S. Colored Infantry. Elliott and Way, *History of the Thirty-Third Regiment Illinois,* 67, 99.
4. Elliott and Way list forty-eight deaths during the stay at Arcadia: Company A, seven; Company B, eleven; Company C, seven; Company D, eight; Company E, one; Company F, one; Company G, five; Company H, three; Company I, five; Company K, none. Elliott and Way, *History of the Thirty-Third Regiment Illinois,* 88–188.
5. See chapter 2, note 2.

Chapter IV

1. Lockwood was William R. Lockwood, who served from October 4, 1861, to March 1, 1862. He resigned for disability. Elliott and Way, *History of the Thirty-Third Regiment Illinois,* 67.
2. Reeves Station was in northern Butler County, near the Black River. It had its own post office from 1859 to 1875. At that time the name of the town was changed to Hendrickson, which had a post office from 1875 to 1975.

3. Steele's orders from General Henry Halleck were dated March 1, 1862. In these orders he was to proceed to Pilot Knob and take command of all the troops in Southeast Missouri, west of the St. Francis River. He was assigned additional units, bringing his command to 4,000 to 5,000 men. With this force, he was to proceed to Pitman's Ferry, Pocahontas, and Jacksonport, destroying all rebel supplies and occupying the territory. He was also to meet and defeat any Confederate forces at Batesville, Arkansas. Ultimately, he was to march to Helena on the Mississippi River and occupy it as a base. All these plans he was to keep a "profound secret" even from his officers. *War of the Rebellion: Official Records*, series 1, 8:578–580. On February 11, Halleck had written to Col. W. P. Carlin, commanding at Pilot Knob, inquiring as to what additional forces he needed to occupy Doniphan, Missouri, and to capture Pocahontas. *War of the Rebellion: Official Records*, series 1, 8:552.

   Steele reported from Pilot Knob on March 23 that the Eleventh Wisconsin and Sixteenth Ohio Battery had arrived and all were moving forward to join the units that had left Pilot Knob on March 1. *War of the Rebellion: Official Records,* series 1, 8:636. Frederick Steele was born in 1819 and graduated from West Point in 1843. He continued in the army, served with distinction in the Mexican War, and attained the rank of major in 1861. He was promoted to colonel of the Eighth Iowa, and then was promoted to brigadier general on January 29, 1862. He moved to St. Louis from mid-Missouri. His new command later became part of Samuel R. Curtis's army. Later he commanded in Little Rock and after the war remained in the army, serving in the Pacific Northwest. He died in an accident in January 1868 and is buried in Colma, California. Warner, *Generals in Blue,* 474.
4. Charles E. Lippincott had served as captain of Company K of the Thirty-third before his promotion to lieutenant colonel (effective March 1, 1862). On September 2, 1862, he was promoted colonel in command of the Thirty-third. He was promoted to brevet brigadier general on February 17, 1865.
5. This may have been at Ringo Ford on the Little Black River in Missouri.
6. Pitman's Ferry was in Arkansas.
7. This is probably Forche Creek, not Focia.
8. New Orleans had been captured on April 25, 1862, after Farragut's fleet had run past Fort Jackson and Fort St. Philip guarding the lower Mississippi. Farragut's Marines actually were the first occupiers of New Orleans. General Ben Butler's troops arrived to hold the city on May 1. The fact that Marshall notes that the news was received on April 30 indicates that telegraphic communication was still in operation, but also that the comment about General Butler was an assumption rather than factual.
9. Jefferson City (or Bird's Point) was not found. Atlases printed between 1855 and 1885 did not show this town, nor do modern maps.

Chapter V

1. General Samuel R. Curtis had been ordered to Southwest Missouri to meet and push back Sterling Price's rebel army. He had succeeded in this task and moved

into Northwest Arkansas near Pea Ridge/Elkhorn Tavern. Price's Missourians had moved further south and united with McCullough's forces (as they had at Wilson's Creek) but this time under the overall command of Gen. Earl Van Dorn. Van Dorn then moved his army north and attempted to cut off Curtis's army, which resulted in the battle of Pea Ridge, March 6–8, 1862. Van Dorn was defeated, McCullough killed, and Price lightly wounded, and the rebel troops widely scattered. After this defeat, Van Dorn was ordered to bring the remnants of his forces to the east of the Mississippi to support the action there around Corinth. General Curtis, unsure of Van Dorn's movements, but concerned that he might attack into Southeast Missouri, began to move his army eastward across essentially trackless Southern Missouri to West Plains and then southward into Arkansas, reaching Batesville on May 3. *War of the Rebellion: Official Records*, series 1, 13:64. Steele's forces began arriving in Jacksonport on May 4. On May 2, General Halleck had notified General Steele, "You will be subject to the orders of General Curtis." *War of the Rebellion: Official Records*, series 1, 13:369) The best book on the battle of Pea Ridge and the subsequent movement of Curtis's army is William L. Shea and Earl J. Hess, *Pea Ridge: Civil War Campaign in the West* (Chapel Hill: University of North Carolina Press, 1992), especially chapter 15. The arrival of Steele's units and the call by Halleck for units to support him in his advance on Corinth caused General Samuel R. Curtis to reorganize his army. Samuel Ryan Curtis Journal, Abraham Lincoln Presidential Library, Springfield, IL, 15:

> May 10
>
> General Halleck telegraphed for me to send part of my infantry to join him. I immediately started Generals Asboth and Davis with ten regiments of infantry.
>
> May 14.
>
> The sending away 10 Inf. Regiments made a reorganization of my forces necessary. I am also relieved of command of the Western part of Missouri. I reorganized as follows:

1st Div. Brig. Gen Fred. N. Steele

Inf.	Cav.	Artillery
11 Wisconsin	1st Ind.	16th Ohio
18 Ind. Col. Patterson	Capt. Dodson's Co.	1st Indiana Battery
8 Ind. Brig. Gen Benton	3rd Iowa Cav.	1st Missouri
33 Illinois. [Col. Hovey]		

2nd Div. Brig. Gen. E. A. Carr

9th Iowa Col. Vandever	4th Iowa Cav.	Elbert's Battery
4th Iowa (Williams)	3rd Ill.	1st Iowa Battery
13th Illinois (Wyman)		

3rd Division, Brig. Gen. P. J. Osterhaus

17th Missouri (Inf.)	4th Mo. Cav.	Welfley Battery
Col. Hassendebel	Col. G. E. Waring	Captn. Martin Welfley
12th Missouri	5th Mo. Cav.	Hoffman's Battery
Lt. Col. O. Schadt	Col. Jos. __mitt	Capt. Lewis H. Hoffman
3rd Missouri	6th Missouri	2nd Ohio Battery
Col. J. f. Shepherd	Col. Clark Wright	T. J. Curlan

> Besides this force I have Bowen's Battalion always my bodyguard and the 24th Mo. Provost Guard under Maj. Weston and the 1st Ill. Cavalry, Col. Bassen guarding posts of Salem and Houston. Col. Boyd camp at Rolla.

This reorganization and the units sent to Cape Girardeau are noted by Curtis. *War of the Rebellion: Official Records*, series 1, 13:390.

2. News of the capture of Memphis reached Curtis on June 10. Since the capture had occurred on June 6, this indicates that at least some communications were reaching Curtis's army. After Island No. 10 had surrendered on April 8, the navy gunboats moved further south along the Mississippi River. The next obstacle on the river was Fort Pillow on the eastern bluffs of the river, not far above Memphis. Attacks on the fort were planned, but on June 5 it was found that the rebel troops had abandoned it and the river was now open to Memphis. On June 6, a small rebel fleet stood off from Memphis to try to stop the approaching Union gunboats and rams. The result was a total defeat for the Confederates. All but one of the rebel gunboats were either sunk or captured. In addition, a number of steamboats moored at Memphis were also captured.
3. Village Creek is located just south of Jacksonport and Newport, Arkansas.
4. The times in Jacksonport were becoming difficult, and not just because of supply problems. The rebel guerrillas were becoming bolder and the townsfolk more resistant. At least one soldier was murdered and roving bands were seen nearby. Colonel Brackett of the Ninth Illinois Cavalry noted that the movement of the army was seen as a retreat by the locals, further emboldening them. *War of the Rebellion: Official Records*, series 1, 13:396.
5. Brigadier General Benton was in command of the Eighth Indiana Infantry and reported to General Steele. William P. Benton was born in 1828, fought in the Mexican War, and was admitted to the bar in 1851. In April 1861 he was elected captain of the Eighth Indiana Regiment and was made colonel of the regiment in August 1861. After service in western Virginia, the Eighth Indiana was ordered to service in Missouri with General Samuel Curtis and fought in the battle of Pea Ridge. Benton was promoted to brigadier general in April 1862. He fought at Vicksburg and Mobile and was brevetted major general in March 1865. He died of yellow fever in New Orleans in March 1867. Warner, *Generals in Blue*, 30.

Chapter VI

1. Reports on the battle at Cache River appear in *War of the Rebellion: Official Records*, series 1, 13:37, 141–151; William Shea, "The Confederate Defeat at Cache River," *Arkansas Historical Quarterly* 52, no. 2 (1993): 129; and Glenn T. Nelson and John D. Squier, "The Confederate Defense of Northwest Arkansas and the Battle of Cotton Plant," *Rivers and Roads and Points in Between* 16 (spring 1989): 5–27. The number of casualties reported seem to differ depending upon whether reported by Union or Confederate officers.

General Hindman in Little Rock had ordered General Rust to proceed with his forces and block the advance of Curtis's army before it could cross the Cache River. For whatever reason, General Rust delayed his march and Curtis was able to get at least part of his army across the Cache. After the crossing, the Thirty-third was acting as scouts looking for Confederates—and they found them. Rush's late arrival certainly gave the advantage to Curtis. But even with that advantage, the results obtained by Hovey's small force against the rebels must be considered to be amazing.

General Albert Rust emigrated to Arkansas from Virginia in 1837. When the war began, he recruited the Third Arkansas Infantry and fought in several battles east of the Mississippi River he was sent back across the river in April 1863. Warner, *Generals in Gray,* 266. He was not held in very high repute by many in the Confederate military. Rust never wrote a report on the debacle at the Cache, and no reports were forwarded from his subordinates. Hindman noted this absence in his reports:

> In that interval Curtis' advance crossed Cache River and attacked General Rust, whose command, after an engagement of about thirty minutes, retreated in great disorder across White River. Many of his men deserted—both Texans and Arkansians. No report of this affair was ever received, though often called for; consequently I am not able to give any of the details. (*War of the Rebellion: Official Records*, series 1, 13:37)

In Curtis's report, the number of casualties reported seems conservative. Colonel Hovey's report and other attached reports estimated two hundred killed. *War of the Rebellion: Official Records*, series 1, 13:141–151. In addition, General Samuel R. Curtis's Journal comments on this battle:

> Battle Near Cotton Plant.
> July 7.
>
> I moved forward to Cache River where my advance under General Steele had been cutting away ______________ arranging [page 38] for forward movement. Sharp skirmishing had occurred on the 6th and the 3rd Iowa Cavalry encountered a few men at the crossing of the Cache, killing several. During the night our pickets had been run in and Col. Baker threw shells into the brush killing three. One man was shot when bathing; a few moments before I rode forward to arrange for placing a pontoon bridge across the stream. I was informed by Gen. Steele that Col. Hovey with part of his Normal regiment and part of the 11th Wisconsin and one little howitzer had been sent forward to skirmish. I arranged matters at the crossing (a thicket of brush and land very gloomy and uncomfortable). And made arrangements for crossing if my trains came up in time. I had hardly dismounted when I heard the sound of the howitzer's repeated several times in the advance.
>
> I directed Major Bowen to remain harnessed but General Steele sent me word that his advance was entirely sufficient. However I had my apprehension excited and ordered Col. Baker of the 13th Illinois to

advance a part of his cavalry with his rifle company. I sent to Gen'l. Steele directions also to second Gen. Washburn command if any necessity existed. The firing increased after Col. Baker (with Lt. Col. Woods) arrived and then I ordered the 3rd Iowa to move and also Brig. Gen. Braton.

My aides soon brought news of the result. Col. Hovey had been attacked by Texian Rangers [page 39] General Rust with men ______ was at Cotton Plant some two miles off. The enemy seems to have been very ill arranged. Col. Hovey was charged on and the Wisconsin troops driven back some distance. The one Howitzer came very near being lost. Col. Hovey got behind a fence and stood the charge, the charge of cavalry repulsing the enemy. About this time Col. Woods came up just in time to open fire with his steel rifle guns and the enemy ran, immediately routed. General Benton as I had ordered, took up the pursuit and the rebels were scattered in all directions.

Our killed is about 4 and one wounded. Some U [blank in ms.]. Among the latter, Major Glendenning of the 1st Illinois wounded severely in the lungs.

The enemy loss in killed must have been near a hundred. Our men buried some 92. They also had a large number wounded.

The victory was a complete one. I ordered large reinforcements to camp on the battleground.

July 8

Our men have been busy burying the dead. I ordered a large cavalry advance to move down the Cache to a ferry, returning by Cotton Plant which is the center of this abominable secesh neighborhood.

Chapter VII

1. Clarendon was truly a disappointment to the weary men of Curtis's army. From late June there had been attempts to reach and resupply the army by means of the White River. The ships, both gunboats and supply steamboats, actually had reached Clarendon just a day or two before Curtis arrived. However, fearing that the river would drop further, the fleet left and steamed back downstream. *War of the Rebellion: Official Records*, series 1, 13:115–119; *Official Records of the Union and Confederate Navies in the War of the Rebellion* (Harrisburg, PA: National Historical Society, 1987), series 1, 23:192–195. Hereafter cited as *Official Records of the Union and Confederate Navies.*
2. The *Acacia* steamboat had been part of the ill-fated White River expedition. It was captured at Memphis after the battle of Memphis, June 6, 1862, and valued at $2,750. It was repaired, taken into service, and used to transport supplies to the exhausted army at Helena. It was noted that it was "sunk in August." *Official Records of the Union and Confederate Navies,* series 1, 23:149, 219, 379, 684.

Chapter VIII

1. Old Town is located a few miles below Helena on the Mississippi River.
2. For a discussion of cotton "confiscation," see Appendix D.
3. Marshall does not identify the wounded man from Company C, but it was probably Henry H. Hays. Elliott and Way list Hays as "wounded at Wimbush's Plantation, 1 Aug., '62." He was discharged for disability February 25, 1863 but re-enlisted February 15, 1864 and was discharged with his regiment in December 1865. Elliott and Way, *History of the Thirty-Third Regiment Illinois,* 114.
4. The wounded and captured men were Cpl. Charles Bovee and Pvts. Selah B. Farwell, Charles D. Montgomery, and Johnson W. Straight. Bovee was as discharged at St. Louis on October 15, 1862, for wounds received at Drisdal's Plantation, Mississippi, on August 4, 1862. Similarly, Montgomery was discharged on February 24, 1863, and Straight on September 6, 1862, from St. Louis Hospital. Farwell was discharged for disability on February 16, 1863. Killed was Cpl. Alvin T. Lewis "near Wilkinson's Landing, Miss." on August 4, 1862. Elliott and Way, *History of the Thirty-Third Regiment Illinois,* 88, 89, 99.

Chapter IX

1. The *Des Moines,* a side-wheel steamer of 297 tons, was chartered as a troopship several times. Charles Dana Gibson and E. Kay Gibson, *The Army's Navy Series,* vol. 1, *Dictionary of Transports & Combatant Vessel, Steam and Sail, Employed by the Union Army* (Camden, ME: Ensign Press, 1995), 85.
2. Fort Pillow, which had been captured June 5, was not manned by Union troops.
3. New Madrid and Island No. 10 had been major blocks against Union movements down the Mississippi River. In a daring move, the *Carondelet* had passed the batteries and anchored at New Madrid, which had previously been taken by General Pope. A few days later the *Pittsburg* repeated the feat. This gave Pope sufficient protection to be able to move his troops across the Mississippi, cut off the defenders at Island No. 10, and force their surrender.
4. Cairo and Mound City, a few miles up the Ohio River, at the southern tip of Illinois had become major naval bases. This area was also the jumping-off place for transporting army units southward.
5. Sulphur Springs was located in Jefferson County, Missouri, and was the most convenient point on the river to connect with the St. Louis and Iron Mountain Railroad to Pilot Knob.
6. Patterson was located twenty-eight miles (as the crow flies) south of Ironton. The road through Brunot also led through a narrow mountain pass called Stoney Battery, which could be easily defended. A small, earthen fort had been erected on the top of a knoll just south of the town. When the Iron Mountain Railroad was extended south from Pilot Knob after the war, it was built west of

Patterson to take advantage of the terrain. A new town, Piedmont, was established, and Patterson lost much of its importance.

7. Timothy Reeves was born in North Carolina in 1812, came to Missouri in the 1840s, and settled on a farm north of Doniphan in Ripley County. He was also a Baptist minister. When war began in Missouri, he sided with the Confederacy and joined the Third Infantry, Missouri State Guard. Upon expiration of his six-month enlistment, he returned to Ripley County and raised a local defense company mustered into the Confederate Army as Reeves' Company, Missouri Independent Scouts. In combination with other units, Reeves' group became part of the Fifteenth Missouri Cavalry Regiment, CSA. Thus, Reeves was not the leader of a "band of thieves and murderers" as described by Marshall, although there were plenty of incidents—on both sides—that could be considered as barbarous. He traveled with General Sterling Price's raid in 1864 and exacted revenge on Union Major Wilson, captured at Fort Davidson–Pilot Knob, for previous events that occurred in Ripley County. After the war, he resumed farming and preaching.
8. The flood event described by Marshall, while rare in its extent, was common in the Missouri Ozarks. The terrain was mountainous in the area with small streams cut deeply and narrowly into the landscape. These small streams often drained large areas, and, with a downpour, could become impassable and dangerous.
9. The "small fort" at Patterson is still in existence, but overgrown.
10. As of December 31, 1862, the Department of Missouri organization, led by Major General Samuel R. Curtis, included the Army of Southeastern Missouri, commanded by Brigadier General John W. Davidson. The Thirty-third Illinois (commanded by Colonel Charles E. Lippincott) was placed in the First Brigade (with the Eleventh Wisconsin) in the First Division (*War of the Rebellion: Official Records*, series 1, vol. 22, part 1, 889–895). General Davidson was born in Virginia in 1824, graduated from West Point in 1845, and served in the West fighting Indians. During the Civil War he first fought in the Peninsula Campaign and was then assigned to the Department of Missouri in 1863. During the war he was brevetted to major general and after the war promoted to colonel of the Second Cavalry in 1879. He died of injuries in 1881 and is buried at Arlington National Cemetery (Warner, *Generals in Blue,* 112).

    General Frederick Steele assumed command of the Army of the Southwest at Helena, Arkansas, on August 29, 1862 (*War of the Rebellion: Official Records*, series 1, 13:605), was promoted to major general March 17, 1863, and served in the Vicksburg campaign. He again served in Arkansas and captured Little Rock in September 1863 (Warner, *Generals in Blue,* 474). Colonel Hovey left the command of the Thirty-third Illinois upon his appointment as brigadier general of volunteers to rank from September 5, 1862. The Senate failed to act on his appointment, which then expired on March 4, 1863. In January 1863 he took part in the capture of Arkansas Post as a brigade commander in Sherman's Corps under Major General McClernand. In that action he was wounded in both arms. He left the service in May 1863. After the war, he became a pension lobbyist in Washington. He died in 1897 and is buried in

Arlington National Cemetery (Warner, *Generals in Blue,* 236; Richard L. Kiper, *Major General John Alexander McClernand* [Kent, OH: Kent State University Press, 1999], 173).

Chapter X

1. Falling Springs is located in northeast Oregon County, feeding Hurricane Creek.
2. John Wynn Davidson (1824–1881) graduated from West Point in 1845. He served on the frontier in Kansas and Wisconsin and in the Mexican War in California. He was promoted to captain of the First Dragoons in 1885. He was appointed brigadier general of volunteers to rank from February 3, 1862. (*War of the Rebellion: Official Records*, series 1, 13:546.) He commanded the Army of Southeast Missouri in 1863 and the Army of Arkansas in 1864. After the war, he remained in the army, serving in the West. He died in 1881 and is buried in Arlington National Cemetery. (Warner, *Generals in Blue,* 112.)

Chapter XI

1. General Davidson's name was applied to the earthen fort that was built near the gap between Pilot Knob and Shepherd Mountain.
2. The name "Fort Curtis" noted by Marshall did not "stick." The name, however, was used by Capt. T. J. Mackey on his map made September 27, 1864, for General Price.

Chapter XII

1. Camp Middlebrook was at the little settlement of Middlebrook, just north of Pilot Knob on the Iron Mountain Railroad.
2. This resolution and the debate stemmed from a Resolution of the Illinois Legislature passed in early January 1863. "Resolved: That the emancipation proclamation of the President of the United States is as unwarranted in military as in civil law; a gigantic usurpation, at once converting the war, professedly commenced by the administration for the vindication of the authority of the constitution, into the crusade for the sudden, unconditional, and violent liberation of 3,000,000 negro slaves; a result which would not only be a total subversion of the Federal Union, but a revolution in the social organization of the Southern States, the immediate and remote, the present and far-reaching consequences of which to both races cannot be contemplated without the most dismal foreboding of horror and dismay. The proclamation invites servile insurrection as an element in this emancipation crusade—a means of warfare, the inhumanity and diabolism of which are without example in civilized warfare, and which we denounce, and which the civilized world will denounce,

as an uneffaceable disgrace to the American people." In November 1862, the Democratic Party captured control of the Illinois State Legislature. Many of these Democrats were "copperheads" and opposed to the war. Resolution from the *Illinois State Register,* January 7, 1863.

3. Eugene A. Carr was born in 1830 and graduated from West Point in 1850. He fought at Wilson's Creek and Pea Ridge. After Steele remained in Arkansas, Carr assumed command. He led troops at Vicksburg, Camden, and Mobile. After the war, he reverted to major, Fifth Cavalry, and commanded units in the West, rising to colonel (1879) and brigadier general (1892). He retired in 1893. He was famous as an Indian fighter. He died in 1910 and is buried at West Point. Warner, *Generals in Blue,* 70.
4. Marshall here uses the phrase of Lincoln that the Mississippi "flows unvexed to the sea" when he was informed of the fall of Vicksburg and Port Hudson in July 1863.
5. The *Illinois* was a side-wheel steamer of 682 tons that was chartered several times, including as a troop transport for the Vicksburg expedition. Gibson and Gibson, *The Army's Navy Series,* 1:158.

Chapter XIII

1. "Down the Mississippi." The Thirty-third was entering upon one of the largest campaigns in the war. The "Anaconda Plan" advocated by General Winfield Scott early in the war proposed a blockade of southern ports and a drive down the Mississippi River to split and strangle the Confederacy. Skeptics scoffed and cartoonists drew a great snake encircling the map of the Confederacy. This plan was, critics notwithstanding, the key to overall Union success in the war. There were several problems. First, many naval officers resigned their commissions and worked to establish a Confederate Navy. Second, many of the navy's ships were on foreign stations, far from the American coast. Third, many of the ships in American waters were obsolete or were in need of repair. Finally, a naval force on the Mississippi River did not exist! But plans were formulated, the coastal blockade initiated, and naval construction begun on the Mississippi and Ohio Rivers. The push down the Mississippi began, but progress was slow through 1861 and 1862, but by the spring of 1863, only a small reach of the river remained in Confederate hands. The river from Port Hudson on the south to Vicksburg on the north was all that was left, and even this saw Union ships braving the heavy cannonades from the fortifications at Port Hudson and Vicksburg. But as long as these fortifications remained, the river was effectively blocked to the commerce so vital to the agricultural Midwest. General Grant began his campaign against Vicksburg and called upon many units that had been stationed in the Trans-Mississippi region. The Thirty-third Illinois Volunteer Infantry was one of these units.
2. General Davidson notes that units have been sent to General Grant's Army near Vicksburg: Brigadier Generals Eugene A. Carr and William P. Benton and the Eighth Indiana, Eighteenth Indiana, Ninety-ninth Illinois, Twenty-second Iowa, Eleventh Wisconsin, Twenty-first Iowa, Twenty-third Iowa, First Indiana

Battery, and the Thirty-third Illinois, Colonel Lippincott commanding. *War of the Rebellion: Official Records*, series 1, vol. 22, part 2, 161.

3. The Army of the Tennessee, commanded by General Grant was made up of the Thirteenth, Fifteenth, and Seventeenth Army Corps. The Thirteenth Army Corps was commanded by Major General John A. McClernand. A division of the Thirteenth was commanded by General Carr, and within that division, the First Brigade, which had the Thirty-third Illinois, was commanded by Brigadier General Benton.
4. These two vessels were "Porter's Boats" in name only. They really belonged to the Mississippi Marine Brigade commanded by Alfred Ellet and were part of the army. The story of this bizarre unit and its actions can be found in Chester G. Hearn, *Ellet's Brigade, the Strangest Outfit of All* (Baton Rouge: Louisiana State University Press, 2000); and Warren D. Crandall, *History of the Ram Fleet and the Mississippi Marine Brigade in the War for the Union* (St. Louis, MO: Society of Survivors, 1907).
5. Colonel Hovey had been appointed brigadier general of volunteers on September 5, 1862, but the Senate failed to act on the nomination within the statutory period and the nomination expired on March 4, 1863.
6. Captain Burnham served Company A. Burnham had served as first lieutenant from the regiment's organization (August 21, 1861) until his promotion to captain (September 5, 1862). He replaced Captain Potter, who was wounded at the battle of Cache River and who was then promoted to major (September 5, 1862). Elliott and Way, *History of the Thirty-Third Regiment Illinois,* 82, 88.
7. The "canal" Marshall mentions was unsuccessful. The hope was that by construction of a ditch across the neck of land in front of Vicksburg, the river would take the "hint" and carve a new channel. However, the river did not cooperate with human attempts to move its channel.
8. Governor Yates, the "War Governor" of Illinois (1818–1873), served from 1861 to 1864. He was known as the "soldiers' friend" and went out of his way to offer support and aid to the Illinois units. As a Republican, he ran afoul of the Democratic-controlled legislature in 1863, leading to great political controversy in the state. See http://history.rays-place.com/governors/il/Yates-r.htm; see also chapter XII, note 2.
9. John A. McClernand was an influential congressman from Illinois who became a brigadier general in 1861. He was known as a "political general" who nevertheless had success leading troops at Fort Donelson and Shiloh. During the Vicksburg Campaign, his political machinations led Grant to relieve him of command. He later served under General Nathaniel Banks, commanding the Thirteenth Corps in the Department of the Gulf. Richard L. Kiper, *Major General John Alexander McClernand* (Kent, OH: Kent State University Press, 1999).

Chapter XIV

1. General Hovey left the army, probably for several reasons. His appointment as brigadier general was not approved by the Senate and expired on March 4,

1863. (Hovey had entered into an argument about credit in the battle of Cache River that, despite the success of the battle, may have stained his reputation.) He took an important part in the capture of Arkansas Post in January 1863, where he was wounded in both arms. These wounds may account for his resignation. After the war he practiced law in Washington, D.C., and specialized in pension lobbying. He died in 1897 and was buried in Arlington Cemetery. Warner, *Generals in Blue,* 236; Kiper, *McClernand,* 173.

2. Bruinsburg was chosen as the point to force the crossing of the Mississippi because it was well below the fortifications that surrounded Vicksburg. Originally, Grant had planned to use another crossing, but then chose Bruinsburg on the advice of a slave who knew the area.
3. Magnolia Hills was an alternate name given to the battle of Port Gibson.

Chapter XV

1. Port Gibson was the site of the first real battle after Grant's forces crossed the Mississippi River. As the army was moving along the Rodney road toward Port Gibson, they ran into Confederate units led by Brig. General John S. Bowen. Unable to stem the tide of superior forces, the Confederates were slowly force to retire from the field.
2. Grand Gulf was initially attacked from the river by David Dixon Porter's gunboats. Because the fortifications of Grand Gulf were elevated, it was very difficult for the gunboats to reach their targets and they were driven off. This reverse led Grant to the decision to move his army further south along the west side of the river to find a crossing point. After the crossing was made and the Confederates dislodged from Port Gibson, the Confederates abandoned Grand Gulf and pulled back to Vicksburg.
3. General Benton was William P. Benton. He served first as captain and colonel of the Eighth Indiana Infantry. He fought at Pea Ridge and was promoted to Brigadier General April 28, 1862. Warner, *Generals in Blue,* 30.
4. General John Alexander Logan was a civilian soldier from southern Illinois (Little Egypt). While this area generally supported secession, Logan was a staunch Unionist. In 1861, Logan returned to southern Illinois and recruited the Thirty-first Illinois, of which he served as colonel. After fighting at Belmont and Fort Donelson, he was advanced to brigadier general (March 21, 1862) He fought at Shiloh and Vicksburg and was named major general on March 13, 1863. He fought in the Atlanta campaign and in the campaign from Savannah to North Carolina. After the war he served as both congressman and senator from Illinois. He died in 1886 (Warner, *Generals in Blue,* 281). For General Carr, see chapter XII, note 3. General A. P. Hovey was a remote cousin of Charles E. Hovey. He served as colonel of the Twenty-fourth Indiana and fought at the battle of Shiloh. He was promoted to brigadier general for his bravery and leadership. He fought in the battle of Champion's Hill. He also commanded the District of Indiana in a recruiting capacity (Warner, *Generals in Blue,* 235).

5. The battle of Raymond was an attempt to delay or deter the Union's march on Jackson. After a long (six-hour) and bloody battle, the Confederate forces were pushed aside and Grant's army held the ground.
6. Peter J. Osterhaus was born in Prussia in 1823. He took part in the revolutions that swept Europe in 1848 and was forced to flee to the United States. He settled in the St. Louis area, where he entered the Civil War as a major in one of the German regiments enlisted by Frank Blair and Nathaniel Lyon. He fought at Wilson's Creek and later commanded a division of Curtis's forces at Pea Ridge. He was appointed a brigadier general of volunteers in June 1862. At Vicksburg he commanded a division and was wounded at Big Black River. After the war he engaged in the wholesale hardware business and was U.S. consul at Lyons, France, and later in the Consular Service in Germany. He died and was buried in Coblenz, Germany, in 1917. Warner, *Generals in Blue,* 352.

Chapter XVI

1. The battle of Champion Hill was one of the key battle in Grant's plan to interpose his army between Pemberton's forces from Vicksburg and assistance that might come from Jackson and eastward. Pemberton was facing east and Grant attacked both from the northeast and east, while A. J. Smith prevented escape to the south.
2. James B. McPherson, born in Ohio, graduated from West Point in 1853. He served as chief engineer to Grant at Fort Donelson. He achieved rank of Major General 8 October, 1862 and commanded the XVII Corps at Vicksburg where he distinguished himself. He died during the battle of Atlanta, 22 July, 1864. (Warner, *Generals in Blue,* 306)
3. Edwards' Station was located mid-way between the sites of the battles of Champion Hill and Big Black River.

Chapter XVII

1. A good reference for this battle and for the battles at Vicksburg, in general, is William L. Shea and Terrence J. Winschel, *Vicksburg Is the Key: The Struggle for the Mississippi Valley* (Lincoln: University of Nebraska Press, 2003).

Chapter XVIII

1. In this chapter, Marshall tells his story of Vicksburg from the private soldier's point of view. For the larger story see Shea and Winschel, *Vicksburg Is the Key;* or Johnson and Buel, *Battles and Leaders of the Civil War,* 3:462–581.
2. Captain Kellogg was Henry M. Kellogg of C Company, killed in action at Vicksburg, May 20, 1863. Elliott and Way, *History of the Thirty-Third Regiment Illinois,* 108, 113.

3. Marshall is in error. Actually, five men of D Company were wounded on May 22, 1863, four of whom died between May 26 and 29, and one died November 14, 1863. Elliott and Way, *History of the Thirty-Third Regiment Illinois,* 119–122.
4. Francis M. DeBoice, Company A, died June 11, 1863, in Memphis of wounds received at Vicksburg, May 21,1863. Elliott and Way, *History of the Thirty-Third Regiment Illinois,* 89.
5. Elliott and Way list six killed, two mortally wounded, and "all the other members of Company E were wounded more or less severely, except three." Elliott and Way, *History of the Thirty-Third Regiment Illinois,* 135.
6. William T. Biggerstaff died on May 22, 1863, and Absalom M. Zartman died of his wounds on May 24, 1863. Elliott and Way, *History of the Thirty-Third Regiment Illinois,* 88, 91.

Chapter XIX

1. Again, in this chapter, Marshall tells his story of Vicksburg from the private soldier's point of view. For the larger story see Shea and Winschel, *Vicksburg Is the Key;* or Johnson and Buel, *Battles and Leaders of the Civil War,* 3:462–581.
2. Marshall does a good job in describing the process of an advancing siege. The "cane rollers" that he describes were sometimes called "sap rollers" and were baskets filled with earth. A similar process was employed in the siege of the Union fort at Lexington, Missouri, except that in that case the sap rollers were bales of hemp, wet down to prevent their burning with hot shot.

Chapter XX

1. Marshall has inserted this chapter in his book to record a talk that he gave in 1866. It breaks no new ground from what appeared previously.
2. The "Few Incidents" section is revealing in that it illuminates the thinking of several different groups of Southerners about the war, Union troops, and slavery.
3. Bowine was John S. Bowen. Bowen was born in Georgia in 1830 and graduated from West Point in 1853. In 1856 he resigned to become an architect in St. Louis. He was captain of militia and chief of staff to General Frost and was captured at Camp Jackson in May 1861. Upon release he organized and became colonel of the First Missouri Infantry. Appointed brigadier general in March 1862, he fought at Shiloh and opposed Grant at Port Gibson in the Vicksburg campaign. He was appointed major general in May 1863. He fought in the battles preceding and in the siege of Vicksburg. Ill with dysentery, he died on July 13, 1863. He is buried in the Confederate cemetery at Vicksburg. Warner, *Generals in Gray,* 29.
4. Marshall's comments on Grant are revealing, not only about his own feelings, but also those of the average private soldier in Grant's army.

Chapter XXI

1. In this chapter, Marshall begins his narrative of the further travels of the Thirty-third Illinois. It was decided that this unit would not follow Sherman and Grant to the east, but rather travel south to New Orleans to take part in operations in Louisiana (and later Texas).
2. Steamer *Gladiator,* tonnage unknown, was used as a troop transport at Shiloh, on the Arkansas River, and during the siege of Vicksburg. Gibson and Gibson, *The Army's Navy Series,* 1:134.
3. General Nathaniel P. Banks was born in Massachusetts in 1816 and was one of the Union's "Political Generals." He was active in Massachusetts and National Politics and was appointed major general of volunteers by Lincoln in January 1861. His contributions were in the realm of recruiting, money, and political support. His military record was abysmal. He was beaten in the Shenandoah Valley and at Cedar Mountain in 1862. After these failures he was "exiled" to the west, at New Orleans, where he botched the siege of Port Hudson, and totally failed in the Red River campaign, where he was relieved of command. His overall command included both Louisiana and Texas. After the war he reentered politics in Massachusetts, serving six terms in the U.S. House of Representatives. He died in 1894. Warner, *Generals in Blue,* 17.
4. Carrollton, Louisiana, was located just north of New Orleans on the east side of the Mississippi River. It was a fashionable location that was absorbed into the city of New Orleans in the 1870s.
5. Richard Taylor, son of President Zachary Taylor, was born in Kentucky in 1826. He graduated from Yale in 1845 after prior study in Europe and at Harvard. In 1850, he established a sugar plantation in Louisiana and entered politics. He was appointed colonel of the Ninth Louisiana Infantry, CSA. He fought at First Manassas, in the Valley Campaign, and in the Seven Days Battles before Richmond. He was appointed brigadier general in October 1861 and major general in July 1862. At that time he was assigned to the District of West Louisiana. Badly outnumbered, he fought Banks in the Red River Campaign, completely defeating him at Mansfield and Pleasant Hill in the spring of 1864. He was promoted to lieutenant general in April 1864. He died in New York in 1879 and is buried in New Orleans. Warner, *Generals in Gray,* 299.

Chapter XXII

1. General Banks had stripped most of his command to send troops to besiege Port Hudson. In so doing, he left the rest of his command woefully undermanned. General Richard Taylor was quick to take advantage of the situation. He attacked Alexandria, Louisiana, and also attacked and took Brashear City. In fact, he attacked along the rail line from Brashear City to New Orleans, reaching a point past Thibodeaux and within twenty miles of

New Orleans. All the points in this southern Louisiana area were undermanned and many convalescent troops were stationed there. Taylor took many prisoners, paroling the enlisted men and sending the officers to prison in Texas until exchanged. This sent shock waves throughout the area. However, once Vicksburg and Port Hudson fell in early July 1863, the Union turned their attention to the problems in southern Louisiana and began to send units to remedy the problems (John D. Winters, *The Civil War in Louisiana* (Baton Rouge: Louisiana State University Press, 1991), 284 ff). On August 31, 1863, Banks reported the organization of his augmented forces. Among these forces was the Thirteenth Army Corps, which was transferred from Vicksburg to Carrollton, Louisiana, August 10–26. Within the Thirteenth Army Corps, the First Division was commanded by Brigadier General William P. Benton. Within the First Division, the First Brigade, commanded by Col. David Shunk, contained the Thirty-third Illinois along with the Ninety-ninth Illinois and the Eighth and Eighteenth Indiana and the First Indiana Battery (O.R., series 1, vol. 26, part 1, 709).

2. Sabine Pass was a disastrous defeat for the Union. Sabine Pass protected Port Arthur and the Sabine River boundary between Louisiana and Texas. A very small garrison with few guns was able to disable and capture two of the four escorting gunboats. The remaining Union forces returned to New Orleans.
3. Cadwallader Colden Washburn was born in Maine in 1818. In 1839 he moved to Wisconsin and in 1842 began a law practice in Mineral Point, Wisconsin. He amassed a fortune in land speculation, lumbering, railroading, and banking. He was elected to Congress in 1854 and served three terms. He was named colonel, Second Wisconsin Cavalry in February 1862 and rose to brigadier general of volunteers (July 1862) and major general (March 1863). He rendered good service while on active duty, first in Missouri under Eugene Carr. After the war, he returned to Wisconsin, served two more terms in Congress and was governor of Wisconsin, 1871–1873. In these years he also organized Washburn, Crosby, and Company—which became General Mills—in Minneapolis. He died in 1882 and is buried in LaCrosse, Wisconsin (Warner, *Generals in Blue,* 542).
4. Berwick was just across the river from Brashear City.
5. On June 20, the Union forces were routed from Brashear City (Winters, *The Civil War in Louisiana,* 285–286).

Chapter XXIII

1. New Iberia.
2. Vermillionville is now Lafayette, Louisiana.
3. Lawler's Brigade was formed by consolidation of the Third and Fourth Brigades of the First Division of the Thirteenth Army Corps on September 23, 1863 (*War of the Rebellion: Official Records*, series 1, vol. 26, part 1, 709.) Brigadier General Michael K. Lawler, commanding the brigade, was probably one of the more "colorful" Union Generals. He was born in Ireland in 1814 and was

brought to America in 1816. He fought in the Mexican War and later farmed in Gallatin County, in far southeastern Illinois. He also kept a general store in Shawneetown, the county seat. Lawler kept discipline in his regiment (Eighteenth Illinois) by "knocking down recalcitrants with his fists, by feeding emetics to drunks in the guardhouse, and by threats of violence to officers and men alike." He was acquitted of these offenses by the department commander, Henry Halleck. He fought and was wounded at Fort Donelson, was promoted to brigadier general (ranking from November 29, 1862), and commanded a brigade in the Vicksburg campaign. After the war he resumed farming in Equality, Illinois, and died in 1882 (Warner, *Generals in Blue,* 276).

4. Colonel David Shunk (1822–1865) and the Eighth Indiana fought at Pea Ridge and at Vicksburg and were then transferred to Louisiana service. They served in Louisiana and on the Texas Gulf Coast and were then transferred to the East and saw service in the 1864 Shenandoah Valley campaign. However, Shunk died, February 21, 1865, in Marion, Indiana. His "arrest" and the reason, therefore, were not noted and probably did not appear in any records.
5. Leonville is/was a small town southeast of Opelousas.
6. Stephen G. Burbridge was born in Kentucky in 1831. He was commissioned colonel of the Twenty-sixth Kentucky (Union) Infantry in August 1861 and brigadier general of volunters in June 1862. He fought at Shiloh, Arkansas Post, and Vicksburg. Early in 1864 he was named to head the Military District of Kentucky, where he engendered considerable hatred. He was relieved of his command in January 1865 and resigned the army in December 1865. He died in Brooklyn, New York, in 1895 and is buried in Arlington National Cemetery (Warner, *Generals in Blue,* 54).
7. Opelousas.

Chapter XXIV

1. The expedition to Texas had several reasons. Both Grant and Banks had wanted to advance on Mobile, one of the last remaining ports in Confederate hands. They were overruled by General Halleck and some of the politicians in Washington for two reasons. First, the French had invaded Mexico and had installed Ferdinand Joseph Maximilian, Archduke of Austria, as Emperor of Mexico. This reflected the French desire for empire and the imperial hopes of Louis Napoleon. Maximilian was supported by the French Foreign Legion troops and a few Mexican loyalists. The timing was chosen with the idea that the United States was too busy with a war of its own to intervene and invoke the Monroe Doctrine. However, Maximilian was also fighting a revolt by Juarez and others. The second reason was that there was considerable trade across the Rio Grande River border. Arms from Europe arrived legally in Matamoras, Mexico, and were then taken a short distance up the river, out of the reach of the Union navy and then transferred to Brownsville or further west into Confederate Texas. Bales of cotton made the reverse trip to fund the arms purchases. Then there was a long difficult trip across Texas (and Louisiana) to

bring the arms to where they were needed. That such a trade actually occurred was an indication of the dire straits of the Confederacy.

2. General Washburn. See chapter XXII, note 4.
3. The steamship *Clinton,* a side-wheel steamer of 721 tons, was chartered on September 1, 1863, and served as a troopship on the Brownsville expedition, October—November 1863. Gibson and Gibson, *The Army's Navy Series,* 1:64.
4. The "steamboat *Warren*" is not to be found in the records.
5. The *Saint Mary's,* a side-wheel steamer of 678 tons, was a sister ship of the *Clinton.* It served on the Mississippi River between Baton Rouge and New Orleans before being chartered for the Brownsville expedition. Gibson and Gibson, *The Army's Navy Series,* 1:283.

Chapter XXV

1. Bank's expedition landed on Brazos Island at the mouth of the Rio Grande and proudly reported to General Halleck, "the flag of the Union was raised on Brazos Island, which is now in our possession" (*War of the Rebellion: Official Records*, series 1, vol. 26, part 1, 397). His troops then occupied Brownsville and the small Confederate force fled the city without a fight. Banks also commented on the turmoil occurring in Matamoras across the border (*War of the Rebellion: Official Records*, series 1, vol. 26, part 1, 399–409). St. Joseph's Island was one of the chain of barrier islands that protected the gulf coast of Texas. All had small garrisons which, as Marshall noted for St. Joseph's Island, rapidly fled from the onrushing Union force.
2. Matagorda Island was one of the larger barrier islands and had a small fort, Fort Esperanza, at its northern tip.

Chapter XXVI

1. At the northern tip of Matagorda Island, in addition to Fort Esperanza, there was a lighthouse to mark the opening into Matagorda Bay. Within the bay were the towns of Lavaca, Saluria, and Indianola. Victoria was some distance inland. For the defense of the fort, Matagorda Bay, and the rest of the Texas Gulf Coast, see Alwyn Barr, "Texas Coastal Defense, 1861–1865," *Southwestern Historical Quarterly* 45 (July,1961): 1–31; Lester Fitzhugh, "Saluria, Fort Esperanza, and Military Operations on the Texas Gulf Coast, 1861–1865," *Southwestern Historical Quarterly* 41 (July 1957): 66–100; and *New York Times,* "The Capture of Fort Esperanza," December 27, 1863, p. 2.
2. Thomas E. G. Ransom was born in Vermont in 1834 and received a degree in civil engineering from Norwich University in 1851. Living in Illinois in 1861, he formed a company which became the Eleventh Illinois. He served as major, lieutenant colonel, and colonel of the regiment. He was wounded at Charleston, Missouri, Fort Donelson, and at Shiloh. He was made brigadier general of volunteers in April 1863 and fought with distinction at Vicksburg.

He also took part in the abortive Red River expedition of General Nathaniel P. Banks, where he was again wounded. He later served in the Atlanta campaign. His wounds were aggravated and he died near Rome, Georgia, in October 1864. For his services he was brevetted major general in September 1864. He is buried in Chicago (Warner, *Generals in Blue,* 389).

3. Pass Cavallo was the entrance to Matagorda Bay.
4. Lt. George H. Fifer "died from wounds [on December 26, 1863] received at Fort Esperanza, Tex. 27 Nov., '63." Elliott and Way, *History of the Thirty-Third Regiment Illinois,* 109, 113.
5. Leon Smith (CSA) to Maj. Gen. J. B. Magruder, November 30, reported, "The enemy charged our rifle-pits on the 28th, at 4 PM and took them, and have since used them against us" (*War of the Rebellion: Official Records*, series 1, vol. 26, part 2, 464).
6. Smith also reported the evacuation of the fort and island, but he did not report the destruction of the powder magazines (O.R., series 1, vol. 26, part 2, 464).
7. These words seem to corroborate the account by Marshall given above.
8. Undoubtedly the correspondent meant Semmes. Raphael Semmes commanded the famous commerce raider, CSS *Alabama.*

Chapter XXVII

1. Indianola was occupied despite orders from the Confederate command in Texas for rebel troops to be sent there (*War of the Rebellion: Official Records*, series 1, vol. 26, part 2, 467). The fact was simply that the Union troops beat the Confederate troops to the town.
2. Actually Decrow's Point, on Matagorda Peninsula, opposite Matagorda Island.
3. Indianola, Texas, on Matagorda Bay was founded in 1846 and at one time was the second largest port in Texas (after Galveston). It served as the port of immigration for many of the German settlers of Texas. It also was the port that received two shipments of camels in 1856 and 1857—the experiment proposed by the secretary of war, Jefferson Davis, for transportation in the American West. Indianola's prosperity continued until two hurricanes struck in 1875 and 1886. The latter completely wiped out the town.
4. The town was first "visited" by Union troops on December 13, 1863, but the troops did not remain after flushing out a few Confederate soldiers. It was noted that "the inhabitants were much frightened when the troops arrived, as great pains have been taken by General Magruder to impress upon them the idea that our troops would burn, ravish, and destroy wherever they go, and acting upon their fears, is endeavoring to induce them to flee from the coast and destroy their property. Before our troops left, their minds were disabused, and they showed considerable friendly feeling" (*War of the Rebellion: Official Records*, series 1, vol. 26, part 1, 853). Full occupation by the First Brigade occurred on December 23 (*War of the Rebellion: Official Records*, series 1, vol. 26, part 1, 879).

5. Fitz-Henry Warren was born in Massachusetts in 1816. In 1844 he moved to Burlington, Iowa, and entered the newspaper business and politics. He was named colonel of the First Iowa Cavalry in June 1861 and served at posts in Missouri against Confederate recruits and sympathizers. In July 1862 he was advanced to brigadier general of volunteers, and in September 1863 he was ordered to the Department of the Gulf. He commanded at Brownsville, Texas. He assumed command of the Thirteenth Army Corps, First Division, First Brigade on November 14, 1863. He replaced Brig. Gen. William Vandever. He was ordered east for health reasons in September 1864 and was brevetted major general of volunteers in August 1865. Later he served as Iowa state senator and as U.S. minister to Guatemala. He died in 1878 and is buried in Massachusetts. Warner, *Generals in Blue,* 540.
6. Pvt. William G. D. Weed served from August 21, 1861, to mustering out on December 6, 1865.
7. This minor expedition receives no mention in the Official Records, but is noted, from the Confederate side, as the battle of Norris Bridge over Chocolate Bayou, in Alex E. Sweet and J. Armoy Knox, *On a Mexican Mustang: Through Texas from the Gulf to the Rio Grande* (Houston, TX: T. N. James & Co., 1884), 483–501.
8. This was Captain Clemente Zapata of the Second Texas Cavalry (Union).

Chapter XXVIII

1. In this chapter, Marshall reviews the events of the year 1863 and comments upon the variety of service that the Thirty-third had seen, from southern Missouri to Vicksburg, to southern Louisiana and finally to Texas.
2. W. M. Berry, editor, was not found on the rosters of either the Thirty-third or Ninety-ninth Infantry Companies.
3. The Thirty-third was asked to re-enlist as officials were concerned about the expiration of their three-year enlistment. The regiment had been established in August 1861, so enlistment expiration was not close at hand at the end of 1863. Nevertheless, reenlistments were taken and with that the regiment went home on furlough. Marshall refused reenlistment for one major reason. As he put it, "For fully two thirds of my army life I had been troubled with the ague." Marshall had been healthier on the Texas Gulf Coast and wished to remain to serve there throughout the remainder of his enlistment or until the Thirty-third returned from furlough and he could rejoin his unit. Officers had offered him hospital time or discharge because of the "ague"—probably malaria—but he refused, wanting to serve out his commitment.
4. Napoleon J. T. Dana was born in Maine in 1822 of a military family and graduated from the Military Academy in 1842. In 1855 he resigned his commission to enter business in St. Paul, Minnesota, but also served as brigadier of Minnesota militia. He was appointed colonel of the First Minnesota in October 1861. He was advanced to brigadier general in the spring of 1862 and was badly wounded at Sharpsburg. After recovery he was

appointed major general to rank from November 1862, and returned to duty in July 1863 but saw no further active service in battles. He was named to command the Thirteenth Army Corps on September 28, 1863. In late December he was reporting on the situation on the Texas gulf coast and inland from Brownsville (*War of the Rebellion: Official Records*, series 1, vol. 26, part 1, 876). He resigned in May 1865 to enter various business enterprises. He died in New Hampshire in July 1905 (Warner, *Generals in Blue,* 111).

5. Marshall did not want to reenlist for another three years with the Thirty-third and yet he did not want a discharge from service. His illnesses (the "ague") that he mentions throughout his narrative had become considerably better with his stay on the Texas Gulf coast, and he wished to remain there. Therefore, he was transferred to the Ninety-ninth Illinois, a unit that had fought near the Thirty-third and one that he was familiar with.

Chapter XXIX

1. The Ninety-ninth Illinois was familiar to Marshall and not just from service in Texas. The Ninety-ninth was organized in Pike County, Illinois, in August 1862 (a year after the Thirty-third). By September 8, it was at Rolla, Missouri. It was stationed at Salem, Dent County (September 17), and Houston, Texas County (November 20). On January 27, 1863, it moved to West Plains, Howell County, Missouri, reporting to Brigadier General Davidson (chapter IX, note 10). At this station, it must have come in contact with the Thirty-third, which was escorting supply trains to West Plains and Pilot Knob. On March 3, 1863, the Ninety-ninth moved to Pilot Knob and thence to Ste. Genevieve along with the Thirty-third. It was assigned, along with the Thirty-third, to General Benton's brigade in General Carr's division. It fought along with the Thirty-third at the battles of Magnolia Hills, Champion Hills, and Black River and in the siege of Vicksburg. Along with the Thirty-third, it was moved to Louisiana and took part in the Teche campaign. Then both regiments were sent to Texas and fought together over Mustang and Matagorda Islands and took Fort Esperanza. On January 27, the Thirty-third left on furlough and the Ninety-ninth remained until June 1864, when they evacuated Matagorda Island and returned to the New Orleans area.
2. "Company A boys" were John D. King, Cyrus A. Bailey, Samuel Smith, and Albert O. Marshall. All were listed as "served by transfer in 99 Illinois. Mustered Out by expiration term of service" Elliott and Way, *History of the Thirty-Third Regiment Illinois,* 88–90.
3. See chapter III, note 3.
4. General Warren. See chapter XXVII, note 5.
5. Edward O. C. Ord was born in Maryland in 1818 and graduated from West Point in 1839. He served in the Seminole and Mexican Wars. Before the Civil War he was on Indian duty in the Pacific Northwest. In 1861, in California, he was appointed brigadier general of volunteers and served in the eastern theater. In May 1862, Ord was appointed major general and served at Corinth and

Vicksburg. Later he had commands in Louisiana and in the Shenandoah Valley. He was wounded in service around Richmond. In January 1865 he commanded the Army of the James and the Department of North Carolina. After the war he was made brigadier general in the regular army and retired in 1881. In 1883, on a ship bound for Vera Cruz from New York, he was stricken with yellow fever and died in Havana. He was buried in Arlington Cemetery. Fort Ord in California (Monterrey area) was named for him (Warner, *Generals in Blue,* 349).

6. The Eleventh Wisconsin was another unit familiar to the Thirty-third. It arrived at Pilot Knob, Missouri, in March 1862 and served along with the Thirty-third throughout northeast Arkansas, fought at Cache River, and, after reaching Helena, returned to Pilot Knob. It also fought in the same organization as the Thirty-third at Vicksburg, in the Teche campaign, and at Fort Esparanza and Indianola (Dyer, *A Compendium of the War of the Rebellion,* 1677–1678).
7. General McClernand, the archtypical political general, had been relieved of command at Vicksburg by Grant during the siege, ostensibly to recruit in Illinois. He returned to the command of the Eight Corps, which by now was widely dispersed in Louisiana and Texas. He finally resigned from the army in November 1864 (Warner, *Generals in Blue,* 293).
8. Benjamin S. Roberts was born in Vermont in 1810 and graduated from West Point in 1835. In 1839 he resigned from the service and entered railroad engineering and construction. He reentered the army with the outbreak of the Mexican War, from his home in Iowa, where he had been practicing law. He then remained in the army serving at various frontier posts, becoming major in 1861. He served in eastern campaigns and then held various minor commands. He was made brigadier general of volunteers in July 1861 and major general of volunteers in 1865. He became lieutenant colonel in the regular army after the war and was assigned as professor of military science at Yale in 1868. He resigned in 1870 and died in 1875 (Warner, *Generals in Blue,* 405).
9. The screw tug *Perry,* 154 tons, was purchased at Philadelphia in December 1863 and was sent to Texas for Banks's Expedition.
10. Probably the *Suffolk,* a steamer of unknown tonnage that was chartered in September 1863.

Chapter XXX

1. These schoolboy-like exercises at least tell us that the units on Matagorda Island were not very busy, as Marshall also noted. Throughout this recounting of "army life" Marshall has made note of the serious nature of many of the soldiers. Remembering that the Thirty-third Illinois was the "Normal Regiment," it should not be too surprising that these college students and teachers were serious about improving themselves through study and reading in their spare time.

Chapter XXXI

1. General Nathaniel Banks had, in the last months of 1863, achieved some success on the Texas coast. Brownsville and several smaller ports had been occupied. But Galveston and the Sabine River were still in Confederate hands. Banks continued to ask for more troops to advance his plans for further coastal attacks and movement inland. Cotton trade through Mexico had decreased, some claimed by more than half, and that which did move was forced to points well west of the Union forces at Brownsville. Much of the cotton trade movements were halted and diverted by order of General Bee, who commanded Confederate forces in the area. However, little cotton had been captured by Banks's army. While Lincoln was pleased with the demonstration at Brownsville and approved of the message that this demonstration had sent to the French occupiers of Mexico, General Halleck in Washington still considered these movements a waste of time and manpower. Halleck's desire was to attack up the Red River in Louisiana, capture Shreveport, and then strike into east Texas, where more cotton was available than in south Texas. This military approach was continually proposed by Halleck to all the military authorities. It was in March 1864 that Ulysses S. Grant became General in Chief of all Union Armies. One of his first acts was to order all posts in Texas with the exception of Brownsville to be evacuated and the troops to be returned to New Orleans.
2. General Alexander Somerville (not Summerville, as Marshall noted) was a brigadier general of Texas militia. In 1842, contrary to orders from Sam Houston, he led forces into Mexico and was defeated.
3. Steamship *St. Mary's,* see chapter XXIV, note 3. It served as a troopship well into 1865. It was a sister ship of the *Clinton.*
4. Steamer *Clinton,* see chapter XXIV note 5
5. "Colonel Parks" was Lt. Colonel Lemuel Parke, who entered service August 23, 1862, and resigned on May 21, 1864.
6. "Demp" King was J. D. King of Company A, Thirty-third Illinois.
7. Carrollton. See chapter XXI, note 4.
8. Donaldsonville was located on the west bank of the Mississippi River between New Orleans and Baton Rouge.
9. Fort Butler was built in Donaldsonville at the confluence of Bayou La Fourche and the Mississippi River as a response to the harassment of shipping. On June 28, 1863, its 300-man garrison was attacked by a superior force of 800 Confederates under General Thomas Green, of the Fifth Texas Cavalry CSA. The Confederates were repulsed and the fort remained guarding the river. This attack was one of the attempts to draw attention away from and to relieve the pressure on both Port Hudson and Vicksburg.
10. See map, chapter XX.
11. Randall Lee Gibson, born in Kentucky in 1832, resided on the family plantation "Live Oaks" in Terrebonne Parish, Louisiana. He graduated from Yale in 1853. In August 1861, he was commissioned colonel of the Thirteenth

Louisiana Infantry (CSA). He was promoted to brigadier general in January 1864. He fought at Shiloh, at Chickamauga, in the Atlanta campaign, and at Mobile. He was elected to Congress (1874–1882) and the Senate (1882–1892). He died in 1892 and is buried in Kentucky (Warner, *Generals in Gray,* 104).

12. It should be remembered that the Emancipation Proclamation that took effect on January 1, 1863, applied only to territory in the hands of the Confederacy. In the territory of slave states occupied by the Union army, slavery had not been ended nor had slaves been emancipated. The procedure described here by Marshall was one of the means used to ameliorate the condition of slaves. Emancipation in Union-held territory was the responsibility of the various state legislatures.
13. Abolitionism apparently ran deep in the Marshall family. A. O. Marshall's grandfather apparently knew Lovejoy, martyred at Alton, Illinois, quite well. This is the first instance that Marshall comments on his own abolitionist sentiments.
14. Charles M. Crocker of Company A on August 19, 1864, was "discharged for disability, Meridian, Mississippi." Elliott and Way, *History of the Thirty-Third Regiment Illinois,* 89.
15. John W. Youngman had joined Company A on February 22, 1864, and on 29 August 29, 1864, was "discharged for disability caused by wounds." Elliott and Way, *History of the Thirty-Third Regiment Illinois,* 91.

Chapter XXXII

1. This chapter marks the beginning of the end of A. O. Marshall's Civil War service. He notes that a large number of the Thirty-third whose enlistments had expired were detailed for guard duty for prisoners that were taken by Admiral Farragut's forces at Fort Morgan guarding Mobile Bay in August 1864. No longer were there to be prisoner exchanges and paroles. Grant had stopped these exchanges upon taking control as general in chief. (He felt that exchange of prisoners helped the Confederacy far more than it helped the Union.)
2. The screw steamer *Cassandra,* 1285 tons, was chartered from March 1864 to July 1865. It was also used to transport troops from New Orleans to reinforce the Army of the Potomac in June 1864.
3. The campaign for president pitted Republican Lincoln against Democrat McClellan. McClellan had failed as an army commander, but he was well-liked by many Democrats, particularly those hoping for negotiations with the Confederacy to end the war. "Copperhead" sympathies were strong in part of the Democratic Party, and when it met in Chicago in 1864 it nominated McClellan, but also supported a platform that called for an "earnest effort [to] be made for peace." The expression in the Democratic Platform was thus: "After four years of failure to restore the Union by the experiment of war." This made for problems for McClellan, who, while an ardent Democrat, was for prosecution of the war. Some in the Union were tired of the seemingly endless

war, but the August victories of Farragut at Mobile Bay, culminating in the capture of Fort Morgan on August 23 and Sherman's capture of Atlanta on September 3, seemed to reignite enthusiasm for the war and doom McClellan's hopes to win the presidency. The enthusiasm was increased by Sheridan's victories in the Shenandoah Valley, the site of so many previous defeats. The final electoral college result was 212 electoral votes for Lincoln and only 21 for McClellan. James Ford Rhodes, *History of the Civil War, 1861–1865* (New York: Dover Publications, 1999), 335–340.

4. The route described by Marshall was the Erie Railroad that ran from Jersey City, New Jersey, through Binghamton, Elmira, and Hornellsville to Buffalo. The connection that he describes at Hornellsville to Dunkirk, New York, was the original route of the railroad.
5. The route from Dunkirk, New York, to Toledo, Ohio, was on the New York Central Railroad.
6. The final leg of Marshall's journey, Toledo, Ohio, to Camp Butler, near Springfield, was on the Toledo, Wabash, and Great Western Railroad (later the Wabash) that ran directly from Toledo to Springfield.

Chapter XXXIII

1. In this last chapter of Marshall's narrative, he describes his last days in the army and his arrival at home. There are the final goodbyes and the joyous homecomings. For his future, see the editor's introduction.
2. James R. Fyffe served as sergeant, August 21, 1861, to March 17, 1863, and was wounded at Cache River. He was promoted to second lieutenant, March 17, 1863, was wounded May 22, 1863, and was promoted to first lieutenant, August 5, 1863, and served until the regiment was mustered out, December 7, 1863. Elliott and Way, *History of the Thirty-Third Regiment Illinois,* 88.
3. Marvin J. Nye served from August 21, 1861, to August 22, 1862, when he was discharged for disability at Helena, Arkansas. Elliott and Way, *History of the Thirty-Third Regiment Illinois,* 90.
4. Edward M. Pike served as sergeant from August 21, 1861, to October 11, 1864, when he was mustered out at the end of his term of enlistment. He was promoted to first sergeant on April 1, 1862. He was voted the Medal of Honor by Congress for his gallantry at Cache River. Elliott and Way, *History of the Thirty-Third Regiment Illinois,* 88.

Bibliography

Government Documents

Civil War Naval Chronology, 1861–1865. Washington, DC: Naval History Division, U.S. Navy Department, 1961–1996. Part I, *1861,* 1961; Part II, *1862,* 1962; Part III, *1863,* 1963; Part IV, *1864,* 1964; Part V, *1865,* 1965; Part VI, *Special Studies and Cumulative Index,* 1966.

Journal and Proceedings of the Missouri State Convention Held at Jefferson City and St. Louis, March, 1861. St. Louis, MO: George Knapp & Co., 1861.

Journal and Proceedings of the Missouri State Convention Held at Jefferson City, July, 1861. St. Louis, MO: George Knapp & Co., 1861.

Official Records of the Union and Confederate Navies in the War of the Rebellion. Harrisburg, PA: National Historical Society, 1987. Reprint edition in 31 volumes. Originally printed by the U.S. Navy Department.

U.S. District Court, Southern District of Ohio. *Henry P. Coolidge v. Columbus B. Guthrie. American Law Register* 17, no. 1 (1869), n.s., 8 (January 1869): 22–28.

U.S. War Department. *The Official Atlas of the Civil War.* New York: Thomas Yoseloff, 1958.

U.S. War Department. *The War of the Rebellion: Official Records of the Union and Confederate Armies.* Washington, DC: U.S. Government Printing Office, 1880–1901. 130 vols.

Papers, Diaries, Letters

Samuel Ryan Curtis Journal. Abraham Lincoln Presidential Library. Springfield, IL.

McCown, Robert A. "Thomas Rescum Sterns at the Battle for Vicksburg." Books at Iowa 39, Iowa City. University of Iowa. 1983.

Thurman Family Papers. Manuscript and Visual Collections. William Henry Smith Memorial Library, Indiana Historical Society. Floyd Thurman to Brother, October 9, 1862.

Other Books, Journal Articles

Allardice, Bruce S. *More Generals in Gray.* Baton Rouge: Louisiana State University Press, 1995.

Barr, Alwyn. "Texas Coastal Defense, 1861–1865." *Southwestern Historical Quarterly* 45 (July 1961): 1–31.

Bragg, Jefferson Davis. *Louisiana in the Confederacy.* Baton Rouge: Louisiana State University Press, 1969.

Bryner, Cloyd. *Bugle Echoes: The Story of the Illinois 47th.* Springfield, IL: Phillips Bros. Co., 1905. Reprint, Salem, MA: Higginson Book Co., n.d.

Burnham, J. H. "The Thirty-Third Regiment Illinois Infantry in the War Between the States." *Transactions of the Illinois State Historical Society* (1912): 77–85. Thirteenth Annual Meeting.

Christ, Mark K., ed. *Rugged and Sublime: The Civil War in Arkansas.* Fayetteville: University of Arkansas Press, 1974.

Christensen, Lawrence O., William E. Foley, Gary R. Kremer, and Kenneth H. Winn. *Dictionary of Missouri Biography.* Columbia: University of Missouri Press, 1999.

Coombe, Jack D. *Gunfire Around the Gulf: The Last Naval Campaigns of the Civil War.* New York: Bantam Books, 2000.

Crandall, Warren D. *History of the Ram Fleet and the Mississippi Marine Brigade in the War for the Union.* St. Louis, MO: Society of Survivors, 1907.

Curtis, Samuel Prentis. "The Army of the South-West, and the First Campaign in Arkansas." Iowa City, Iowa. *Annals of Iowa* 7, no. 3 (July 1869). This section describes the Battle of Cache River. The entire presentation begins with vol. 4, no. 2 (April 1866), and continues to vol. 7, no. 4 (October 1869).

DeBlack, Thomas A. *With Fire and Sword: Arkansas, 1861–1874.* Fayetteville: University of Arkansas Press, 2003

Dougan, Michael B. *Confederate Arkansas: The People and Policies of a Frontier State in Wartime.* University: University of Alabama Press, 1982.

Duden, Gottfried. *Report on a Journey to the Western States of North America.* Columbia: State Historical Society and University of Missouri Press, 1980.

Dyer, Frederick H. *A Compendium of the War of the Rebellion.* 2 volumes. Dayton, OH: Morningside Books, 1994.

Elliott, Isaac H., and Virgil G. Way. *History of the Thirty-Third Regiment Illinois Veteran Volunteer Infantry in the Civil War.* Gibson City, IL: n.p., 1902. Reprint, Salem, MA: Higginson Book Co., 1998.

Engel, Stephen D. *Yankee Dutchman: The Life of Franz Sigel.* Fayetteville: University of Arkansas Press, 1993.

Erickson, Edgar L., ed. "Hunting Cotton in Dixie, from the Civil War Diary of Captain Charles E. Wilcox." *Journal of Southern History* 4 (1938): 493–513.

———. "With Grant at Vicksburg, from the Civil War Diary of Captain Charles E. Wilcox." *Journal of the Illinois State Historical Society* 30 (1938): 440–503.

Fitzhugh, Lester. "Saluria, Fort Esperanza, and Military Operations on the Texas Gulf Coast, 1861–1865." *Southwestern Historical Quarterly* 41 (July 1957): 66–100.

Foulke, Joseph W. *Struggle for the Heartland: The Civil War along the Mississippi Corridor.* Pittsburgh, PA: Dorrance, 2001.

Gibson, Charles Dana, and E. Kay Gibson. *The Army's Navy Series.* Vol. 1, *Dictionary of Transports & Combatant Vessel, Steam and Sail, Employed by the Union Army.* Vol. 2, *Assault and Logistics: Union Army Coastal and River Operations.* Camden, ME: Ensign Press, 1995.

Gillespie, Michael L. *The Battle of Lexington, 1861.* N.p.: n.p., 1995.

Goodspeed's History of Southeast Missouri. 1888. Reprint indexed ed., Cape Girardeau, MO: Ramfre Press, 1978.

Grabau, Warren E. *Ninety-Eight Days: A Geographer's View of the Vicksburg Campaign.* Knoxville: University of Tennessee Press, 2000.

Guernsey, Alfred H., and Henry M. Alden. *Harper's Pictorial History of the Civil War.* New York: McDonnell Bros., 1894.

Harper's Weekly. "*Confiscation of Anglo-Rebel Cotton.*" May 2, 1863, 273, 286.

Hearn, Chester G. *Ellet's Brigade, the Strangest Outfit of All.* Baton Rouge: Louisiana State University Press, 2000.

Hess, Earl J. "Confiscation and the Northern War Effort: The Army of the Southwest at Helena." *Arkansas Historical Quarterly* 44, no. 1 (1985): 56–75.

Hinze, David C., and Karen Farnham. *The Battle of Carthage.* Campbell, CA: Savas Publishing Co., 1997.

Ingenthron, Elmo. *Borderland Rebellion.* Forsyth, MO: Ozark Mountaineer Press, 1980.

Johnson, Ludwell H. *Red River Campaign: Politics and Cotton in the Civil War.* Kent, OH: Kent State University Press, 1993.

Johnson, Robert U., and Clarence C. Buel, eds. *Battles and Leaders of the Civil War.* 4 vols. New York: The Century Co., 1887.

Kerby, Robert L. *Kirby Smith's Confederacy.* New York: Columbia University Press, 1972. Reprint, Tuscaloosa: University of Alabama Press, 1991.

Kiper, Richard L. *Major General John Alexander McClernand.* Kent, OH: Kent State University Press, 1999.

Kohl, Rhonda M. "This Godforsaken Town: Death and Disease at Helena, Arkansas, 1862–1863." *Civil War History* 50, no. 2 (2004): 109–144.

Laughlin, Sceva Bright. *Missouri Politics during the Civil War.* Salem, OR: n.p., n.d. This material also appeared in the *Missouri Historical Review* (1929–1931): vol. 23, 400–426, 583–618; vol. 24, 87–113, 261–285; vol. 25, 164–165.

Lossing, Benson J. *Pictorial Field Book of the Civil War.* 3 vols. 1876. Reprint, Baltimore, MD: Johns Hopkins University Press, 1997.

Marcy, Randolph B. *The Prairie Traveler.* New York: Harper and Brothers, 1859.

Moat, Louis S. *Frank Leslie's Illustrated Famous Leaders and Battle Scenes of the Civil War.* New York: Mrs. Frank Leslie, n.d.

Monaghan, Jay. *Swamp Fox of the Confederacy: The Life and Military Services of M. Jeff Thompson.* Tuscaloosa, AL: Confederate Publishing Co., 1956.

Moore, Frank. *Rebellion Record.* New York: G. P. Putnam, 1861. Reprint, New York: Arno Press, 1977.

Nelson, Glenn T., and John D. Squier. "The Confederate Defense of Northeast Arkansas and the Battle of Cotton Plant." *Rivers and Roads and Points in Between* 16 (spring 1989): 5–27.

New York Times, "The Cotton Court of Inquiry," May 24, 1863, 2.

New York Times, "Military Governor of Arkansas," July 21, 1862, 5

New York Times, "The Capture of Fort Esperanza," December 27, 1863, 2.

Peckham, James. *Nathaniel Lyon and Missouri in 1861.* New York: American News Company, 1866.

Phillips, Christopher. *Damned Yankee: The Life of General Nathaniel Lyon.* Columbia: University of Missouri Press, 1990.

Piston, William Garrett, and Richard W. Hatcher III. *Wilson's Creek: The Second Battle of the Civil War and the Men Who Fought It.* Chapel Hill: University of North Carolina Press, 2000.

Ponder, Jerry. *The Civil War Battle of Fredericktown, Missouri.* Mason, TX: Ponder Books, 1996.

Rainwater, P. L. "The Letters of James Lusk Alcorn." *Journal of Southern History* 3 (1937): 196–209.

Rhodes, James Ford. *History of the Civil War, 1861–1865.* New York: Dover Publications, 1999. This edition is a reprint of a 1961 edition of the original 1917 Pulitzer Prize winning book.

Ryle, Walter. *Missouri: Union or Secession.* Nashville, TN: George Peabody College for Teachers, 1931.

Scharf, J. Thomas. *History of St. Louis City and County.* Philadelphia, PA: Louis H. Everts & Co., 1883.

Shea, William. "The Confederate Defeat at Cache River." *Arkansas Historical Quarterly* 52, no. 2 (1993): 129.

Shea, William L., and Earl J. Hess. *Pea Ridge: Civil War Campaign in the West.* Chapel Hill: University of North Carolina Press, 1992.

Shea, William L., and Terrence J. Winschel. *Vicksburg Is the Key: The Struggle for the Mississippi Valley.* Lincoln: University of Nebraska Press, 2003.

Slack, Kent. *The Thirty-Third Illinois Volunteer Regiment, Company C.* Internship paper, Bloomington, IL., McLean County Museum of History, 1981.

Stanton, Donal J., Goodwin F. Berquist, and Paul C. Bowers, eds. *The Civil War Reminiscences of General M. Jeff Thompson.* Dayton, OH: Morningside Press, 1988.

Stevens, W. W. *Past and Present of Will County, Illinois.* Chicago, IL: S. J. Clark Co., 1907.

Surdam, David G. "Traders or Traitors: Northern Cotton Trading during the Civil War." *Business and Economic History* 28 (winter 1999): 301.

Sweet, Alex E., and J. Armoy Knox. *On a Mexican Mustang, Through Texas from the Gulf to the Rio Grande.* Houston, TX: T. N. James & Co., 1884.

Townsend, Stephen A. *The Yankee Invasion of Texas.* College Station: Texas A&M University Press, 2006.

Warner, Ezra J. *Generals in Blue.* Baton Rouge: Louisiana State University Press, 1992.

———. *Generals in Gray.* Baton Rouge: Louisiana State University Press, 1987.

Wheeler, Richard. *The Siege of Vicksburg.* New York: Thomas Y. Crowell Co., 1978.

Winter, William C. *The Civil War in St. Louis.* St. Louis: Missouri Historical Society Press, 1994.

Winters, John D. *The Civil War in Louisiana.* Baton Rouge: Louisiana State University Press, 1991.

Wright, Marcus J. *Official and Illustrated War Record.* Washington, DC: n.p., 1899.

Theses

Futrell, Robert F. "Federal Trade with the Confederate States, 1861–1865: A Study of Governmental Policy." PhD. diss., Vanderbilt University, 1950.

Hixon, Marion. "Fremont's Hundred Days." Master of Arts thesis, Washington University, 1926.

Keltner, Herbert L. "The History of the 33rd Illinois Volunteer Infantry Regiment." Master of Arts thesis, Illinois State University, 1968.

Koelling, Harry Carl. "The Civil War in Missouri during 1861." Master of Arts thesis, Washington University, 1937.

Lambie, Agnes L. "Confederate Control of Cotton in the Trans-Mississippi Department." Master of Arts thesis, University of Texas, 1915.

LeDoux, Louis H. "The Civil War in Missouri in 1862." Master of Arts thesis, Washington University, 1949.

Westover, John G. "The Civil War Experiences of General M. Jeff Thompson in 1861." Master of Arts thesis, University of Missouri, 1941.

Internet Sites

Army of the Tennessee, Thirteenth Army Corps. Organization. http://www.ehistory.com/uscw/features/regimental/Indiana/union/49thindiana/13corps.cf.

Battle of Cotton Plant. http://www.arkansaspreservation.org/publication/archive.asp?ID=19&t=Battlefield.

Battle of Fredericktown. http://www.rosecity.net/civilwar/batfred.html and http://www.cr.nps.gov/hps/abpp/battles/mo007.htm.

Camp Butler, Illinois. http://www.illinoiscivilwar.org/campbutler.html.

Cavallo Pass Handbook of Texas Online, s.v. "CAVALLO PASS." http://www.tsha.utexas.edu/handbook/online/articles/view/cc/RKC10.html.

Civil War Era Population Statistics. http://www.census.gov/population/documentation/twps0027/tab09.txt (accessed July 2006) and http://www.civilwarhome.com/population1860.htm (accessed July 2006).

Fort Esparanza Handbook of Texas Online, s.v. "FORT ESPERANZA." hppt://www.tsha.utexas.edu/handbook/online/articles/view/FF/acf2.html and http://www.fortunecity.com/victorian/pottery/1080/fort_esperanza_tx_26nov63.htm.

Illinois State University (Normal). http://www.mlb.ilstu.edu/ressubj/subject/isuhist/presidents2.htm and http://www.normal.org/AboutNormal/History.htm.

Illinoistown (East St. Louis). http://www.compu-type.net/rengen/stclair/1881estl.htm and http://archive.ncsa.uiuc.edu/Cyberia/RiverWeb/Projects/Ambot/Society/SOC1.htm and http://archive.ncsa.uiuc.edu/Cyberia/RiverWeb/Projects/Ambot/Society/SOC4.htm.

Indianola, Texas Handbook of Texas Online, s.v. "INDIANOLA, TX." http://www.tsha.utexas.edu/handbook/online/articles/view/II/hvi11.html.

Matagorda, Texas Handbook of Texas Online, s.v. "MATAGORDA ISLAND." http://www.tsha.utexas.edu/handbook/online/articles/view/MM/rrm2.html and http://www.tpwd.state.tx.us/news/magazine/matagord.htm.

Ninety-ninth Illinois Infantry Regiment. http://www.illinoiscivilwar.org/cw99-agr.html and http://www.rootsweb.com/~ilcivilw/history/099.htm and http://www,riitsweb,cin/~ilcivilw/dyers/099inf.htm and http://www.rootsweb.com/~ilcivilw/f&s/099-fs.htm.

Stewart's Independent Illinois Cavalry Company. http://www.rootsweb.com/~ilcivilw/dyers/cav-stew2.htm and http://www.illinoiscivilwar.org/cwindcav.html.

Thirty-third Illinois Infantry Regiment. http://www.civilwararchive.com/Unreghst/unilinf3.htm#33rd and http://www.civil-war.com/searchpages/result.asp?name=33rd&category=Infantry&subm.

Twenty-first Illinois Regiment. http://www.rootsweb.com/~ilcivilw/history/021.htm and http://www.rootsweb.com/~ilcivilw/reg_html/021_reg.htm.

Index

Page numbers in italics refer to illustrations.

Albert O. Marshall was born in 1840 on a farm in Illinois. He served in the Thirty-Third Illinois Regiment for three years, after which he became a lawyer and was elected to a four-year term in the state senate and later to the county court as a circuit court judge.

Robert G. Schultz teaches history at East Central College in Union, Missouri, and has published numerous articles on local and regional history and postal history.